# Videoblogging

**Jay Dedman and Joshua Paul**

WILEY

Wiley Publishing, Inc.

*This book is dedicated to the different people in the Videoblogging Community who care enough to fight for what they believe in.*

*—Jay Dedman*

*For my mother, who somehow finds time for everyone.*

*—Joshua Paul*

**Videoblogging**

Published by
Wiley Publishing, Inc.
10475 Crosspoint Boulevard
Indianapolis, IN 46256
www.wiley.com

Copyright © 2006 by Wiley Publishing, Inc., Indianapolis, Indiana

Published simultaneously in Canada

Manufactured in the United States of America

10 9 8 7 6 5 4 3 2 1

1B/QW/QW/QW/IN

For general information on our other products and services or to obtain technical support, please contact our Customer Care Department within the U.S. at (800) 762-2974, outside the U.S. at (317) 572-3993 or fax (317) 572-4002.

Library of Congress Cataloging-in-Publication Data
Dedman, Jay, 1973-
Videoblogging / Jay Dedman and Joshua Paul.
    p. cm.
 Includes index.
 ISBN-13: 978-0-470-03788-1 (paper/website)
 ISBN-10: 0-470-03788-1 (paper/website)
 1. Blogs. 2. Digital video. I. Paul, Joshua. II. Title.
TK5105.8884.D43 2006
006.7--dc22

                              2006012927

# Credits

**Executive Editor**
Chris Webb

**Development Editor**
Maryann Steinhart

**Technical Editor**
Gene Sullivan

**Production Editor**
Felicia Robinson

**Copy Editor**
C.M. Jones

**Editorial Manager**
Mary Beth Wakefield

**Production Manager**
Tim Tate

**Vice President and Executive Group Publisher**
Richard Swadley

**Vice President and Executive Publisher**
Joseph B. Wikert

**Project Coordinator**
Ryan Steffen

**Graphics and Production Specialists**
Carrie A. Foster
Lauren Goddard
Denny Hager
Joyce Haughey
Barbara Moore
Lynsey Osborn
Stephanie D. Jumper
Julie Trippetti

**Quality Control Technician**
John Greenough

**Proofreading**
Techbooks

**Indexing**
Sherry Massey

**Cover Design**
Anthony Bunyan

# About the Authors

**Jay Dedman** started his career as a lover of punk music and Hi-8 cameras. He became a TV journalist, working for local news and eventually CNN International. Jay also worked as free-lance photographer in the Democratic Republic of Congo before becoming a videoblogger. In 2004 he created the Videoblogging Group with Peter Van Dijck, where they formed a community that began teaching others how to post and distribute video in their blogs.

Jay lives in San Francisco, where he is a founding partner in FireAnt.tv. He also works with Node101.org, setting up public spaces around the world to help teach people how to videoblog. His personal blog can be found at www.momentshowing.net.

**Joshua Paul** has more than 10 years of experience delivering video entertainment for both cable and network television. He has produced primetime specials for Fox Television, worked as a pro-ducer for Sony Pictures Entertainment, and produced a variety of broadcast and online projects for companies throughout Los Angeles. During the past decade, he has witnessed, participated in, and pushed the growth and adoption of digital video within the entertainment industry.

Joshua is an active member of the Producers Guild of America, an author, and a public speaker. He is fluent in a number of computer programming and scripting languages and can often be found hunched over a keyboard hacking on code. When not consumed by work, he lives, loves, and enjoys life with his wife and son. His personal blog can be found at www.joshpaul .com/blog.

# About the Contributing Authors

**Adrian Miles** teaches the theory and practice of hypermedia and networked interactive video at RMIT University, Australia. He has also been a senior new media researcher in the InterMedia Lab at the University of Bergen, Norway. His academic research on videoblogs and networked interactive video has been widely published and exhibited internationally. Adrian's research interests also include appropriate pedagogies for new media education, digital poetics, and the use of Deleuzean philosophy in the context of digital poetics. He is likely the first videoblogger, having started his experimental "vog" in November ,2000.

**Andreas Haugstrup Pedersen** is a graduate student at Aalborg University, Denmark, where he studies videoblogging as a medium and cultural phenomenon. After dark he moonlights as a coder. He has been making tools to ease the lives of videobloggers since 2004. Andreas blogs at `www.solitude.dk`.

**Clint Sharp** lives in Redmond, Washington. He's worked in the technology industry for more than 8 years, and his site (`http://clintsharp.com`) is where he presents his thoughts on technology and his life. He's a committed blogger and videoblogger, and has been active in Internet communities for more than 10 years. Clint frequently posts on the Yahoo Videoblogging group.

**Dave Huth** is a teacher, storyteller, picture maker, and whistler of jaunty tunes. He is presently a professor of visual communication and media arts at Houghton (N.Y.) College. You'll find him at colleges, conferences, and creative gatherings, provoking discussion about how community conversation is a good way to explore art, theology, culture, politics, and just about any good idea you can think of. You can follow Dave's adventures in videoblogging at `www.davemedia.blogspot.com`, and his other projects in visual communication at `www.davidhuth.com`. E-mail him at dave.huth@yahoo.com.

**David Meade** has been running some form of his web site since 1994. Today visitors to `DavidMeade.com` will find text blogs, audio blogs, and, of course, video blogs. David started video blogging in April of 2005 and has since enjoyed being an active member of the videoblogging community, working with vloggers from around the country on various projects both online and in the real world.

**Dave Slusher** was the longtime host of the SF-themed radio talk show *Reality Break*, beginning in 1992. *Reality Break* started in Atlanta on Georgia Tech's WREK-FM and from there metastasized onto the NPR satellite system. Dave is a software consultant who has worked for DRM and ebook companies, online health companies, computer security firms, online travel companies, and a number of startups. He was an early podcaster, and the first person to use the term "podcast" inside of a podcast. He continues to encourage the use of Bittorrent in podcasting, the independence of podcasters, and candor in communication. He lives in coastal South Carolina.

**Duncan Speakman** is a sound and video artist who works in both live and mediated spaces using emergent technologies. His work has been exhibited internationally at festivals including ISEA, Futuresonic, ArteAlmeda, and Navigate, and he has created pieces for a number of large-scale site-specific events. In 2002 he received the Clark Trust Award for Digital Arts from the Watershed in Bristol, following this he worked with Hewlett Packard designing networked sound installations for their mobile computing research. He is currently a visiting lecturer in technology and performance at Dartington College of Arts, U.K.

**Greg Smith** is a member of the RSS Advisory Board and the developer of FeederReader, the Pocket PC program used to download all things RSS for personal or enterprise use. Greg's extensive background in software development, electrical engineering, project management, and business financial systems along with occasional bouts of training, consulting, and amateur musicianship qualifies him to muck around in a lot of different areas. He is currently attempting to change the world using a Pocket PC, Visual Studio, and C#; and has been known to throw gobs of Perl, HTML, and C into vats of Solaris, Linux, and Windows. Greg lives with his beautiful wife and two kitties in Clinton, Mississippi.

**James A. Donnelly** has worked on dozens of television productions and recently added two 2005 Telly Awards to career honors that include 2 Emmys, an Iris Award, and 11 Addy Awards. Check out his videoblog, podcast www.Dummycast.com, and www.PetsOnBoard.com, one of the first online pet adoption web sites. Donnelly has recently joined the PodShow Podcast Network, bringing new, entertaining, informative, and humorous podcasts to the premier network of independently produced audio and video content.

**Josh Leo** has been videoblogging since March 2005 and has quickly made a name for himself. He has a number of blogs and vlogs featuring his own work and the work of others at www.joshleo.com. He is also the assistant editor for the videoblogging news site We Are The Media (http://wearethemedia.com). A professional radio producer, Josh Leo continues pushing the boundaries of videoblogging with each video he posts.

**Joshua Kinberg** is an artist, hacker, and visionary. In 2004, his protest performance *Bikes Against Bush* earned international acclaim. Afterward, he began experimenting with media distribution and aggregation via RSS, and released a small program in October 2004 to automatically download video files from a list of RSS subscriptions and assemble them into a media playlist. Joshua's personal videoblog can be found at www.JoshKinberg.com.

**Kath O'Donnell** is a broadcast television engineer who dabbles in Internet technologies and Australian electronic music, hip hop, and arts communities in her spare time. She works on projects as AliaK and can be found at www.AliaK.com

**Matt Savarino** is the creator of VlogMap.org, the world map of video.blogs. Matt has been doing web and database development since 1997. Some of his past projects include ESPN.com, XGames.com, and ScottUSA.com.

**Michael Sullivan** (sull) helped launch www.Ourmedia.org and is the creator of www.vlogdir.com, one of the first videoblog directories; www.videobloggers.org, a project hosted with ibiblio.org to offer free hosting for vloggers; and more recently worked to create SpreadTheMedia.org, a project to help commingle the people and the tools useful to the Open Media Revolution. Michael also is a moderator on the Yahoo! Videoblogging Group, and came up with the new name Mefeedia for Peter Van Dijck's me-tv.com site.

**Michael Verdi** is a videoblogging pioneer and the co-creator of FreeVlog.org, an online videoblogging tutorial. He's also co-founder of NODE101, a network of grass-roots media centers, and co-author of the book *Secrets of Videoblogging*. His personal videoblog is at www.michaelverdi.com.

**Nathan Freitas**' career has spanned the academic, corporate, and non-profit worlds, solving difficult problems through the thoughtful application of technology over the last 10 years. His work has been built into Palm handhelds, on display at SIGGRAPH, included in Wikipedia, and covered in media ranging from Boing Boing and Slashdot, to the New York Times and

Howard Rheingold's book *Smart Mobs*. He began programming at the age of 6 on a Radio Shack TRS-80 computer, and founded his first technology company, ThinAirApps with Jon Oakes, just 18 years later. Nathan also provides guidance and assistance to non-profits, as a volunteer and Board Member to groups such as the Students for a Free Tibet and MobileActive. His latest work is the open-source media aggregator I/ON and a new business venture, Open Network Television (`http://openvision.tv`).

**Pete Prodoehl** is a hacker of many things...he started using computers in 1980, started a weblog (`http://rasterweb.net/raster`) in August of 1997, started podcasting in August 2004, and started videoblogging (`http://tinkernet.org`) in May 2005. He is always interested in new technology, and in new ways to use the Internet and open-source software for communication, collaboration, and occasionally just for fun.

**Peter Van Dijck** is a Belgian information architect and is one of the early cheerleaders of the idea of independent videoblogging. He writes at `http://poorbuthappy.com/ease` (first videoblog entries in 2004), and he's the founder of Mefeedia.com, the first video aggregator. You can find contact information at `http://petervandijck.net`.

**Richard Hall** is a professor of Information Science and Technology, and director of the Laboratory for Information Technology Evaluation at the University of Missouri–Rolla (`www.umr.edu/~rhall`). He videoblogs at `www.richardshow.com`.

**Ryanne Hodson** (`http://ryanedit.com`) is a BFA graduate of the Studio for Interrelated Media at Massachusetts College of Art. She started her career as a video editor at WGBH PBS Boston and in Boston public access television. Another disillusioned producer struggling to get distribution for artists and media creators, she's made videoblogging her medium of choice for uncensored, unmediated communication. She envisions a huge population transforming itself from media consumer to media producer. From Amsterdam to San Francisco to New York, Ryanne has taught diverse audiences the hows and whys of videoblogging. With co-creator Michael Verdi, she runs Freevlog.org, the essential resource for teaching videoblogging over the web in 8 easy steps.

**Shawn Van Every** is a Media Researcher and Adjunct Professor at NYU's Interactive Telecommunications Program. His research is focused on emerging technologies related to media creation, distribution, and interaction. His projects generally involve development of tools that help to make low-cost media making, distribution, and interactivity possible. Shawn holds a Master's degree in Interactive Telecommunications from NYU, and a Bachelor's degree in Media Study from SUNY at Buffalo. You can see all his work at `www.walking-productions.com/shawn.html`.

**Steve Garfield** is one of the most active and pioneering folks in the videoblogging space, and has spent countless hours helping people get started in videoblogging, including, perhaps, the first elected politician. Steve talks at a variety of events, teaches videoblogging, is a correspondent for Rocketboom and We Are the Media, and hosts a couple of helpful and entertaining videoblogs including Vlog Soup (`http://stevegarfield.blogs.com/videoblog/vlog_soup`), a free tour of the vlogosphere. See him at `http://stevegarfield.com/`.

**Tim Whidden** is an arist and web technologist working at the intersection of the web and digital video. He is Creative Director for Wavexpress, Inc., the makers of TVTonic (`www.tvtonic.com`) and his artwork has been presented internationally in museums, galleries, and festivals. Learn more about his personal artwork at `http://mteww.com`.

# Acknowledgments

I would like to thank Chris and Maryann, who edited this book and were patient and pushing where necessary. I must point out that Josh Paul's experience was the engine in this whole process. I'm also grateful to his wife and young son, who put up with us while I stayed at their home for a week while writing.

This book would not be possible without all the listed contributors, as well as the rest of the community that spends countless hours defining and practicing this new art form.

I'd like especially to shout out to my girlfriend, Ryan Hodson, who helped me keep calm when I was simultaneously trying to write and work a full-time job. She would want me to tell everyone how important it is for each of us to start making our own media and join the conversation. A technical book such as this one is often a challenge to write because services and process are always evolving. But you have some of the best videoblogging tips and tricks in your hands that, if practiced, will make you a pro.—Jay Dedman

I want to thank my wife and son for tolerating my disappearance, yet again. I love you both more than you'll ever know. I also want to thank my family for all of their love and support, day in and day out.

This book would not exist without the numerous contributors and the videoblogging community as a whole. Each of you has made this book possible, and I truly thank you. Also, I want to thank Gene Sullivan for looking over our shoulders and making sure this book is technically sound. Your input was invaluable.

The Wiley staff was exceptionally understanding with Jay and me as we raced to stay ahead of this ever-changing landscape. Specifically, thank you Chris and Maryann. Your patience with us was greatly appreciated. Now, go make media.—Josh Paul

# Contents at a Glance

# Contents

## Part I: Preproduction

## Part II: Production

## Part III: Post-Production

## Part V: Find and Watch Videoblogs

# Introduction

You will hear many terms for what this book is about: video podcasting, vlogging, vidcasting, vodcasting, and others. But they all refer to the same thing: a video in a blog or, more correctly, *videoblogging*. The big deal about videoblogging is how open, powerful, and revolutionary it is for anyone, anywhere in the world, to distribute video.

## Blogging, Digital Video, and Broadband in Brief

To get to videoblogging, it helps to understand the mindset of bloggers—people who use web logs, which are similar to online diaries. People—regular people, citizens, and community members like you—started blogging in the late 1990s. A blog enables a person to publish thoughts, ideas, and opinions (usually accompanied by links to referenced content on the web) quickly and easily. Unlike building a complicated web site, the software that runs a blog does all the technical stuff automatically, enabling a blogger to focus on writing instead of on details such as valid HTML code. By commenting on and creating links between blogs, people began holding dynamic, public conversations online. As time passed, bloggers started to post photos and audio files to their blogs.

In the mid-1990s, during the Internet's financial boom, it seemed as though everyone was trying to do video online, but it didn't really work well. What happened primarily was that office workers and college students emailed funny videos to each other because they were the ones who typically had fast Internet connections and could download videos quickly and easily.

At the same time, digital video (DV) became widely available. DV file formats and hardware advancements like FireWire empowered people to shoot and edit high-quality video at affordable prices. DV enables anyone to record video, import it to a home computer, and edit it using professional-quality tools. Early on, though, large file sizes and bandwidth restrictions limited where a finished video could go from there.

As DVD-authoring software became more accessible, more and more amateurs began creating pro-quality packages for their videos. Still, the most common Internet access was too slow to handle the high bandwidth requirements of video, and there were limited outlets for personal video that didn't fit into narrow categories. Digital video film festivals tried to fill the void, yet many videographers, editors, and artists simply piled their personal creations (see Figure 1) or threw them in the closet for "later."

Times have definitely changed since the 1990s. More than half of Internet users in North America have broadband connections, allowing large video files to move across the net easily. Other industrialized nations are adopting fast connections as well, many even more quickly than the United States (see Figure 2). This has enabled Internet video distribution to a worldwide audience.

FIGURE FM1: If you own a video camera, this may be a familiar sight.

In 2004, it became apparent to a small knot of video enthusiasts that you could place video in a blog. The group formed an online community, spread the word, and actively began documenting their ideas, experience, and lives using video online. It was a culture that supplied its own producers and audiences to this unique new medium. The viewers were also the stars (and still are).

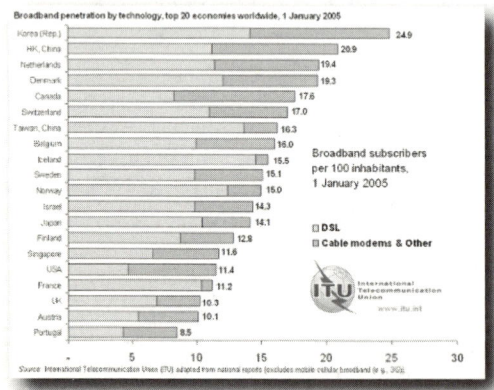

FIGURE FM2: Broadband access to the Internet is becoming widespread.

Cultural and geographic barriers began to fall away because people were sharing videos of their lives. You could watch a video created by someone in another part of the world (see Figure 3), send a message directly to the creator, and begin a conversation with the person whom you would not have met otherwise. Because the medium is video, the communication tends to be personal.

As one videoblogger said: "...video technology brings to the Internet a more human side, which was missing."

FIGURE FM3: Videoblogging is worldwide.

# Diving into the World of Videoblogging

Until recently, few people were able to have their videos broadcast or distributed locally, much less internationally. National and cable networks, television stations, and other media outlets (collectively Hollywood), have always been very selective of the content they produce and distribute. Yet, now, anyone with a connection to the Internet can easily distribute video worldwide. The potential audience is larger than that of familiar names such as Adelphia, Comcast, COX, and DirecTV.

Yes, the little fat girl in Ohio[1] is now on even footing with multi-billion-dollar corporations . . . and competing for the same eyeballs. Anyone on the planet with an Internet connection can put his video out there for the public, right with the biggest media conglomerates in the world. This book provides you the knowledge to participate in this unprecedented phenomenon.

---

[1] In reference to Francis Ford Coppola's famous quote from *Hearts of Darkness*.

As we write this book, more and more people are obtaining video entertainment from the Internet. Some of it continues to come from traditional media outlets such as CBS and ESPN, primarily through the iTunes Music Store (see Figure 4). But the videos being watched could just as easily be yours.

The technology behind videoblogging has leveled the playing field. A viewer has as much of a chance to watch a video made by an independent producer, like "Tiki Bar TV," as one made by Disney, like "Deperate Housewives." People are no longer dependent on what media companies produce. There is a tremendous amount of choice and opportunity.

You can now be a consumer and a producer. Plus, through videoblogging, you can be an active part of the conversation; after all, video is simply another medium through which to communicate.

## Why Make a Videoblog?

A lot of people have video they've recorded over the years—video of their children's birthdays, parents' anniversaries, engagements, events, little movies they made aspiring one day to put together the family story.... If you have a video camera, you have video. The question shouldn't be why make a videoblog, but why *not* make a videoblog?

Nevertheless, people ask why, so here are a few answers:

- You want to document moments in your life in video so your grandkids can see what you were like when you were their age.
- You want to connect your family that is spread throughout the country, or even the world, through video.
- You want to record a project over time, using the videoblog as a documentary in parts.
- You want to show people behind the scenes of your business, creating a conversation with your customers.
- You want to make a short TV show that people can subscribe to and watch regularly.
- You want to contribute, create, and collaborate with the rest of the world.
- You want to create your own definition of what a videoblog is.

More than likely you'll discover that your videoblog will take on a life all its own, mixing various genres of video, some traditional and some experimental. It will grow, and change, just as you do.

## Is a Videoblog like a Podcast?

Yes. A podcast is simply an audio file on a blog instead of a video. Apple made a big splash in 2005 by promoting the use of the iPod with audio shows to which you could subscribe. Apple released its video iPod in late 2005, making it possible for people to download television shows and movies. But it also enables people to subscribe to and download videoblogs.

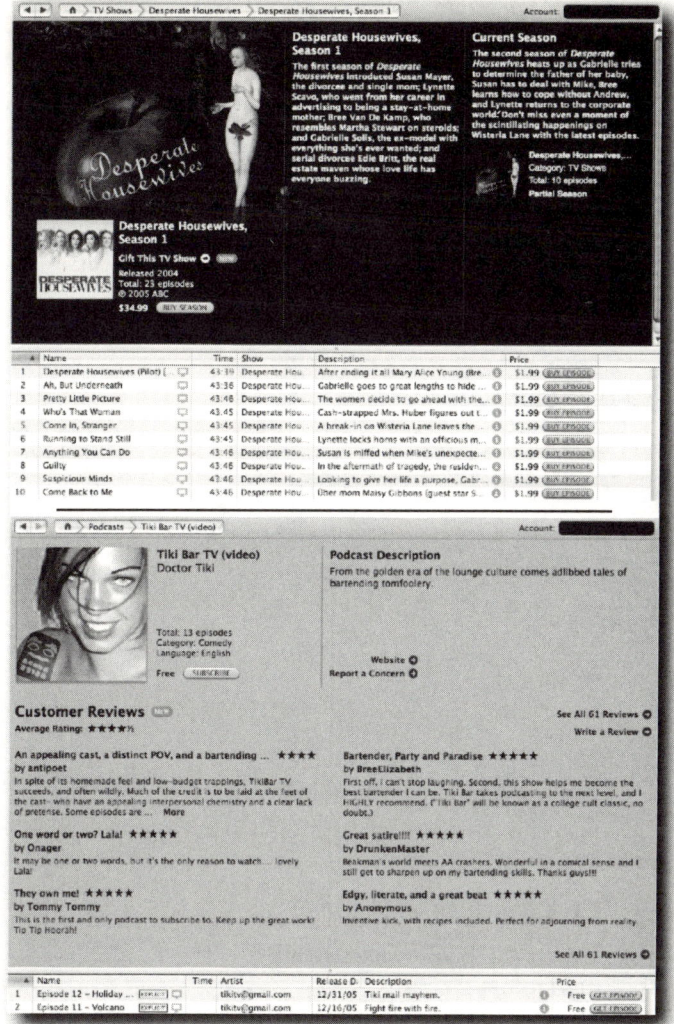

FIGURE FM4: Both "Desperate Housewives" and "Tiki Bar TV" can be obtained via iTunes.

By using a digital videocamera, a video-editing program, and a videoblog, you can distribute video to anyone in the world with a connection to the Internet. More creativity, more choices...see Figure 5.

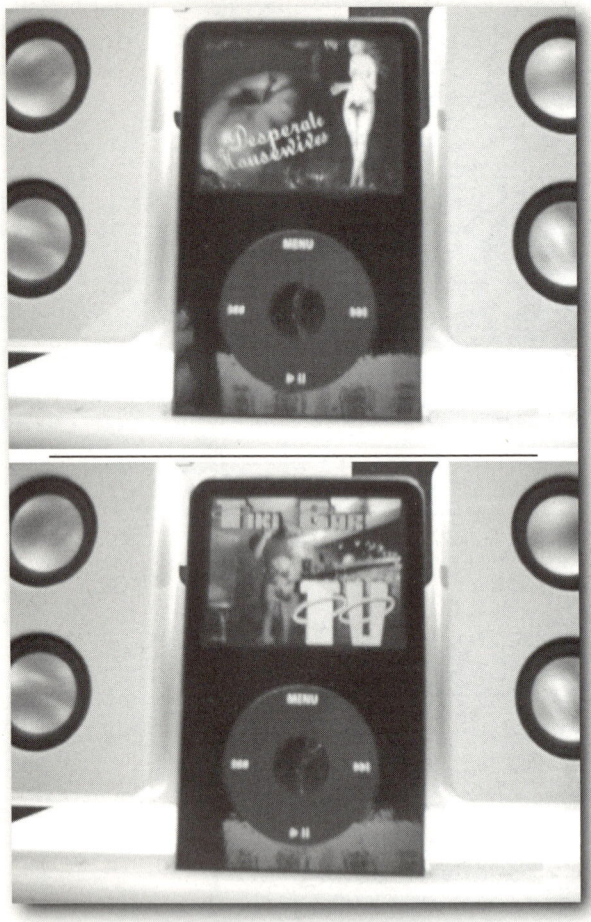

FIGURE FM5: There's not much difference between a "traditional"
television show and an independent one.

## Why Is This Happening Now?

Broadband Internet connections are becoming more widespread, due to the increasing availability of cable modems and DSL connections. Because of this, an enormous number of people
can now download video quickly. In addition, connection speeds are getting faster and cheaper.

Really Simple Syndication, primarily known as RSS, is the magic that makes videoblogging
happen. RSS allows people to subscribe to your videos using an aggregator, which collects all of
a person's subscriptions in one place and automatically downloads new videos whenever they
are available. You'll do a lot of work with RSS in this book.

Besides RSS and faster Internet connections, videoblogging is exploding because there is a
growing, highly supportive community that wants videoblogging to happen. There is a hunger

for clear, unfettered voices. Technology and media companies are also pushing hard to make video on the web a reality and to create new distribution channels. For a price, you may soon be able to download any TV show or movie online and then watch it on your TV, a portable device like the iPod, or even your cell phone.

# Video on a Web Site versus Video in a Blog

What is the difference between a video on any web site and a video in a blog? Most web sites are static; each page is created individually and the video just "sits" there. In a blog, however, every video can be linked to, downloaded, and archived, and most of this process is automated. A blog, much like a television series, will produce many videos over time, and anyone who likes the blog can subscribe to it through RSS. By subscribing, the viewer is guaranteed to receive the latest content because the subscriber's computer automatically updates and downloads new videos as they're released.

A blog also has a template that allows authors to simply type something, which is then placed online, without the author needing to worry about technical details. This is commonly known as *posting* (see Figure 6). The blog software automatically arranges posts and creates an instant archive of all the published content. Then, people anywhere, at anytime can comment on or link directly to each post, including those with video.

A videoblog is not about one video. A videoblog is made up of a collection of videos that grows over time. Usually these videos are short and simple to make, but they don't have to be. An audience will get to know your work over time. It is thrilling when your audience leaves comments on your video posts, allowing you to respond to them. Conversations grow organically.

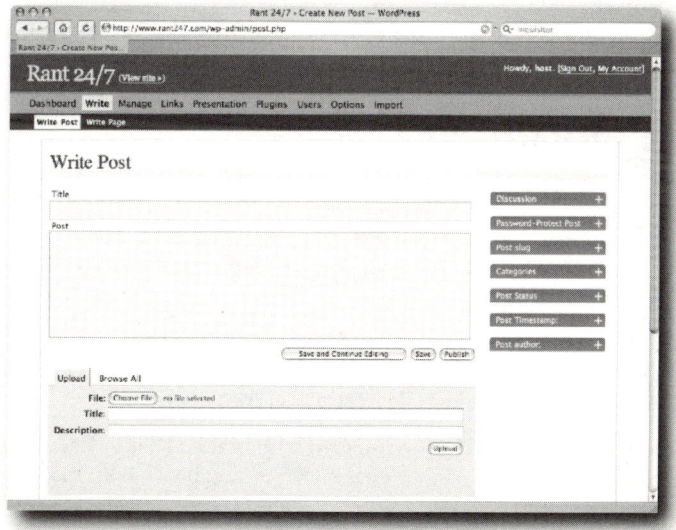

FIGURE FM6: Blog software makes creating and maintaining a web site very easy.

# Remixing Culture

For those artistically inclined, many videobloggers grant permission for you to download their videos, remix them (creating new combinations and ways of viewing the media), and upload them to your own blog. This is unlike traditional media, where strict control over audio-visual images is the norm.

Videoblogging is a new medium, completely unprecedented and unscripted. The rules about how media is created, distributed, and consumed are changing.

# Whom This Book Is For

This book is for anyone interested in finding, viewing, or creating video on the web.

If you're a beginner, this book will show you how to make a videoblog from scratch...and even make you an advanced user. If you are already a blogger and know the basics, you can use your existing skills and really take advantage of this new medium. Each chapter begins with "the simple way," which enables you to become productive quickly. The rest of the chapter takes you through a range of solutions, from easy to advanced, and a variety of challenges.

Following one rule will help you at every step. You must ask questions. Questions lead to responses, which lead to more questions, which become extensions of the robust and often surprising conversation permeating this amazing new form of communication. If you don't know any computer geeks, online communities of helpful videobloggers are ready to hear what you are trying to do and very willing to offer their help and advice. One of the main places to get help is the original online videoblogging discussion group: `http://groups.yahoo.com/group/videoblogging`.

Don't be timid; become a contributor in the personal media revolution! We'll see you online.

# How This Book Is Organized

In Part I, "Preproduction," you lay the foundation for your videoblog and start your own blog.

The three chapters in Part II, "Production," teach you many ways to acquire video—both with and without a camera. You also learn some techniques for creating professional-looking videos on a shoe string.

Part III, "Post-Production," takes you into the nitty-gritty of working with the video you've captured—from editing tips, to using text, to transcoding, to creating interactive videos. You'll be armed with tools that can help you successfully release your own creativity.

When you've completed your video, you'll want to share it with others. That's where Part IV, "Distribution," comes in. How can you host your own video? What about syndication? Can you embed your video in a web page? This part of the book answers all those questions and more.

Part V, "Find and Watch Videoblogs," shows you how to find and subscribe to videoblogs and explores your viewing options. The final chapter in this part delves into myriad ways in which you can customize your videoblog to present your work in the best possible way.

So you like videoblogging and want to take it a step further. Part VI, "Pimp Your Vlog," covers the bases for you, from tagging your videos to other methods of letting folks know about your feed. You'll also see how you can track statistics for your site and how you might make some money with it, too. Finally, the burgeoning worldwide videoblogging community really wants you to be involved, and the last chapter explores ways in which you can easily be part of this exciting media.

# Conventions Used in This Book

The following conventions are used throughout this book.

## Key Combinations

When you are instructed to press two or more keys simultaneously, each key in the combination is separated by a plus sign. For example:

Ctrl+Alt+T (Command+Option+T)

The preceding tells you to press the three listed keys for your system at the same time. You can also hold down one or more keys and then press the final key. Release all the keys at the same time.

## Menu Commands

When instructed to select a command from a menu, you see the menu and the command separated by an arrow symbol. For example, when instructed to execute the Open command from the File menu, you see the notation File→Open. Some menus use submenus, in which case you see an arrow for each submenu, as follows: Insert→Form Object→Text Field.

## Typographical Conventions

New terms may appear in *italic* type.

A special typeface indicates HTML or other code, as demonstrated in the following example:

```
<html>
<head>
<title>Untitled Document</title>
</head>
<body bgcolor="#FFFFFF">
</body>
</html>
```

This code font is also used within paragraphs to designate tags, attributes, and values, as well as filenames and URLs.

The code continuation character ⊃ at the end of a code line indicates that the line is too long to fit within the margins of the printed book. You should continue typing the next line of code before pressing the Enter (Return) key.

## Icons

Occasionally, icons appear in the text to assist you. They indicate important or especially helpful information. This book includes the following types of icons:

Tips provide you with extra knowledge that separates the novice from the pro.

Notes provide additional or critical information and technical data on the current topic.

Cautions point out procedures for which you need to be extremely careful, as well as pitfalls that you can avoid.

# Preproduction

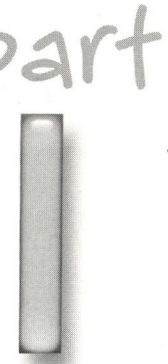

part

# Get the Vlog Mindset

**N**ew videobloggers often have the same questions:

➤ What should my videoblog be about?

➤ Should I record my life?

➤ Should I make a TV show?

➤ Will I make money from putting videos online?

➤ How much will this cost me?

➤ Who will be watching?

➤ How many viewers can I get?

This chapter answers those questions and more, preparing you for the rest of the book.

## Videoblogging: The Big Picture

When it comes to videoblogging, the best way to understand the medium is to see what other people in the community are doing. Whether you love or hate what you see, it'll give you a sense of the diversity and abundance of approaches people take to creating videoblogs. The best way to locate and view videoblogs is to take some time looking through the current batch of what's available in the following directories:

➤ www.FireAnt.tv

➤ www.Mefeedia.com

➤ www.VlogDir.com

➤ www.VlogMap.org

Mefeedia was the first directory devoted specifically to videoblogging. Peter Van Dijck started it in 2004, and it has grown to track more than 6,000 videoblogs as of this writing. Figure 1-1 shows the Mefeedia home page.

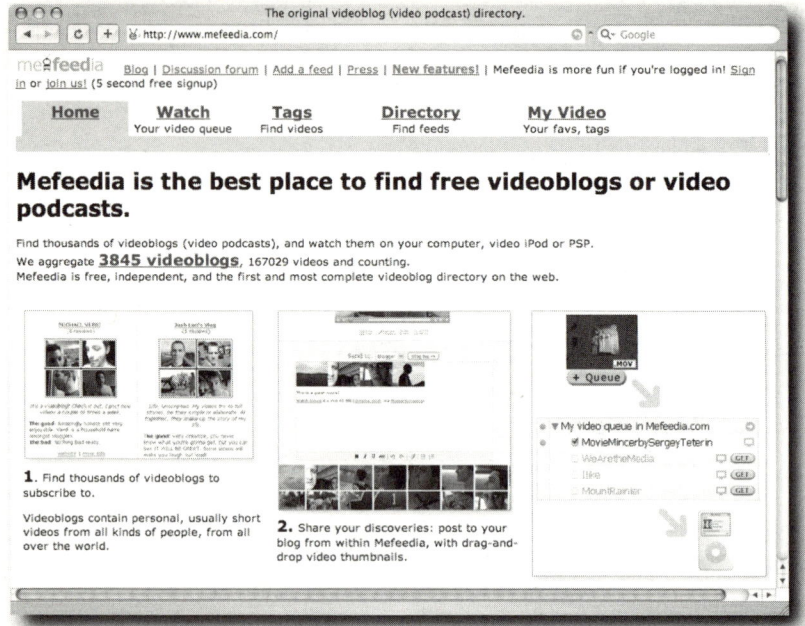

FIGURE 1-1: Mefeedia was the first place to track videoblogs.

You may also want to look in the Podcasts section at the iTunes music store to find and view different videoblogs as well. (Follow the Podcasts link under "Inside the Music Store" on the main page.)

Videoblogging sprang from the drive of people who communicate visually. Writing is a great way to communicate, but not everyone can write well. In addition, writing can't always express the true intent of the author — written sarcasm, for example, can sometimes lead to unintended consequences, misunderstandings, and hurt feelings.

With videoblogging, however, each person can express herself in a personal and highly effective manner. In the brief history of videoblogging, journalists like to ask, "Who needs millions of hours of home video on the web?" They plant the idea that there is enough to read and watch already, so we don't need more media made by inexperienced people.

Every new medium goes through this stage of being blown off: talkies, color movies, television, and the web. All of the aforementioned were supposed to fail, yet all of them have overcome their initial roadblocks. In 1957, Francois Truffaut (Figure 1-2) said, "The film of tomorrow will not be directed by civil servants of the camera, but by artists for whom shooting a film constitutes a wonderful and thrilling adventure . . . it will be enjoyable because it will be true and new. . .the film of tomorrow will be an act of love."

FIGURE 1-2: "The film of
tomorrow will be an
act of love." — Francois Truffaut.

Throughout history, practitioners of an old medium make fun of the practitioners of a new medium, as the early adopters learn their craft and explore its boundaries. Often, the new medium grows, culture adopts it, and a new industry is born.

A national television network can play only a certain number of shows in a day, one after the other. Newspaper and magazines have only a couple hundred pages they can fill in a given day. Videoblogging gets in no one's way. If you don't want to see someone's videos, don't type that URL.

## A Global Community

The web is nearly infinite in its capacity for distributing information. The videoblogging world is one of vision and shared experiences. Every person can have his own videoblog. This is beautiful because a person's voice and vision is important whether he wants to post videos of his baby growing up, make a weekly comedy show with friends, or do video reporting of important events in his neighborhood. Politicians (see Figure 1-3) are even videoblogging to connect with their constituents on a more personal level.

Why is video so powerful on the web? Much of what we know and interpret is done through visual communication. When someone talks to you, you are learning and interpreting her intentions through her unspoken gestures, such as facial expression and speech patterns, as much as through what she actually says. With a videoblog, all of this unspoken expression is communicated.

Video creates empathy, and videoblogging enables people from opposite sides of the world to see what life is like in another country, through the eyes of another ordinary citizen. People in the United States can watch videos made by people in Iran. People in Japan can watch videos made by people in Chile. This is unprecedented.

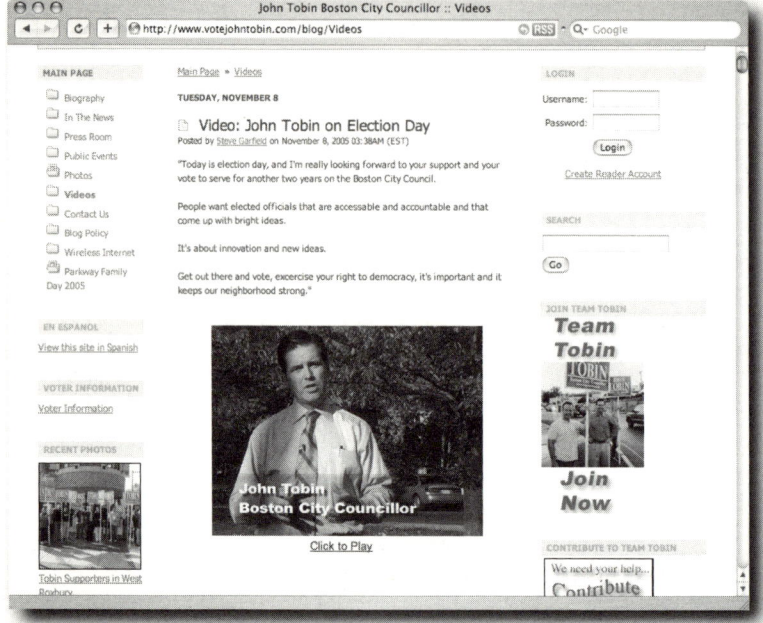

FIGURE 1-3: Boston City Councillor John Tobin's videoblog.

Videoblogging enables person-to-person communication, with no gatekeeper in between. It breaks down geographic and cultural barriers. Even in China, a country physically and metaphorically walled off from the world, blogs enable individuals to communicate on a global scale.

## Videoblogging: Up Close

What does it takes to make a videoblog? The rest of this book goes into greater detail about the specifics, but here's a simple outline to get you started:

1. Have an idea.

2. Record a video.

3. Transfer the video to your computer.

4. Edit the video.

5. Make a screenshot of your video.

6. Set up a blog.

7. Upload your video to a server.

8. Post the screenshot and video to your blog.

9. Create a feed on your blog so people can subscribe.

10. Tell people about your post and videoblog.

FreeVlog.org (`www.freevlog.org`) is a great site that walks you through the steps of setting up a videoblog, and its own videoblog provides tutorials. Michael Verdi and Ryanne Hodson, who created the site in the spring of 2004, run it.

## Interview with Ryanne Hodson of FreeVlog.org

*What made you create freevlog.org? What were your motivations?*

Michael and I had been getting so many emails asking how we had actually posted video to a blog, what was RSS (Really Simple Syndication), where did we host videos, etc. Some folks had dismissed videoblogging as a tool only viable for video professionals. Since both of us came from an art background, we decided it was time to set the record straight and illustrate the steps it took to videoblog and, most importantly, how to do it for free.

*What kind of people do you see using your tutorial?*

We see lots of different people using the tutorial, from techie nerds to artists to moms and dads to teenage kids. This is one of our goals, to make the tutorial easy enough for your grandma to understand.

*What are some of the unique videoblogs that you've seen made?*

One of the videobloggers who came through FreeVlog was Alan Larson, who created Alan's Bird Cam Blog (`http://birdcamblog.blogspot.com`). Alan's an avid birdwatcher who videotapes and describes birds at his window feeder. The vlog is so simple and beautiful, anyone would be interested to watch.

Another interesting vlog is A Pilot's Life (`http://lear60.blogspot.com`), which is an in-depth look at the life of an airline pilot in the US.

*Since you came from commercial TV, what do you see in videoblogging that isn't in TV?*

Videoblogging was like my saving grace from a life of editing for television. I found that TV is severely limiting for artists because there are no open distribution methods, no chance for feedback, and no dialog with viewers. Plus, there is such a high barrier to entry.

Videoblogs allow individuals to produce video with no censorship, there no producers manipulating content for ratings or sponsors. Artists and non-artists alike have a level playing field for producing and expressing themselves through a visual medium in a way never before available. Videobloggers can have their voices heard just as loudly as any network television show.

# Videoblogging Motivations

So why do you want to make a videoblog? All good videoblogs start with a strong idea. Remember, a videoblog is made up of many videos that build up over time. You are not making a movie (although you could), so you shouldn't feel pressured to have it "right" in one video. Very often, you will write text along with your video to give it context.

A videoblog can be that of a couple documenting their first baby, extreme videos such as the beheadings that occurred in the Middle East, a fictional story of hunting the Loch Ness monster, a girl interviewing her grandparents about their lives, a. . .well, you get the picture.

Maybe you'll choose to distribute video of the things that happen to you daily, or your business, or a specific hobby you do on weekends. Through a videoblog, you are sharing your ideas with other people. Choose a topic that you are really interested in. Doing so will help you stay focused and motivated.

Videoblogging is not necessarily another form of TV. Most videobloggers post short videos because they don't have time for anything longer and because most people don't want to sit through more than a few minutes of "web video." And as with most rules, every guideline presented here can be broken.

# Documenting the World Around You

Personal videoblogs are about the people who make them. They use the blog to keep up with ideas, share what's going on in their lives, and comment on things they've seen on the web and in the world. A personal videoblog is really just for the person who makes it, but it can help friends and family keep up and in touch.

If you choose to create a personal videoblog, you'll probably meet people online with similar personalities. But ultimately, you are keeping a record of your life and ideas. Steve Garfield is a prolific videoblogger known for producing "The Carol and Steve Show" (http://stevegarfield.blogs.com/videoblog/carol_and_steve_show), which is about his and his wife's life together, among other videos.

---

### Interview with Steve Garfield

*Steve, you posted a video in January 2004, declaring that year to be the "year of the videoblog." This turned out to be true. No one else was posting video like this. What prompted the idea of videoblogging?*

I'd been posting videos to web pages and blogging but hadn't combined the two. Thinking back on it, it might have come to me in a dream. It was New Year's 2004, and I wanted to challenge myself with something. Figuring out how to add video to a blog was something that I felt should be easy but wasn't. So I decided to post a video to my blog, declaring 2004 as The Year of the Videoblog. Little did I know what would follow.

*You have extensive experience doing professional video; why do you videoblog?*

A lot of times my professional projects need to be perfect. Some videos need to be edited down to the frame level for accuracy for broadcast (that's 1/30th of a second). With videoblogging, it doesn't have to be that way. In fact, video for videoblogging has no rules! That's what's so exciting about it.

The audience also does more than just sit back and watch. They respond. I'll get comments on my videoblog and emails from as far away as Australia. That's what's so different from doing traditional video. With videoblogging, there's an ongoing conversation that can happen about the work.

*Do people understand what you're doing? How do you explain it at a party?*

Most people don't understand what I'm doing. A lot of them are not interested. Most of the time people want to talk about themselves. Once in a while I might meet someone who gets it. Maybe an artist looking to expand the audience for his work, or a band that wants to get greater exposure. But when I hit it right, and explain it to someone who is receptive to the idea, then the magic happens.

I explained it to Boston City Councillor John Tobin. He became the first U.S. elected official to video blog. He loves it, and his constituents love it, too.

*Do you have any advice for new videobloggers?*

My advice for new videobloggers is to look at videoblogging as a continuum. There are four steps: Watch, Learn, Create, and Teach.

First, go out and watch some video blogs. See who is out there and watch what they are doing. Leave some comments on people's sites. Second, learn how to create a videoblog. Then third, create one for yourself. After you've gone through these steps, help others start their own. That's what I've done. It's very rewarding.

Now get out there and become a videoblogger. Send me a link and I'll be watching.

So pick up a camera. Even a digital still camera that records video clips can be a highly effective tool for videoblogging. If you record a bunch of the little moments that happen in any given day, edit them together on your computer, and post them regularly, you'll have an incredibly amazing record of your life that anyone can see.

With videoblogging, you can be anonymous or attempt to become a superstar. You can videoblog for free. . .or spend a lot of money. You can have an audience of 5, 50, or 50,000 people. . .maybe more.

The majority of those who do videoblog do so with no aspirations of making money from their work. Others actively try to create revenue models that will let them videoblog fulltime. Remember, you don't need permission to videoblog. It's essentially free, open, and without rules.

As with any open system, you will get stuff of varying quality, which holds different relevance based on who is looking at it. If I make an unappealing videoblog, no one needs to watch. They simply don't have to type the URL. But someone, somewhere, may like and be interested in what you find unappealing. The point is: Videoblogs are available for whoever wants to see them. You can pick and choose what to watch and when to watch it.

Blogging is a culture of sharing. People comment, link to each other, remix each other's work, and quote each other. This helps the community grow. . .and growth leads to a global conversation. By videoblogging, you are joining this culture.

# Making a Show

Commercial producers are starting to see Internet distribution as just another way to showcase their existing content. You already can purchase episodes of the television shows "Lost" and "Desperate Housewives" for $1.99 through the iTunes music store. The concept is that people will download these shows so they can watch them on their TV or portable device such as Sony's PlayStation Portable or Apple's iPod.

## Interview with Andrew Michael Baron of Rocketboom

*How did you discover videoblogging? What inspired you to do Rocketboom?*

I didn't really discover videoblogging; I just figured out on my own that it would be another dimension for blogging. I was volunteering for John Edwards in the primaries already in 2003, and in the spring of 2004, I was creating a site for Senator John Edwards' DVD. I noticed after making the site that people were able to view the video without problems. For the first time, I noticed, most people didn't complain about plugin or buffering problems.

So it dawned on me that the time for video online was now. I decided I would create a videoblog and that I could use it as a tool to help defeat Bush. Well, I got side-tracked because I was hired at M.I.T that summer, but I used those months to brainstorm my plan and save up money and create one when I got back to NYC and that this is what I would do after the election was over (because it would take me almost until then to launch it). I also thought to myself that it would be really big, so I figured that I would be able to realistically, somehow, sustain from it (mostly from other opportunities it would bring, I thought).

*What other formats did you think about doing?*

I considered how Rocketboom could be great for people in general and how it could be used in so many ways, but I was interested mostly in apolitical things, actually, like computers, art, design, and Internet culture. So, I knew that it would be short wit commentary because that's what I was inspired by, stylistically, in the other blogs that I liked to read and also wrote for.

*Do you have any professional video background?*

I co-created and designed the Motion Capture/Motion Tracking Lab at Parsons (School of Design), where I taught grad students for a couple of years. My mission statement and site design are still the same on the current site, at `http://a.parsons.edu/~motion/`.

What most people don't realize is that they can do essentially the same thing. Budding filmmakers can now make a videoblog to showcase their work. Also, they can submit their videoblog to iTunes and enable people to subscribe to their videos from the iTunes store. This presents a possible future where even the worst movie will be seen by at least several hundred people. Now that is a huge audience that couldn't have existed just a few years ago.

Filmmakers do not need to appeal to a mass audience but can instead tell stories for specific audiences. Niche audiences are becoming the norm.

Many people want to make documentaries. Videoblogging enables people to tell stories in segments, which are perfect for documentaries. No longer does a producer have to limit her documentary to less than two hours, because she can produce a story that spans years, told over the same amount of time. Again, this is unprecedented.

Another option people can choose is to make a regular TV-like show, in the form of episodes and storylines. As with TV, you choose a topic, choose a host or characters, choose a format, and publish the video on a regular basis. Through this format, a videoblog can build an audience of people who know what to expect and when to expect it.

One example of this model is Rocketboom (`www.rocketboom.com`). Andrew Baron started the Rocketboom (see Figure 1-4) videoblog at the beginning of 2005. Each day of the week he posts a three-minute video where Rocketboom's host, Amanda Congdon, shows some cool stuff they've found on the web. As of this writing, the show has more than 250,000 downloads a day and is also distributed via TiVo (`http://research.tivo.com/rocketboom`).

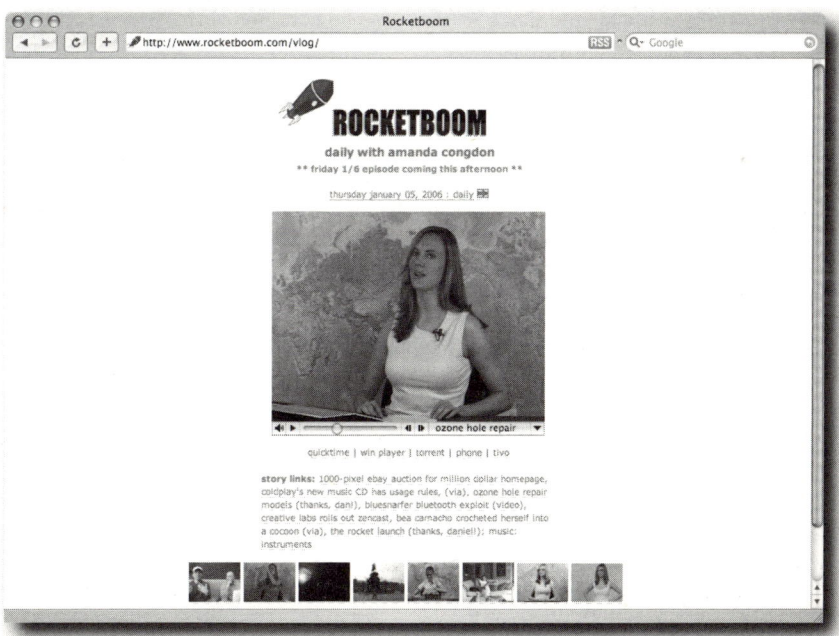

FIGURE 1-4: Rocketboom is hosted by Amanda Congdon and viewed by more than 100,000 people daily.

The funny thing is, Rocketboom is shot in Andrew's apartment, using a simple DV camera, audio microphones, and small lighting kit. He does all of the editing on a laptop. Yet Andrew has a larger audience than that of some cable television shows. Rocketboom proves that if a videoblog is regularly distributed, with content that is interesting, large numbers of people will subscribe and watch.

So, where's all the money in this? No one has that answer yet. But if you can get lots of people to watch your videoblog regularly, making money just becomes a detail.

# Distributing Worldwide (or Just to Your Neighborhood)

Never before in human history could a regular person create and distribute video worldwide for little or no cost. Your audience may be half the planet or half your family. There is no difference in your videoblogging process.

For example, my girlfriend is eating dinner, and I think she's beautiful. I pull out my little camera and record her. When I get home, I import the videoclip on my computer, edit it a little, and upload it to my videoblog. The whole process takes about 10 minutes. Now, all my friends and family around the world can see what I saw that night and know why I'm so happy. In fact, anyone can watch this video. Maybe someone will link to it because he can understand where I'm coming from, and he and I start a conversation and become friends. . .and he's halfway around the world.

Videoblogging breaks down barriers and borders and opens lines of communication. When you start videoblogging, you may find that you have more in common with someone who lives in another country than you do with your next-door neighbor. It happens, often.

# Making a Video Viral

Once you post a video to a blog, anything can happen. You are putting it out there to the world. You may one day be (un)lucky enough to have one of your videos linked to and emailed around the world and watched by hundreds of thousands of people in a single day. This phenomenon is called *viral video*.

It happened to Gary Brolsma, who distributed a video of himself dancing (see Figure 1-5). The video became known as the "Numa Numa Dance" and has been downloaded more than 1 million times from www.newgrounds.com/portal/view/206373. It has also been emailed to countless people around the world and has appeared on "Good Morning America" and "The Tonight Show with Jay Leno" as well as being parodied on a number of web sites and television shows.

A video can become viral if it is compelling and resonates with the people who view it. It also needs to be small enough to be emailed, which means it should be less than 10MB and preferably 5MB or less. Whether it's humorous, heart warming, or gut wrenching depends on your personal taste and that of the people who find it worthwhile to email it to their friends.

FIGURE 1-5: Gary Brolsma performing the Numa Numa Dance.

# Archiving for Future Generations

When you make a videoblog, your videos live online so people can find them at anytime. Taking this to the extreme, your videos could be stored online and available in 50 years. If you videoblog, your grandkids will be able to see and hear the world through their computers in a way that traditional news, whether written or televised, never could because people from around the world can choose what they want to show.

This is opposite of traditional "big media," which follows a top-down model. Traditional news media starts with raw material and filters it for you, deciding which stories are important to fill a certain amount of space (such as the pages of a newspaper or time of a news broadcast). The web, however, is bottom up — everyone has access to the same raw material, and anyone can decide how to arrange it with essentially no limit on the amount of space of time they fill.

The web is a huge archive that lets you arrange the pieces anyway you want. If you don't want to be your own editor, sit back and relax. . .there are plenty of people with interests similar to yours who will do it for you.

# Explaining to Others What You're Doing

Videoblogging is still a couple years from becoming mainstream, which is why it's so exciting to be involved in it right now. People will look at you like you're crazy when you talk about putting video of your life online and technology such as Really Simple Syndication (RSS). The best way to talk about videoblogging is to talk about how people use the web currently.

Most people go online, check their email, and check a couple of their favorite web sites. They more than likely use a search engine like Google to find things they are researching or interested in. But there's a new way to consume information that is on the web. It is through the use of an RSS reader, and it enables people to subscribe to sites they want to follow. Some video-capable RSS readers, also known video aggregators, are iTunes (`www.apple.com/itunes`), FireAnt (`www.fireant.tv`), I/ON (`http://openvision.tv/home/ion.html`), and Democracy (`www.getdemocracy.com`). With a video aggregator, you can subscribe to videoblogs, and the application will download a new video whenever one's available. When using the web this way, a person simply opens the aggregator of his choice, and any new posts are automatically brought to him. It's all made possible through RSS.

So with videoblogging, not only can you create your own video channel, but you can also subscribe to the feeds or channels of those you want to keep up with. All a person has to do is open his aggregator and watch.

## Summary

To become a videoblogger, you need to get into the right state of mind, or, as Ty Webb (Chevy Chase) says in Caddyshack, "Be the ball." To "Be the ball" in videoblogging, you need to understand the technology behind it at a very basic level.

# Get Your Tech On

**T**o videoblog, you have to deal with a variety of technologies; however, the technology isn't intimidating. Nor should it be. If a stay-at-home mother of two (http://nealey.blogspot.com) can videoblog, so can you. Figure 2-1 shows Erin's videoblog's home page.

So, what technology do you need? Well, it depends. For most situations, a video camera, a computer that can capture video, and an Internet connection are the bare minimum. Additional items you'll likely want are a video editing application, lights, and a whole lot of creativity. But, first things first.

This chapter provides you with the technical preparations you need for camera and computer, along with advice that stores won't give you.

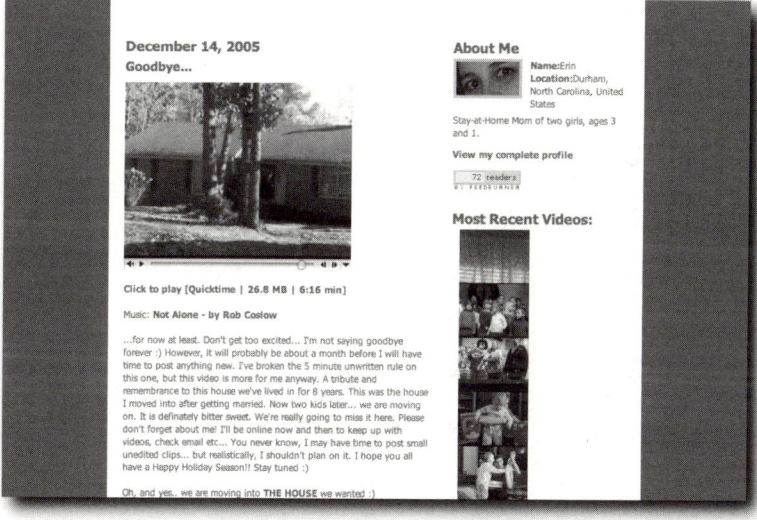

FIGURE 2-1: Erin videoblogs. So can you.

# Choosing a Video Camera

The primary reason to videoblog is to distribute video via the Internet. To do so, you need to acquire video somehow. Although there are sources for free video, such as the Internet Archive (www.archive.org), you'll find videoblogging a lot more fun if you distribute video you've shot for yourself.

One problem with choosing a video camera is simply that there are so many choices. Many people feel there are, in fact, too many choices. To help narrow down your options, you'll need to ask yourself a few questions. They aren't difficult, but they do require you to be honest with yourself about your real requirements.

## Usage

How you intend to use your camera can help narrow your choices dramatically.

Will you always record video while near your computer? If so, a webcam such as Logitech's QuickCam ($29.95+, www.logitech.com) might fulfill your needs. If not, you can pretty much eliminate a webcam from the equation. Most people want to record and distribute video that they obtain while out of their home or office, such as children playing sports, local events like parades, and common daily activities. Although you could tote around a laptop computer along with a webcam, that's not really practical. Webcams are available in different shapes and sizes, as shown in Figure 2-2.

FIGURE 2-2: A couple of webcams.

Will you record video for Internet distribution only? If so, you may find that a digital camera with video capabilities such as the Sanyo Xacti (Figure 2-3) is the perfect fit. Many of these cameras offer exceptional digital-quality images for still pictures, while adding the capability to record video. The downside is that the video is often suitable only for Internet distribution. If you plan to use your video for independent film making, you'll almost certainly want to look at a camera that utilizes tape, such as DV or HDV cameras.

If you want to have every distribution option available to you, tape-based cameras provide the most versatility. In addition, videotape is a cheap, reliable medium for acquiring and archiving footage, whereas digital storage (hard drives, flash drives, and so on) can be expensive and volatile. As of this writing, a mini-DV tape costs about $10 and has a capacity of approximately 13 gigabytes (GB). This is about the same price per GB for hard drives at $1 per GB and much less than CompactFlash disks at $100 per GB.

FIGURE 2-3: The Sanyo Xacti is the preferred choice of many videobloggers.

An alternate choice, which a few videobloggers are experimenting with, is to use a video-enabled cell phone. That's still an emerging technology, however, and the quality of such video is usually quite low, so it isn't covered in-depth in this book.

## Size and Weight

Of the three available types of cameras, only tape-based cameras come in a wide variety of sizes. Webcams and digital still cameras almost always fit in one hand and can be carried in a pocket or small bag.

Tape-based cameras, on the other hand, range in size from those that can fit in your pocket to those weighing 10 pounds or more. Unless you're planning to shoot an independent feature film and enter it in film festivals, you'll probably want to stick with the smaller, lighter cameras, such as the Sony DCR-P55 shown on the right in Figure 2-4.

When evaluating cameras of equivalent size and weight, you'll want to compare the final image quality that each camera can acquire.

FIGURE 2-4: Video cameras come in a range of sizes (Canon XL-1 and Sony DCR-P55).

## Video Quality

When it comes to video "quality," the term is purely subjective, but there are some guidelines that can help you determine what fits your needs. Keep in mind that acquiring higher-quality video initially will result in a higher-quality video in the end.

A typical videoblog is distributed at a resolution of 320 pixels high by 240 pixels wide (320x240). The 320x240 size is in essence half the size of the visible portion of a standard television signal in North America (also known as NTSC). Also, most videoblogs distribute video that displays at 15 frames per second (fps). This is, again, essentially half of an NTSC signal.

Distributing your video at a resolution of 320x240 and a frame rate of 15fps means your camera must record at least at that resolution and frame rate. Fortunately, almost all current video-enabled devices — whether cell phone, digital camera, or video camera — can record such video. Keep in mind, though, that you will more than likely wind up compressing your video, therefore degrading its quality. You learn more about compression in Chapter 9.

Most video-enabled still cameras are capable of recording video at 320x240 and 15fps. Many can even record higher resolution images at 640x480, and many can even reach 30fps. However, the overall image quality isn't great compared to that of tape-based cameras.

The DV format is by far the most popular consumer, and pro-sumer, format on the market. DV can record video at 720x480 and 29.97fps (NTSC), or 720x576 and 25fps (PAL). Many cameras also offer various features that enable DV to look more "film-like" by changing the way each image is captured to a frame of video, altering the frame rate, and even providing control over details such as chroma. Not only is the DV format an excellent choice for acquiring video for videoblogging, but it can also be displayed on a television at broadcast quality.

Over the past couple of years, the HDV format, a video format capable of recording high-definition video on mini DV videotape, has gained some attention. Its "native" sizes are 1280x720 and 1440x1080, but it can record at various resolutions and frame rates. The method that HDV uses to record video is quite technical and, once you scratch the surface, can become daunting. Suffice it to say that HDV looks beautiful and is a higher resolution than "standard" DV (720x480).

Another decision you'll need to make when choosing a camera is how many Charged-Coupled Devices (CCDs) you'd like. Without getting too technical, CCDs are computer chips that can sense light and help record images. CCDs come in various sizes, and manufacturers take different approaches to distinguish themselves. In a nutshell, the more CCDs in the camera, the better your image will look. (Higher-quality cameras, for instance, have three CCDs.)

## Compression

The nature of compressing video requires a drop in quality from the original footage. This occurs because you are trying to "squeeze" the video into a smaller file. To do so, a trade-off has to occur. Besides changing the video's height, width, and frame rate, compression changes many of the color properties. If you can acquire high-quality video, you'll see a difference in the resulting compressed video.

## Options

When researching video cameras, you'll find options galore. Some of the options include the capability to shoot video in the dark (by using infrared light); the capability to edit "in-camera," including adding effects and titles; various recording speeds to allow you to record 90 minutes of footage on a 60-minute tape; and audio inputs for professional microphones (known as XLR connections).

## Price

Cameras can range in price from a couple hundred dollars to tens of thousands of dollars. As with most purchases, don't spend money on features you aren't going to use. On the other hand, don't skimp on features you may use. It's cheaper to spend a little more on a camera and get the feature(s) you plan to use than to discover a few months after your purchase that you want to buy a different camera. A good source for information and reviews of digital video cameras is www.camcorderinfo.com.

The following table covers the major pros and cons of the three types of video cameras.

| Video Camera Selection Considerations | | |
|---|---|---|
| *Type* | *Pros* | *Cons* |
| MPEG | Ultra-portable | Image quality |
| | Examples: | Sony Cyber Shot DSC-T7 ($350) |
| | | Sanyo Xacti DMX-C6 ($500) |
| DV | Tape-based | Not pocket-sized |
| | Examples: | Panasonic PV-GS250 ($350) |
| | | Sony DCR-PC55 ($500) |
| HDV | Incredible image | Require carrying case |
| | Examples: | Sony HDR-HC1 ($1,500) |
| | | JVC GR-HD1 ($2,500) |

Ultimately, you need to do some research and make the final decision. New camera models and features are probably going to be released 24 hours after this book is printed. (Technology's just that way, isn't it?)

### FireWire and USB

Selecting a camera can be a confusing process. An additional point of uncertainty for many people is the method of connecting a camera to their computer. Most of the currently available cameras offer either an IEEE-1394 (FireWire or i.LINK) or Universal Serial Bus (USB) connection. The primary difference between the two is the process they use to transfer information to the computer.

USB requires a computer to act as a controller. Because of this, processes and applications running on the computer can affect the performance of a USB device. FireWire allows peer-to-peer device communication without using your computer's resources, so its data transfer is much more reliable. Therefore, it is well suited for transferring data off of a tape, which is why you often find a FireWire connection on a tape-based camera.

Here's what the different cables look like:

**A FireWire cable (left) and a USB cable.**

# Cheap Lighting Solutions

Lighting video is both art and science. Many people earn a living just mounting, pointing, adjusting, and controlling lighting. That should tell you that it's not a simple task. Entire books are dedicated to explaining the intricacies of lighting. None of this, however, means you can't successfully light your video, even cheaply.

## Reflectors

Professional photographers often use reflectors to help balance out light and fill in shadows (see Figure 2-5). Such reflectors can cost from as little as $10 to more than $200. However, there are a number of cheap alternatives, some possibly lying around your house.

A reflector does just that: reflects light. A variety of household items can reflect light. A mirror is probably the most obvious choice, but you can't gain much control over its reflected light (which is usually quite concentrated), decent-sized ones aren't really portable, and if you break one, well . . .

### Aluminum Foil

Instead of a mirror, try using aluminum foil. Its reflective properties are similar, but it's easier to control, much more portable, and meant to be broken (torn). Also, it has two sides, one more reflective than the other.

FIGURE 2-5: Using a reflector enables you to fill shadows. The facial features are much easier to see in the picture on the right, for which reflected light was used.

To create an aluminum foil reflector (see Figure 2-6), simply tear off a piece of foil at the desired length, crumple it slightly, and flatten it.

FIGURE 2-6: An aluminum foil reflector.

By crumpling the foil, you create a variety of ridges that disperse the reflected light. This provides a more natural-looking light on your subject. You can also attach the foil to a piece of cardboard to provide a more rigid backing.

### Windshield Shade

Another wonderful item that can work double-duty as a reflector is an automobile windshield shade. There are generally two types of shades: cardboard and fabric. A cardboard shade usually has one side that is predominantly white, which is the side you will want to use for reflecting light. Auto shades often do a good job in a pinch.

The fabric-type windshield shades often have a metallic side — similar to the fabric used in professional reflectors — that can work as a really effective reflector.

## Dimmers

Every once in a while you have a light that is simply too bright. By placing a dimmer on the light, you can gain control over its intensity. A variety of dimmers are available, but the most functional are those that simply plug into an AC outlet and then allow you to plug in a light (see Figure 2-7).

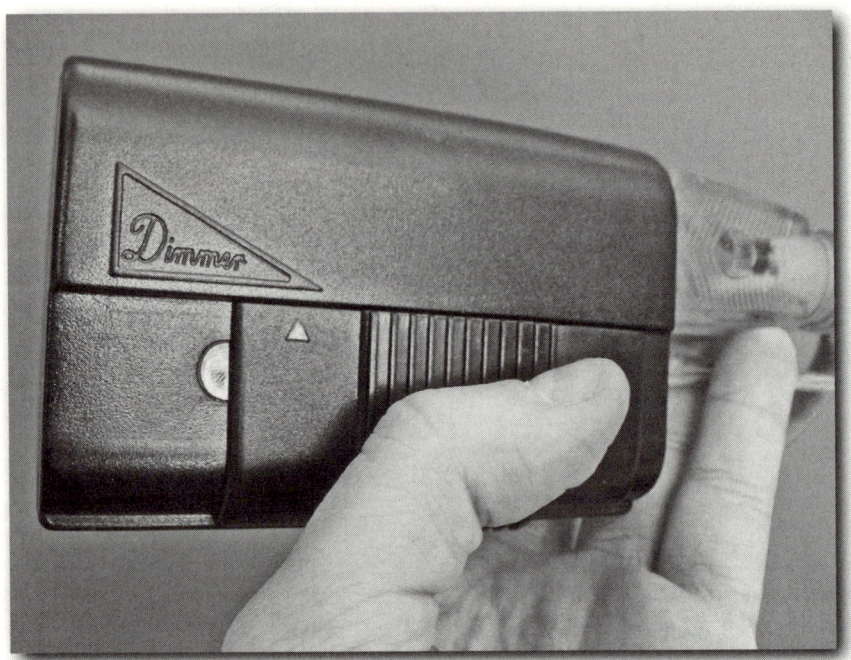

FIGURE 2-7: A lamp dimmer.

You can find dimmers at common household goods stores such as Wal-Mart and Target and home improvement stores such as Lowe's and Home Depot. Some dimmers, called Triac dimmers, reduce the brilliance of a light by turning it on and off really fast (sometimes up to 120 times per second). As most bulbs aren't designed for such abuse, this approach can often generate a hum or buzz. The hum is caused by the light's filament vibrating.

Quite obviously, a hum in your video is undesirable, so test your dimmers before using them. You may also have more success — no hum or buzz — by using a rheostat or variable transformer (Variac) dimmer to control your lights. These types of dimmers can be quite expensive, however.

Note    You can learn more about rheostat and voltage control, including how to make a rudimentary rheostat, at www.energyquest.ca.gov/projects/rheostat.html.

Companies such as Impact and Cool-Lux offer professional dimmers that can be purchased through B&H Photo (www.bhphotovideo.com) and other photo/video retailers.

## Diffusion

Diffusion is a very effective method of softening light. It scatters light, making it less intense. A simple example of this is to hold up a piece of white paper in front of a light; notice that the light becomes less intense and softer.

One good option for easy diffusion is to use baking or parchment paper, opaque papers manufactured to withstand the high heat of an oven. A roll of baking paper can be purchased at most grocery stores for less than $5. Figure 2-8 illustrates its use.

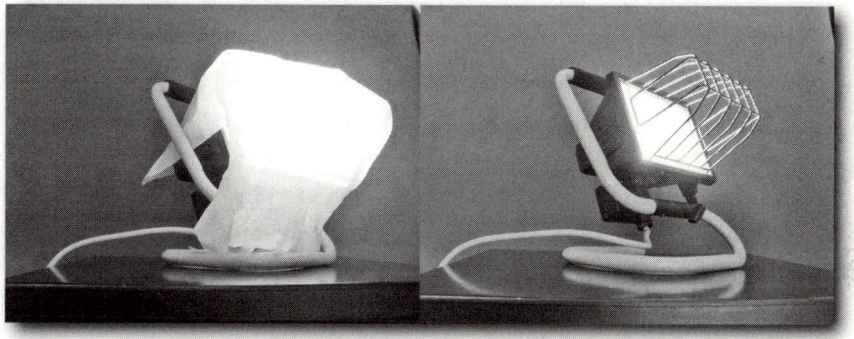

FIGURE 2-8: A light with and without baking paper diffusion.

 Be aware that baking paper is not wax paper; the two are quite different.

You can purchase professional diffusion products from places such as Filmtools (www. filmtools.com) and B&H Photo. When searching these sites, simply use the word "diffusion" and you'll discover a wide range of options.

You can also use some cheap alternatives to create diffusion; some items are probably lying around your house. Be aware, however, that using diffusion involves light and that light generates heat. Therefore, using diffusion can be a fire hazard.

## Lights and Lamps

Although traditional lights are sufficient for shooting video, "lighting" can help enhance the images you plan to capture. Even adding one simple light can make a tremendous difference in the look and feel of your video, as seen in Figure 2-9.

FIGURE 2-9: A simple shot using available lighting (left) and additional lighting (right).

### Paper Lamps

Using paper lamps, sometimes called Chinaballs, is a great way to create soft, even light. The lamps are so effective that you can even purchase them from professional film and video retailers such as Filmtools. You can often purchase them at swap meets, novelty shops, and even online.

### Work Lights

An extremely effective — and affordable — method of lighting is to use work lights. These lights are often very bright (100W–500W) and exceptionally durable, because they're designed for use in workshops and at contract sites. They can be purchased at most home improvement stores such as Home Depot and Lowe's.

If you find that a work light is simply too bright for a certain situation, covering it with some baking paper will likely solve the problem. Ultimately, you'll learn how to "light" for video through practice. When lighting, be creative in what you try, but most of all, have fun.

## Quick Kit

If you want to assemble a quick, portable, and cheap lighting kit, simply gather the following items:

> A roll of aluminum foil
>
> A roll of baking or parchment paper
>
> A couple of dimmers
>
> A couple of work lights

A couple of extension cords (for running power to lights, when and where needed)

A handful of wooden clothespins (for attaching baking paper to lights, foil to items, and so on)

A backpack to hold everything

For $50–$100, you can assemble a pretty decent lighting kit that you can take almost anywhere.

# Choosing a Computer

This book covers the major operating systems — Windows XP/2000 and Mac OS X — along with a few Linux tips when possible. The choice of a computer is a personal one, but no matter which system you choose, you should strive to obtain some minimum requirements:

| Operating System | Mac/Windows/Linux |
| --- | --- |
| Chip/Speed | G4, 1GHz+ for HDV<br>Pentium 4/Athlon, 3GHz+ for HDV |
| Disk/Space/Speed | 13GB per hour of DV/HDV; varies with other formats; 7200 rpm or better |
| RAM | 512MB+ |
| FireWire/USB | Depends on your camera selection; if you can get a computer with a FireWire port, do so. |

# Selecting Editing Software

There is a wide variety of video-editing applications available, ranging in price from free to more than $100,000. If you are just getting started with video editing, it is recommended that you start with one of the free applications available for your particular operating system. If you've recently purchased a computer, it more than likely came with one bundled (see Figure 2-10): iMovie on Mac and Movie Maker on Windows.

FIGURE 2-10: Apple's iMovie (left) and Microsoft's Movie Maker (right) are included with most new computers.

The following table outlines some of the distinguishing features of the more popular editing applications:

| Application (by operating system) | Cost | Features |
| --- | --- | --- |
| **Mac** | | |
| Apple iMovie | free | Works with DV/HDV; integrated with iTunes/iPhoto/iDVD |
| Apple Final Cut Express | $299 | Works with DV/HDV; includes Soundtrack/LiveType |
| Apple Final Cut Studio | $999 | Works with DV/HDV/HD; aimed at professionals using HD/HDV |
| **Windows** | | |
| Microsoft Movie Maker | free | Works with DV; integrated with WindowsXP/2000 |
| Adobe Premiere Elements | $99 | Works with DV/MPEG-4/DVD/cell phone |
| Adobe Premiere Pro | $999 | Works with DV/HDV/HD; aimed at professionals using HD/HDV |
| Sony Vegas | $449 | Works with DV/HDV/HD; aimed at prosumers and professionals |
| **Cross-Platform** | | |
| Apple QuickTime Pro | $30 | Works with most video types; quick and dirty |
| Avid FreeDV | free | Works with DV; introduces user to Avid interface |
| Avid XpressDV | $1,499 | Favorite within Hollywood circles |

If you plan to edit video for your videoblog only, iMovie or Movie Maker will more than suffice. As you become more proficient in editing, you may discover that you would like features that aren't available in those applications, such as the capability to matte using a greenscreen. Fortunately, plenty of companies offer applications to help you explore your imagination.

## Summary

Once you've trudged through the world of digital video, you'll reap the rewards of it. Not only will you be able to create video masterpieces at home, but you'll also be able to show them to the world. How? By creating a video channel of your own on the web—your videoblog.

# Starting a Blog

**Y**our blog is the basis for everything you will do. With a blog, you aren't required to know HTML to create web pages. Your blog automates all of the tasks that used to eat up time when publishing to the web. Everything is easy.

This chapter leads you through the steps to create your videoblog. The rest of this book goes into great depth on all these steps and actually builds upon them. Yet you can set up a videoblog without really knowing what the techno-jargon means.

A videoblog is a blog that distributes video using an RSS feed. To understand a videoblog, then, you really just need to understand a blog. Figure 3-1 provides a visual overview of a typical blog.

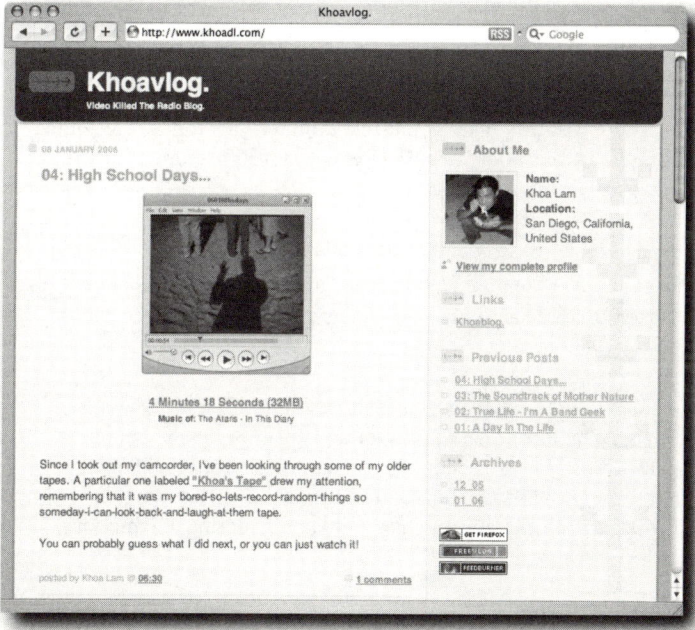

FIGURE 3-1: A sample blog.

# Creating a Videoblog for Free

Creating a videoblog is actually quite easy. In less than 30 minutes you can be distributing video on the Internet.

Here are the simple steps for setting up your videoblog:

**1.** Set up a blog.

**2.** Upload your video to a server.

**3.** Create your first videoblog post.

**4.** Create an RSS feed.

Believe it or not, that's all there is to it — and it's all easy to do!

Many good blogging services are available. You can use an all-in-one service such as TypePad (`www.typepad.com`), for which you must pay a fee each month, or a simple text-based blog system such as Blogger (`www.blogger.com`), which is free. (Blogger is run by a little company called Google. You may have heard of it.)

We recommend Blogger because it's easy to use, reliable, hosts your blog, and even stores photos for free. Another site gaining popularity among videobloggers is WordPress (`www.word press.com`) because it offers free hosting using the popular open-source blogging software WordPress (`www.wordpress.org`). Both sites work well for videoblogging purposes.

Setting up a blog at most sites is quite easy and takes about five minutes. Just follow the simple step-by-step instructions. For simplicity, this book uses Blogger.com for its examples; most sites work similarly. Figure 3-2 shows a page from the set-up process.

 **Note** You need to open accounts on various systems, so you may want to make it easier on yourself by using the same username/password for all of them. If you're more security conscious, feel free to do your thing. Either way, you'll need to create a username and password for each service, along with a name for your blog.

First, you create an account and accept the terms of service. Click Continue, and then you choose a name or title for your blog. The best titles are those that explain what the blog is about, such as Joe's Burger Reviews. You can also select a title that reflects your nickname, a brand name (one you create, not someone else's), or something simple like My Thoughts. Whatever you choose is up to you, and you can always change it later. Entering a name for a blog is easy, as shown in Figure 3-3.

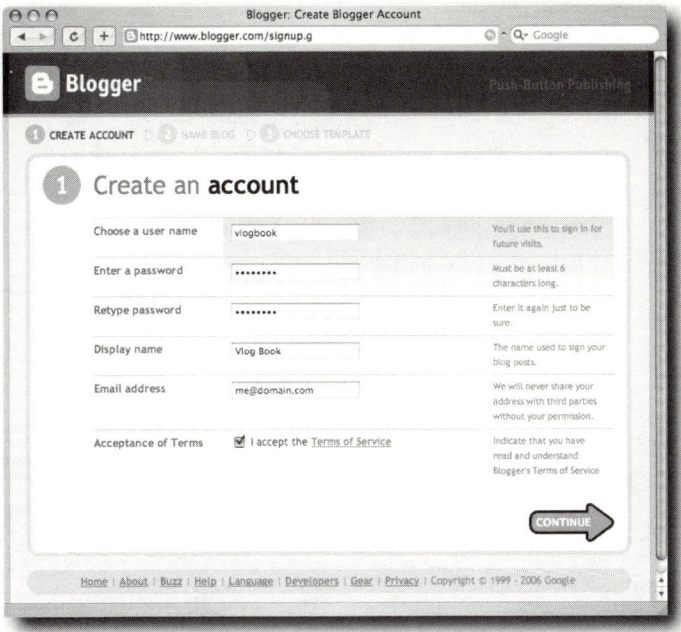

FIGURE 3-2: Signing up for a Blogger account.

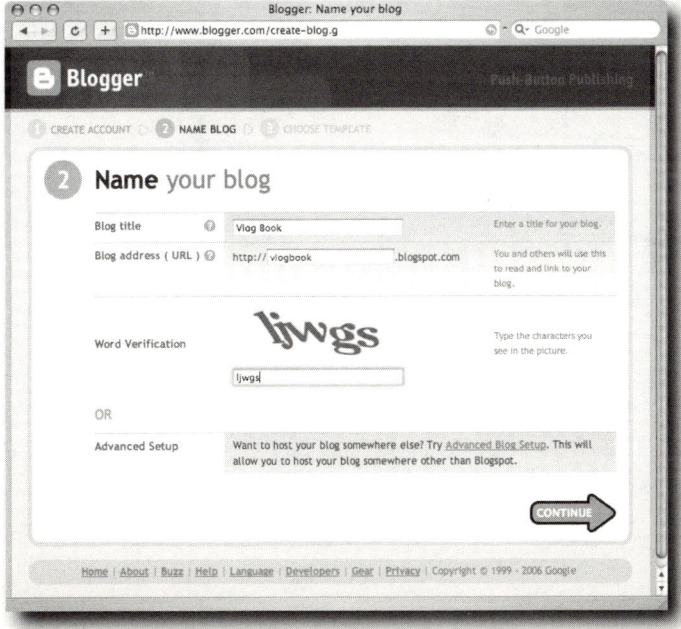

FIGURE 3-3: Naming your blog.

Next you need to decide on a URL. For instance, if you choose `ryanedit`, your URL would become `http://ryanedit.blogspot.com`. The difference between the title of your blog and the URL is that the title is just the large words on your blog, while the URL is the address someone types into his browser to read your blog. Once you've chosen the URL, the only way to change it is to create a new blog, so choose wisely. If you absolutely must change the URL, you can always link the original to a domain name that you buy. Click Continue.

Next, select a template, as shown in Figure 3-4. A template affects only the look of your blog, not the content, so don't fret over your choice. You can always change the template later.

Click Continue and Blogger creates your blog. Create a test post by typing some text and actually posting it to your blog, as shown in Figure 3-5. If all goes well — and it should — you have a blog!

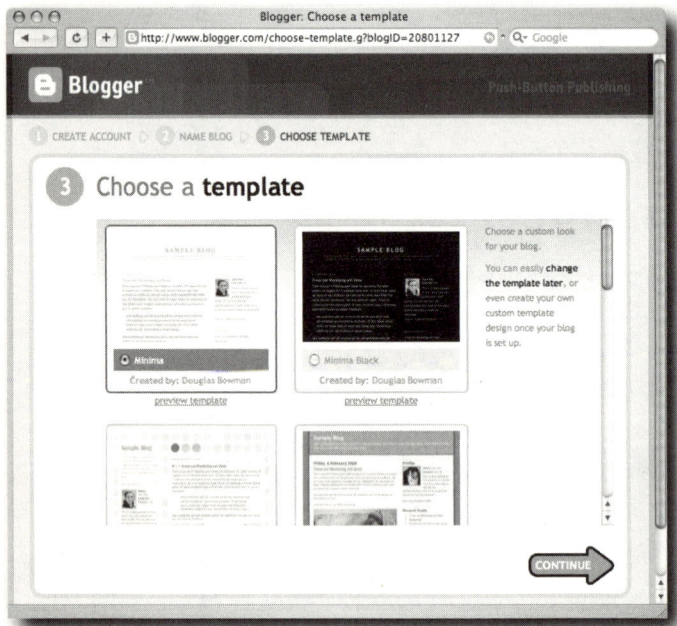

FIGURE 3-4: Selecting a template.

Blogger and blog systems in general are designed for ease of use. They're designed for control, too, so remember: You can edit and delete posts any time in the future.

Although Blogger is free, the site doesn't store video files, so you will need to host your videos on another server. The good news is that video hosting can also be free.

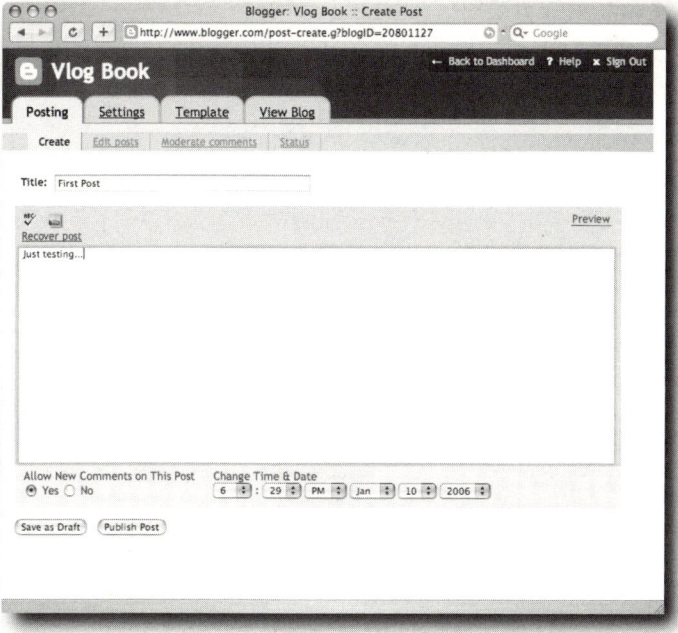

FIGURE 3-5: Testing an initial post.

# Uploading Your Video to a Server

Because you're interested in videoblogging, you must have video to distribute via the Internet. Everything in videoblogging depends on your having a little video file on your computer. To distribute it, though, you need to transfer the video to a server for hosting.

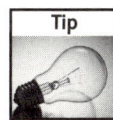

**Tip**   We recommend that you use short video clips smaller than 30MB. That's a size that most people can easily download from the Internet, without having to wait an unreasonable amount of time.

### What Is Video Hosting?

For people to be able to download your video at anytime, from anywhere, it needs to reside on a computer connected to the Internet 24 hours a day, 7 days a week. The computer should also utilize a fast connection to the Internet. When placing your video on such a computer, it is "hosted" on the computer. Later, when you link to the video, anyone can reliably download it from that server.

Unfortunately, most hosting companies charge a monthly fee for storage and transmission of files. In addition, they place limits on the amount of storage you have, as well as the amount of data you can transmit. So if you post a popular video, it will actually cost you more money as more people watch it. Furthermore, once you stop paying your monthly hosting fee, your video will be removed from the server and be unavailable. Paid servers make sense for businesses and for people who want complete control over their files.

**The Internet Archive**

The Internet Archive has been archiving nearly everything on the open web since 1996. The Archive maintains its own site, but nearly all of Ourmedia's user-generated media will be stored on the Internet Archive's ultra-large servers (racks of Petaboxes, actually; `www.archive.org/web/petabox.php`). The Archive's founder, Brewster Kahle, has pledged to preserve these materials for generations to come. You can read about Brewster Kahle at the Wikipedia page: http://en.wikipedia.org/wiki/Brewster_Kahle.

Many paid hosting services are available, and they all offer different services and pricing structures. As a videoblogger, you'll be most interested in three things: availability of blog software, storage space, and bandwidth allocation. As of this writing, DreamHost (`www.dreamhost.com`) is offering a great package for $7.95 per month, which includes WordPress blog software, 20GB of drive space, and 1TB of bandwidth per month. (For readers of this book, DreamHost will provide up to $97.00 off its service if you use the promotional code `vlog`.)

### Use a Free Video Host

The good news is that free servers are available. The Internet Archive (`www.archive.org`) and Ourmedia (`www.ourmedia.org`) have teamed to offer free storage to anyone producing original video. One caveat: Once you upload your video through Ourmedia, you give permission to the Internet Archive to make your work publicly available (which is probably what you want, right?). You can choose appropriate licenses for how accessible you want your video to be beyond simple viewing, similar to copyright but with more options.

To set yourself up on Internet Archive or Ourmedia, just follow the appropriate instructions on the sites, or check out Freevlog's video tutorial at `http://freevlog.org/#step3`. After you acquire a hosting account, just follow the steps to upload your video.

There are also other free video-hosting sites, such as BlipTV (`www.blip.tv`).

Make sure you write down the URL provided for your video. That is where your video will reside and where people have to go to download it. This is important.

## Create Your First Videoblog Post

Okay, you've got the two essential parts of a videoblog: your own personal blog space and your video on a server. Now you just need to put them together.

Most videobloggers take a screenshot of their video and post it to their videoblog entry to indicate that a video exists for the post. They then link the video to the screenshot. To make a screenshot, open the video you are going to use, locate a section that you like, and follow the steps for your operating system (see Chapter 5 for more in-depth discussion):

- Mac:

    1. Press Command+Shift+4, and then press the space bar.

    2. Click the video.

    3. Locate the image on your Desktop.

- Windows:

    1. Press the Print Screen key.

    2. Open the Paint application.

    3. Select Edit→Paste.

    4. Crop the screenshot to just your video window.

    5. Save the image to your Desktop.

Blogger is really easy to use; just log in and create a New Post. Use the Photo Upload tool to add the screenshot you created, and then use the Link tool to connect the screenshot to the URL of video that you uploaded to your video host. Finally, add some text for your Post to give the video some context, and add links to the things you talk about and show.

Now when someone goes to your videoblog, he can click the screenshot and watch your video.

## Create an RSS Feed

Publishing videos to your blog is only half of the magic of videoblogging. The other half is syndicating your videos using Really Simple Syndication (RSS), which basically means people can subscribe to your videos. It's kind of like TiVo for Internet video.

Practically every blog provides an RSS feed. You can find them by looking for hyperlinks with names like Subscribe, RSS, RSS2, Atom, or XML. Often, the links are represented by graphics containing the aforementioned words, usually in the color orange, or with the community-accepted standard RSS icon (hey, even Microsoft agreed to it!), shown in Figure 3-6.

### Freevlog and Other Resources

Another resource for learning about videoblogging is Freevlog (www.freevlog.org), a great web site that has video tutorials to walk you through the steps of setting up a videoblog for free. It's a videoblog that teaches you how to videoblog.

Also, you can always ask real videobloggers technical questions on the Yahoo! Videoblogging group at http://groups.yahoo.com/group/videoblogging/.

Figure **3-6:** The RSS icon.

When you use RSS, your audience automatically downloads to their computers any new video you post. To subscribe, all a person has to do is click the RSS link in your blog. That's it. She doesn't have to do anything but watch from that point forward!

You now have a videoblog that lets you post video. . .and anyone on the planet with an Internet connection can subscribe to it and watch it. Remember that you can post anything you want. You can even have multiple videoblogs at once. It's the Wild West.

In the following chapters, you'll learn tricks and tips for making your videoblog an amazing place for people to visit.

# Moving a Blog from Blogger

If you've set up your videoblog using Blogger, at some point you may want to gain more control over your videoblog. Then you need to migrate to a different blogging system. There are a lot of free blog software applications, but the most widely used are MovableType (`www.six apart.com/movabletype`), TextPattern (`www.textpattern.com`), and WordPress (`www.wordpress.org`). These are freely available, and some web hosts even provide them.

When switching from one blog system to another, your new system won't automatically be aware of your previous videoblog posts. It's just the way things go. Moreover, moving from Blogger can be a little more difficult because it uses the Atom syndication format instead of RSS, which most other blog systems use. Fortunately, there are ways to import your prior feeds easily.

Be aware that not all systems can import comments that have been left by visitors to your videoblog. Also, if you've assigned categories to your posts, the new system may not import them. Again, sometimes that's just the way things go.

If importing comments and/or categories is a requirement for you, make sure you research to find out if your choice of blog system will import to your satisfaction. After you've determined which blog software you are going to use, follow the appropriate instructions for a successful transition. Instructions for importing feeds for the more popular blog systems are as follows:

## Choosing a Host for Your Videoblog

There are a lot of web-hosting companies. A lot. (No, really. There are *a lot*.)

When evaluating a host, you should keep four things in mind:

- Monthly cost and additional overage fees
- Ease of blog software installation
- Amount of storage for your videos
- Amount of bandwidth to distribute your videos

- MovableType: `www.sixapart.com/movabletype/docs/3.2/01_installation_and_upgrade/mt_import.html`

- TextPattern: `http://textpattern.com/faq/114/can-textpattern-import-entries`

- WordPress: `http://wiki.wordpress.org/BloggerImport`

Don't be intimidated. All of the instructions are laid out in a very friendly, easy-to-follow manner. People have ventured down the migration path to make it easier for others. Let them lead the way.

# Summary

After you've acquired the equipment to shoot and edit video, a blog site, and a place to store your video online, you're pretty much done with the basics. You've got a videoblog. Luckily there's much more to learn, explore, and experiment with, including shooting video in different and unusual ways. Here's where it starts to get fun.

# Production

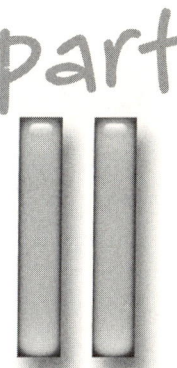

part

# Tricks for Acquiring Video with a Camera

**A**lthough there are a number of steps required to produce a video for distribution on the Internet, none is more important than actually acquiring the raw footage. Doing so almost always involves the use of a camera. Options abound for recording video, including the use of tripods, simple handheld shots, crane shots, hidden cameras, and even car mounts. Some people have even attached cameras to their pets! Just don't attach your camera to your pet and then mount him on your car.

## Shooting Video While Walking

Videobloggers often capture unplanned video on the go. Videobloggers like to travel lightly, usually with just a small camera, so they can document life as it happens. Often it seems as though most opportunities arise to record something while simply walking down the street. If there is one situation where it's hard to get a steady shot, walking is it.

In such circumstances, when there isn't the time or opportunity to employ something like a stabilizer or tripod, there are a few tricks you can use to make the best of a difficult shooting situation.

## Steadying a Shot

Unfortunately, the "steady shot" feature on most cameras isn't enough to stabilize a shot while walking. Also, a stabilizer or tripod is too heavy and time consuming to carry around all the time. Fortunately, there's something you can do to minimize the "Blair Witch" effect that's common in video recorded while walking.

This technique of shooting requires you to hold the camera almost at arm's length, in front of your body. Palm up, you can simply rest the camera in your hand (see Figure 4-1). If your camera has a handle on top, you could just "suspend" it by holding the handle. Holding the camera using a handle may make acquiring footage more comfortable for you.

---

**in this chapter**

☑ Shooting While Moving—On Foot or in a Car

☑ Using a Digital Still Camera to Capture Video

☑ Creating Slow-Motion Footage

☑ Can You Moblog?

FIGURE 4-1: Arm-stabilizing a shot.

This technique enables you to let the camera float as you walk. Realize, however, that the farther your arm is extended, the heavier your camera will feel. Do use the hand-strap provided with your camera — those who don't end up with a lot of broken cameras.

## Face the Direction You're Walking

The most important thing to do is to remember to face the direction in which you are walking. People trying to remain "behind the camera" often end up walking sideways or even backward. First, without someone guiding you, you're likely to have an accident. Second, walking sideways or backward actually increases the shakiness of your shot!

When recording a video while walking, face forward and point the camera at the action. This is the best way to produce a smooth shot. If you have a camera with a flip-out LCD screen, focus your attention on it (because it represents your actual footage).

### Shooting to the Side

If you want to record a shot of the person walking next to you, by himself, flip the LCD screen around so that it faces outward and is flush against the side of the camera. Doing so will enable you to cradle the camera perpendicular to your body (see Figure 4-2).

## No LCD? No Worries

What if you're shooting with a digital still camera and your LCD screen doesn't rotate? Although this can be a problem, it can be managed with a little practice. To accomplish the shot, hold your camera in the same manner.

With your camera in hand, gather a few friends and simply shoot some footage. After a few practice shots, you'll have a good sense of how to aim your shots. With a little practice, you'll find that you can shoot on the go without making your viewers nauseaus.

FIGURE 4-2: Shooting to the side.

To record footage that includes you and someone walking next to you, you'll have to swivel the LCD screen out from the side of the camera. Use the LCD screen to line up the shot, and then have your arm "remember" the location so you can watch where you are going. Holding the camera out in front at a slight angle is enough to place you and the person walking next to you in frame.

## Shooting Behind

Face forward, flip the LCD screen out, and turn the camera around to record footage of people behind you. Hold the camera in front and slightly to one side, and then point the camera behind while you walk forward (see Figure 4-3). You'll discover that this is much easier than trying to walk backward.

FIGURE 4-3: Shooting action behind.

## Shooting Yourself

Getting yourself into a shot is a little tricky, but it can be done. A classic videoblogger shot simply involves "speaking to the camera." To create the shot, just look at the lens — not at the LCD screen — and talk directly to it (see Figure 4-4). This gives your audience the perception that you are talking directly to them.

Ultimately, it's important to find a comfortable distance to hold the camera from your body. You will probably want to keep your arms loose and extended but not so far as to blur your shot. The object is to use your arms as shock absorbers, for which they do a surprisingly good job.

FIGURE 4-4: Self-referential shooting.

# Shooting Video with a Digital Still Camera

Chances are you already have the equipment to videoblog. All you need is a digital still camera that records video clips, which most current camera models do. Although these cameras usually record at less than DV (digital video) quality, the result is perfect for video on the web.

## Understanding Digital Still Cameras

Using a digital still camera provides several advantages, such as the fact they are reasonably priced. Some, such as the Canon PowerShot, can be purchased for less than $200. In addition, you may already have one for still photos and just haven't realized it can take video (or you've not had a reason to use it for video).

Digital still cameras are also very small and portable. Personal videoblogging is often at its best when it captures those fleeting moments in life. With a small camera, you can record video almost anywhere. Plus, because most people usually "clam up" once they see a big camera pointed at them, you can record footage that you might otherwise be unable to acquire. More often than not, people overlook someone with a little digital still camera, especially when they don't know video is being recorded.

Digital still cameras are also tapeless, which means that they record directly onto a memory card, so you don't need to do any digitizing to get footage onto your computer. The workflow is easy: record, copy, edit (if you want), and upload to your blog.

**Tip**  Although Flash and SD cards are available in sizes up to 4GB (as of this writing), you may want to simply use a 512MB card. The reason is that you can easily archive your footage from a 512MB card onto a 700MB CD. If you're using a larger card, you won't be able to take advantage of the cheap storage that CDs provide.

Even though the video is not DV quality, it's okay. Because most videoblogs distribute compressed video, your audience won't mind (and may not even notice) the difference in quality. Ultimately, what matters is the quality of the moments you capture.

## Determining Whether a Camera Can Record Video

There are several ways to determine if your camera can record video. First and foremost, you can check the manual that came with it. More than likely there's a section on video if your camera has that feature.

If you don't have the manual, perform a search online for your camera's make and model or check the manufacturer's web site. You should be able to determine its available functions from the search results.

You can also just scroll through the camera's functions using its various buttons (the preferred method of men everywhere). If the camera has a video recording function, you usually find a menu item with the title "Video" or "Movies."

## Using the Camera

Once you have a video-capable camera, try recording "a day in the life;" it's the easiest and coolest way to make a hip videoblog. To record your entry, keep the camera in your pocket/bag and take it with you as you go about your day. Whether you're at home, at school, at work, or running errands, make sure you have your camera with you.

Every so often, record a minute of what's going on around you. Whether you record yourself, your friends talking, or simply something happening around you, don't worry about it making any sense. "A day in the life" is about telling a natural story as you record your day as it unfolds.

## Getting the Video onto Your Computer

Most cameras come with a dock or cable that connects the camera to your computer. Others require you to remove the storage card (where the video files exist) from the camera and use a specific device to transfer the files to your computer. More often than not, connecting the camera or card to a computer is trivial, and the files can be easily (if not automatically) transferred.

 **Note** The video files may be in any number of formats, depending on the type of camera used. The common formats include Windows Video, QuickTime, and MPEG-4. If you plan to edit the video, you may need to transcode (discussed in Chapter 9) the video to work with your editing system of choice.

After you transfer the video to your computer, the question is: to edit or not to edit? You could very well upload individual clips to your videoblog as is — more than likely the files are already compressed decently for Internet distribution. You may, however, find it best to do some simple editing, if only to add some theme music.

To finalize your "day in the life" video, import the clips you recorded throughout the day into your editing software. Then put the videos on the timeline in the order they occurred, trim the clips you like, and delete the clips that don't make sense. Keep the timing of the clips tight and succinct, and remember that editing is really just a process of getting rid of the stuff that's not compelling. When you're finished you'll have a great little movie of your day and a complete understanding of how your camera works in a variety of situations.

# Creating a Slow Motion Video

Slow motion can look cool. It can let you see short events in more detail, and it can change the emotional impact of a video clip. If you've ever tried slowing things down when using editing software, you will have probably noticed that at a certain point, it starts to get jerky. Fear not; you can get the most detail possible and elegantly capture slow motion the old fashioned way . . . by using your digital still camera.

Cameras are available that can film up to 50,000 frames a second. Those are the ones people use to produce all of that smooth footage of insects' wings and light bulbs exploding. Unfortunately, those cameras are quite expensive. Luckily, there are a variety of digital still cameras that can film at 60fps, which means they can obtain smooth slow-motion footage (although far from 50,000fps. Such is life.).

Importing 60fps footage into a standard video-editing package can be tricky, though, because most editing systems are set to ignore all those nice, extra frames.

Ingenuity should tell you that there's a way to get around an editing system's shortfalls . . . and there is.

## Acquiring Slow-Motion Footage

Most digital still cameras offer different modes for shooting footage. For example, the Canon PowerShot offers a sports or fast shutter mode that causes the shutter of the camera to open and close very quickly, which is ideal for capturing slow motion, while the Kodak EasyShare V570 offers 22 different scene modes, including a "sport" mode. You should look in your camera manual to see if your camera can do it. In addition to your camera, you'll need QuickTime Pro (www.apple.com/quicktime; $29.99).

## Slowing Down Video

Video, just like film, works by taking a series of still images (known as frames), usually at 30 per second in North America. The speed of video is referred to as the number of frames per second (fps). When the speed of a video is reduced by half, each frame is basically displayed for twice the amount of time. For example, if you slow 30fps footage to half speed, it becomes footage at 15fps with each frame doubled, therefore reaching the required 30fps speed.

At 30fps, a person's eyes are tricked into seeing the sequence of still images as motion. As footage is slowed down, a person's brain is able to process the images individually. Eventually, as the frame rate gets lower, the viewer interprets the frames as still images. Hence, the "jerkiness" of slower footage, such as video you may have found on the Internet in the mid-1990s.

### Capture and Transfer

Obviously, if you want to create a slow-motion video, you need some footage. So, grab your camera, set it to use a fast shutter mode, and record something. You may find that recording a moving object results in a more pronounced slow-motion effect. When you've finished recording, simply transfer it from your camera to your computer and open the file using QuickTime.

**Tip**    If you're not sure whether the footage is recorded at 60fps, select File ➜ Show Movie Info in QuickTime to find out.

Create a folder called slowmotion (you can name it anything you like, actually) on your Desktop, and use it to contain your video while you're creating your slow-motion effect.

### Export

Exporting to a series of images provides individual frames for use in your slow-motion video. Note that exporting as a series of images results in still images only, not in audio.

Once you've opened your footage, here's what to do:

1. Select File ➜ Export ➜ Movie to Image Sequence.

2. Click the Options button. The Export Image Sequence Settings window opens.

3. Select BMP for the image format.

4. Set the Frames Per Second to 60. If you have a camera that records video at frame rates higher than 60fps, change this setting to match the frame rate of your camera.

5. Click the Options button and set the quality to Best Depth.

6. Click the OK button.

Save the image sequence—a series of still images, one for each frame in your original video—to the slowmotion folder on your Desktop.

## What Is Interlacing?

To make video production all the more confusing, there is something called "interlacing" that you may have to deal with at some point. Video actually takes two images (called "fields") for each frame. Interlacing is the process by which the picture is scanned onto a video screen so that the lines of one scanned field fall evenly between the lines of the preceding field, resulting in a single video frame. Each field is displayed at a different time, and each is referred to as lower (even) and upper (odd), respectively.

On rare occasions, fields become an issue and can cause a strobe-like effect, most often because the fields are being rendered in the opposite order than they were recorded (DV is always rendered lower (even) field first). If you are working with DV footage and you discover that a strobe-like effect is occurring, examine your video settings and make sure your computer isn't rendering the fields in the wrong order.

### Create a Video File

After QuickTime has exported the images, close the original video file. Then select File→ Open Image Sequence. Locate the slowmotion folder on your Desktop, select the first image inside, and click the Open button.

Now for the important part: QuickTime requires you to select a frame rate. If you are in North America (NTSC video), choose 29.97. If you are in Europe (PAL), choose 25. After making your selection, you can play the resulting video, which should play about 50-percent slower than the original.

If you want to edit the slow-motion video with editing software, save the file as a self-contained video. If not, you can simply export the video for the web and put it straight on your videoblog.

# Shooting Video from a Car

Gathering footage from a car, especially when it's moving, can be exhilarating for you, while recording, and for your audience. There are a couple problems, however, with recording footage from a vehicle in motion. First and most obvious is the safety concern, because holding a camera with one hand implicitly means you have only one hand free for driving. Second, rigging a camera mount can be difficult and expensive.

Enter PowrGrip (www.powrgrip.com), a powerful suction cup offered with a camera mount. PowrGrip provides the same suction-cup technology used to move large pieces of glass by a minimum number of people (sometimes just one!). You can locate distributors of the camera-mount version from the PowrGrip web site (in the Sporting Goods and Photography product line).

The rest of this section describes how to use PowrGrip and your camera to shoot video from your car.

## Preparing the Area

You can use a PowrGrip to mount your camera to the inside or outside of your car or anywhere you can find a flat surface. When selecting an area on which to mount your camera, look for a level, smooth surface. Glass is a perfect example of a flat, smooth surface, and it's also plentiful on a car. You can also attach a PowrGrip to various body panels on a car, such as a fender.

As with all suction cups, any debris on the surface you are attaching to can cause the vacuum created by the suction to be ineffective, so thoroughly clean and dry the area where you plan to attach the mount. Before actually recording footage, make sure you have a good seal.

## Mounting the Cleat

PowrGrip has designed the plunger, which helps create the vacuum, to show when a "good" seal exists by using a simple red line. To attach the mount, place the suction cup against the surface and "pump" the grey plunger until the red indicator is no longer visible. After doing so, you can confidently attach your camera, knowing that the mount is firmly affixed to your car.

## Attaching the Camera

PowrGrip uses a standard 1/4-20-thread screw for attaching a camera to it, so simply thread the camera onto the mount. Then make any necessary adjustments to align the shot you want to acquire. Some models, such as the LJ45PHC Cleat, have arms that enable you to adjust the angle and rotation of the attached camera.

## Recording Footage

With your camera attached to your car, you're ready to record footage. One problem you may run into is how to actually start recording. How you go about getting your camera to record depends on its features and where you've mounted the PowrGrip.

If the camera is mounted close to you, you may be able to simply press the requisite buttons to start recording when necessary. If the camera is mounted out of your reach, you may be able to use a remote control to start recording, if your camera offers such a feature. If all else fails, you can always start recording footage early and simply edit out the fluff. Once you've attached your camera, you can actually drive with it attached.

Periodically check on the PowrGrip's red indicator to make sure you still have a secure seal. Stopping your car and pumping the plunger a few times is a lot cheaper, and safer, than watching in astonishment as your camera detaches from the car and goes bouncing down the street at 35MPH.

## Removing PowrGrip

After recording your footage, you can very easily remove the PowrGrip from your car by simply pushing on the small tab on the suction cup. You'll be amazed how a simple push on the tab can release what a mere second before was practically glued to your car.

# Exploring Mobile Videoblogging

Numerous cell phones have integrated cameras, and several even have the capability to capture and send video. In fact, in 2005 there were more camera phones than cameras sold worldwide. One can easily imagine that in the near future video-enabled phones will be outselling video cameras, too.

If you've got a video-enabled cell phone, you'll probably be tempted to use it for mobile videoblogging — or moblogging. Through the use of a little Perl script, you can video moblog from anywhere you have your cell phone and a decent signal.

## Determining if You Can Moblog

Before starting, you should be aware of some possible "gotchas" with moblogging. First, you must use the Multimedia Messaging Service (MMS) from your phone to send the video to your blog. Because of the sheer number of phones on the market and the differences among them, you will have to determine how to send an MMS using your particular phone. Be aware that some mobile service providers charge for MMS; if you are going to be doing this a lot, you might be financially better off by getting a plan that includes it as a part of the service.

Most providers in the United States also offer the capability to send MMS messages to regular Internet email accounts. Unfortunately, they don't all do this in the same manner. Some providers send the MMS message in an email including HTML, displaying the content directly in the recipient's mail program, while other providers simply attach the content of the message as a MIME email. Fortunately, most of these situations can be accounted for, so once you get the settings right, you'll be able to moblog.

## Setting Up

The first step in setting up a system to post MMS messages automatically to your vlog is to arrange for a dedicated email account for this purpose. The Perl script for moblogging is written to utilize a standard POP3 email account, as offered by most web-hosting companies. Be aware that most webmail providers, such as the free version of Yahoo! Mail, do not offer POP3 (Post Office Protocol 3) access.

## What is MMS?

MMS is an acronym for Multimedia Message Service, which, like SMS (Short Message Service), is a standard employed by mobile phone service providers. MMS enables users to send images, text, audio, and video to other mobile phones. Various providers market this capability slightly differently under special names. For example, Verizon calls its service Video & PIX Messaging, while Sprint calls it PCS Vision. The major providers in the United States — Cingular, T-Mobile, and Sprint — all offer MMS and have agreed to interoperate with each other.

There are several reasons to use a dedicated email account. The most important reason is that you don't want to accidentally publish your personal email to your public blog. You also don't want your blog overloaded with spam (how do they get all our addresses?) or have the Perl script delete an important email before you've had a chance to read it.

## Writing the Script

The Perl script in Listing 4-1 retrieves and parses email from a dedicated email account. In addition, it retrieves text, images, audio, and video from email or MMS messages. After parsing a message, it automatically posts it to your blog. The script relies on your blog supporting XML-RPC with the metaWeblog API, which the vast majority of blog software does.

**Note**    Although an enterprising Perl coder could rewrite the script to utilize IMAP (Internet Message Access Protocol) or even to use one of the free webmail provider accounts, such options are beyond the scope of this project. (You might keep an eye out for such a script, though.)

The script is commented with explanation throughout, so you'll know what's going on. Any time you see a #, the text following it is a comment and is human readable. Knowing this may help you better understand what's going on in the code. Open a simple text editor such as Notepad (Windows) or TextEdit (Mac), and enter the script, or simply download it from this book's web site.

---

**Listing 4-1:** Moblog.pl

```perl
#!/usr/bin/perl -w

###
# Perl modules that need to be installed
###
use MIME::Parser;
use MIME::Entity;
use MIME::Base64;
use Net::POP3;
use XMLRPC::Lite;

###
# User Configurable Variables
###
my $username = "xxxx"; ## CHANGE THIS LINE
my $password = "xxxx";  ## CHANGE THIS LINE
my $mailserver = "xxx.yourdomain.com"; ## CHANGE THIS LINE
my $temp_folder = "...."; ## CHANGE THIS LINE
my $attachment_output_folder = ""; ## CHANGE THIS LINE
my $attachment_output_folder_relative = "xxxx"; ## CHANGE THIS LINE
my $blog_xmlrpc_url = "xxx"; ## CHANGE THIS LINE
my $blog_id = 2; ## CHANGE THIS LINE
my $blog_username = "xxx"; ## CHANGE THIS LINE
my $blog_password = "xxx"; ## CHANGE THIS LINE
```

```
###
# Other Variables that *may be* changed
###
my $pop = Net::POP3->new($mailserver, Timeout => 15);
my $max_chars = 70;  # Number of chars to allow in a line of text from an
incoming message
my $delete_messages = 1; # Delete messages from your inbox as they are processed
my $delete_temp_files = 1; # Delete temporary files that are created
my $print_output = 1; # Print output
my $post_to_blog = 1; # Post to your blog?
my $use_gif = 0; # 1 to allow GIFs as attachments, 0 to not allow them
                 # (T-Mobile issues)
my @bad_attachments = ("masthead.jpg"); # A list of attachment filename regular
                                        # expressions that you don't want included
my $umask = '0002';  # File creation to 775, 0022 would be 755

my %mime_types = ("image\/jpeg", "jpg",
                  "image\/jpg", "jpg",
                  "image\/gif", "gif",
                  "video\/3gpp", "3gp",
                  "audio\/x-wav", "wav",
                  "video\/mp4", "mp4",
                  "video\/3gpp2", "3g2",
                  "video\/mpeg", "mpg",
                  "video\/quicktime", "mov",
                  "video\/x-quicktime", "mov",
                  "video/x-msvideo",  "avi"
             ); # A list of the attachment mime types to extract

###
# Parsing Subroutine
###
sub parseMessageParts
{
   my @messageParts = @_;

   my $partnum = 0;
   my $is_mime_message = 0;

   while(my $part = shift(@messageParts))
   {
      $is_mime_message = 1;  # Yes we have a mime message
      my $known_type = 0;  # Did we find the type yet?

      # Get the Mime type of the part
      my $type=$part->head->mime_type || $part->head->effective_type;

      ## Loop through the types we understand
      foreach $valid_type (keys %mime_types)
      {
```

*Continued*

Listing 4-1 *(continued)*

```
    if ($type =~ $valid_type)
    {
        $known_type = 1;

        for (my $i = 0; $i <= $#bad_attachments; $i++)
        {
            if ($part->head->recommended_filename =~ $bad_attachments[$i])
            {
                $skip = 1;
            }
        }

        if (!$skip)
        {
            my $attachment = $part->bodyhandle->as_string;
            my $file_name = "attachment_" . time() . "_" .⤵
int(rand(1000)) . "\." . $mime_types{$valid_type};
            my $image_file = $attachment_output_folder . $file_name;
            my $fh = new FileHandle "> $image_file";
            if (defined $fh) {
                print $fh $attachment;
                $fh->close;
            }

            $attachments[++$#attachments] = $file_name;
            $attachments_type[++$#attachments_type] = ⤵
$mime_types{$valid_type};
            $attachments_relative[++$#attachments_relative] = ⤵
$attachment_output_folder_relative . $file_name;
        }
    }
}

    ## Not in the list; check for text or multipart messages
    if ($known_type == 0)
    {
        if ($type =~ /text\/plain/i)
        {
            my $message_bodyhandle = $part->bodyhandle;
            $mime_message_body = $message_bodyhandle->as_string;

            @mime_message_array = split('\n',$mime_message_body);

            foreach $message_line (@mime_message_array)
            {
                if ($message_line =~ /^\n/ ||
                    $message_line =~ /^\s*\n/ ||
                    $message_line !~ /\w/)
                {
                    # Ignore blank lines
```

```
            }
            else
            {
                $body .= $message_line;
            }
        }
    }
    elsif ($type =~ /text\/html/i)
    {
        # Plain Text portions or attachments
        my $message_bodyhandle = $part->bodyhandle;
        $mime_message_body = $message_bodyhandle->as_string;

        @mime_message_array = split('\n',$mime_message_body);

        foreach $message_line (@mime_message_array)
        {
            $message_line =~ s/<.*>//gi; # Strip out any HTML tags

            if ($message_line =~ /^\n/ ||
                    $message_line =~ /^\s*\n/ ||
                    $message_line !~ /\w/)
            {
                # Ignore blank lines
            }
            else
            {
                $body .= $message_line; # Only grabbing first line
            }
        }
    }
    elsif ($type =~ /multipart\/.*/i || $type =~ /message\/.*/i)
    {
        # Multipart Message, Parse This Again
        # Thanks again T-Mobile
        my @otherparts=$part->parts;
        &parseMessageParts(@otherparts);
    }
    else
    {
        if ($print_output)
        {
            print "Other Type: " . $type . "\n\n"; # OUTPUT
        }
    }
    }

    $partnum++;
}
return $is_mime_message;
}
```

*Continued*

**Listing 4-1** *(continued)*

```
###
# Main Program Execution
###
if ($print_output)
{
   print("Running at: " . localtime() . "\n");
}

if ($pop->login($username, $password))
{
      $umask = oct($umask) if $umask =~ /^0/;
      umask $umask;

      if ($print_output)
      {
         print("Logged into mailserver\n");
      }

      # Create the parser object
      my $parser = MIME::Parser->new();
      $parser->output_dir($temp_folder);

      my $msgnums = $pop->list; # hashref of msgnum => size
      foreach my $msgnum (keys %$msgnums)
      {
            my $msg = $pop->get($msgnum);

            my $entity = $parser->parse_data($msg);

            ###
            # GET MESSAGE HEADER
            ###
            my $msg_head = $entity->head;
            my $subject = "";
            my $to = "";
            my $from = "";

            ###
            # MESSAGE Related Vars
            ###
            $body = "";
            @attachments = ();
            @attachments_type = ();
            @attachments_relative = ();

            ##
            # GET MESSAGE SUBJECT
            ##
            if ($msg_head->count('Subject') > 0)
            {
```

```perl
      $subject = $msg_head->get('Subject');
   }

   ##
   # GET MESSAGE FROM
   ##
   if ($msg_head->count('From') > 0)
   {
      $from = $msg_head->get('From');
      if ($from =~ /<(.*)>/)
      {
         $from = $1;
      }
   }

   ##
   # GET MESSAGE TO
   ##
   if ($msg_head->count('To') > 0)
   {
      $to = $msg_head->get('To');
      if ($to =~ /<(.*)>/)
         {
            $to = $1;
         }
   }

   ###
   # GET MESSAGE PARTS (BODY AND ATTACHMENTS)
   ###
   my @parts=$entity->parts;
   my $is_mime = &parseMessageParts(@parts);
   ## Calling the parse subroutine

   ##
   # IF IT ISN'T A MIME MESSAGE (NO ATTACHMENTS)
   ##
   if (!$is_mime)
   {
      ###
      # GET MESSAGE BODY LINES
      ###
      $msg_body = $entity->body;
      foreach $message_line (@$msg_body)
      {
         if ($message_line =~ /^\n/)
         {

         }
         else
         {
            $body .= $message_line;
```

*Continued*

**Listing 4-1** *(continued)*

```
          }
        }
      }

      chomp($to); # REMOVE TRAILING LINE BREAKS
      chomp($from);
      chomp($subject);
      chomp($body);

      if ($post_to_blog)
      {
          my $attachment_html = "";
          for (my $i = 0; $i <= $#attachments; $i++)
          {
              my $attachment = $attachments[$i];
              my $attachment_type = $attachments_type[$i];
              my $attachment_relative = $attachments_relative[$i];

              if ($attachment_type eq "jpg" || $attachment_type eq "gif")
              {
                  $attachment_html .= "<img src=\"$attachment_relative\">\n";
              }
              elsif (
                      $attachment_type eq "3gp" || $attachment_type eq ⮌
"wav" || $attachment_type eq "mp4" ||
                      $attachment_type eq "3g2" || $attachment_type eq ⮌
"mpg" || $attachment_type eq "mov" ||
                      $attachment_type eq "avi"
                    )
              {
                  $attachment_html .= "
                    <OBJECT CLASSID=\"clsid:02BF25D5-8C17-4B23-BC80-⮌
D3488ABDDC6B\" WIDTH=\"320\" HEIGHT=\"257\" CODEBASE=⮌
\"http://www.apple.com/qtactivex/qtplugin.cab\">\n
                      <PARAM name=\"SRC\" VALUE=\"$attachment_relative\">\n
                      <PARAM name=\"AUTOPLAY\" VALUE=\"false\">\n
                      <PARAM name=\"CONTROLLER\" VALUE=\"true\">\n
                      <EMBED SRC=\"$attachment_relative\" WIDTH=\"320\" ⮌
HEIGHT=\"257\" AUTOPLAY=\"false\" CONTROLLER=\"true\" PLUGINSPAGE=⮌
\"http://www.apple.com/quicktime/download/\"></EMBED>\n
                    </OBJECT>\n
                  ";
              }
          }

          my $postresult=XMLRPC::Lite
                  ->proxy($blog_xmlrpc_url)
                  ->call('metaWeblog.newPost',$blog_id, ⮌
$blog_username,$blog_password,
                      {
                          'title'=>$subject,
```

```
                    'description'=>$body . $attachment_html,
                    'mt_allow_comments'=>1,
                    'mt_allow_pings'=>1
                },
                1
            )
            ->result;

            if ($print_output)
            {
                print "Message To: $to\n";
                print "Message From $from\n";
                print "Message Subject $subject\n";
                print "Message Body $body\n";
                for (my $i = 0; $i <= $#attachments; $i++)
                {
                    print "Message Attachment $attachments[$i] . ⤶
 " - " . $attachments_type[$i] . " - " . $attachments_relative[$i]\n";
                }
                print "Post to Blog Result: " . $postresult . "\n";
                print "-------------------------\n";
            }

        }
        elsif ($print_output)
        {
            print "Message To: $to\n";
            print "Message From $from\n";
            print "Message Subject $subject\n";
            print "Message Body $body\n";
            for (my $i = 0; $i <= $#attachments; $i++)
            {
                print "Message Attachment $attachments[$i] . ;
 " - " . $attachments_type[$i] . " - " . $attachments_relative[$i]\n";
            }
            print "Not Posted to Blog";
            print "-------------------------\n";
        }

        if ($delete_messages)
        {
            $pop->delete($msgnum);
        }

    }

    if ($delete_temp_files)
    {
        $parser->filer->purge;
    }
}
$pop->quit;
```

If you've entered the script by hand, save the file as a plain-text document with a `.pl` extension. `Moblog.pl` (the name of the download file) is just fine. Next, you'll want to customize the script for your own use.

The Perl script uses the `<object>` tag to place video in a web page. On April 11, 2006, Microsoft released an update for Internet Explorer 6 that changed how the browser loads certain elements, including those that use the `<object>` and `<embed>` tags. Because of this change, viewers using the patched version of the browser will have to confirm that they want to view the video by clicking through a dialog box that states "Click to run an ActiveX control on this webpage." If you would prefer your video to load without this requirement, refer to the "Using JavaScript to Embed Video" section in Chapter 13. Other browsers such as Firefox (`http://www.mozilla.com/firefox`) and video aggregators are not affected.

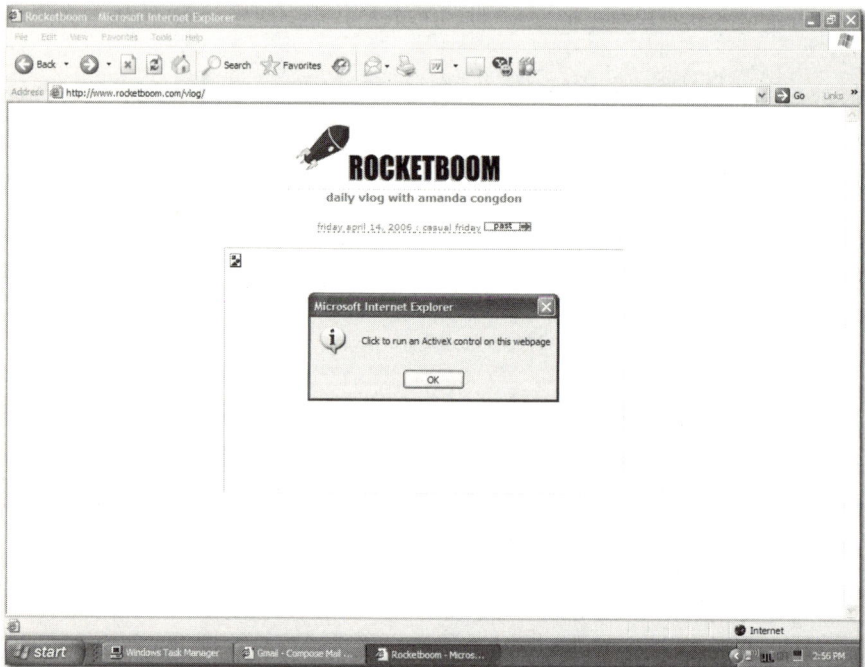

Figure 4-5: An ActiveX dialog requesting permission to play a video.

## Customizing the Script

Most of the lines that need to be changed are located near the top of the script and can be found by searching for `## CHANGE THIS LINE`.

**Tip**

You can always download the latest version of this script from www.walking-productions .com/parseMailScript/parseMailScript.zip. It's a good idea to keep up to date.

The first item to change is my $username = "xxxx"; ## CHANGE THIS LINE. Simply change the xxxx between the quotes to your email account username. Leave the quotes because that's how Perl determines the text to be an email address. Some hosting providers force you to use your complete email address — username@yourdomain.com — and others require you to use only your username to retrieve email. Check with your email provider for the correct way to format this line.

The next line is my $password = "xxxx"; ## CHANGE THIS LINE. Just replace the xxxx with your email password, and the script will handle the rest. Following that, you need to specify your mailserver (for retrieving email, sometimes referred to as your POP server).

You also need to change my $mailserver = "xxx.yourdomain.com"; ## CHANGE THIS LINE to reflect the mailserver you are using, such as mail.domain.com. You can obtain this information from your mail provider.

You should also set up a couple of folders for storing your videos: a temporary folder for processing and an attachment output folder. You can configure the folders in the following lines:

```
my $temp_folder = "....";  ## CHANGE THIS LINE
my $attachment_output_folder = "";  ## CHANGE THIS LINE
my $attachment_output_folder_relative = "xxxx";  ## CHANGE THIS LINE
```

The temp_folder should be set to a writable directory, where the script can create work files. For the output folders, set the attachment_output_folder to a directory that is writable and is accessible via the web, and set the attachment_output_folder_relative to the relative path from your web server to the attachment_output_folder.

Finally, configure the script to actually make a post to your vlog. In the line my $blog_xml-rpc_url = "xxx"; ## CHANGE THIS LINE, change the xxx to the URL of the XMLRPC page you need to access. For example, if you are using WordPress, your URL may resemble http://www.domain.com/wordpress/xmlrpc.php. The URL will depend on your blog software and its configuration.

You also need to configure your blog id, username, and password for your blog. These can be configured in the following lines:

```
my $blog_id = 2;  ## CHANGE THIS LINE
my $blog_username = "xxx";  ## CHANGE THIS LINE
my $blog_password = "xxx";  ## CHANGE THIS LINE
```

The script does have a few defaults built in for text parsing. If your MMS messages come through email with a subject line that will be used for the title of your blog post, any text found in the message will be utilized for the body of the post. On the other-hand, if you would rather specify a title separate from the subject line, use the following syntax within the body of the MMS message itself:

```
Title: Your custom title
Body: Your body text
```

Using this manner of specifying the `body` and `title` of your post greatly decreases the chance of including information in your post that you don't want to be included. More specifically, you can utilize this option to avoid posting text that your mobile provider might add onto the message when sending it through email (such as marketing or advertising material).

## Uploading the Script

The next step is to gain access to an account from your hosting provider from which you can execute a program to check your newly set-up email account. Most web-hosting companies offer `ssh` (secure shell) access to their servers, and it's highly recommended that you use `ssh` for these purposes as well. Of course, if your hosting company offers only `telnet` (an insecure remote shell application), offers none at all, or you are using a Windows server, the following instructions may be modified to work with your setup, although you'll be more or less on your own.

If you're unfamiliar with using the command line of a computer, be very careful. A seemingly innocent command like `rm -rf /*` can erase everything on your hard drive. Even long-time users have been known to run destructive commands accidentally.

Remember, when you're not sure about a command, you can always type `man <the_ command>` and view a reference of its use.

Once you have access to a shell account, you will want to upload the script to the server. For security reasons, place the script somewhere in your user directory that is not publicly accessible (that is, do not place it in your web documents or cgi-bin directories). That will help protect your email and blog accounts' username and password combinations. You may also want to change the access permissions to the script, for an additional measure of security.

Depending on the type of services provided on the server, you may be able to automate the execution of the script on a periodic basis. For example, on Unix-like systems, there is usually a utility called `cron` that can perform a variety of functions on a set schedule. If you're unfamiliar with `cron`, typing `man cron` on the command line provides a reference manual. One way to use `cron` would be to add the following entry to the `crontab`, which is a file that cron uses to schedule its tasks:

```
* * * * * perl /path/to/my/script/parseMessages.pl >> @@>
    /path/to/my/output/log/output.log
```

This entry can be understood as: Run the following command every minute of every hour of every day of every month of every year (`* * * * *`). The command that is run is `perl/ path/to/my/script/parseMessages.pl` and the output of the command is redirected to a file at `/path/to/my/output/log/output.log`. For help with `cron`, simply search the web for cron.

Voilà! Now you can send MMS messages via email and have them show up on your vlog. All it took was a little Perl code . . . the duct tape of the Internet.

### Troubleshooting

Check your spelling and punctuation. Computers don't do what you mean; they do what you say. A single misplaced quotation mark can cause hours of head/wall interaction.

Look at log files. They usually tell you (even if cryptically) what's going on.

Check the documentation. The major blogging software packages have large, active user bases and a lot of online documentation. You're probably not the first to run into a problem.

Search engines are your friends; all of these technologies are moving targets—things change quickly, and effective searching usually turns up your answer.

## Summary

How you capture your footage ultimately results in a certain "feeling" being evoked. If you don't subscribe to the artsy world of video production, you'll at least capture your footage from a certain perspective (if only in the absolute physical sense). Or you may not want to change your perspective at all and just sit in front of your computer. If so, you can still videoblog.

# Obtaining Video Without Leaving Your Computer

**B**elieve it or not, you don't need a video camera to acquire video. There are a variety of sources for video, including stock footage (images other people have captured), historical footage, or even your own computer. Some third-party sources may charge you, require you to use the footage a certain way, or simply give you free reign. You can take videos that your friends and family email you and re-edit them (called remixing). Remember that you are working with digital video, which means you can use any kind of media that can be imported into your editing application. If you are a fan of documentaries, you may have noticed that many of them are simply images with voiceovers strategically placed. The key is to be creative.

## Screencasting

Screencasting is the term people use for video of a computer's screen while it's being used. Most screencasts are created to help explain in visual terms how to accomplish something on a computer or to show what problems are being experienced. For example, the screencasts at www.freevlog.org (Figure 5-1) help explain, visually, how to create a videoblog for free.

Screencasts are a very effective tool for communicating the abstract world of computing, such as mouse movements, menu selections, and virtual folder navigation. But they can also be used in artistic ways, too. There are a variety of ways to create screencasts, the most obvious being recording a computer screen with a video camera. However, using a computer to make a video of itself is just too cool (and geekily recursive) to pass up.

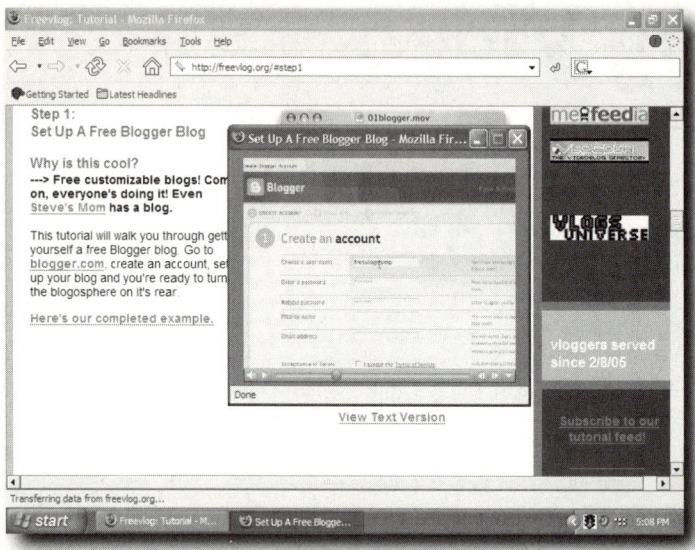

FIGURE 5-1: A screencast from Freevlog.org.

## General Screencasting Best Practices

To make your screencast easy to view, there are a handful of steps you can take before you record it.

- If possible, resize the windows and text of the application you are recording to slightly larger than you normally use them. That'll make it easier for your viewers to see what you're doing.

- Have only the applications that you are using actually running, or "hide" any other applications that you may have open. You do this so that those other applications don't get in the way during your screencast and confuse your viewers.

- Use a single color background for your desktop image, preferably white or black. This helps focus the attention of your viewers on what you are attempting to communicate.

- If you are screencasting a web site, hide personal information such as bookmarks and tabs of other web sites (unless they are used in the screencast).

- If you are recording an audio track, make sure you speak clearly. There is no need to rush through the screencast. And don't eat or drink while screencasting.

Finally, remember that you can always re-record a screencast or even edit it. If you find that your video has long pauses in it (for example, as a result of a slow Internet site), you can edit the pauses out of your final video.

## Snapz Pro X (Macintosh)

Ambrosia Software (www.ambrosiasw.com) distributes a wide variety of software, from games to utilities. The application Snapz Pro X ($69), which is preinstalled on certain Macintosh models, enables users to capture images, audio, and video of their computers easily. The application operates in the background while you work. When you need to record something, you simply press Command+Shift+3 and SnapzPro springs into action, ready to work.

### Features

Snapz Pro X enables you to constrain the recorded area of your screen in a variety of ways, such as to a specific window, area of the screen, or even by following your mouse. Because of its flexibility and configuration options (Figure 5-2), the application is perfect for screencasting. Plus, it's easy to use.

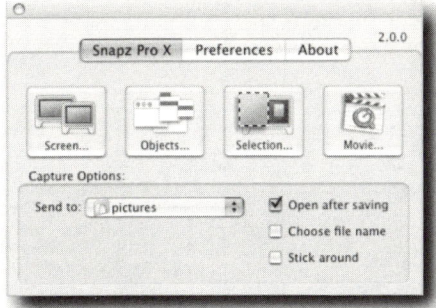

FIGURE 5-2: Snapz Pro X configuration window.

### Recording Video

To record a video, invoke Snapz Pro X (Command+Shift+3) and then click the Movie tab. You have the opportunity to set the camera mode, angle, audio, and additional recording options. For the camera mode, you have three choices:

- **Fixed Camera** — Records a specific section of the screen. If action occurs outside of the section, it does not appear in the video.

- **Follow Cursor** — Records video in a specified range, around the mouse cursor on screen. The video follows the cursor around the screen, keeping it centered in the video.

- **Smooth Pan** — Records video much like Follow Cursor, but the mouse is given a certain amount of room to move before the camera follows. This setting attempts to create a video that is easier to view by giving the mouse "wiggle room."

You can decide whether Snapz Pro X should record audio, too. If you are willing, it's recommended that you record a voiceover or narration track after you've recorded your video. There are two reasons why:

- You will be able to concentrate on one portion of the screencast at a time: video and then audio. Doing so enables you to avoid a lot of "umms" and "uhs" in your audio, as well as being able to fine-tune the final video without having to disrupt your audio.

- It is easier for Snapz Pro X to record only video, because it requires less CPU power to do so. By placing fewer requirements on your CPU while recording, you free it to work more efficiently. Ultimately, this results in Snapz Pro X's recording the smoothest possible video.

Another option that may be of interest is Use Movie Guides. If you elect to use this option, a small box appears around the area that Snapz Pro X is recording. This can be exceptionally helpful when you are first getting used to the application and want an indication of what's being recorded while it's being recorded, as seen in Figure 5-3.

FIGURE 5-3: Recording video with movie guides.

After setting your options, select an area of the screen to capture and either press the Return key or double-click in the selected area to start recording video. Then simply go through your demonstration. Snapz Pro X will record the screen as expected.

## Saving Video

To stop recording, type the hot key combination (Command+Shift+3) again. Snapz Pro X will then provide you the ability to name the video file that was recorded, if the option was selected, and choose the compression settings for the final video, as seen in Figure 5-4. A nice feature is that Snapz Pro X provides a suggestion for the best compression setting for your final video, which may fulfill your needs.

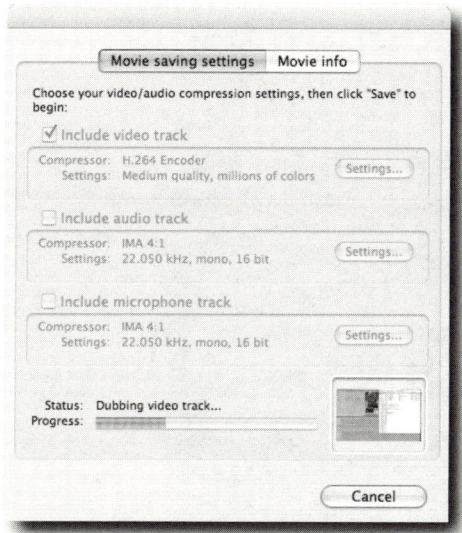

FIGURE 5-4: Saving a video from Snapz Pro X.

If you plan to edit a video using the screencapture as a portion of it, select the DV codec appropriate to your system (most likely DV/DVCPRO - NTSC), 44.1kHz for audio (if audio was recorded), and a frame rate of 29.97FPS. Otherwise, choose an MPEG-4 or H.264 codec, audio compression of IMA 4:1, and a frame rate of 15. You learn more about QuickTime compression settings later in this book.

# CamStudio (Windows)

CamStudio (www.camstudio.org) is a free, open-source screen recording application available for Windows. It is able to record in either Flash (.swf) or Audio Video Interleave (.avi) format. Most videobloggers are interested in recording to .avi because it's easier to work with.

## Setting Up to Record

CamStudio enables you to record the screen in a few different ways: Region, Fixed Region, and Full Screen. Each of these selections can be found under the Region menu item, and each has advantages and disadvantages. Which one you select will depend on what you are attempting to communicate. Unless you are planning on distributing a very large file, both in resolution and file size, you will probably not use the Full Screen option to create a screencast for your videoblog.

If you want to record a specific section of the screen, select the Region option. It enables you to outline an area of the screen for recording, as shown in Figure 5-5. You can set the area numerically or by simply clicking and dragging the cursor to outline the specified area.

FIGURE 5-5: Setting a Region using CamStudio.

Selecting the Fixed Region option is only slightly different, in that while you are recording, you can drag the recording area to a different section of the screen to record the new area. If you plan to record different areas of the screen, however, select the Autopan option, which causes CamStudio to follow your mouse cursor around the screen while recording. To enable this feature, select Options ➜ Enable Autopan.

In addition, you can set:

- Video options — Includes the video codec used and overall quality.
- Cursor options — Allows you to hide the cursor, use a custom cursor, or highlight the cursor.
- Record audio from microphone option — Determines whether audio will be recorded using a microphone.
- Autopan speed — Establishes the speed at which CamStudio will pan.
- Keyboard shortcuts — Allows you to set your own keyboard shortcuts.

Should you choose, you can also add annotations to the screen, similar to a watermarking or captioning, or to the video as a picture-in-picture.

### Recording Video

To start CamStudio, all you need to do is click the Record button. You can also select File ➜ Record from the application's menu or type the keyboard shortcut (F8 is the default). You can pause the recording in a similar manner, only by using the Pause command.

### Saving Video

When you have completed the screencast, you just need to click the Stop button to halt the recording. CamStudio then prompts you for a filename and location to save the video file. After saving, the video opens, enabling you to view your handiwork immediately.

Welcome to the wonderful world of screencasting! Now if we could only book-cast . . . .

## Screenshot Your Media Player

Most videobloggers place a screenshot of the requisite video for every post they make to indicate to viewers that there is an associated video and to provide a simple preview of the video's content, as seen in Figure 5-6.

FIGURE 5-6: A standard screenshot of a video.

How you create a screenshot depends on which operating system you are using.

## Macintosh

Apple has the built-in capability to take screenshots through a non-obvious key combination. By enabling the Caps Lock key and then pressing Shift+Command+4, you enable the Screen

Shot feature, specifically the Copy Picture of Selected Area as a File feature, as seen in Figure 5-7. You can view other screenshot shortcuts, as well as other keyboard shortcuts, by selecting System Preferences ➔ Keyboard & Mouse ➔ Keyboard Shortcuts.

FIGURE 5-7: Performing a screen capture of a window.

Your new screen capture image will be on your Desktop, likely named Picture 1. Double-click it to open it in Preview.

After opening the image, select File ➔ Save As from the application's menu items at the top of the screen. Select JPG from the Format drop-down menu, and move the slider to the Best setting. Finally, name your file accordingly and click the Save button.

When all is said and done, upload the image to your videoblog and link it to your video. . .just like all the cool kids.

## Use Grab

Apple also provides an application called Grab, of which most people are unaware. It can capture a selection of your screen, a specific window, the entire screen, or what's called Timed Screen. Timed Screen simply starts a timer and allows you to interact with the computer for a short period of time before Grab actually captures an image.

## Windows

Microsoft has designed the capability for users to take screenshots easily, although the vast majority of users don't know how. So, here's the trick: Press Alt+Print Screen. (The Print Screen key is often called F13.)

That's it! After you press the key combination, the screenshot will be in the computer's memory on the Clipboard.

Because the screenshot is on the Clipboard, and you want to use the image, you'll need to use an image-editing application to alter and save it. The easiest application, which is installed with every copy of Windows, is Paint. Launch the Paint application by selecting Start → Programs → Accessories → Paint. With Paint open, select Edit → Paste, which places the image into the Paint document (see Figure 5-8).

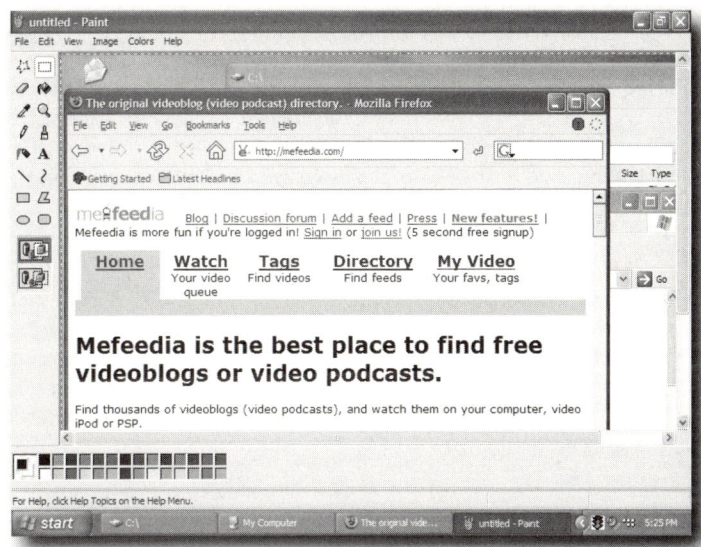

FIGURE 5-8: A screenshot in Windows' Paint program.

Use the Select tool (dotted-line square) from the application's Tool menu on the left side of the screen to crop your screenshot. Select the tool and then click and drag around the area you want to keep. Select Edit → Copy, create a new document by selecting File → New, and then select Edit → Paste. Finally, select File → Save, and save the image as a .jpg file.

When you're ready, upload the image to your videoblog and link it to your video. Easy.

### Linking the Screen Capture to a Video

Videobloggers who do screen captures of their videos normally enable the image of the video to be clicked to enable viewers to easily download the associated video. The HTML code to do this is:

```
<a href="http://www.domain.com/location/of/video"><img src="
http://www.domain.com/location/of/screen_capture.jpg"></a>
```

For the link to work, just alter the URLs appropriately. After adding the HTML code to your videoblog post, viewers can simply click the screen capture image to start downloading the linked video.

# Finding and Using Footage

Even if you don't have a video camera, you can still acquire footage to use on your videoblog. A wide variety of footage is available through places such as the Internet Archive (`www.archive.org`), Ourmedia (`www.ourmedia.org`), and even NASA (`www.nasa.gov/multimedia/videogallery`). Also, many videobloggers release their footage under a Creative Commons license, which allows other people (like you!) to use their footage in creative ways. You can learn more about the Creative Commons at `www.creativecommons.org`.

### Finding Video

Quite obviously, before you can download and use video, you need to find it. A great place to start to find video you can use is through the Creative Commons Find page at `www.creativecommons.org/find`. From the page you can find audio, images, video, and other formats that are shared for free; you use either Google or Yahoo! search engines. You can also browse a variety of collections, most notably the Prelinger Archives, which contains more than 1,000 videos that you can use and remix.

---

#### Nothing So Strange

The independent movie *Nothing So Strange* is about the fictional assassination of Bill Gates. The movie is shot in an obvious homage to the Zapruder film of the assassination of President John F. Kennedy. In an unusual move, the producers released the footage, including audio files, under an open-source license (specifically Creative Commons Attribution 1.0), allowing others to create their own version(s) of the movie as long as attribution for the footage is given to the producers.

Although the producers do charge for access to the footage, it is exceptionally reasonable at less than $5 for all of the video, audio, and original music. You can learn more from the Nothing So Strange web site at `www.nothingsostrange.com/open_source`.

**Interview with Ourmedia's J.D. Lasica**

*Why did you start Ourmedia?*

We saw early on that while the tools for creating digital media were coming down in price and becoming easier to use, it was still hard to *share* media. I would visit friends and colleagues and see astonishing videos, animations, and artwork they created, but which was locked away on a laptop or private network.

When Brewster Kahle of the Internet Archive offered free storage, free bandwidth, and free preservation for anyone willing to share their works in a global library, it was too good an offer to pass up. We partnered with the Archive and created the first social media network for sharing multimedia works. In effect, we're a hub for citizens' media.

*What kind of people are using Ourmedia?*

We began with a large contingent of videobloggers. Then podcasters joined the bandwagon, often because the free bandwidth saves them from having to pay hundreds of dollars to their Internet service providers. Today it's a broad cross-section of the public, including students, musicians, artists, political activists, ministers—anyone who wants to create and share digital media.

*What is the craziest or most unique video you've seen on Ourmedia?*

A 20-something member from Colombia created a trippy video of a surreal soccer game, combining a filmmaker's prowess with a young person's computer skills and storytelling sensibility.

*How do you think traditional media outlets will adapt to this new form of communication?*

Traditional media have no choice but to embrace these emerging forms of citizens' media. Society's expectations are changing. Many of us will no longer accept traditional roles as passive recipients of Big Entertainment media flowing down one-way pipes. The Digital Generation expects to produce and design its own media. They also want to remix and interact with traditional forms of media—movies, television, music, games—from the world they've grown up in.

Other great places to search for video-usable footage are at the Internet Archive's and Ourmedia's home pages. On the Internet Archive's home page, select Moving Images from the Search popup menu, enter your search terms, and then click the Go button. At Ourmedia, you can simply enter a search term in the Search form and click the Dig It! button. In either case, you receive a list of relevant videos.

## Downloading Video

Before selecting a video to use, make sure that you have the right to use it in the manner you plan. Understanding copyright and "fair use" is a subject best covered by lawyers, but if you use a video licensed under a Public Domain license, you can rest assured that you haven't violated any laws. The next best license is one of the many Creative Commons licenses.

Prior to downloading a file, however, make sure that you can actually use the file — some videos are encoded in a format that your editing system may not be capable of reading. For example, if you download an MPEG-2–encoded file and your editing system can't understand it, you've wasted time and bandwidth. Figure 5-9 shows an Internet Archive video with different download choices.

**Note**

You can transcode a file from one encoding to another through tools such as FFmpeg (www .ffmpeg.org), which is discussed more in Chapter 9.

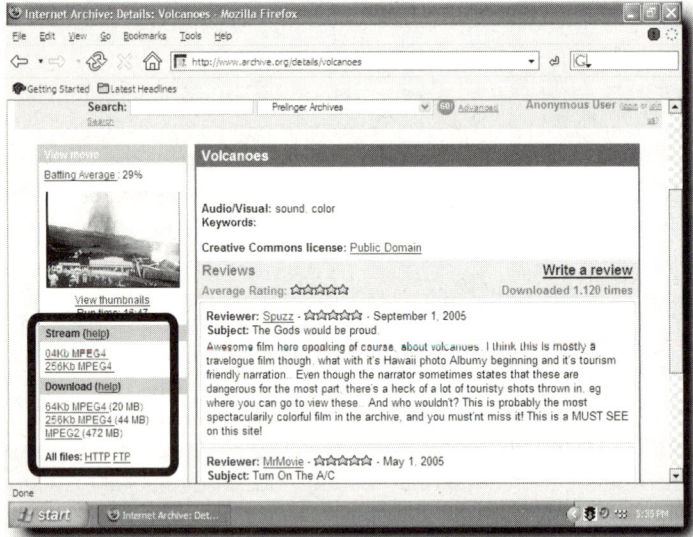

FIGURE 5-9: Various download choices through the Internet Archive.

Once you've located a video you would like to use, you need to download it. Most sites offer only one version/quality available for download, but others, such as the Internet Archive, offer a variety of qualities. If you have the option to download different qualities, opt for the best quality you can use, which almost always is the largest available file.

# Recording an iChat Conversation

With the advent of video chat, people can now realize the sci-fi vision of talking face-to-face with someone, even when the people are on opposite sides of the world. In addition, recent advances in video compression have enabled multiple people to chat at the same time, as shown in Figure 5-10. Apple's iChat, which is standard on every Mac OS X computer, is capable of handling video chat easily and, with the right hardware, can handle up to four people chatting at one time. The simple interface of iChat, in addition to its ease of use, makes it a perfect candidate for recording interview or debate footage or even just general conversation.

FIGURE 5-10: Multiple people conversing in iChat.

A standard feature of iChat enables you to save a transcript of each chat in which you participate. However, the transcript is text only. Therefore, Ecamm Network created the Conference Recorder application (www.ecamm.com/mac/conferencerecorder; $14.95) to make it possible for people to record audio and video of iChat conversations in real-time. Ecamm Network also offers an application called PowerBoost ($8) that allows older Macs (as old as G3 800MHz) to participate in multiple-person video chats.

## Setting Up for a Video Chat

Conference Recorder provides a variety of settings (see Figure 5-11) that enable you to control the quality of the resulting video: Image Size, Frame Rate, Video Quality, and Audio Quality.

### What if You Don't Use iChat?

If you are on a PC or using video-chat software that's different from iChat, you may be able to use the technique of screencasting, discussed earlier in this chapter.

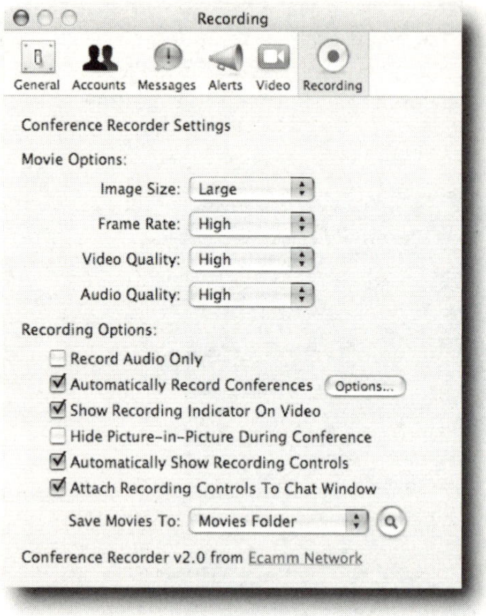

FIGURE 5-11: **Conference Recorder settings for recording.**

The Image Size setting offers Small, Medium, or Large options. Unfortunately, such descriptions leave much to be desired, and the resulting dimensions aren't available from within the application.

- Small: 110x134
- Medium: 176x144
- Large: 320x262

The Frame Rate setting is similar:

- Low: 5 frames per second
- Medium: 15 frames per second
- High: 20 frames per second

You can set the Video Quality for Space Saver: Low, Medium, or High. The technical numbers behind these settings aren't available, but they control the data rate (compression level) of the resulting movie, so the higher the quality setting, the higher the data rate and file size.

The Audio Quality setting offers Normal or High as the choice.

Following are the best settings for videoblogging:

- Image Size: Large
- Frame Rate: Medium
- Video Quality: Medium
- Audio Quality: High

An additional setting, the Show Recording Indicator option, is on the Recording tab in the Settings. When enabled, it places a flashing red dot in the chat window to indicate to the participants that they are being recorded. This is done for possible legal reasons, so if you turn it off, make certain that the participants are aware they are being recorded.

## Recording a Video Chat

After setting up Conference Recorder, you're ready to actually record a video chat. To do so, simply start a chat with one or more people, and then click the Record button. You can also set Conference Recorder to automatically record all of your chats by checking the Automatically Record All Conversations preference in the Recording tab settings. By default, all videos are saved in your Movies folder, but that too can be changed.

After recording a chat, you can either post it directly online or import it to your editing system for finessing.

# Revlogging

Revlogging. There we go, making up words again.

Revlogging is blogging about other videobloggers, creating a web of links between videoblogs and videos, and making videoblogs much easier to discover. Videoblogging needs revlogs.

Text blogs have something called a bookmarklet that makes quoting another person's blog a simple one-click process. For videoblogs, however, there isn't really such a mechanism, which generally means that most videobloggers don't link to other videobloggers' videos and sites.

Peter Van Djick originally attempted to bridge this gap through his QuoteThis tool in Mefeedia (www.mefeedia.com). It enabled you to create an SMIL video file that contained a quote from another video and then post that to your videoblog. Although the attempt was a good idea, it had two problems: The SMIL movies would often play very slowly (a limit of the technology), and there was no one-click sending to your blog.

Peter's second attempt at encouraging revlogging is the BlogThis tool in Mefeedia. BlogThis posts directly to your videoblog, and you can even drag and drop thumbnails of the video in your post. It's actually a WYSIWYG (What You See Is What You Get) editor! With BlogThis, it's easy to browse through Mefeedia and revlog.

To use BlogThis, you first need to inform Mefeedia about your videoblog so that cross-communication can occur. Then, while viewing a video, you can click the BlogThis icon, which opens a small text editor in a new window (see Figure 5-12). Just type whatever your comment is, and Mefeedia takes care of the rest.

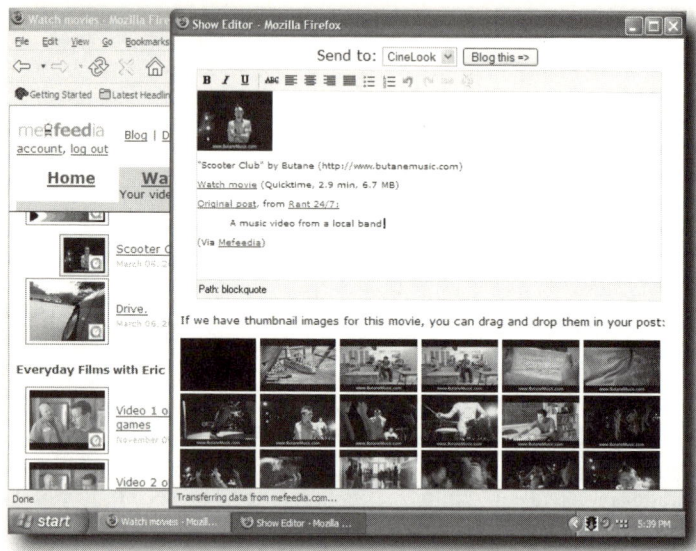

FIGURE 5-12: Revlogging using Mefeedia's BlogThis tool.

The really nice thing about Mefeedia is that it has a fairly complete archive of all videobloggers and a pretty good tagging/keyword feature set. Also, you can BlogThis from anywhere on Mefeedia. The experience can be a memory trip: You browse through tags and feeds you know, rediscover old videos, and revlog them to your site. The whole thing just works.

Peter believes BlogThis still needs improvement, but the basic experience is solid and can only get better. Try it out for yourself, and let Peter know what you think.

# Using del.icio.us for Video

The web site del.icio.us enables its users to keep, share, and discover other sites on the Internet. It is a community-driven web site, where people can "tag" other sites on the Internet. One way to think about it is that it enables you to bookmark a site and then relate keywords to it. So, a del.icio.us user might choose to bookmark the web site "ryanedit.blogspot.com" and then add the tags "videoblog," "ryanne," and "editing."

The site is community driven in that users share their bookmarks and enable them to be searched by tag. So, if someone searched for "videoblog," then "ryanedit.blogspot.com" would be a part of the results. It is a wonderful site that really becomes indispensable once used.

## Limiting del.icio.us Results to Video

Using your preferred web browser, go to `http://del.icio.us`. You can then add information to the end of the URL in your browser to limit the type of links that del.icio.us provides. For example, adding `/tag/system:media:video` to the URL restricts the result list to only video:

`http://del.icio.us/tag/system:media:video`

Adding /tag/system:filetype:mov restricts the results to only QuickTime files:

`http://del.icio.us/tag/system:filetype:mov`

Similarly, adding /tag/system:filetype:wmv restricts the results to Windows Video files:

`http://del.icio.us/tag/system:filetype:wmv`

## Further Restricting Results

You can also place additional restrictions on the results by adding metadata to the end of the URL, such as `+funny`:

`http://del.icio.us/tag/system:media:video+funny`

Placing such a restriction would result in videos that have been "tagged" with the word funny. You can also trust your fellow del.icio.us users and simply try out the most popular videos using the URL `http://del.icio.us/rss/popular/system:media:video`.

## Subscribing to del.icio.us

So, what good is a video search if you can't subscribe to it using RSS (as discussed in Chapter 3)? Well, the great folks behind the site allow you to easily subscribe to other users' links as well as search results. At the bottom of your result page, you'll find an orange RSS button. Simply click it and your aggregator should handle the rest. If it doesn't, you can copy the RSS link information and then paste it into your aggregator as a new subscription. Once you subscribe, you get a fresh feed of new videos, suited to your taste, daily.

Truly, delicious.

# Summary

Just because you don't own a digital video camera doesn't mean you can't participate in the videoblogging world. With a variety of options available, you can easily download, link to, and record video using just your computer. After working with it for a while, you'll soon discover that your computer is really just a tool to help you communicate with the rest of the world.

# Using Technology Creatively

**D**igital video is a great technology that has enabled millions of people to acquire, edit, and distribute high-quality video cheaply. But shooting video using a camera is just the beginning. There are a number of ways to be creative with digital video, from transferring old analog (VHS) footage to digital, adding motion to still images, and even using a broomstick to change the angle of your shots.

## Shooting a Television or Monitor

Once in a while, you might find it worthwhile to record video while your monitor or television is in the background. This can be very useful when you're trying to "quote" a video source. The problem is that you most likely will see the screen "flicker" in the background. The reason is that the monitor or television is refreshing the image very quickly. In fact, that's how televisions create the illusion of movement—by showing a series of images in fast succession.

Because the flicker can be distracting and is easy to overcome, you might as well take a couple of steps in preparation to create a better viewing experience for your audience: stabilizing your shot and changing your camera's refresh rate.

## Stabilizing the Shot

Practically every video camera sold today has some type of image-stabilization feature. Sony calls it Steady Shot, Panasonic calls it Electronic Image Stabilization, and others simply call it "image stabilization." Whatever it's called, the feature helps keep an image centered and compensates for the shakiness that occurs when people shoot footage using a handheld camera.

Unfortunately, image-stabilizing technology enhances the flicker you see when shooting a television or monitor. To help reduce the flicker, you need to turn off image stabilization on your camera.

If you're planning to shoot without automatic image stabilization, you can compensate for your loss of this helpful technology by using a tripod. By doing so, you remove shakiness from the equation.

## Changing the Refresh Rate

To remove — or at least drastically reduce — the flicker of a monitor, you can change the refresh rate (in addition to turning off image stabilization on your camera). If you are in North America, or a country that broadcasts using the NTSC standard, you'll want to change the refresh rate to a multiple of 30 (or as close to 30 as possible). For example, if your monitor is set to refresh at 120Hz, you will see less flicker than if it is set to refresh at 100Hz.

Although it seems minor, reducing the monitor flicker (and stabilizing your shot) will help keep your audience's focus on the content of your video, not on your technical skills (or lack thereof).

# Converting Analog Video to Digital

If you have some VHS tapes with footage that you never got around to doing anything with, join the gang. Millions of households around the world have analog footage acquired in days past . . . and the footage is begging to have a breath of life again. Using a small video-conversion tool called a *breakout box*, you can easily transfer your analog video to digital video.

## Buying a Breakout Box

There are a wide variety of breakout boxes on the market, in a wide range of prices. How you choose a breakout box depends on the source of your original footage, its quality, and the quality you want to extract. For the majority of people, almost any breakout box will do. A couple of the more popular options are:

- Canopus ADVC-110 (www.canopus.com; $249.00). This FireWire-powered box offers excellent conversion quality and great audio synchronization.

- Miglia Director's Cut Take 2 (www.miglia.com; $269.00). This FireWire-powered box ignores Macrovision (a copy protection scheme that garbles the picture) and has two analog outputs that enable you to attach a TV to it for use during editing sessions.

If your footage is in less-than-optimal quality or if you're a professional, with footage on beta, 3/4-inch, or Hi-8 tape, you may want to look at some of the more feature-rich boxes. For example, a breakout box with a built-in Time Base Corrector can improve the visual quality of your video. A couple of suggestions are:

- Canopus ADVC-500 (www.canopus.com; $1,499.00). This box offers balanced audio (XLR), image control (brightness, contrast, hue, saturation, hue, sharpness), and component video connections.
- Datavideo DAC-10 (www.datavideo.us; $499.00). It offers component video connections, video color adjustments, and a blackburst generator.

You should note that when using a breakout box, you will not have control over your VHS machine. This is a very minor issue and shouldn't lead to any problems.

## Converting Your Video

Once you've obtained a breakout box, the actual conversion process is straightforward. Connect your VHS machine's outputs to the breakout box's inputs. Then connect the breakout box to your computer using either FireWire or USB. Once everything is connected and turned on, launch your editing software, set it to capture video, and hit play on your VHS machine.

### Using a Camera to "Pass Through"

Some DV cameras allow for an analog signal to "pass through" and be converted to digital. The best way to find out if your camera allows pass-through is to test it. Here's how:

1. Connect your camera to your computer via FireWire.

2. Connect your VCR (or other analog device) to your camera.

3. Turn on your camera and VCR, and launch your video editing/capture application.

4. Put your camera in VCR/VTR/Playback mode and play your VHS.

5. Finally, try to capture video using your computer; you'll know almost immediately if it works, because you'll see the video on your computer screen. If you're able to capture video, congratulations; your camera allows for pass-through. If not, you'll probably have to break down and buy a breakout box.

More often than not, you'll be using a DV codec to capture video, unless you set your software to use something else. The DV codec uses 13GB of drive space for every 60 minutes of footage, so you should plan accordingly.

Being able to transfer old footage that you never did anything with and then editing and distributing the video on the web can be a great way to get into videoblogging. Imagine putting your son's first birthday on the web as a gift . . . for his 21st birthday. What you do with your footage is up to your imagination, but breathing life back into the footage can be a thrill in itself.

# Creating a Videoblog Using Only Photos

Videos are basically a collection of still images displayed quickly. So why can't you take a still image and add motion to it to create a video? You can.

The process of adding motion to a still image is called *motion control*. Less than 10 years ago, creating a motion-control video was exceptionally expensive. But as digital acquisition methods such as scanners became cheaper and computer hardware became more powerful, motion control slowly became possible for anyone with a computer. Today, practically every video-editing program provides some type of motion-control capability, even those that are free.

To create a motion-control video, you need two things: digital photos and motion-control software.

## Acquiring Digital Photos

There are a variety of ways you can acquire digital photos, the most obvious being through a digital still camera. You can also use a scanner to transfer your physical pictures to your computer. Scanners range in price, with many high-quality scanners — such as the Epson 3490 (www.epson.com) and the Canon CanoScan 4200F (www.canon.com) — available for less than $100.00. Also, many companies now offer multifunction printers that are also capable of faxing and, yup, scanning.

Another method of obtaining digital images is to look online using, for example, Google's image search (www.google.com/imghp) or Flickr (www.flickr.com) (see Figure 6-1). This can be exceptionally useful when you're looking for shots of nature, tourist attractions in foreign countries, or just generic images that you don't have time to shoot for yourself. Remember, when using images you locate online, make sure that you have the right to use them.

### Jonathan Coulton

In late 2005, Jonathan Coulton created a well-received music video (www.jonathancoulton .com/2005/12/22/thing-a-week-14-flickr). The video used images he found on Flickr (www.flickr.com). All of the images that Jonathan used are licensed under a Creative Commons license that allowed him to create his video. He wrote the song *Flickr*, which can be downloaded separately from the video at www.jonathancoulton.com/songs for $1.00.

FIGURE 6-1: Flickr.com.

## Using Motion-Control Software

After you've acquired the images you want to use in your video, insert them in a video timeline and add any desired motion. How you import the images and add the motion depends on your software, but most applications follow a similar workflow:

1. Launch the editing software.

2. Select File → Import.

3. Locate the images you'd like to use.

4. Place an image on your video timeline.

5. Add a resize, motion, or "Ken Burns" effect to the image.

6. Add music or sound effects.

7. Render.

8. Repeat for additional images.

When you're satisfied with the look of your video, export it and upload it to your videoblog. Using still images is just another means to get creative with digital video in an unexpected way.

## Photo to Movie

LQ Graphics (www.lqgraphics.com) offers software designed specifically for motion control. It's called Photo to Movie and is available for Mac OS X and Windows XP for $49.95. The software enables you to import photos and create truly stunning and complex motion paths easily. The software also offers the capability to import sound and create great-looking titles. If you plan to create more than a couple of videos that use motion control, it would be well worth your time to evaluate Photo to Movie.

# Automating a Videoblog Entry on a Mac

Through the use of Apple's Automator and QuickTime Pro, you can easily record, upload, and create your videoblog. Placing your videoblog on the net can be a tedious process: Record your video, compress your video, upload your video, open your blog site, type your post, and, finally, submit it. Through the use of Apple's Automator and QuickTime Pro, you can create your videoblog much more easily.

When Apple released OS 10.4, also known as Tiger, it unveiled a new technology called Automator. Tiger Automator enables you to create Workflows to help reduce the amount of time you spend doing tedious tasks, thereby freeing you to be more productive (or, maybe, to get outdoors). So, why not create a Workflow to help you create your videoblog?

Because of the effort involved, you may even put off posting to your videoblog for the simple reason that it just takes too much time. But what if you could simply click your mouse a few times and be done with it? You can.

 **Tip** To make this solution work effectively, connect a webcam such as Apple's iSight to your computer. You can also use a DV camera, if you have one. Some MPEG-capable digital cameras can also work.

## Starting the Workflow

Find Automator in the standard Applications folder on your computer and launch it. Create a new Workflow (if one hasn't already been created for you). You're going to use QuickTime player for your video capture, which is really quite easy to do.

## Automating the Video Capture

After creating your new Workflow, add your first Action. Click the Run AppleScript Action, listed in the Library Action pane under the Automator item, and drag it to the Workflow window. Then add the following to text area in the Run AppleScript Action:

```
on run {input, parameters}

    (* start QuickTime *)
    tell application "QuickTime Player"
        activate
    end tell

    return input

end run
```

This script will launch the QuickTime Player application.

Select QuickTime Player from the Library pane. From the Actions pane, click the New Video Capture Action and drag it to your Workflow. The Workflow, as it should appear, is shown in Figure 6-2.

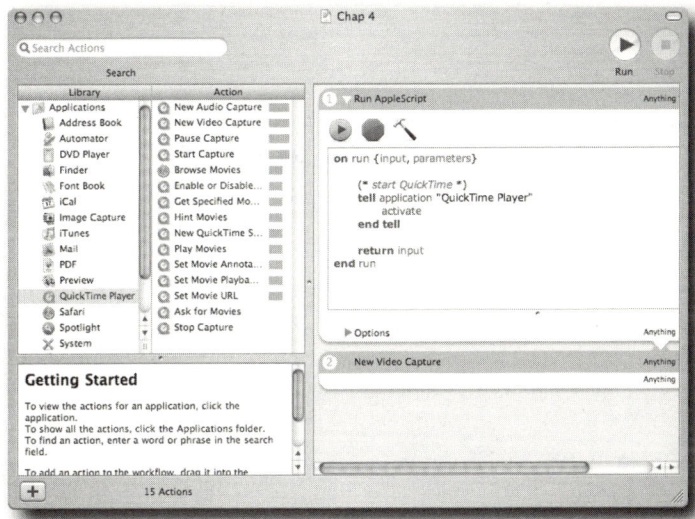

FIGURE 6-2: A Workflow set to begin a Video Capture session.

Next, select the Wait for User Action from the Automator Library and drag it to your Workflow. The Action enables you essentially to pause a Workflow for a specified amount of time or until the user clicks a button.

When the Workflow crosses the Wait for User Action, it opens a window and displays whatever message you enter in the Message text area. For example, to automatically stop the Workflow after five minutes, check the appropriate box and enter the number of minutes you want to stop the Workflow after (see Figure 6-3). The Wait for User Action enables you to frame yourself in the video before you actually record. It also provides enough time to

QuickTime Player to focus and adjust your webcam. If you allow the Workflow to stop, you have to click the Start button for it to run again.

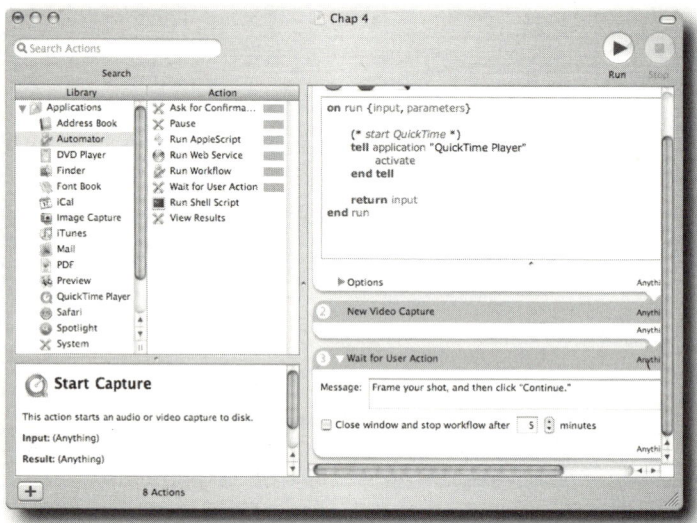

FIGURE 6-3: Wait for User Action configured to never stop the Workflow.

For example, say you're about to record a videoblog entry and the phone rings. You walk away from your computer to answer the phone. After a 30-minute conversation with your mother about today's happenings on *Dr. Phil*, you return to your computer. Because of the Wait for User Action, and the automatic stop, your computer didn't record 30 minutes of who-knows-what and post it to your videoblog.

Now add the Start Capture Action, which can be found in the QuickTime Player Library. It causes QuickTime to actually start the video-recording process. If you were to run the Workflow immediately after adding the Start Capture Action, QuickTime Player would open, wait for you to click a Continue button, and then start recording whatever video it's being fed.

Obviously, you want the video to stop recording at some point, which is where you use a Stop Capture Action. However, if you use Stop Capture immediately following the Start Video Capture Action, you won't acquire much video (probably less than a second). You'll simply start recording video and stop recording video quickly. Fortunately, you can use Wait for User Action to pause the Workflow.

After adding the Wait for User Action, select QuickTime Player in the Library and drag the Stop Capture Action to your Workflow. So the last three steps in your Workflow should be:

1. Start Capture

2. Wait for User Action

3. Stop Capture

**A Stop Capture Bug**

If you are using OS X 10.4.5, the Stop Capture Action will halt the Workflow. To work around this issue, substitute a Run AppleScript Action for the Stop Capture Action and enter the following code:

```
tell application "QuickTime Player"

    stop movie 1

end tell
```

Finally, test your Workflow by clicking the Play button. It should launch QuickTime Player, start recording video, wait for you to click the Continue button (or a specified amount of time), and then stop recording. Upon completion, a video called Movie.mov appears on your Desktop.

## Renaming the Video File

To make the Workflow of any long-term use, it should rename the resulting video to something unique. But how? By using a tool you already have at your disposal but probably don't know about.

The uuidgen tool is a command that can create a unique series of characters. Using uuidgen, the Workflow can create a unique name for your file. To use uuidgen, drag another Run AppleScript Action to the Workflow. Then add the following code:

```
on run {input, parameters}

    (* stop movies in QuickTime *)
    tell application "QuickTime Player"
        stop every movie
    end tell

    (* create a unique filename *)
    set fileName to do shell script "uuidgen"

    (* determine the current user's name *)
    set username to do shell script "whoami"

    (* Upload to FTP requires the full path to the movie *)
    set input to ("/Users/" & username & "/Desktop/" & fileName &
".mov")

    (* rename the file by moving it *)
    do shell script "mv ~/Desktop/Movie.mov " & input

    return input
end run
```

The AppleScript stops any movies currently playing in QuickTime Player, creates a unique filename (by using the `uuidgen` tool), determines your username (by using the `whoami` command), and finally renames the file (using the `mv` command).

## Copying the Video to a Server

There are a variety of ways you can copy your video file to a server. Most web hosts provide access to the server through FTP, while others enable more secure access through SCP. There are Automator Actions available for FTP and SCP online:

- FTP: `http://editkid.com/upload_to_ftp`
- SCP: `http://douglas.stebila.ca/code/automator/upload_with_scp`

This book uses the FTP method. Here's what to do:

1. Download the Upload to FTP Action from `http://editkid.com/upload_to_ftp` and install it.

2. Quit and relaunch Automator (so it will recognize the new Action).

3. Select Upload to FTP from the Action pane and add it to your Workflow. (You can locate the Action easily by entering **ftp** in the Search dialog above the Library and Action panes.)

4. Enter the requisite information in the appropriate text fields (see Figure 6-4). At the very least, you should enter your Server, Username, and Password.

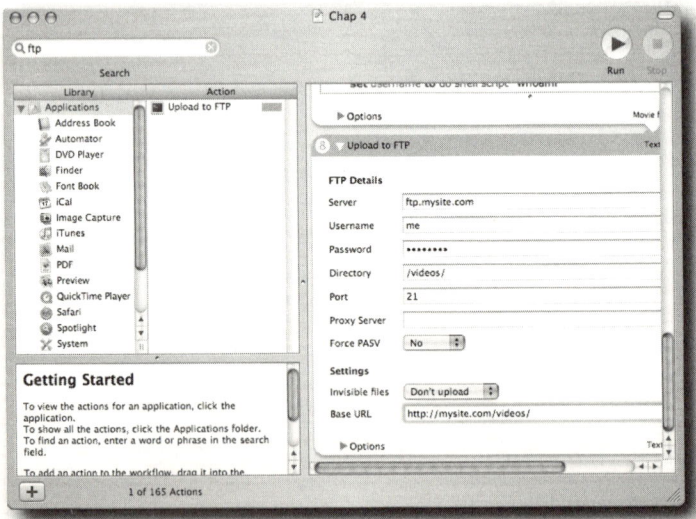

FIGURE 6-4: The Upload to FTP Action configured to upload to mysite.com in the videos directory.

**Being Secure**

Secure Copy (SCP) is the preferred method for the security conscious. To use it, you should be familiar with how to use SSH and how to set up Public Key Authentication. Information is available on Douglas Stebila's SCP web site (`http://douglas.stebila.ca/code/automator/upload_with_scp`), as well as through web searches (search for "Public Key Authentication").

Although the results from the action of recording video are technically Movie Files, and Upload to FTP technically requires Text, the process still works.

## Posting to Your Blog

You'll probably want to add a little text information about your video, if only to provide your audience some context. To do so, add a Run AppleScript Action to your Workflow and add the following code:

```
on run {input, parameters}

    (* open TextEdit *)
    tell application "TextEdit"
        activate

        (* create a new, clean document *)
        make new document at end of documents

        (* add some outline text *)
        (* this is all one line! *)
        make new paragraph at end of front document with data
"<title>" & (current date) & "</title>YOUR POST HERE<br/><a
rel=\"enclosure\" href=\"" & input & "\"><img
src=\"http://www.domain.com/path/to/quicktime/image\"
alt=\"QuickTime\"/></a>"

    end tell

end run
```

The AppleScript opens TextEdit, creates a new document, and then adds some text for you. The text is HTML, which is what web browsers interpret. There are two items to note:

- When you run the work flow, you'll need to place your text in place of YOUR POST HERE. Do not alter any of the other text.

- Replace `http://www.domain.com/path/to/quicktime/image` with the actual web address for a QuickTime image.

To not have Automator step on your toes, add another Wait for User Action to your Workflow to provide you time to type whatever you choose for your post.

Next, add a Get Content of TextEdit Document Action from the TextEdit Library. This Action simply copies your post and passes it to the next Workflow Action. Simple and easy, huh?

## Creating the Videoblog

Ah, the final step, where your video and your blog come together to make a videoblog. Again, you use the power of AppleScript to accomplish your goal.

Most blog software allows for Remote Procedure Calls (RPC), which enables people to write other software to interface with the blog. AppleScript has the capability to create and send RPC through the call xmlrpc feature. In addition, the way to communicate with blog software is freely available through Application Programming Interfaces (APIs) published on the Internet.

The call you are going to use is newPost from the Blogger API, which most blog software supports. To implement the XMLRPC communication, add a Run AppleScript Action, as you have done previously. Then enter the following code:

```
on run {input, parameters}

    (* initialize a stub of terms *)
    using terms from application "http://www.apple.com/placebo"

        (* set up the required parameters *)
        set appKey to "0123456789ABCDEF"
        set blogId to 1
        set myUsername to "username"
        set myPassword to "password"
        set myContent to input
        set publish to true

        try
            (* make a connection to the blog *)
            tell application "http://www.domain.com/xmlrpc.php"
                (* call the actual xmlrpc *)
                call xmlrpc {method name:"blogger.newPost", ⤶
parameters:{appKey, blogId, myUsername, myPassword, ⤶
myContent, publish}}
            end tell
        on error e
            (* display the error to the user *)
            display dialog e
        end try

    end using terms from

    return input
end run
```

In this code, change the username and password to what you use with your blog and the `http://www.domain.com/xmlrpc.php` to the XMLRPC end point (which you can find out from your blog software; just search for XMLRPC). After you enter the code, your Workflow is complete (see Figure 6-5).

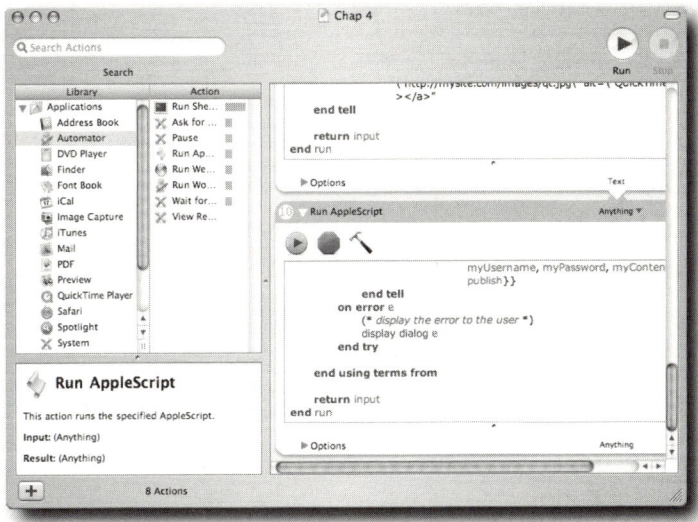

FIGURE 6-5: The completed Automator Workflow, ready for use.

The AppleScript connects to your blog and adds your post to it. It automatically links to your video, too. That's it. You're done.

Go. Vlog. You have no excuses.

**Note**   If your blog software doesn't support the Blogger API, it may support MetaWeblog, which is just as easy to implement. Information on the MetaWeblog API is at `www.xmlrpc.com/metaWeblogApi`. Simply look for how to post an entry.

# Creating a Camera Crane

A crane shot is often used in major motion pictures. You've probably seen it hundreds of times, consciously or unconsciously. Basically, the camera zooms in on a subject and then moves out, away from the subject, going higher to allow the audience to see more of the subject's surroundings. For the shot to be dramatic, however, it needs to continue moving away from the subject as far as possible.

In the movie *Garden State*, Zach Branff uses a crane shot to emphasize the loneliness and feeling of loss of the characters. The shot occurs in a scene with a pet cemetery, where two characters are sitting on the ground. As the shot begins, the audience is shown how small the cemetery is. Then the camera moves higher, until it finally moves so high that the actors look like little toy dolls. It's a very effective shot.

Although you can purchase a semiprofessional crane from ProMax (`www.promax.com/Products/Cat/Cranes`; $299.00 and higher), you can also create your own crane by using a broomstick and some ingenuity.

Steve Garfield did exactly that to create *The Carol and Steve Show: Episode 17 — Car Wash* (`http://stevegarfield.blogs.com/videoblog/2005/04/the_carol_and_s_2 .html`), and viewers really liked it. To create your own crane, you'll need a few items:

- A small digital camera that can accept a tripod attachment.
- A tripod. (Recommend: REI UltraPod; $10.00 from `www.rei.com`).
- A Velcro strap.
- A broomstick.

To assemble the crane, you need to follow a few simple steps:

1. Attach the tripod to the camera (see Figure 6-6).

FIGURE 6-6: Attaching a camera to a tripod.

**2.** Attach the broomstick to the tripod using the Velcro strap (see Figure 6-7).

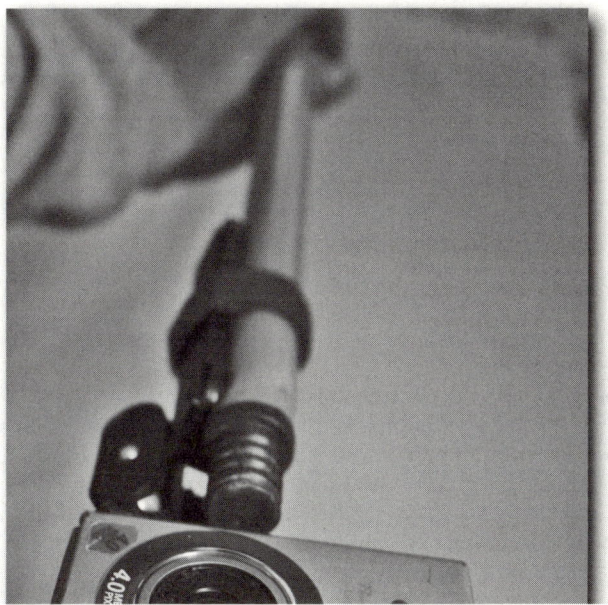

FIGURE 6-7: Using Velcro to affix tripod to broomstick.

**3.** Turn on the camera and start recording.

It's basic yet highly effective. To create the most convincing shot, use as smooth a motion as possible. It helps if you plan your shot ahead of time and practice it a few times. You may also want to use a cheap, disposable digital video camera, like the one sold through CVS/pharmacy stores.

# Reusing a CVS Digital Camera

In 2005, the CVS/pharmacy chain began selling a line of one-time-use video camcorders. These cameras are manufactured by Pure Digital Technologies, and the intention was that, after shooting the video, the customer would return the camera to the store for processing. In exchange for a $14.00 fee, the customer would receive a DVD with the acquired videos. Shortly after the release of this device, however, the hacker community sprang into action and discovered a way to reuse it. (Here, the term *hacker* is used in the traditional sense of "a person who enjoys exploring the details of programmable systems and how to stretch their capabilities.")

## John Maushammer

John Maushammer, an embedded systems engineer, had previously disassembled the CVS/pharmacy digital still photo camera, also manufactured by Pure Digital. By reusing a lot of the work from his previous effort, he quickly discovered how to access the internals of the digital video camera version as well. With collaboration from many contributors at the Camera Hacks forum (`http://camerahacks.10.forumer.com/index.php`), a solution was created to get the files from the video camera and on to a computer as unencrypted video files (technically, they're XViD AVI format).

You can find John Maushammer's CVS/pharmacy Camcorder site at `www.maushammer.com/systems/cvscamcorder`.

There are numerous ways to hack the CVS/pharmacy digital video camera, and a web search for "cvs camera hack" locates many of the alternatives. The approach presented here is particularly good for a few reasons. Most important, it does not actually involve disassembling the video camera itself and thus is low risk for damaging the electronics of the device. Also, this solution uses easily and cheaply found parts. In fact, many people will have the necessary spare parts already tucked away in a drawer or closet. Finally, it is simple; a novice with a soldering iron can successfully accomplish the tasks required.

Required materials:

- A 10-pin connector, such as those found on the sync cables for Palm III devices
- A USB cable with full-sized USB-A connector
- A soldering iron
- A Dremel tool or sharp knife
- (Optional) Wiring heat wrap
- (Optional) A multimeter for checking connections

## Getting Started

To get started, pop open the shell of the 10-pin connector. Then, using a soldering iron, remove all the wires attached to the backside of the pins. In most cases, the cable should lift out of a notch in the connector. If there is a rubber or plastic stress relief piece that clips into that notch, set it aside for later use.

Next, remove the printed label from the top of the CVS camcorder, exposing the 10-pin connection. See if your connector will fit into that gap so that the pins mate up. Most connectors will be too large and will require whittling or cutting some of the hard plastic off of the shell with a knife or Dremel tool. Figure 6-8 shows a connector that's been whittled on the top.

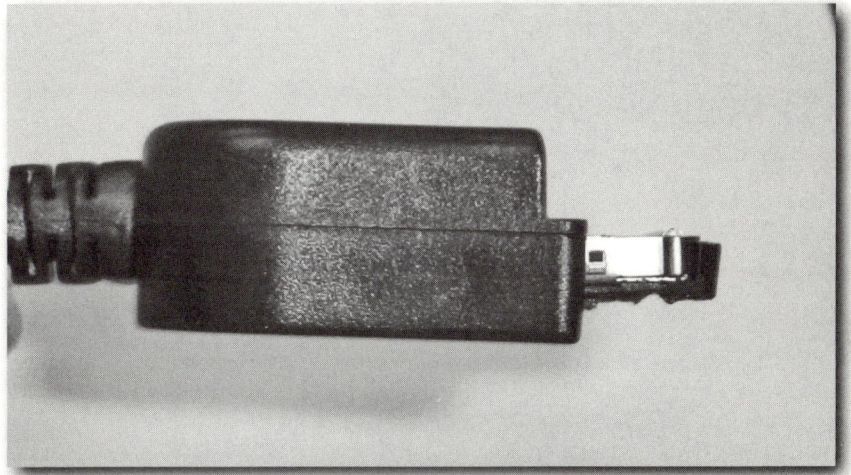

FIGURE 6-8: A modified 10-pin connector.

When removing part of the plastic, be patient. Do it in several passes, if necessary. If you get the connector cut just right, it will fit perfectly and snugly in that space (see Figure 6-9). If you cut too little, the pins will not be able to make a good connection. If you cut too much, the connector will fit too loosely. When just right, the two pieces will snap together and hold securely.

FIGURE 6-9: Testing the 10-pin connection.

Next, take the USB cable, identify the end with the full-sized USB-A connector (the one that you plug into your computer), and cut off the other end of the cable. Carefully slit the outer insulation of the cut end of the USB cable and remove about $1^{1}/_{2}$ inches of it, leaving the four internal wires free. Then strip each of the four wires so that they have about $^{1}/_{4}$ inch of wire exposed. If you plan to use wire heat wrap, slide it on now, before you attach the wires to the connector.

## Creating the Connections

To create the necessary connections, place the connector face down so that the back of the pins are facing up (see Figure 6-10), and solder the wires in this order. (With the connector on your left, and the cable leading off to the right, count from the top):

1. Pin #6 — Red Wire (+5 volts)
2. Pin #8 — Green Wire (positive data)
3. Pin #9 — White Wire (negative data)
4. Pin #10 — Black Wire (ground)

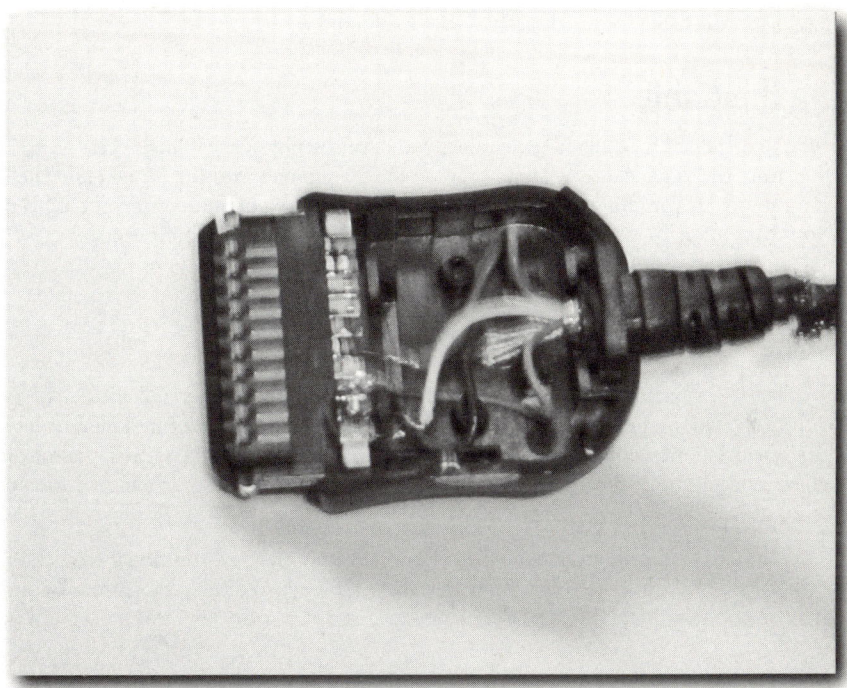

FIGURE 6-10: A newly soldered 10-pin connector.

If you want to verify your soldering job with a multimeter, test a connection between the following pairs of pins (looking into the USB connector with the pins down, count the pins from right to left):

- USB Pin #1 to Pin #6
- USB Pin #2 to Pin #9
- USB Pin #3 to Pin #8
- USB Pin #4 to Pin #10

If you are using heat wrap, use a blow dryer or hot air gun now to shrink it around the wires. You can also use rubber pieces from the original wiring, or a small amount electrical tape, to build up some stress relief. When you click the plastic connector shell back on, you don't want any tugging on the cable to pull directly on your soldered wires.

## Using the Cable

Once you've successfully soldered your cable, you have the physical cabling necessary to extract your files from the video camera. To do so, plug the 10-pin end into the camera and the USB connector into your computer. You should be able to see the camera mounted as a USB device from your computer. To extract the video files, you need a computer application:

- Macintosh OS X: PureRead (`www.maushammer.com/systems/cvscamcorder`)
- Windows or Linux: Ops (`http://pv2devkit.sourceforge.net`)

PureRead and Ops enable the downloading of videos to your computer and the deleting of videos from the video camera. In addition, Ops enables more advanced functionality, including changing various options of the camcorder such as the resolution of the videos, the maximum allowable recording time, the frame rate, and even the sounds the camera makes during certain operations.

In recent revisions of the video camera's firmware (3.62 and greater), additional protections were added to prevent reusing the camera. However, there are ways to disable those, too. Look at `http://camerahacks.10.forumer.com/viewtopic.php?t=1577`.

# Summary

The size of digital video cameras, along with the capability to easily manipulate digital footage and to import various types of files, opens a whole new realm of digital-video creativity to those who want to explore. Transferring footage, adding still images, getting creative with mounting solutions, and even physically opening a camera are simply beginning steps to what can be done. The limits are yours to discover.

# Post-Production

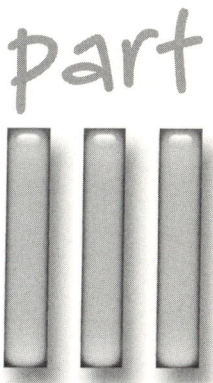

part
III

# Editing Tricks

**U**nless you just post video exactly how you shoot it, you'll need to edit your video. Although the process can be tedious and daunting, it doesn't have to be. In fact, it can be a lot of fun.

## In-Camera Editing

Making a video for your blog can be easy. If you edit as you shoot, you don't even need editing software. This process is called *in-camera editing* and essentially requires that you record only the video you want to keep. Also, you shoot your footage in the order you want it to play.

For example, let's say that your sister is graduating today, and you want to post a video of her big day as soon as possible, specifically for your family who can't attend the ceremony. You'll want to make the video available as soon as possible and therefore don't want to spend time — hours, days, or possibly even weeks — digitizing and editing it. You also want to upload a fairly short yet entertaining video because you know your family doesn't have much of an attention span. To accomplish this, all you have to do is visualize. . .and use the edit-search feature on your camera.

Many digital video cameras have an edit-search feature. It enables you to move forward or backward on your tape one frame at a time. The Edit-Search button, such as the one in Figure 7-1, is much more accurate than the Rewind and Fast-Forward buttons on a camera because you can see the video as it's moving frame-by-frame instead of just hoping you stop the tape in the right place. It lets you perform very exact edits as you're shooting.

So, you're recording your sister explaining how she feels about graduating, and you figure that you've recorded too much. You know that your audience will get the point after the first 30 seconds, but you've managed to record much longer than that. You can use the edit-search feature of your camera to locate a point that you think is appropriate to end her talk about her feelings. Afterward, when you start recording again, the next shot begins exactly where you left it, without any jump in the image.

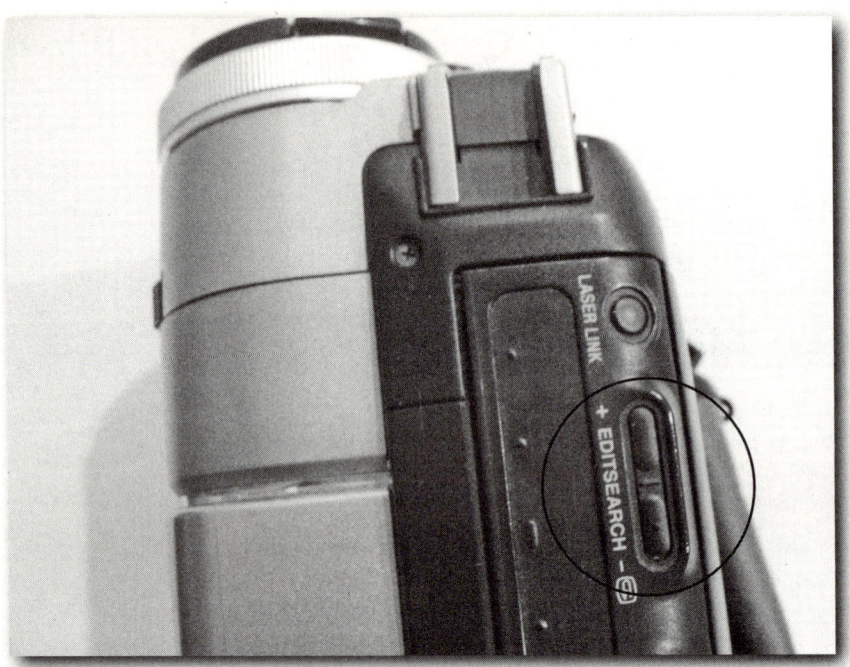

FIGURE 7-1: An Edit-Search button on a video camera.

Whenever shooting a video using the edit-search feature, always try to stay one step ahead in your vision for the final video. Anticipate what's next, emotionally and visually. For instance, in your graduation video, you might first show the graduate-to-be putting on her gown at home. You might grab a moment of her arriving at the event and later record her saying how she feels just before the ceremony starts. During the ceremony, you would record her walking across the stage to get her diploma and then show her celebrating at the end. At the end of the day, the video would be complete — it would require no additional editing, because it would have been recorded with only the necessary footage.

Using in-camera editing enables you to shoot, compress, and post your video all in the same day. Once you get a handle on the simple tools you have and learn to visualize the moments you're trying to share, videoblogging can easily become a part of your daily life.

## Editing with QuickTime Pro

Using the Swiss Army knife of video tools, QuickTime Pro ($29.99; www.apple.com/quicktime/pro), you can easily edit a video with some quick-and-dirty cuts. QuickTime Pro is the advanced version of the free QuickTime Player (www.apple.com/quicktime)

for Mac and Windows. The free version is bundled with iTunes, and the Pro version enables you to perform simple edits using cut-and-paste commands. The advantage to having these features is that you can do a quick edit, using easy-to-create cuts, without having to import files or render as you do in most editing-software applications. Plus, you can easily export the final video for your videoblog directly out of the application itself.

## Selecting Media to Edit

There are a couple ways to select the portions of your media that you want to edit. First, you can slide the small, gray selection indicators (Figure 7-2) to their approximate in and out points with your mouse. This is not always accurate, but it's good for a quick chop.

Selection indicators

FIGURE 7-2: Selection indicators used for marking in and out points.

Another way to select a clip is to play a selection while using key commands to do the work. To do so, position the playhead at the beginning of where your clip should start; then press Shift+Command+➜ (Macintosh) or Shift+Ctrl+➜ (Windows). The video will play until you release the keys. The in point is where the playhead started, and the out point is where your playhead stopped. You can also do this in reverse by using the ← instead of ➜.

### Performing an Insert Edit

Once you've selected a clip of your video, you'll probably want to use it in another video. To insert the clip in an existing video file, it's easiest just to copy and paste it.

### Performing a Trim Edit

If you want to trim the beginning and end out of a clip but keep a particular section, a great choice is to use the Trim to Selection feature. To use it, first select a portion of the video, and then choose Edit ➔ Trim to Selection (Figure 7-3).

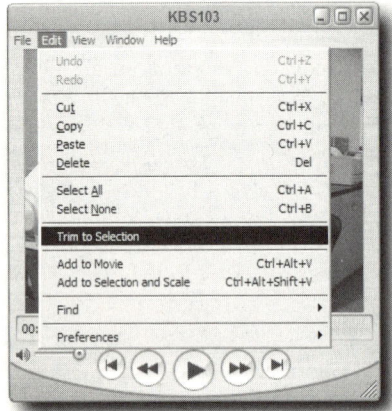

FIGURE 7-3: Using the Trim to Selection feature.

The new version of the video will be created, using only the length of your selection.

## Edit and Save the Video

To create the edit, select the portion of media from Video 1 using the aforementioned clip-select method. Then select Edit ➔ Copy. To place the clip into another video, position the play-head in Video 2 where you want to insert Video 1's media (that's currently on your Clipboard), and select Edit ➔ Paste. After pasting the video, you will have made the simplest "insert edit" on Earth.

---

### Beware of Different Codecs

If you can't Paste your selection, you may be working with different codecs. This occurs, for example, if you're using two videos, one using the MPEG-4 codec and the other using the MPEG-2 codec. To resolve this problem, simply transcode one video to match the other. You learn about transcoding in Chapter 9.

To save the file while preserving your original, select File ➜ Save As. Use a different file name from your original so that the original is not accidentally deleted (you'll also be able to distinguish between the two at a later date). When saving, choose the Save as a Self-Contained Movie option, so that you have a complete file. If you don't choose to create a self-contained movie, you wind up creating a reference file, which just points to the media you have edited. Basically, if you were to email a reference file to a friend, she wouldn't be able to see any of the video, because it would still be on your computer.

## Using a Timeline

If you're used to editing in a program with a timeline and would like to try a similar method, create an empty video file by selecting File ➜ New Player. This method provides a blank slate for you to insert clips, much like on timeline. To add clips to the timeline, use the copy-and-paste method. You can create a completely separate document from your original source clips, so you can start with any footage you want. Unlike other methods of editing using QuickTime, you can use File ➜ Save because you've created a completely new file from scratch, so there is no risk of overwriting any original material.

## Working with Audio

QuickTime also enables you to work with audio files. As a bonus, QuickTime treats audio in a similar manner to video, so all of the editing tools (playhead, in point, out point) work the same way. Once you get the hang of working within QuickTime, you can edit audio and video, either separately or together.

### Adding an Audio Track

Adding an audio track such as a voice-over or background music to a video is easier than you might think. First, open your audio file using QuickTime by selecting File ➜ Open and navigating to the file you would like to use. You can select audio files from music CDs in addition to those stored on your computer.

With your file open, you can select the entire range of audio or just a section of it. Copy your selection to your Clipboard by selecting Edit ➜ Copy. Then change the active file to the one you plan to add the audio to, and position the playhead where you want the music to begin. Finally, select Edit ➜ Add to Movie. Your video will then contain the new audio track, along with any audio that was initially there.

If your newly inserted audio track is much longer than your video clip, you'll want to trim the excess. For instance, adding a three-minute MP3 music track to a 30-second video extends the video by two minutes and 30 seconds — quite a bit too much. Use the trim-to-selection method mentioned previously to cut the excess media. Your in point should be the very beginning of the video; your out point should be the very end. Slide your selectors using whichever method works best for you, the mouse or the key commands Shift+Command+➜ (Macintosh) or Shift+Ctrl+➜ (Windows). After your selection is made, choose Edit ➜ Trim Selection. That eliminates the excess audio.

### Altering the Audio's Properties

To change the volume, balance, bass, or treble of an audio track, select Window ➔ Show Movie Properties. In the Movie Properties dialog box, click the Sound Track you want to change, and then select the Audio Settings tab (see Figure 7-4). Use the provided sliders to adjust the relevant settings.

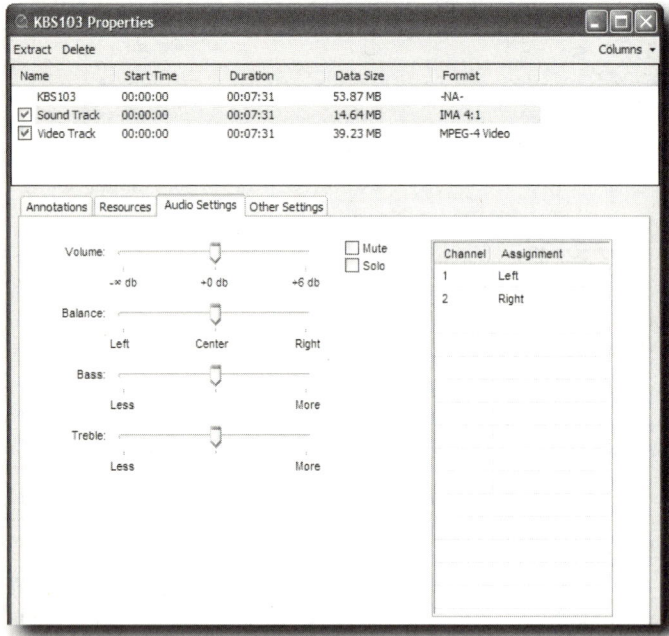

FIGURE 7-4: Altering the audio properties.

### Removing an Audio Track

At some point you may want to remove the original audio and keep only the new audio you've placed. To do so, select Window ➔ Show Movie Properties. Then click Sound Track 1, which is almost always your original audio track. Under the first column titled Enabled, uncheck the box; that will disable the audio track.

## Reviewing and Exporting

After editing your video, you may want to check a specific section of the video to make sure it plays as you envisioned. QuickTime makes this easy, and utilizes the familiar in/out point metaphor. To isolate a section, use the selectors to mark in and out points, and then choose

Play Selection Only from the View menu. After selecting it, you'll notice that a checkmark appears to the left of that item. Now, when you play the video, QuickTime will play only the selection you've indicated.

When reviewing your edited video, the cuts will sometimes play "choppy" or display flashes. This effect is simply an oddity in the way QuickTime handles the process and does not affect the final compressed video output.

After you've edited the video to your liking, you'll want to export a final version using QuickTime compression settings. These and other compression settings are discussed later in this book.

# Converting Camera Files to DV Format

Numerous digital still cameras are capable of capturing video in addition to still images. However, the video is often in a format that isn't friendly to video-editing software, which often works best with DV format files. Fortunately, there are easy ways to convert to the DV format.

If you haven't already discovered, QuickTime Pro is a nearly indispensable tool for video-bloggers. Not only can it be used for editing, captioning, and simply viewing a range of video, but it can also be used to convert one video format to another.

## Using QuickTime Pro

To convert the format of a video, launch the QuickTime application and select File → Open. Using the dialog provided, select the video you want to convert. QuickTime then presents the video, as it would any other file it can play.

---

### Recording to WMV?

Some cameras are capable of recording WMV files (Windows Media), but be aware that the WMV format is not well suited for editing. Even Microsoft, the creator of the WMV format, has publicly acknowledged that in its Knowledge Center (see `www.microsoft.com/windows/windowsmedia/knowledgecenter/mediaadvice/0065.mspx#E2C`). If you have software that can edit WMV natively, you're good to go, but most software is designed to work with more standard formats, such as MPEG, DV, or even AVI (although it's outdated).

If your camera can record in another format—and practically all of them can—you may want to switch to a more standard format for compatibility among your various software packages and portable devices.

Next, select File ➜ Export. You are presented with a set of export options (Figure 7-5), from which you should select the following:

- **Export:** Movie to DV Stream
- **Use:** DV NTSC 44.1kHz

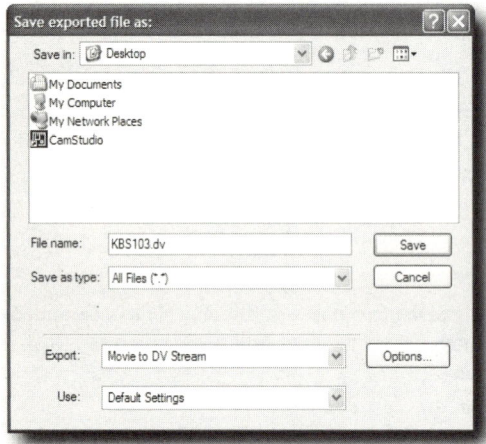

FIGURE 7-5: Exporting a video to DV.

Choose where to save the resulting file, click the Save button, and wait for QuickTime to perform the conversion. The amount of time it takes to convert depends on the size of the video file, as well as the horsepower of your computer.

## Automating the Process

If you have a lot of files that need to be converted, you can automate the process using the appropriate technology for your platform. If you're the resourceful type, you may be interested in programming your computer to handle the conversion for you.

### Macintosh — AppleScript

Apple provides a set of programs — really it's a set of AppleScripts — that can help you work with your video in creative ways. The scripts can be downloaded from www.apple.com/applescript/quicktime. The Convert to DV Stream script will convert a QuickTime-compatible video to DV. However, that script doesn't handle MPEG-4 video as a default. The following script fixes that limitation.

```
-- the list of file types which will be processed
-- need to use Apple's resource type
-- eg: {"PICT", "JPEG", "GIFf", "TIFF"}
```

```
property type_list : {"MooV", "TvoD", "MPEG"}
-- since file types are optional in OS X,
-- check the name extension if there is no file type
-- NOTE: do not use periods (.) with the items in the name extensions list
-- eg: {"txt", "jpg"}, NOT: {".txt", ".jpg"}
property extension_list : {"mov", "mp4", "mpg", "mpeg"}
property default_preset : "NTSC 44.1 kHz"

global target_folder, temp_folder

on run
    display dialog "Convert to DV Stream" & return & return & "This script ⤴
will convert dragged-on movie files to DV Stream QuickTime movies." ⤴
buttons {"OK"} default button 1

    -- ENABLE THESE LINES FOR TESTING
    --set these_items to (choose file) as list
    --open these_items
end run

-- This droplet processes both files or folders of files dropped onto the applet
on open these_items
    -- this routine uses the gestaltVersion_info() sub-routine
    copy my gestaltVersion_info("qtim", 8) to {QT_version, QT_string}
    if the QT_version is less than "0502" then
        display dialog "This script requires QuickTime 5.0.2 or higher." ⤴
& return & return & "The currently installed version is: " & QT_string ⤴
buttons {"Cancel"} default button 1
    end if
    -- create a unique temp folder
    repeat
        set this_name to (random number from 100000 to ⤴
999999) as string
        tell application "Finder"
            if not (exists folder this_name of the desktop) then
                set the temp_folder to (make new folder at desktop with ⤴
properties {name:this_name}) as alias
                exit repeat
            end if
        end tell
    end repeat
    --set the target_folder to choose folder with prompt "Destination ⤴
folder for the converted files:"
    repeat with i from 1 to the count of these_items
        set this_item to (item i of these_items)
        set the item_info to info for this_item
        if folder of the item_info is true then
            process_folder(this_item)
        else if (alias of the item_info is false) and ⤴
((the file type of the item_info is in the ⤴
type_list) or the name extension of the item_info is in the extension_list) then
            process_item(this_item)
```

```
         end if
      end repeat
      -- delete the temp folder
      tell application "Finder"
         delete temp_folder
         empty trash
      end tell
end open


-- this sub-routine processes folders
on process_folder(this_folder)
   set these_items to list folder this_folder without invisibles
   repeat with i from 1 to the count of these_items
      set this_item to alias ((this_folder as text) & (item i of these_items))
      set the item_info to info for this_item
      if folder of the item_info is true then
         process_folder(this_item)
      else if (alias of the item_info is false) and ⊃
         ((the file type of the item_info is in the ⊃
type_list) or the name extension of the item_info is in the extension_list) then
         process_item(this_item)
      end if
   end repeat
end process_folder


-- this sub-routine processes files
on process_item(this_item)
      NOTE that the variable this_item is a file reference in alias format
      -- FILE PROCESSING STATEMENTS GOES HERE
   with timeout of 3600 seconds -- one hour per movie time limit
      tell application "QuickTime Player"
         launch -- bypasses promo movie
         activate
         my toggle_suppress(true)
         try
            stop every movie
            close every movie saving no
            open this_item
            if saveable of movie 1 is false then
               error "This movie has previously been set so ⊃
that it cannot be copied, edited, or saved."
            end if

            tell application "Finder"
               set the file_name to the name of the this_item
               set the target_folder to the container of the this_item
               if exists file file_name of the temp_folder then ⊃
                  delete file file_name of the temp_folder
               set the new_file to ((temp_folder as text) & file_name & "DV" )
            end tell
            if (can export movie 1 as DV stream) is true then
```

```
                -- export the movie as DV stream movie
                export movie 1 to file new_file as DV stream using ⤸
default settings
                -- close the source movie
                close movie 1 saving no
            else
                error "This movie cannot be exported as a DV stream."
            end if
            tell application "Finder"

                move file new_file to the target_folder with replacing

            end tell
            my toggle_suppress(false)
        on error error_msg
            my toggle_suppress(false)
            display dialog error_msg buttons {"Stop", "Continue"} ⤸
default button 2
            set the button_pressed to the button returned of the result
            close movie 1 saving no
            if the button_pressed is "Stop" then error number -128
        end try
      end tell
    end timeout
end process_item


on toggle_suppress(status_flag)
    tell application "QuickTime Player"
        set ignore auto play to the status_flag
        set ignore auto present to the status_flag
    end tell
end toggle_suppress


on gestaltVersion_info(gestalt_code, string_length)
    try
        tell application "Finder" to copy my NumToHex((system attribute ⤸
gestalt_code),string_length) to {a, b, c, d}
        set the numeric_version to {a, b, c, d} as string
        if a is "0" then set a to ""
        set the version_string to (a & b & "." & c & "." & d) as string
        return {numeric_version, version_string}
    on error
        return {"", "unknown"}
    end try
end gestaltVersion_info


on NumToHex(hexData, stringLength)
    set hexString to {}
    repeat with i from stringLength to 1 by -1
        set hexString to ((hexData mod 16) as string) & hexString
        set hexData to hexData div 16
```

```
      end repeat
      return (hexString as string)
end NumToHex
```

## Windows — VBScript

If you install Windows Media Encoder 9 Series (www.microsoft.com/windows/
windowsmedia/9series/encoder/default.aspx; free), you will have a handful of
tools at your disposal for capturing and manipulating digital video. The Windows Media
Encoder SDK provides additional low-level access to the Windows Media structure. The following code will transcode an MPEG file to a DV file and should be compiled using Microsoft
Visual Basic Studio.

```
' Create a WMEncoder object.
  Dim Encoder
  Set Encoder = New WMEncoder

' Retrieve the source group collection and add a source group.
  Dim SrcGrpColl
  Set SrcGrpColl = Encoder.SourceGroupCollection
  Dim SrcGrp
  Set SrcGrp = SrcGrpColl.Add("SG_1")

' Add a video and audio source to the source group.
  Dim SrcVid
  Dim SrcAud
  Set SrcVid = SrcGrp.AddSource(WMENC_VIDEO)
  Set SrcAud = SrcGrp.AddSource(WMENC_AUDIO)

' Identify the source files to encode.
  SrcVid.SetInput "C:\InputFile.mpg"
  SrcAud.SetInput "C:\InputFile.mpg"

' Choose a profile from the collection.
  Dim ProfileColl
  Dim Profile
  Dim i
  Dim lLength

  Set ProfileColl = Encoder.ProfileCollection
  lLength = ProfileColl.Count

  For i = 0 To lLength - 1
    Set Profile = ProfileColl.Item(i)
    If Profile.Name = "Windows Media Video 8 for LAN, Cable Modem, or xDSL" Then
        SrcGrp.Profile = Profile
        Exit For
    End If
  Next

' Fill in the description object members.
  Dim Descr
```

```
Set Descr = Encoder.DisplayInfo
Descr.Author = "Author name"
Descr.Copyright = "Copyright information"
Descr.Description = "Text description of encoded content"
Descr.Rating = "Rating information"
Descr.Title = "Title of encoded content"

' Add an attribute to the collection.
Dim Attr  Set Attr = Encoder.Attributes
Attr.Add "URL", "IP address"

' Specify a file object in which to save encoded content.
Dim File
Set File = Encoder.File
File.LocalFileName = "C:\OutputFile.wmv"

' Crop 2 pixels from each edge of the video image.
SrcVid.CroppingBottomMargin = 2
SrcVid.CroppingTopMargin = 2
SrcVid.CroppingLeftMargin = 2
SrcVid.CroppingRightMargin = 2

' Start the encoding process.
Encoder.Start

' Wait until the encoding process stops before exiting the application.
' You can do this by using the WMEncoder object to create an event sink.

' For this example, simply monitor the size of the output file and
' use a message box to indicate when to close the application.
MsgBox ("Click OK when encoding has stopped.")
```

Quite obviously, there are a lot of options when directly accessing the Windows Media toolbox.

## Conversion Applications

There are a number of conversion applications on the market to help convert one format to another, so if you're not inclined to actually program your computer, you're in luck. Here's a sampling:

- AutoDesk (www.autodesk.com) distributes Cleaner (Macintosh, $599.00) and Cleaner XL (Windows, $599.00). The application, shown in Figure 7-6, has long been a standard tool used by compression professionals because it offers a wide range of default compression schemes, as well as complete control over the compression process.

- FFmpeg (ffmpeg.sourceforge.net/index.php; free, open source) is a cross-platform audio- and video-encoding tool that is exceptionally powerful but can be intimidating to those who aren't comfortable using a command-line tool.

- Sorenson Squeeze (www.sorensonmedia.com, $449.00) is available for Macintosh and Windows and offers a tremendous number of features, including the capability to encode video to Flash.

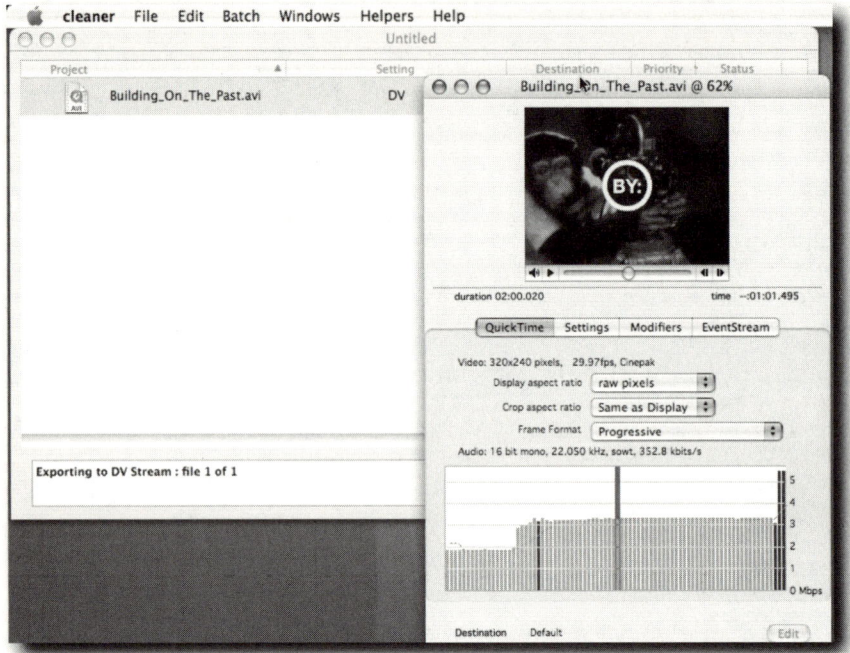

FIGURE 7-6: Using Cleaner to transcode a video.

Whatever method you choose to transcode your video files, you can relax knowing that no matter what format you use to acquire your video, with the right tools, you can always convert it to suit your needs.

# Taking a Screenshot and Automatically Posting It

Most videobloggers like to place a screenshot of their video on their blog to inform people that there is a video available, and its format. The traditional — and tedious — process involves taking a screenshot of the video, using an image editing application to crop the screenshot, using FTP to upload the screenshot to a server, and finally typing the requisite HTML into a blog entry. Why go through all of that when there's an application that can do it all for you?

ImageWell (Mac, free; www.xtralean.com/IWOverview.html) provides an easy means to get a screenshot of a video onto your blog. ImageWell is exceptionally adept at taking selective screenshots of your completed video to use as images on your blog.

Here's how to use it:

1. Select Preferences from the ImageWell menu, and then in the pop-up dialog, choose a Location in which to store your images. See Figure 7-7.

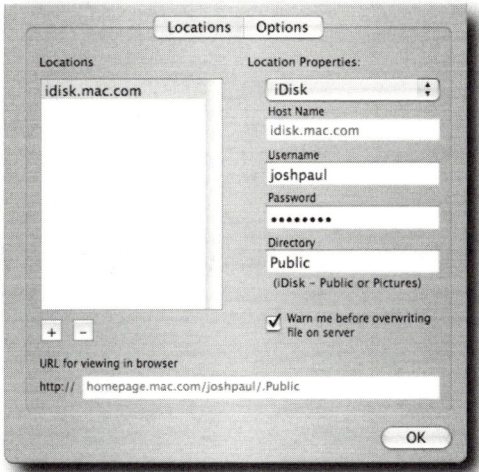

FIGURE 7-7: The ImageWell Preference window.

You can choose from iDisk, FTP, or WebDav for the method of storing your images. After you enter your Location, enter your Username, Password, and the Directory in which you would like to store your images. Click OK when you are finished.

2. ImageWell offers a feature that creates the appropriate HTML to embed the image in your blog, so that it displays to your visitors. Just click the More button at the bottom-right of the main ImageWell window, and select html <img> from the pop-up button for the Url To Copy To Clipboard setting. Using this feature copies the necessary HTML to your Clipboard, which saves you from having to type the HTML (and possibly mistyping something). Then you simply paste the HTML in your blog post to embed the image.

## Create a Clean-Looking Image

Avoid having other applications, documents, or even a busy desktop image behind your video; those can create an "unclean" image. By having a uniform background—preferably white—nothing gets in the way of your image capture.

3. To capture the image you want, open your video using your video player application, and then locate the frame of video you want in the screenshot.

4. In ImageWell, choose Tools → Grab Selection (see Figure 7-8).

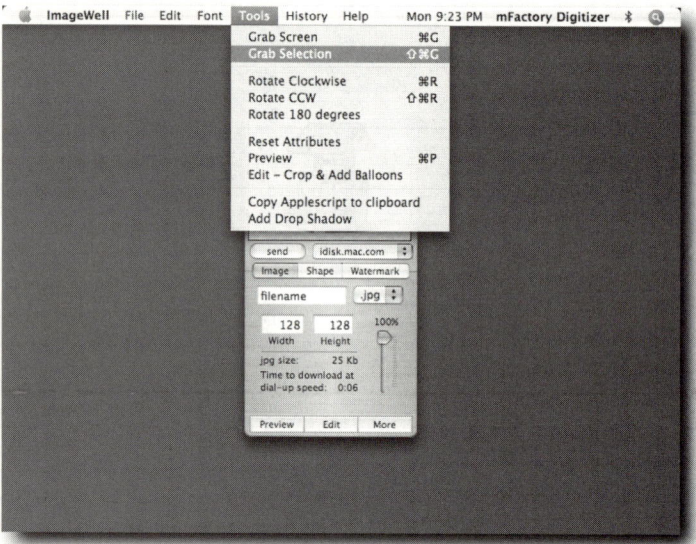

FIGURE 7-8: Grab Selection.

5. Simply click and drag around the video player's window to select your image.

6. Modify the size of your image, name it appropriately, and add a watermark, if you like, using the controls provided in the main ImageWell window.

7. ImageWell makes sending the final image to your server really, really, really easy. Ready?

   Click the Send button (Figure 7-9).

8. Go to your blog, create a new entry, and press Command+V (or select Edit → Paste). The code for referencing the image is automatically generated and pasted directly into your blog. The resulting HTML code looks similar to this:

   ```
   <img src="http://homepage.mac.com/stevegarfield/.
   Pictures/imagewell_logo.jpg" width="128" height="128"/>
   ```

   Then type whatever else you want for your entry, ensuring that you do not overwrite or edit the ImageWell-generated HTML.

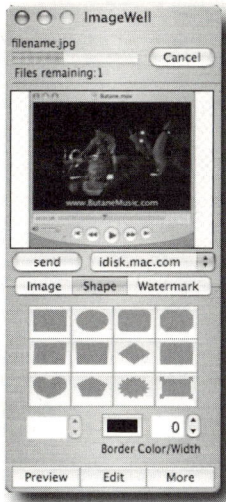

**FIGURE 7-9: Sending an image doesn't get any easier than this.**

After using ImageWell once, you'll probably never go back to the "old way."

# Adding Clickable Links Inside QuickTime Videos

QuickTime has the capability to add clickable links inside your video instead of, or in addition to, the links in your accompanying blog post. LiveStage Professional ($450, www.totallyhip .com/livestage.asp) is a QuickTime authoring application that can do truly amazing things with QuickTime movies, including adding links. The bad news is that it costs $450. The good news is this solution can be accomplished with QuickTime Pro ($30, www.apple.com/ quicktime) and a text editor (free).

**Note**

After getting a taste of interactive video by using Clickable Links, you may want to download a demo version of LiveStage Pro. We guarantee that you'll discover something new about QuickTime that will blow your mind.

If you have a video that uses a graphic as a link (Figure 7-10), you can easily add an HREF track to the QuickTime movie. An HREF track makes the graphic "clickable" and active within the video. When you're finished, a viewer can click the graphic, and the video will open a specific web page.

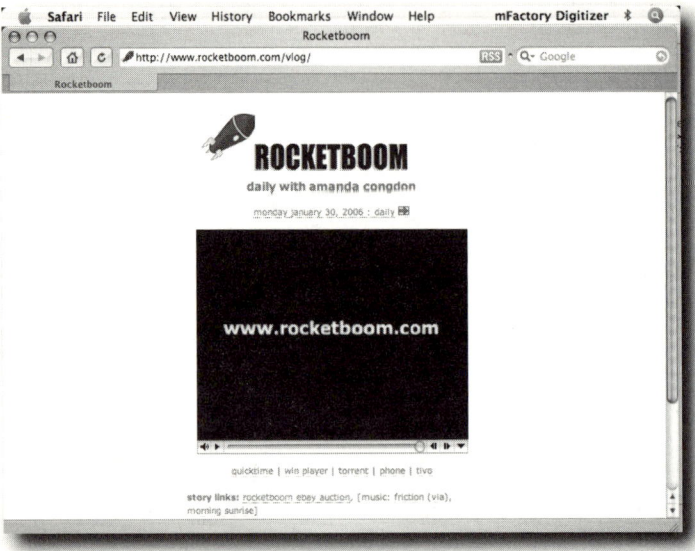

**FIGURE 7-10: Video that utilizes a graphic link.**

Here's what to do:

1. In a text editor such as TextEdit (Mac) or Notepad (Windows), create a new plain-text document. What you are about to create is a text track that you will later change to an HREF track. All text tracks start with the descriptor `{QTtext}` followed by a number of other descriptors that let you customize the display of text in the QuickTime movie. In this case, your text will be hidden so you don't have to spend any time formatting it.

2. Begin your document like this:

   ```
   {QTtext}{timeScale:1000}{timeStamps:absolute}
   ```

3. Move the playhead to the start of your video. Select Window ➜ Movie Info and note the Current Time. Type it into your text document, followed by two hard returns (press Enter or Return twice) — one to end the line containing the time and the second to create a blank line:

   ```
   [00:00:00.00]
   ```

   This inserts blank text into the track or, in this case, no hyperlink.

4. Play your QuickTime movie to the frame where you want the link to begin. Note the time at that point, and add it to your document like this:

   ```
   [00:00:34.00]
   <http://www.domain.com>T<_blank>
   ```

## A Variation of the HREF Variety

Placing a capital A before the URL tag will make the link open automatically when the video reaches that point in time. It should look like this:

```
A<http://www.domain.com>T<_blank>
```

In this example, `_blank` is a placeholder for the URL that you want to take people to (the URL will go between the brackets <>). The T indicates the target frame you want the URL to display in, which can be useful if you are using the video in a web page containing frames.

**5.** Decide where you want the link to end, note the time at that point, and add it to your document, followed with two hard returns (one to end the line containing the time and one to insert a blank line). Your document should now look something like this:

```
{QTtext}{timeScale:1000}{timeStamps:absolute}
[00:00:00.00]

[00:00:34.00]
<http://www.domain.com>T<_blank>
[00:00:43.00]
```

**6.** Add the ending timecode of the movie to the end of the document. The whole thing looks like this:

```
{QTtext}{timeScale:1000}{timeStamps:absolute}
[00:00:00.00]

[00:00:34.00]
<http://www.domain.com>T<_blank>
[00:00:43.00]

[00:01:17.00]
```

Do not add a hard return after the final timecode. If you add one, your HREF track will more than likely not work.

**7.** Save your document, switch back to QuickTime Pro, and open the document from the File menu. The text file will open like a small QuickTime movie (see Figure 7-11), with the text `<http://www.domain.com>T<_blank>` displayed between the times specified (if you're following along, that would be between 34 and 43 seconds into the video).

**8.** To convert the text to an HREF track, choose Edit → Select All and then choose Edit → Copy.

**9.** Switch from the text video to the video you want to make clickable, and place the playhead back to the start.

FIGURE 7-11: Text as imported to QuickTime.

**10.** Select Edit ➔ Add to Selection & Scale. This adds the text on top of your video. You can visually check that it's in the correct place in time by scrubbing through the video.

**11.** Now select Window ➔ Show Movie Properties. You should see a new Text track in the list at the top of the window.

**12.** Click twice on the Text track and change its name to HREFTrack, exactly like that (uppercase and lowercase, no space). Then deactivate the track by clearing the Enabled box next to the track. The track will still work — disabling an HREF track simply makes the text invisible.

**13.** Select File ➔ Save As, and choose Save as a Self-contained Movie. Otherwise, the HREF track will not be included in the new video file.

Now your video is ready for posting on your videoblog.

There is also another way to create an HREF track. It uses a hyperlink in a plain-text track and is a great option when you don't already have an image built into the video.

Here's what to do:

**1.** Create a new plain-text document in your text editor. The text will be displayed this time, so you want to include some style information at the top of the document. Here is a sample:

```
{QTtext}{font:Ariel}{bold}{anti-alias:off}{size:16}{textColor: ↩
0, 0, 0}{backColor: 65535,65535,65535}{justify:center}↩
{timeScale:1000}{width:320}
{height:20}{timeStamps:absolute}{language:0}{textEncoding:0}
```

**Note**  You'll find a whole list of QuickTime text descriptors and what they do at www.apple.com/quicktime/tutorials/textdescriptors.html.

**2.** Open your video in QuickTime and select Window ➔ Movie Info. Note the Current Time property, which you'll use in your document.

3. Just like an HREF track, your document will consist of a time followed by the text you want to display. You can also enter a time and a blank line to insert no text. When adding a target URL, enclose the link text in the {HREF:}{EndHREF} tags. Any text outside of those tags will display as text formatted according to the descriptors laid out at the beginning of the document.

4. Once you've added your links, your document will look something like this:

```
{QTtext}{font:Ariel}{bold}{anti-alias:off}{size:16}{textColor: ⤴
0, 0, 0}{backColor: 65535, 65535, 65535}{justify:center}⤴
{timeScale:1000}{width:320}
{height:20}{timeStamps:absolute}{language:0}{textEncoding:0}
[00:00:00.00]

[00:00:34.00]
{HREF:<http://www.domain.com>T<_blank>}Click Here{EndHREF}
[00:00:43.00]

[00:01:17.00]
```

Do not add a hard return after the line with the final time. If you add one, your link(s) probably won't work.

5. Switch to QuickTime Pro and open the text file that contains your link(s). Choose Edit → Select All, and then choose Edit → Copy.

6. Switch back to the QuickTime movie that you want to add the links to, and make sure the playhead is at the start. Choose Edit → Add to Selection & Scale. This adds the text track on top of your video (see Figure 7-12).

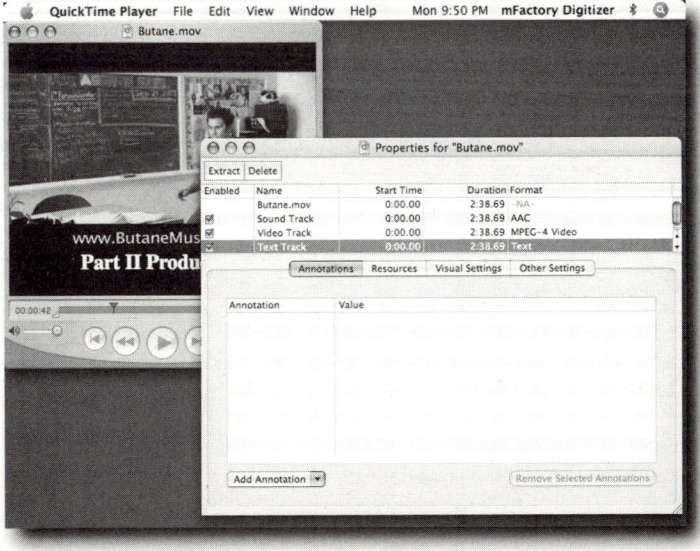

FIGURE 7-12: A QuickTime video with a new text track.

7. By default your text is placed at the top of the movie. If you'd like to position it at the bottom of the screen (like a subtitle, for example), you can edit the track in the Movie Properties window. To do so, select Window ➔ Show Movie Properties. Then select the text track and click the Visual Settings tab.

   The text box is 20 pixels high (defined by the text descriptors), so you can move it to the bottom by determining the difference between the height of your video and the height of the text box. For example, if your video is 240 pixels high, and the text box is 20 pixels high, you can offset the top of the box by 220 pixels, thereby pushing the text box to the "bottom" of the video.

8. Be sure to save your video as a Self-contained Movie. Otherwise, it won't contain the links you worked so hard to create.

# Summary

Editing is more of an art than a science, and every artist needs a set of tools and a medium to express himself. Exceptionally good, and lucky, artists are given a gallery to show their work. As a videoblogger, video is your medium, your computer is your tool, and the Internet is your gallery.

# Using Text in Video

Editing video is a fairly straightforward process. As you become a more proficient editor, however, you'll discover that adding text and graphics can help give your videos a polished, professional feel. Using the right combination of audio, video, and graphics, you can even change the emotion a video evokes.

## Place Subtitles in Your Video

Adding subtitles to your videos is a time-consuming process. A few applications are available to help make the process easier, but they cost thousands of dollars. WGBH helped to create MAGpie (`http://ncam.wgbh.org/webaccess/magpie`, free), which runs on both Macintosh and Windows, to provide an affordable subtitling tool, but it hasn't been updated since 2003. Thankfully, a hack can be done fairly easily with a text editor and QuickTime Pro.

It's possible to add subtitles directly to a video from within most editing applications. Sometimes, doing so is the easiest and fastest way to create subtitles, especially if you're just adding a few of them.

## Using a Text Track for Subtitles

Subtitling an entire video, especially one with a lot of dialog, can become quite tedious, and it also attaches another layer of complexity. Because the text becomes part of the video when you compress it, the results aren't always legible, either. Moreover, if want to add subtitles in multiple languages, you'd have to create a separate video for every language.

QuickTime has many types of tracks within a file, including video tracks, audio tracks, timecode tracks, HREF tracks, sprite tracks, and text tracks. Tracks have multiple advantages, one of which is the capability to be enabled or disabled. By using multiple text tracks and enabling or disabling them as appropriate, you can include different language subtitles in one video. Text tracks also scale dynamically with your video so that if it's seen at a larger size, the text remains crisp.

## Getting Started

To begin, open up a new text document using a text editor such as TextEdit (Macintosh) or Notepad (Windows). Make sure that the document you create is simple (not rich text). QuickTime expects text without font changes, colors, or formatting (such as bold) applied. Using the default plain-text settings for your application should suffice.

All text tracks need to start with the descriptor {QTtext}, followed by a number of other descriptors that let you customize the look of the text QuickTime displays. Here's what the start of your document should be like:

```
{QTtext}{font:Arial}{plain}{size:14}{textColor: 65535, 65535, 65535}
{backColor: 0, 0, 0}{justify:center}{timeScale:1000}{width:320}
{height:35}{timeStamps:absolute}{language:0}{textEncoding:0}
```

This creates a black box that's 320 x 35 pixels in dimension, with white, 14-point Arial text. The 35-pixel height should provide enough space for two lines of text. There are a number of ways you can modify these settings — Apple has an entire list of QuickTime text descriptors and what they do at www.apple.com/quicktime/tutorials/textdescriptors .html.

The rest of the document will consist of a series of timecodes, with the text that should display at each time interval. It's simple, although it can appear intimidating at first. For workflow, you may find it easiest to just transcribe the movie first, then go back to break the transcript into one or two line sections, and finish up by assigning a timecode to each section.

## Assigning Timecodes

If there is a section of video that you'd like to be clear of any text, simply enter a blank line after the timecode. This basically displays a line of text with nothing in it. When you have entered all of the appropriate text and timecode combinations, add the last timecode of the movie to the end of your text document. For efficiency, you may want to set up your work environment so you can watch the video while typing, as shown in Figure 8-1.

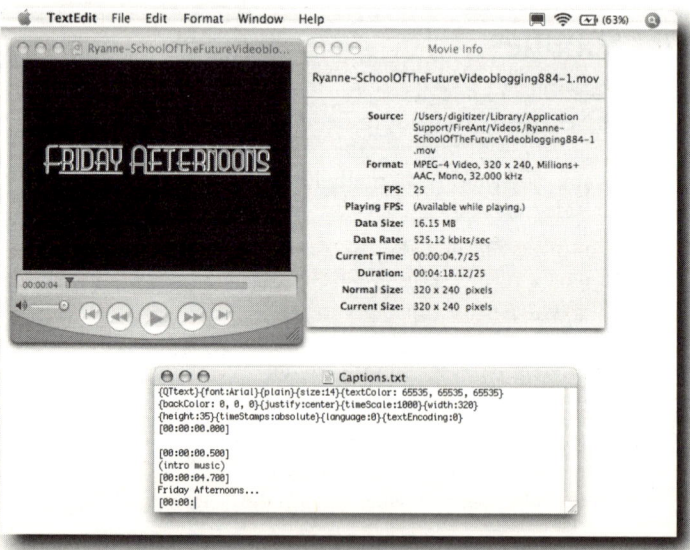

FIGURE 8-1: A good working environment can make the process easier.

Here's an example of a complete text track:

```
{QTtext}{font:Arial}{plain}{size:14}{textColor: 65535, 65535, 65535}
{backColor: 0, 0, 0}{justify:center}{timeScale:1000}{width:320}
{height:35}{timeStamps:absolute}{language:0}{textEncoding:0}
[00:00:00.000]

[00:00:00.500]
(Rocketboom intro music)
[00:00:02.750]
Michael:
Good Wednesday, April 6, 2005
[00:00:05.500]
I'm Michael Verdi and I'm in NEW YORK CITY!
[00:00:09.000]
Look, check it out. That's not Texas out there.
[00:00:12.000]
(Music - Nina Hagen, New York)
[00:00:19.500]
Michael:
Pretty cool huh?
[00:00:21.750]
(singing: "New York, New York")
[00:00:36.000]
```

Note that there is no extra carriage return after the final timecode entry.

Save your file, switch to QuickTime Pro, and open the text document from the File menu. The text file opens as a small QuickTime movie; play it and see the text changing accordingly. In a sense, QuickTime just treats the text as another type of video.

Next, choose Edit → Select All, and then select choose Edit → Copy. Switch the active video to the video you would like to caption, and place the playhead at the start. Choose Edit → Add to Selection & Scale. This adds the text track on top of your video and adjusts the time of the text so that it fits your video. This is necessary, as text by itself doesn't have "time" associated with it.

## Changing the Position of the Captions

By default the text is placed near the top of the movie. To position it near the bottom of the screen, like most subtitles, you have to edit the track in the Movie Properties window (Window → Show Movie Properties).

Select your text track and click the Visual Settings tab. This tab enables you to set the Scaled Size and, more important, an Offset. For example, if a text box is 35 pixels high (defined by the text descriptors in the text file) and the video is 240 pixels high, you can move the caption to the bottom of the screen by offsetting it by 205 pixels (math: 240 − 35 = 205). Once you change a text track's offset, the text box moves to its new position within the video's frame. Figure 8-2 shows the default text placement and the text repositioned with Offset.

## Adding Transparency

The Visual Settings in QuickTime allow more than just size and offset modifications to be made to tracks. For example, you can alter a track to become slightly transparent by switching the Transparency popup to Blend and then adjusting the Transparency Level slider. You can Flip/Rotate a track, too.

FIGURE 8-2: A video with the default text setting (left) and the text placed with an offset (right).

After your subtitles are configured to your liking, select File ➔ Save As — and make sure you select the Save as a Self-Contained Movie option so that the text track is included in the new video file.

That's it. Your newly captioned video is ready for posting on your videoblog.

# Using Typography in a Video

Used wisely, text can enhance your videos and give them a little something extra. There are five basic principles of typography to consider:

- Choice of font
- Choice of color
- Understand the meaning
- Understand time and space
- Be concise

The following pages provide examples of each of these basics, as well as solutions to common problems. With typography, pictures speak a thousand words, so pay close attention to the figures provided.

## Choose a Font

In the days of hand-inked printing and movable type, changing a typeface involved hours of stooping over the press bed, squinting at thousands of tiny pieces of lead with letters embossed on them. Not to mention, all the letters were backward!

Since the desktop publishing revolution of the 1980s, and the invention of small computer files called fonts, switching one typeface to another takes no more effort than pointing and clicking. While still involving some risk (carpal tunnel is no picnic), type is much more fun to work with now than it was in the old days (ink poisoning was no picnic, either).

Because changing type is so easy now, there's a lot more experimentation.

- Good news: Experimentation eventually leads to innovation.
- Bad news: Most experiments blow up.

Unusual fonts are fun for short titles or phrases, but don't overdo it (see Figure 8-3). If you use all kinds of cool and unusual fonts in your video, it'll likely look amateurish and be hard to read.

FIGURE 8-3: Even on a still image, this font is difficult to read.

You'll do better by toning it down and balancing experimental coolness with practical readability (see Figure 8-4).

FIGURE 8-4: A readable font punctuated
with an unusual one.

If you're using a font called Circus Monkey Hair Explosion Sans over a black background, it is probably going to be difficult for your viewers to read. When the type is surrounded by moving pictures, or if it is moving itself, it will be even harder! So here's an important rule of thumb: *Words want to be read.*

In video, an audience has only a few seconds to read what you've put on screen. Weird shapes and weirder combinations of fonts merely make it close to impossible for your viewers to read your text at all. Simply choose familiar fonts, and limit yourself to a total of a couple fonts. Every time the text in your video changes to a different font, it causes your viewer's brain to try to figure out what is happening and why. A viewer's attention is precious. Don't waste it on frivolous fonts!

**Tip**

The Grandmother Test: If you're in doubt about the readability of your video text, show it to your grandmother. If she complains about the lines of dancing worms getting in the way when you ask her about the text, chances are it's time to tone it down a bit.

## Choose a Color

Believe it or not, reading typography takes a lot of mental heavy lifting. In video, where the type is often appearing, disappearing, and moving around on screen — all while surrounded by other moving pictures — the eyes and brain can really get a workout. Fewer distractions to readability result in maintaining your viewers' attention. Color can really help, or really ruin, a viewer's ability to understand your text.

Just because you can make your text all the colors of the rainbow doesn't mean you should (see Figure 8-5). If your typography uses all the pretty colors that dazzle the senses but nobody can read what it says, you've made a mistake. You want, and need, to be understood.

Quite often, using black and white text is the smartest choice. They can generally be seen clearly against the colors in your video. Figure 8-6 shows an example.

FIGURE **8-5**: Colorful text can result in illegible captions.

FIGURE **8-6**: Using simple black and white can make text more legible.

Contrast between the text and the background is what will create the most readable text. It's best when the text is the darker of the two colors (as you can see at the bottom of Figure 8-6), but if the background is dark, going lighter on the text provides a better result. For example, white text on a dark blue background can work for short titles (see Figure 8-7).

FIGURE **8-7**: Light text on a dark background works if the text is short.

## Use a Color Wheel

Have you seen a color wheel (see figure) before? The rough rule is that colors on opposite sides of the wheel are complementary and that colors that differ in brightness have a contrasting value.

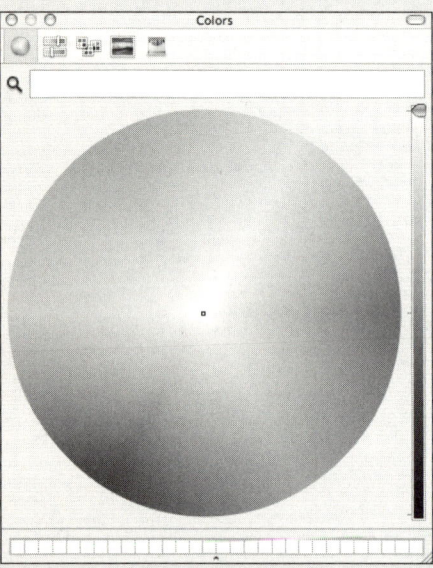

Blue and green, for example, are near each other on the color wheel and look terrible together, much like orange and yellow, which are also close together. However, blue and yellow are farther apart from each other on the wheel, so they are more complementary. If you select a light yellow and a dark blue, you'll have the right value contrast for a complementary combination.

You can use a color wheel to easily discern color combinations that will work together. Do a web search for "color wheel" and you'll find images of color wheels and learn how to understand them.

The exception is if there is a lot of text appearing on screen; in that case, dark text on a light background is clearly best. Figure 8-8 shows an example of too much light-on-dark text.

Create your titles with colors that have a contrasting value yet are complementary, and they will be easy for your viewers to read.

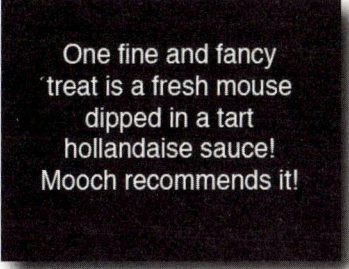

FIGURE 8-8: Too much light-on-dark
reading can start to hurt the eyes.

## Understand the Meaning

Typography used well plays a supporting role in a video, but it should not become the main event. Sometimes it helps to think of typography as music. If you want to confuse your audience, or get an effect from your video you did not plan, use the wrong typographical "soundtrack" for what your video is about. You need to adjust your font choice as appropriate for the content of your vlog post.

For example, a somber tribute video for a recently deceased literary hero won't feel right if the text is displayed in a Comic Sans font, but Circus Monkey Hair Explosion may be the perfect font for the title of a home movie called "Our Day at the Circus." (Just don't overdo; see the "Choose a Font" section earlier in this chapter.) Compare the "feel" of the text in Figures 8-9 and 8-10.

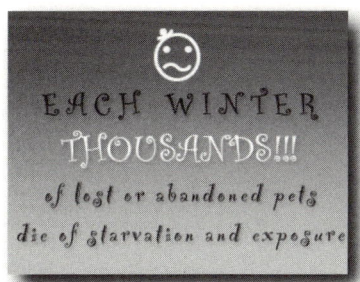

FIGURE 8-9: Happy party fonts and somber
subject matter do not mix well.

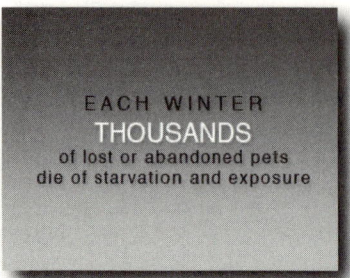

FIGURE **8-10: The emotional feel of a font should match the emotional content of the video.**

When selecting a font, think about what typeface can help the emotion of the video be consistently communicated. The look and feel of a font and the way it is animated can support the look and feel of the rest of your vlog post.

## Understand Time and Space

Here's a simple rule: Do not slap text on the screen. Plan the placement of text carefully and in context of the video, and avoid text and video combinations that are too cluttered to read or have jerky motion that makes the text difficult to understand (compare the text in figures 8-11 and 8-12).

FIGURE **8-11: Too much motion and shaky animation can obscure meaning.**

Here's a painfully obvious statement: Using typography in your videoblog is more complex than typing words on a blank sheet of paper. The images around your text are constantly changing through cuts and edits. Everything is in motion. . .sometimes the text itself! Because of this, you must always be aware of how the visual character of your video is changing frame by frame.

FIGURE 8-12: Try to match the right type
to the right background and motion.

For example, if you're adding text in the lower-left corner of your video, over the black shirt of the person you're interviewing, you might choose a white font color (see the "Choose a Color" section earlier in this chapter). But if the person leans right to expose a white wall in the background while the text is still on screen, you'll lose the contrast and the text will be unreadable. In this case, you can use a drop shadow or outline (see Figure 8-13) to help maintain the visibility of the text.

Sometimes there may be too much going on in the video to find screen real estate where the font can be displayed with good contrast. In such situations, you can create a solid area like a color bar or gradient mask, often called a backplate, and place it behind the text. You can often add a more professional look to your video by using a basic backplate and font combination throughout your video.

FIGURE 8-13: A drop shadow or outline can
help text stand out on a background.

## Be Concise

Many people become easily bored with video, and they tune out very quickly when boredom sets in. One thing that loses the attention of a lot of people is a lot of reading. Reading is cool, but books and web pages will always be better for that than videoblogs can be.

Knowing what will help your viewers interested, and what will make them want to leave, is crucial to building a loyal audience. Reading takes time and requires more mental effort from an audience than watching pictures alone. So, choose your words sparingly, and when in doubt, cut down on your word count.

It takes patience to sharpen your videoblogging skills, yet most audiences don't have much patience at all. People watch video expecting a different kind of experience. A helpful rule of thumb is "less is more."

The text is there to support the story, not to tell it. Here are some pointers for how to reduce the amount of onscreen reading you are asking of your viewers:

■ **Don't be redundant.** If your text simply states the obvious, you don't need it. Let your typography provide new information. For example, don't add a caption to a shot of a toddler blowing out birthday-cake candles with the text "She blew out the candles." Your audience will be better off if you inform them of something they can't tell from the images, like the child's name and age. Or try to tell a piece of the story that will give a more complete understanding of the whole narrative, like "It was the first time she didn't spit on the cake!" Figure 8-14 provides an example.

■ **Proofreading can only help.** Take a few minutes to edit what you want to say to be more concise. Use a thesaurus to find shorter words that mean the same thing. Ask a friend who's good with words to suggest ways to say more with less. You may also want to ask your friends or family to watch the video and offer suggestions about how to shorten the text. Sometimes simply typing what you want to say, leaving it, and then coming back to it a half hour later can give you a different perspective on the text. Figure 8-15 is a good example of "less is more."

■ **Try a voiceover.** If you just can't get all the extra information across that you need in a few short sentences, try using a voiceover track. A simple voiceover, in conjunction with some text or image on screen type, can help tremendously when you don't have enough footage to get it all across in images and text alone. A voiceover could also replace text (see Figure 8-16).

■ **Ask yourself: who cares?** This can be hard, but editing is a brutal process. One way to cut down on the amount of text onscreen is to just cut it! Always ask yourself whether the text being displayed is really that important. If the choice is between boring your audience and finding something to remove, what can you remove? Don't put it onscreen unless you have to.

Finally, remember that while typography in a video can be a good thing, you can have too much of it. In this way, onscreen typography is like poetry: It's all about the economy of words and is the sort of skill that can be learned only through trial and error. Fortunately, you're now armed with a little knowledge that you can apply.

FIGURE 8-14: Don't use text just to repeat the action; provide some new information.

FIGURE 8-15: Re-wording long sentences can help you be more concise.

FIGURE 8-16: Adding a voiceover can eliminate text completely.

# LiveType: Quick and Dirty

When making a title or graphic for your video, the key is to grab your viewers' attention, give them the proper information, and yet not distract them. Creating animated typography and transitions using Apple's LiveType can be fast, fun, and look great. Simply put, LiveType rocks!

LiveType is part of Apple's amazing suite of video-production tools and comes bundled with Final Cut Express HD (Mac OSX; $299.00) or Final Cut Studio (Mac OSX; $1299.00). Not only is LiveType able to export video files that can be dragged directly into a Final Cut workspace, but the two applications integrate seamlessly. For example, should you want to make changes to a LiveType-created video, you can select it in a Final Cut timeline and subsequently re-open it in LiveType. Any changes made in LiveType automatically occur in Final Cut, too. To truly appreciate this feature, you have to experience it. . .but let me just say, it's a major time-saver.

## LiveType Workflow

There are a few ways to work in LiveType. You can work directly with typography by entering text, choosing a font, and applying various animation effects. You can work with LiveType's special Live Fonts, which are letter-shaped QuickTime movies that can be colored or scaled. You can also use LiveType's prebuilt templates (see Figure 8-17), which are customizable, to create combinations of animated text and graphics. Or you can create your own graphics animations by importing images and then applying animation effects.

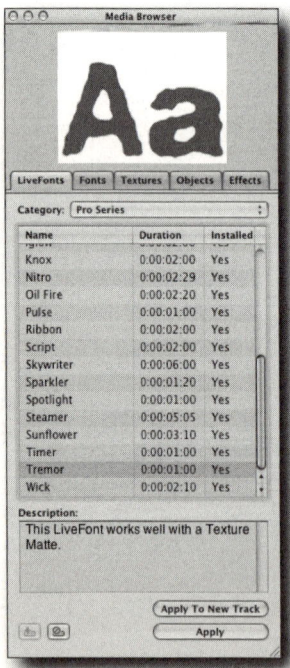

FIGURE 8-17: A variety of templates are provided in LiveType.

LiveType enables you to quickly create text animations against a transparent background. Later, when you import the rendered text into Final Cut, you can reposition it, scale it, or alter the speed settings on the fly. This approach requires some extra rendering while working, but it saves some of the time and hassle of exporting a reference video from Final Cut and importing the reference video to LiveType.

Some vloggers export their edited video from Final Cut for use in LiveType as a reference video. A reference video enables you to work with your video as a background, so you can more accurately place your text and animations. Although using a reference video can be more time consuming than simply using a blank background, it can greatly help in the placement and timing of the final LiveType animation.

However you choose to create your animation, LiveType is exceptionally flexible and customizable. Even using it in simple ways can give your videoblog a lot of sizzle and professionalism.

## Use LiveType as a Basic Animation Tool

Most people don't know it, but LiveType animates more than just text. Anything you select or import into LiveType is treated as a glyph and can be animated (see Figure 8-18). So, if you want to animate pictures, graphics, and clips in a video but don't have time for all that timeline keyframing, LiveType can help.

FIGURE 8-18: Each character can be animated individually.

### Keyframes

Keyframes, also expressed as Key Frames, are places in time-based media used as reference points for a computer program to base a motion calculation. For example, if you want to move a ball from the left side of the screen to the right side of the screen over a period of one second at 30fps, you need 30 distinct images of the ball in different locations. To create this motion manually, you'd need to create the 30 images. But by using keyframes you can simply set a point on the left side of the screen at the start and another at the end. The computer then calculates and creates the remaining 28 images for you.

The magic of the amazing text effects that you can accomplish in LiveType happens because the application "understands" font information as a series of "glyphs" along a keyframed animation path. Essentially, individual letters become the primitive building blocks of an animation. What's groovy about this is that glyphs don't have to be letters.

To animate something other than text in LiveType, you need an external element. You can create a graphic element in an image-creation program, or simply use an image you already have, whether from a digital still camera, clip art package, or elsewhere. Import the element into LiveType, apply one of LiveType's effects, and voilâ! Done.

Do you want a picture of your cat to zoom onto the screen, jiggle around, and then fade away? You could painstakingly keyframe this in Final Cut or some other editing application, although you wouldn't get the smooth acceleration and deceleration that would make it super slick. Or you can just import the picture into LiveType and then apply the Zoom In, Wobble, and Fade Out text effects. The animation is done for you automatically, with the polish and professional characteristics of all of LiveType's sophisticated animations.

After you output the LiveType file, by rendering it as a `.mov` file, drag it into your Final Cut timeline. It's a single self-contained video clip (with transparency!) that Final Cut treats just as any other video. Seamless.

## Quickly Combine Effects to Create New Animations

Just like working with text effects, the animations applied to your imported graphics can be tweaked for timing, direction, and position and can be combined with other effects to create even more unique animations. There are tricks to combining effects in unexpected ways and tweaking their parameters to make them all yours. By choosing several effects (see Figure 8-19), you can avoid having your effects look like everyone else's. After all, you're unique, and your effects should be, too.

It's possible to keyframe the glyphs in LiveType text animations. But keyframing can be quite time consuming. Videoblogging is an immediate and fast-moving medium. The point for many is to get a video done quickly and done right.

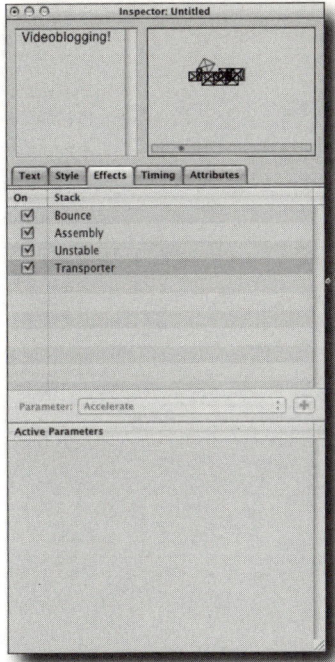

FIGURE **8-19: Combining effects.**

The prebuilt LiveType animations displayed in the effects palette are some of the sweetest, smoothest, most expressive and useful animations any vlogger could want. The trouble is that everyone who uses LiveType knows how cool the prebuilt animation effects are, and they use them all the time. What you want to do is take full advantage of what is available already yet add some flavor of your own. The challenge, therefore, is to take advantage of LiveType's amazing set of features, while customizing them for yourself.

The following are a handful of ways to approach animation effects so that the combinations and tweaks you apply result in great, customized text animations.

## Listen to the Pros

The designers of LiveType provide suggestions about the way many effects can be customized. Under the Effects tab, in the Description box, there are often a couple of sentences about ways that timing, direction, randomness, or combinations can be tweaked to get more interesting results (see Figure 8-20). These appear in plain view, but most people seem to miss them. Just click once on the name of the effect in the list and then read the description box for any insider advice.

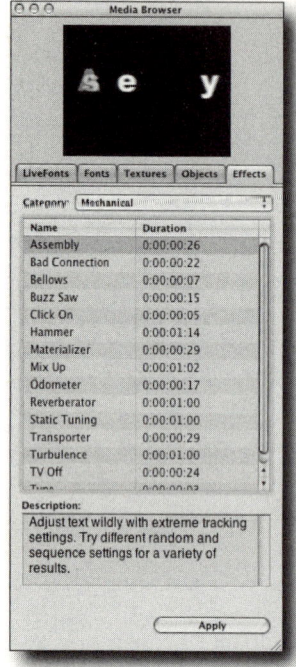

FIGURE 8-20: Suggestions from the pros.

Many of these suggested customizations could be just what you're looking for, and you won't need to spend the time thinking them up yourself!

### Try Something Random

LiveType is so easy and flexible that you can sit down any time and simply start throwing combinations together. Quite often, you'll come up with something unique and interesting in no time. Keep track of your experiments, because just messing around can produce awesome results.

A little organization ahead of time can help you create a unique library of effects, combos, and tweaks. One way to start is by creating a folder (perhaps inside your Documents folder) in which it's convenient for you to store a lot of LiveType files. Then, when you create a combination of effects, or an interesting settings adjustment, you can save the LiveType .ipr file to your folder. Don't just render the movie and throw the project file away! You'll need the .ipr file for future reference.

### Speed

Changing the speed of an effect can alter the entire character of the final animation. The Timing tab in the Inspector palette contains the settings that determine how fast or slow an effect unfolds. If you change the speed of the animation, the aspects of it can change so dramatically that the templates that have been used are unrecognizable to others who are familiar with them.

There are a couple ways you can adjust the animation's speed: by dragging the Speed slider in the Timing tab (see Figure 8-21) or by making changes in the timeline window. Dragging the Speed slider is the quickest and most direct way to slow or quicken the animation. The slider runs from 0 percent to 200 percent of the default speed. The keyframes of the animation are then lengthened or condensed accordingly.

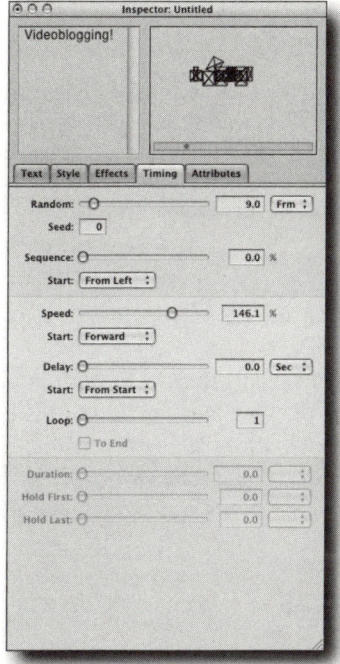

FIGURE 8-21: Changing the speed of an animation.

Directly changing the timeline is less predictable but can produce even more interesting results. By clicking and dragging one end of the purple bar, which represents an effect, you are able to alter the speed. Individual keyframes can also be manipulated, which provides fine-grained control over the speed.

## Reverse and Other Settings

Effects never look quite the same when they run backward. A nice feature of the Timing tab is that effects can be reversed with just the click of a button. Do you like the way the Bounce Track effect works but are worried that everyone has seen it before? Simply click the drop-down menu under Speed and select Reverse. You get a similar traveling and bouncing feel but with an altered animation. . .not to mention a cool fade out, as opposed to the normal Bounce Track, which is a fade-in effect.

There are other ways the Timing tab makes adjusting the animation parameters fast and easy. Many people overlook experimenting with the Speed slider and the Sequence drop-down, which let you change the starting location of the animation. There are also a variety of randomizing controls you can use to experiment.

All of these settings can modify your animations in a way that makes them unique. Experiment and enjoy.

## Quick Pointers for Every Vlogger's Needs

You know how at the start of a film at the theater, there is a series of short animated graphics? The production companies, studio, and distributor all have slick, animated logos that quickly identify the companies. Many vloggers do the same thing, and it's a great way for viewers to recognize your work immediately when they begin to play your video. These are very short, typically five or ten seconds long, but it's like adding a professional visual signature to your work.

### Be Aware (Beware) of the Timeline

When working with LiveType, keep an eye on the in and out points in the top portion of your timeline (the blue arrows and lines). If you slide the starting point of the animation (the left end of the purple bar), the effect will start somewhere in the middle of the animation. Dragging the purple animation bar past the out point means that the rendered animation will end before the effect has completed, so the section of animation that occurs after the out point never appears on screen.

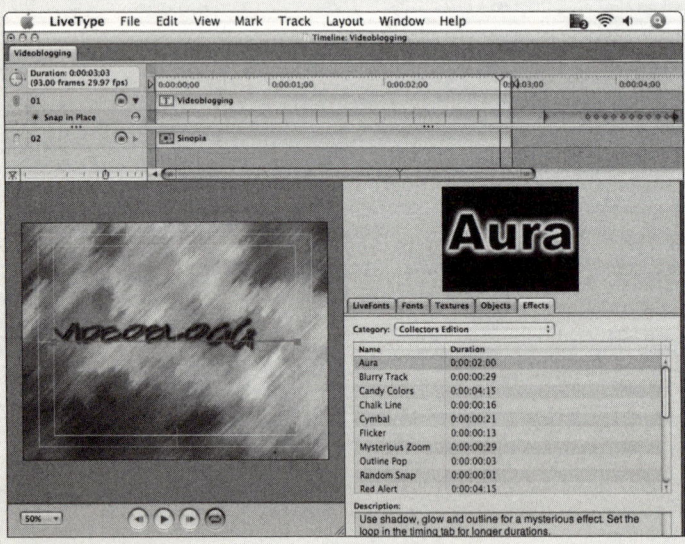

Animated title fails to complete.

Depending on your vision, this can be something you want, because it will make the animation look unique. However, it could also cause the final animation to end before all the letters appear onscreen.

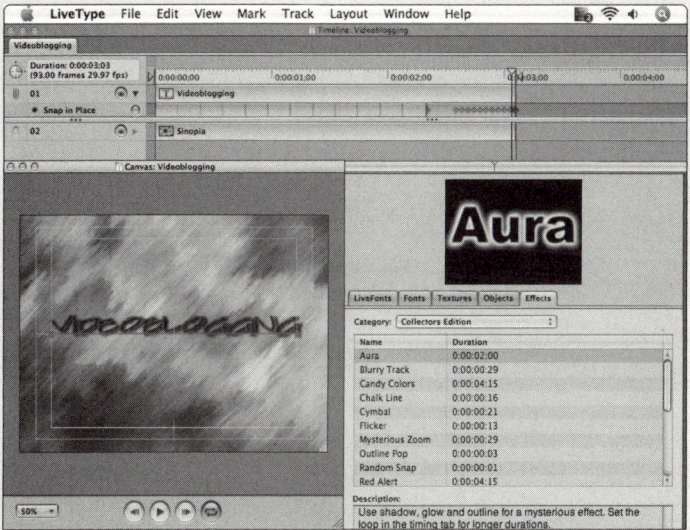

**Animated title falls within in and out points.**

### Create a Logo

Even if you're not a sophisticated computer animator, LiveType can animate a logo for you, plus add any necessary text and effects. To create a logo, you need three things: a logo graphic or image, some text (possibly your name or a title for your videoblog), and a short sample of sound or music. Before you start designing your logo, spend time thinking about the "feel" (theme) that you would like to convey. Should it be quick and snappy or slow and reflective? When you start to animate your elements, keep the theme in mind.

Create a graphic in an image-creation application like Adobe Photoshop or Illustrator, and then import it into LiveType. Animate your graphic using an effect that fits your theme. Add some text and combine several effects to give it a unique look. Finally, render a `.mov` file and import it into Final Cut, iMovie, or Soundtrack Pro to add a bit of sound or a music loop. When you've finished, you'll have an easily recognizable, personal, and professional-looking logo that you can use for each of your videos.

### Create an Opening Title

If you know what you want to convey in your opening titles — the name of your video blog, an episode title, a cast of characters, or other information — and have a plan for how you would like it to look, LiveType can display and animate it for you. A little preparation before you sit down to build your titles will help tremendously. Do you want white text on a black background? Do you want to include graphics? Or are you going for an Academy Award for hottest opening sequence? Whichever you choose, you want to place it at the beginning of your video as an introduction. Figure 8-22 shows an example.

If the opening title you are envisioning is complicated, you can import a rendered video from your editing system to place on LiveType's background layer. That puts the video in view to use as a guide for the placement of your text. On the other hand, if you are flexible and would like to save a little time, LiveType handles alpha channels superbly. It can easily render video with an alpha channel that you can arrange over your video footage later.

When building your titles, keep in mind that you don't have to create the entire sequence all at one time. You can do it in pieces, one line (or even one word) at a time. It really depends on your creative vision, as well as your patience in bringing it to life.

After creating the pieces, you can layer the individual video pieces in your video's timeline. This will allow you to rearrange each layer until you have an arrangement that you like. Also, if you like the first part of your sequence but don't like how the last part animates, you can change just the last piece instead of re-rendering the entire title sequence. When you're satisfied with the look of your video, simply render it and you're done.

FIGURE 8-22: An opening title from a videoblog.

## What Is an Alpha Channel?

An alpha channel is an area of an image that certain computer applications will treat as transparent. The presence of an alpha channel essentially indicates the absence of color in certain locations within an image. Using an alpha channel enables you to composite images in layers, so that one layer can appear on top of (or in front of) another. When creating titles for a video, an alpha channel can help make the sequence look professional, especially if you are using many layers.

## Contact Information

People will collect and view your videos in a number of ways, including by RSS subscriptions. Your videos may also be forwarded through email or linked from other blogs. In addition, if you host your video using a service with its own searchable index, such as Ourmedia and the Internet Archive, viewers may download and watch your video from a source other than your videoblog.

Many vloggers add a simple, short indicator (see Figure 8-23) at the beginning or end of their video clips. The indicator doesn't have to be fancy — a URL or email address that identifies you as the creator of the video and tells people how to find you is sufficient. If you want to build an audience and would like your videoblog to be found, including contact information assures you that anyone who sees your video has a quick way to locate your online presence.

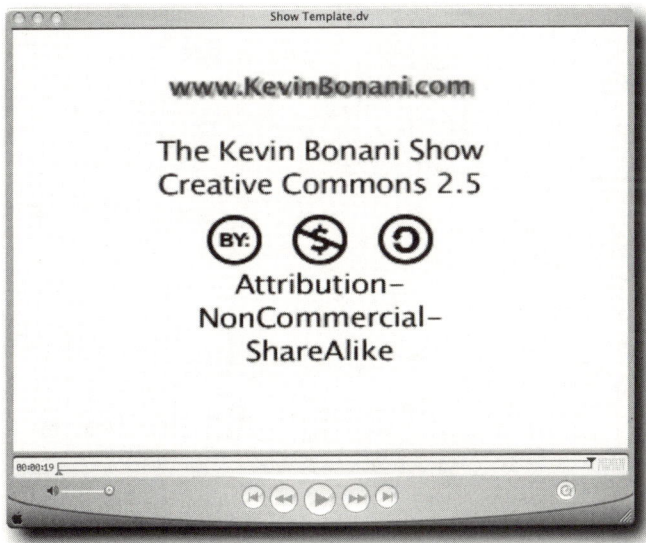

FIGURE 8-23: Contact information from a videoblog.

Because your video may take on a wandering life of its own, taking the time to add visual contact information will enable viewers to contact you about your video or to see more of your work.

## Summary

Adding text to your video can provide a variety of artistic outlets, in addition to helping you reach deaf and foreign-speaking viewers. Although adding text and graphics adds time to the editing process, the results are well worth the effort. Once you've got the hang of adding text and graphics, the process simply becomes part of your workflow.

# Transcoding and Compressing

T he vast majority of video distributed online is compressed, which means it has been altered from its original format to another, specifically to make the resulting video file smaller. This is sometimes called *transcoding*, especially when converting a previously compressed video file to a different format (such as converting from Windows Media to QuickTime). Even television shows purchased through Apple's iTunes are compressed, so you can rest assured that compression is not a bad thing. To most people, compression seems like a daunting and complicated process to learn. It isn't.

## Using FFmpeg

Converting video from one format to another is often restricted to a limited number of formats. For example, Windows Media doesn't allow you to transcode to QuickTime, and vice versa. Fortunately, a group of computer programmers from around the world have collaborated to create FFmpeg (`http://ffmpeg.sourceforge.net/index.php`), a cross-platform video recording, conversion, and streaming tool. It is free, and the source code is open.

After you've downloaded and installed FFmpeg, which requires you to build it (instructions are included), you'll discover that there is no GUI to use. Yes, that's right; FFmpeg is a command-line tool. To use it, you need to use a Command Line Interface (CLI):

➤ Macintosh — Launch the Terminal application, located in the Utilities folder at /Applications/Utilities/.

➤ Windows — Select Start ➔ Run, type CMD, and click OK.

To use FFmpeg, you type a couple of commands and let the application take care of the details. In the simplest form, here's the syntax for converting one video format to another:

```
ffmpeg -i original.avi converted.mpg
```

### Graphical User Interfaces to FFmpeg

If you're uncomfortable using a CLI, there are a couple of downloadable GUI applications that utilize FFmpeg and related technologies. For Macintosh, you can use FFmpegX (`http://homepage.mac.com/major4`); for Windows, MeWiG is available from `http://mewig.sourceforge.net`. Both applications are terrific options, especially if you are just starting to learn about transcoding and don't need all of the options that FFmpeg offers.

The `ffmpeg` runs the application; `-i` indicates the video to be used for the conversion (`original.avi`, for this example). You then follow the command by the location of and name of the converted video file (`converted.mpg`). Based on the file extension, FFmpeg determines the format to which you want to convert the video. For example, to convert the file `mycat.avi` to `mycat.mpg`, you would type `ffmpeg -i /path/to/mycat .avi/path/to/mycat.mpg`.

There are a plethora of options available when using FFmpeg, including the capability to output to multiple files and formats during a single conversion pass. For example, you could convert a video to MPEG, FLV, ASF, and MOV formats in one pass. You can learn more about the variety of options and how to use them by reading the FFmpeg documentation at `http://ffmpeg.sourceforge.net/ffmpeg-doc.html`.

# Using QuickTime Pro

Apple's QuickTime can open a wide range of video files, and the Pro version (`www.apple.com/quicktime`; $29.99 Macintosh, Windows) can export to a variety of video formats as well. QuickTime works with the following video formats:

| | |
|---|---|
| Animation | Graphics |
| Apple BMP | H.261 |
| Apple Pixlet (Mac OS X v10.3 only) | H.263 |
| | H.264 |
| Apple Video | JPEG 2000 |
| Cinepak | Microsoft OLE (decode only) |
| Component video | Microsoft Video 1 (decode only) |
| DV NTSC | Motion JPEG A |
| DVC Pro NTSC | Motion JPEG B |
| DV PAL | MPEG-4 (Part 2) |
| DVC Pro PAL | Photo JPEG |

| Planar RGB | Sorenson Video 3 |
| PNG | TGA |
| Sorenson Video 2 | TIFF |

In addition, QuickTime can work with other formats through the use of plug-ins. For example, 3ivx (www.3ivx.com) distributes an MPEG-4 encoder that integrates seamlessly with QuickTime.

To use QuickTime to transcode a video, launch the application and select File → Open File. Then choose the video file you want to convert; QuickTime presents it in a playback window. Finally, select File → Export and choose the appropriate setting (see Figure 9-1) for the video.

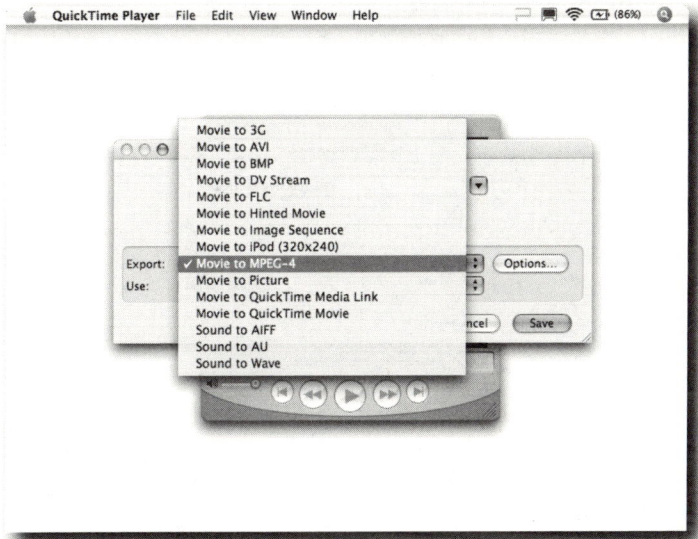

FIGURE 9-1: Export options when using QuickTime Pro.

A nice feature of the export process is that you can have more than one export process occurring at one time. Because QuickTime can export to a variety of formats, this feature can be quite useful when you are distributing across multiple outlets (such as cell phone, iPod, and web). To reach the largest audience, you should offer multiple formats of your video, and using QuickTime can ease this burden.

To transcode your video for use on various devices, simply select an Export option and then select a preset from the Use popup. For the most compatible video, select the Movie to MPEG-4 setting. To distribute a video for a cell phone, simply select the Movie to 3G export setting. To distribute video for the iPod, select the Movie to iPod (320 x 240) setting.

## Exporting Flash Video

Flash is a multimedia technology and, according to Macromedia (the company that created the technology), is installed on approximately 98 percent of computers accessing the web. Because of Flash's penetration and its capability to deliver video content, many people have chosen to distribute video using this technology. If you want to distribute Flash content, you may want to take a look at FlixExporter (Macintosh, Windows; $149) from On2 Technologies. A demo of FlixExporter can be downloaded from `www.on2.com/downloads/flix-demo-software`.

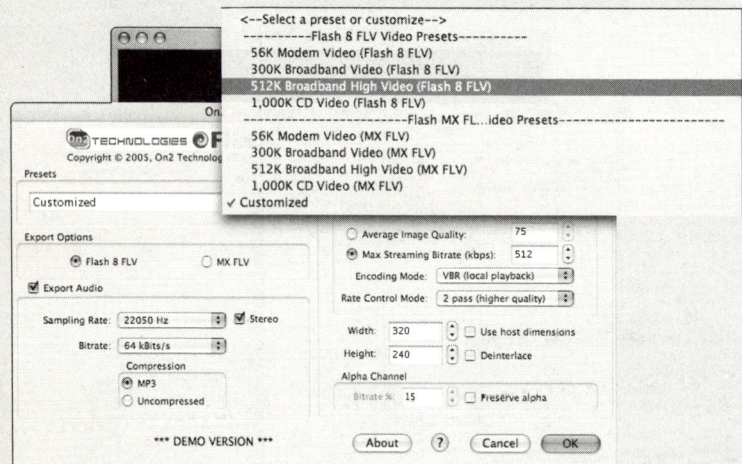

**FlixExporter.**

Once installed, FlixExporter places additional options into the Export popup menu, which enables you to transcode video to either the FLV or SWF formats. On2 recommends that longer videos be encoded using FLV. The two formats are indistinguishable from one another to most people. The biggest drawback to using FlixExport is that the actual process of converting to Flash takes a long time.

On the plus side, any application that uses the QuickTime engine automatically utilizes FlixExporter. So, if you're using Final Cut Pro, Avid Xpress, or Adobe Premiere, you have complete access to the tools necessary for creating Flash video.

QuickTime's default presets, such as those shown in Figure 9-2, work sufficiently in most instances.

As you become more proficient (and picky) with video transcoding, you'll probably want to control the settings manually by clicking the Options button. The Options provide you with complete control over the audio and video settings, including which codecs, bit rates, keyframe rates, filters, and frame rates are used. At that point, your options are nearly unlimited.

FIGURE 9-2: Default settings work for most videos.

# Using QuickTime Pro Without QuickTime Pro

QuickTime Pro is well worth its price, but, if you're comfortable using Mac OS X's Unix Terminal and want to save the $30, there's a solution for you!

All of QuickTime Pro's functionality is already included with the basic QuickTime Player — it's just locked from the QuickTime Player application until you apply a license key. Other applications such as iMovie and Final Cut Pro use QuickTime's export dialogs, so the functions are there. . .deep inside OS X. This solution gives you full access to the entire suite of QuickTime Pro's functions directly from the Terminal application.

## Download and Install QT Tools

To get started, you need to download QT Tools (www.omino.com/~poly/software/ qt_tools), a suite of tools that includes qt_export, qt_proofsheet, qt_info, qt_thing, and qt_atom. The latest version of QT Tools is available from the bottom of the page. Of the suite of tools, the one of interest is qt_export. To quote part of the QT Tools page that explains qt_export:

Here are some cool and useful things you can do with qt_export, all shell scriptable:

  - Convert an MPEG movie to a QuickTime movie.

  - Convert a batch of MPEG movies to QuickTime movies.

  - Convert an MP3 file to an AIFF file.

  - Convert an AIFF file to a whole folder full of other AIFF files each at a different sampling rate.

- Use rsh and network file servers to script the conversion of many QuickTime movies to other formats, farming out each rerender to an Xserve.

- And, lastly: recompress a movie without paying the whopping $30 for QuickTime Pro! (You cheap thug.)

After downloading and opening the disk image, save the contents to a folder on your Desktop. Then navigate to the QT Tools directory using the Terminal application. Here's how:

1. Launch the Terminal application, which can be found in the Utilities directory (\Applications\Utilities\).

2. In the Terminal window, type cd followed by a space.

3. Drag the folder where you saved the QT Tools file into the Terminal window and press Return.

4. To install QT Tools, type the following into the Terminal window and hit Return:

   ```
   sudo ./install.sh
   ```

5. You are prompted for your password. Enter it, and the QT Tools command line utilities are installed in the directory /usr/local/bin. This directory is normally hidden from view in the Finder but can be easily accessed using Terminal.

## Use QT Tools

With QT Tools installed, you'll want to see what it can do! Change back to your Home directory by typing the following in the Terminal window and press Return:

```
cd
```

Next, create and save a settings file for future use. Here's how:

1. Launch a QuickTime Export dialog — without QuickTime Pro — from the command line by typing:

   ```
   qt_export --dodialog --savesettings=filename.dat
   ```

   If the command doesn't work for you, you can also access the qt_export tool directly by typing:

   ```
   /usr/local/bin/qt_export --dodialog --↵
   savesettings=filename.dat
   ```

2. The command launches a dialog window, similar to the one shown in Figure 9-3.

3. Select a predefined collection of export settings, or customize the settings to suit your specific needs. When you're satisfied with the settings, click the OK button. The settings are saved to a file named filename.dat in your Home folder.

Following is the syntax for exporting a video using your settings:

```
qt_export --loadsettings=/location/of/settings/file ↵
/location/of/original/video /location/of/exported/video
```

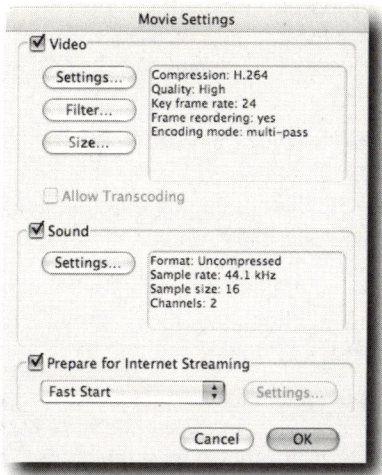

**Movie Settings**

☑ Video
Settings...  | Compression: H.264
Filter...    | Quality: High
             | Key frame rate: 24
Size...      | Frame reordering: yes
             | Encoding mode: multi-pass

☐ Allow Transcoding

☑ Sound
Settings...  | Format: Uncompressed
             | Sample rate: 44.1 kHz
             | Sample size: 16
             | Channels: 2

☑ Prepare for Internet Streaming
Fast Start ▾    Settings...

Cancel    OK

FIGURE 9-3: A QuickTime export dialog box.

## Terminal Tips

You can always drag and drop files in the Terminal window to get the path to the file, rather than typing the whole string. Just as you dragged the QT Tools folder onto the Terminal window, you can simply drag and drop any file onto the Terminal window, instead of typing `/Users/my_name/Desktop/my_file.dat`. This can be especially helpful if you're not familiar with or comfortable using Terminal.

The ~ can also be used as a shortcut to your Home directory. So:

    /Users/my_name/Desktop/my_file.dat

is the same as

    ~/Desktop/my_file.dat

In addition, there is a PATH used by Terminal that tells it where to locate applications you want to run. You can set the PATH to include other directories by creating two files in your Home directory: .profile and .login. The `.profile` file should consist of two lines:

    PATH="/usr/local/bin:$PATH"

    export PATH

and the `.login` file should consist of one line:

    set PATH = ( /usr/local/bin:$PATH)

Terminal automatically reads those two files and looks in the directory /usr/local/bin for any applications, such as qt_export.

The qt_export command causes QuickTime to load a video file and then export the video using the settings you specified. So, to export the MyVideo.mov video in your Movies folder to a video named MyNewVideo.mov in your Movies folder, you'd type the following in a Terminal window:

```
qt_export --loadsettings=~/filename.dat ~/Movies/MyVidco.mov ↵
~/Movies/MyNewVideo.mov
```

There are a variety of options and tools in the QT Tools package. Explore, experiment with, and enjoy them. . .and go buy something nice with the $30 you saved.

# Using Windows Media Encoder

Windows Media Encoder 9 Series is a free set of utilities for creating digital media. The files can be downloaded from www.microsoft.com/windows/windowsmedia/forpros/encoder/default.mspx. For transcoding video, the tool of most interest is Windows Media Encoder, which can be launched by selecting Start ➜ Programs ➜ Windows Media ➜ Windows Media Encoder.

The application launches, presenting you with a handful of Session Wizards (see Figure 9-4), including a template to Convert a File.

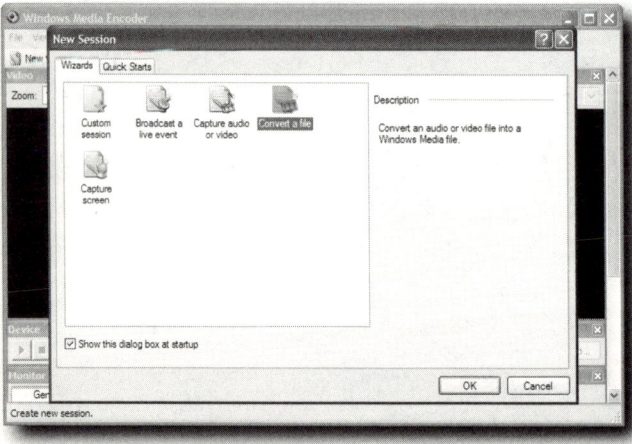

FIGURE 9-4: Windows Media Encoder Session Wizards.

Windows Media Encoder can work with the following file formats:

```
.wav    .asf    .mp3

.wma    .avi    .bmp

.wmv    .mpg    .jpg
```

Selecting Convert a File, locate a file to convert, and select a location in which to save the converted file. Then select the type of distribution method you are going to use (see Figure 9-5); your choice determines which options are available for encoding. For distributing via your videoblog, select Web Server (Progressive Download). If you would like more control over the default settings, deselect the Start Encoding When I Click Finish checkbox and then edit the appropriate properties.

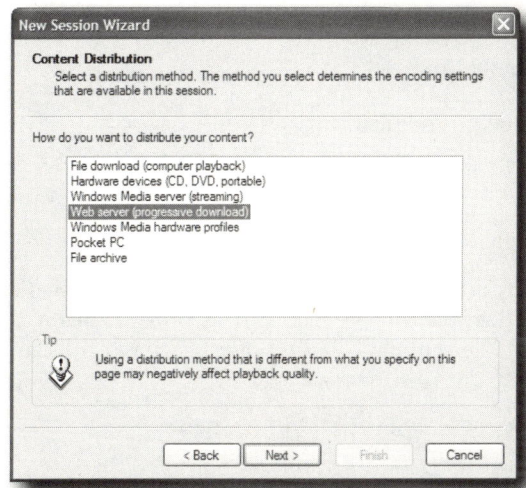

FIGURE 9-5: Content Distribution options.

Next, select your Encoding Options (see Figure 9-6). For videoblogging, select Full Screen Video (CBR) with the 500kbps option. This choice greatly reduces the size of the video file you are distributing, while maintaining a decent quality.

After you configure your distribution method, Windows Media Encoder transcodes your video. When it's finished, you have the opportunity to view the final video, create another video, or quit the application. For a free tool, Windows Media Encoder is exceptionally useful and should be a standard application in your videoblogging arsenal.

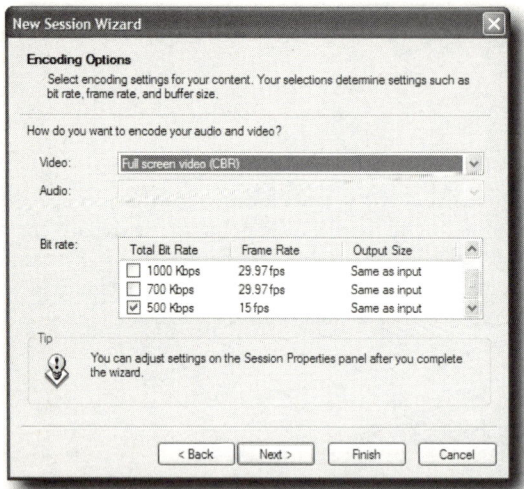

FIGURE 9-6: Full screen distribution at 500kbps selected.

# Using PSPWare

Sony's PlayStation Portable (PSP) is more than just a gaming machine. It can play music, videos, and even surf the web. But getting your content in the correct format so that it can be played on the PSP isn't straightforward. Fortunately, NullRiver offers PSPWare for Macintosh and Windows. PSPWare is $15, and the download sites are:

- Macintosh—`www.nullriver.com/index/products/pspware`
- Windows—`www.nullriver.com/index/products/pspware.win`

Converting video using PSPWare couldn't be easier. After launching the application, select the Movies tab. Then simply add the videos you would like to convert. You can make minor alterations (see Figure 9-7) to the resulting video by clicking the Options button; just click Close when you're finished.

After you set your options, you just wait for PSPWare to complete its video conversion (see Figure 9-8). During this time, you can work on other things, like customizing your videoblog.

PSPWare alerts you when the videos are ready, and you can locate them by clicking the teardrop button (far left bottom button), which opens the directory where the converted videos are saved. Because the videos that PSPWare creates are MPEG-4 compliant, you can open them using any MPEG-4–compliant player and view the video's properties. Doing so will reveal some of the technical details (see Figure 9-9) behind the conversion, such as the resolution (320 x 240), data rate (~300kbps), frame rate (29.97fps), and audio setting (AAC codec at 24kHz).

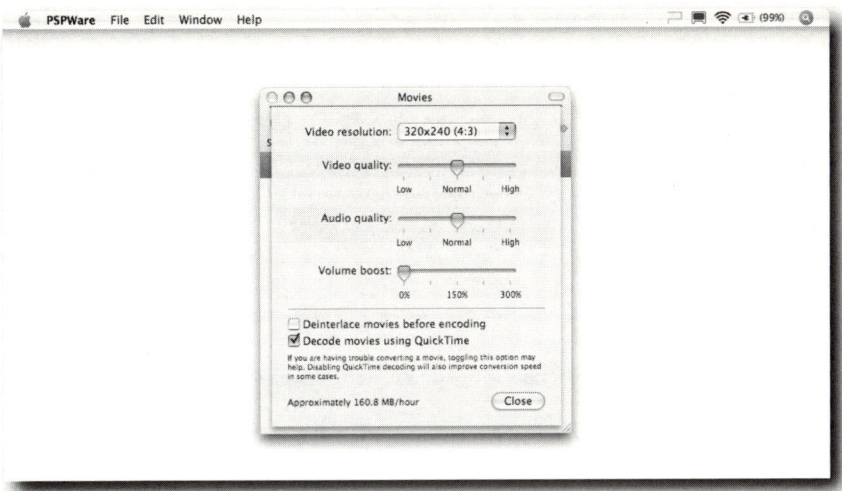

FIGURE 9-7: Options for fine-tuning the converted video.

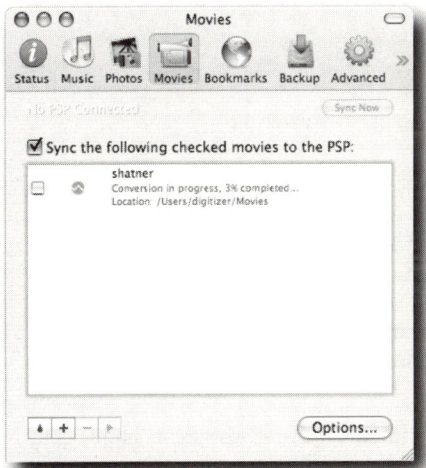

FIGURE 9-8: PSPWare converting a video.

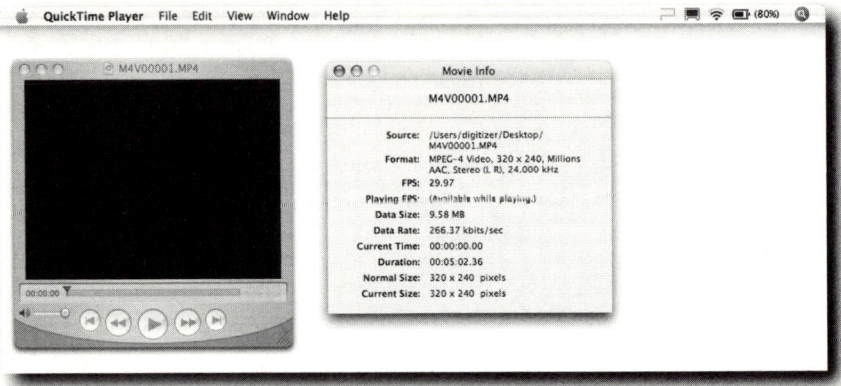

FIGURE 9-9: The technical data of a PSPWare converted video.

Understanding these technical details will help you better comprehend the world of digital video, especially the widespread acceptance of the MPEG-4 standard. Although technically you can use other tools to transcode video for PSP use, PSPWare goes far beyond just converting video for playback, because it is optimized for the PlayStation Portable. If you own a PSP, you're well advised to check it out. If you don't, at least understanding it will help you better appreciate a portion of your audience.

## Using iTunes

Most people don't realize it, but Apple's iTunes (www.apple.com/itunes; free, Macintosh, Windows) is capable of transcoding video. This feature is not really "hidden," but it's not really advertised either. The real beauty of the feature, however, is its relative simplicity.

To import video to iTunes, you can just drag and drop a file to your Library (see Figure 9-10).

Then, to locate your file, type its name in the Search box in the upper-right corner of the screen. Once you've located it, select it, right-click (Control+click if using a single button mouse), and choose Convert Selection for iPod (see Figure 9-11).

The newly converted video is saved in your iTunes library. To distribute it, simply copy it from your Library and upload it to your videoblog by clicking the video and dragging it to your Desktop (or another folder on your computer). You can also right-click (or Control+click for a one-button mouse) on the video and select Show Song File from the menu, revealing the actual file on your computer.

Sometimes black-and-white pictures just can't make the statements that color pictures can. The figures on these pages give you a better "picture" of some of the aspects of videoblogging.

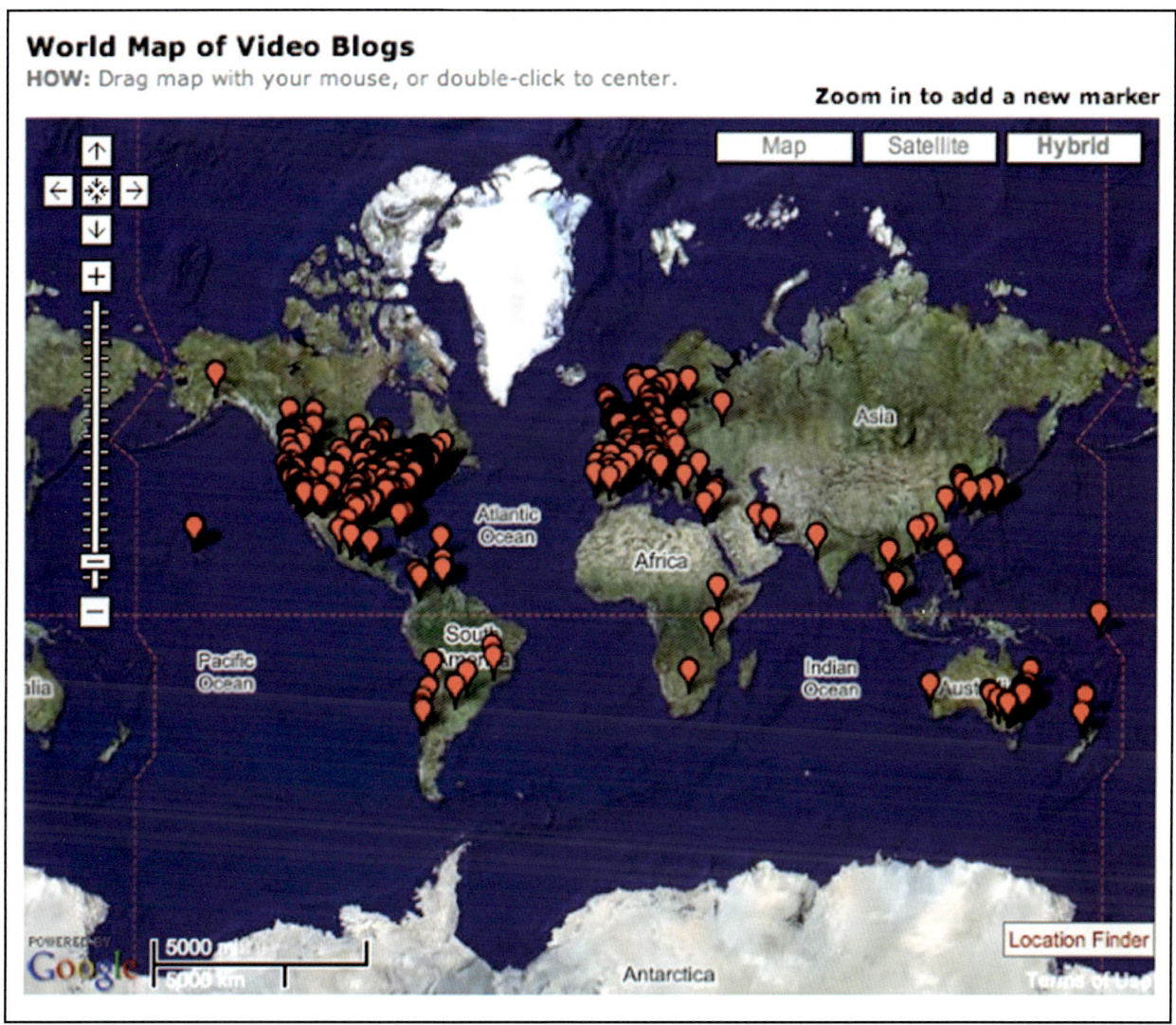

**World Map of Video Blogs**
HOW: Drag map with your mouse, or double-click to center.
Zoom in to add a new marker

Among its many features, VlogMap.org helps you locate videobloggers around the world. You can add your site to the world map, too.

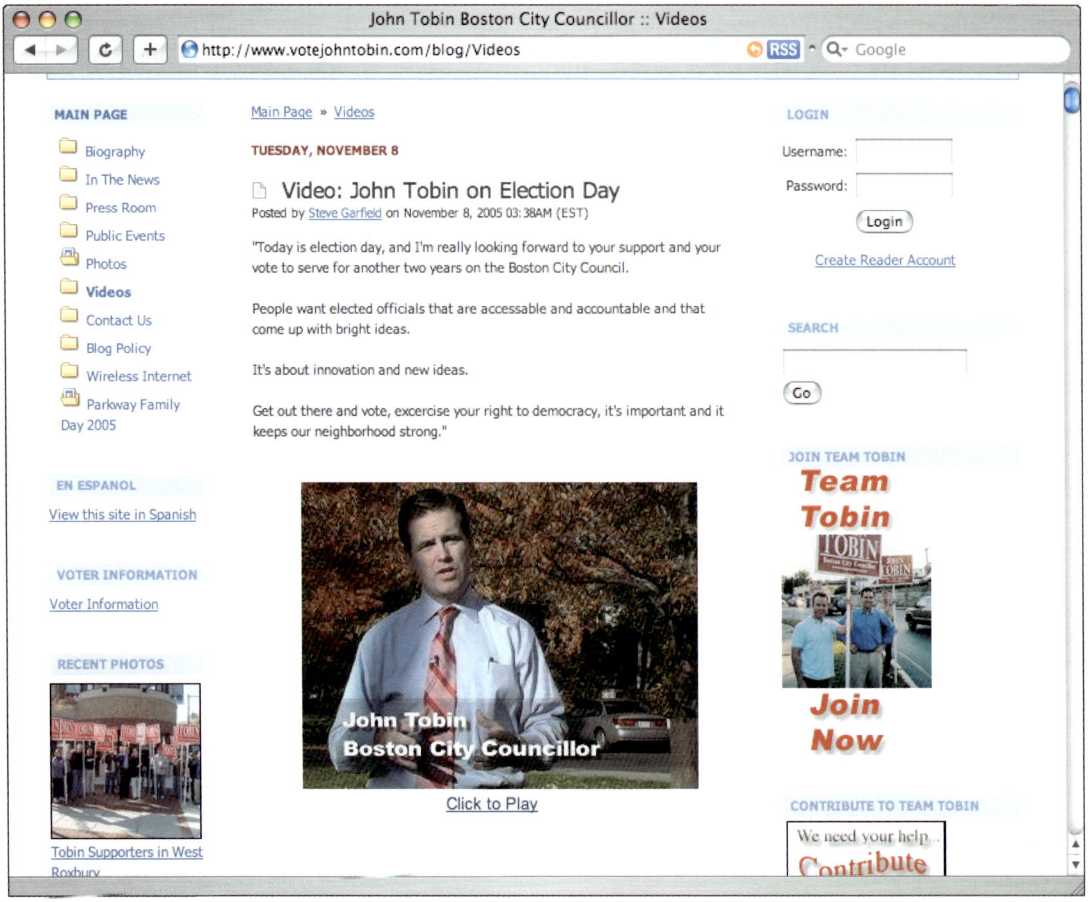

Videoblogs have moved into the political arena, providing additional means for voters to get to know their candidates and helping elected officials keep in touch with their constituents.

Reflectors help balance out light and fill in shadows. See how much clearer the facial details are in the photo on the right. The photographer used reflected light to help balance the existing light and fill in shadows. You can buy reflectors although there are a number of cheap alternatives such as aluminum foil and auto windshield shades that you may already have sitting around house.

"Rainbow" text is pretty, but your viewers will have a difficult time reading it. Hold it to one or two colors for best results.

Black and white can often be the best color choice for text — black against light colors and white against dark colors in your video.

Definitely too much of a good thing. Unusual fonts can be fun, but they're also hard to read.

A readable font punctuated with an unusual one is a good choice. It's creative yet easy for your viewers to see.

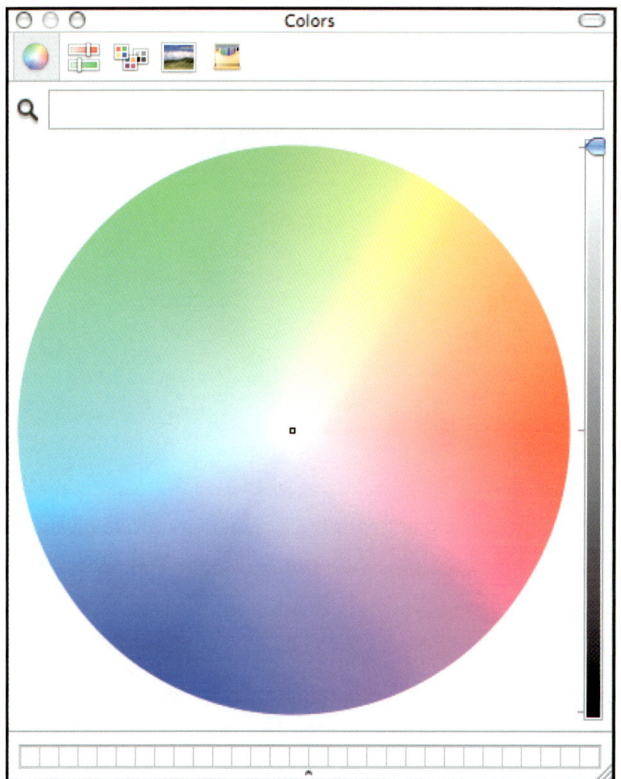

You can use a color wheel to easily discern color combinations that will work together. Do a web search for "color wheel" to find images of color wheels and learn how to understand them. The rough rule is that colors on opposite sides of the wheel are complementary, and colors that differ in brightness have a contrasting value. This information can help you choose the right color(s) for text and titles against the background in your video.

A drop shadow or outline may help make your text more readable. You wouldn't be putting text into your video if you didn't want viewers to see it, right?

Traditional lights are sufficient for shooting video (left), but "lighting" can help enhance the images you capture. Even adding one simple light (right) can make a tremendous difference in the look and feel of your video. Be creative; try out lots of different kinds of lighting.

Recording footage that includes you and someone walking next to you is a little tricky, but still manageable. Swivel the LCD screen out from the side of the camera, use the screen to line up the shot, and then have your arm "memorize" the position so you can watch where you are going. Holding the camera out in front at a slight angle is enough to place you and the person walking next to you in the frame.

LiveType is great, but you must watch the In and Out points in the top portion of your timeline (the blue arrows and lines). If you slide the starting point of the animation (the left end of the purple bar), the LiveType effect will start somewhere in the middle of the animation. Dragging the purple animation bar past the Out point means that the rendered animation will end before the effect has completed, as this figure shows.

Of course, it may be your vision that the animation not complete so that your video is unique. Just remember that a side effect is likely to be that all of the letters won't appear onscreen. This figure shows a LiveType animation within the timeline — with the result that all of the letters are visible to your viewers.

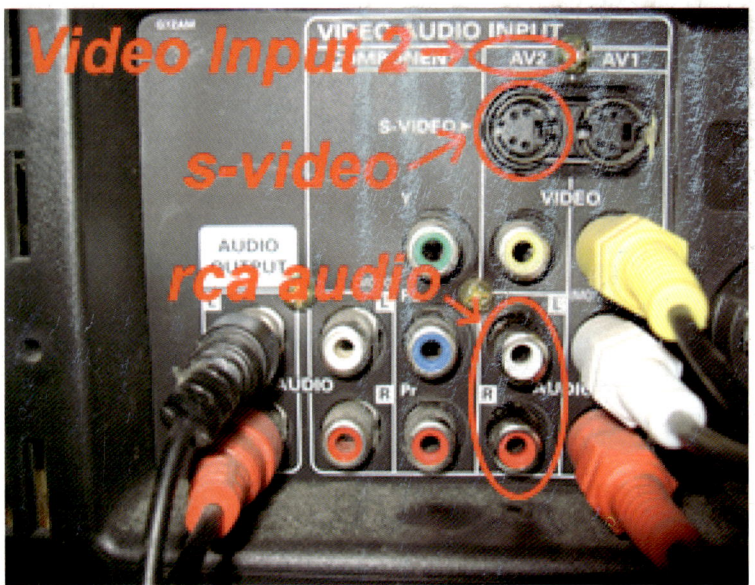

Video Input 2
VIDEO AUDIO INPUT
AV2
AV1
S-VIDEO
s-video
VIDEO
AUDIO
rca audio

You can watch your videos on your TV by connecting your computer to your TV. Everything you need to do is explained in Chapter 15.

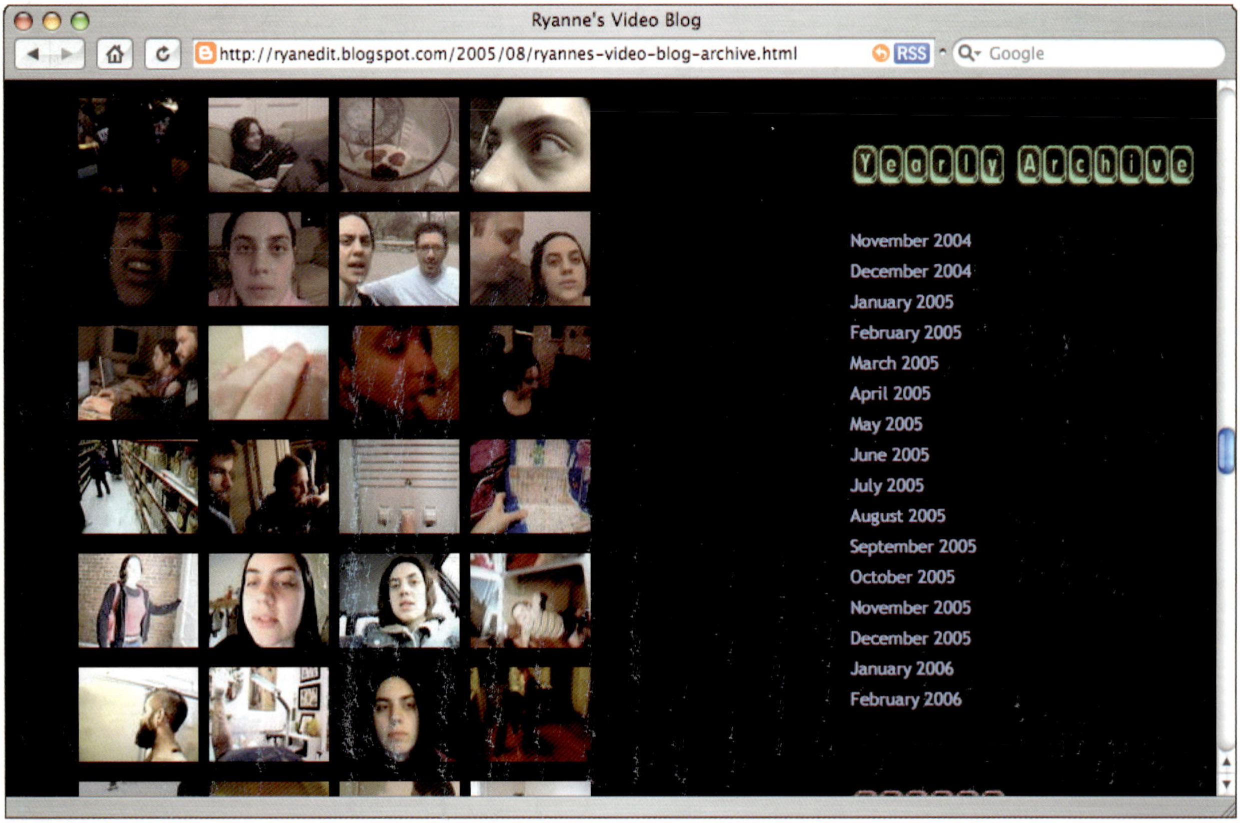
Ryanne's Video Blog
http://ryanedit.blogspot.com/2005/08/ryannes-video-blog-archive.html
RSS
Google
Yearly Archive
November 2004
December 2004
January 2005
February 2005
March 2005
April 2005
May 2005
June 2005
July 2005
August 2005
September 2005
October 2005
November 2005
December 2005
January 2006
February 2006

A video archive can be quite dramatic. Each thumbnail links to the video it represents. This figure also shows a textual archive (on the right). Archives enable viewers to easily check out the videos you've posted on your vlog.

FIGURE 9-10: Importing a DV video into iTunes by dragging it into the Library.

FIGURE 9-11: Selecting to transcode a video.

# Summary

No matter what format you use to acquire your video, you can use a number of technologies to transcode your video to another format. Being able to change from one format to another with relative ease is a wonderful aspect of the medium and means that you can reach a wide and varied audience. Whether your audience is using a web browser, video aggregator, iPod, PlayStation Portable, cell phone, or some other device, you are limited only by your creativity and ambition.

# Creating Interactive Videos

One major advantage online video has over traditional broadcast video is the opportunity to include interactive elements in the video. With interactive video, you can include clickable links in your video that open web pages. You can also include videos that interact with other videos. In addition, you can enable areas within a video to react to user input, such as mouse clicks. The area of interactive video is still in its infancy, and people are discovering new methods of creating interactive experiences on a seemingly daily basis.

## Use QuickTime Media Links

Once you're publishing your videoblog and have a few subscribers, you may wonder, "Now that people are getting my videos delivered in so many different ways, how can I include a link back to my web site that will travel with the video itself?" Fortunately, there are a number of ways to do just that! Some of the methods are easier than others, naturally, but they are all do-able.

### QuickTime and Interactivity

If you publish your videoblog in a QuickTime format, you'll be pleased to know that QuickTime enables video producers to explore a completely new medium of interactive video that allows for active links to be added to a video. The links are much like hyperlinks on web pages.

Using a couple of downloadable tools, you can create a small QuickTime file that has a clickable link back to your web site. Some people call this a *comment frame* because it's a frame, attached at the end of a video, that users can click. Clicking takes the user to a web site, usually the originating videoblog, to leave a comment about the video he just watched. You can append a comment frame to each of your videos and rest easy knowing that no matter how your viewers receive your video content, it's prepackaged with a link back to your web site.

## Using eZediaQTI

The tool most people use to create a comment frame is eZediaQTI (www.ezedia.com; $49.95). eZediaQTI is available for both Macintosh and Windows systems. Although the full version requires a license, the demo version allows for all the functionality required to create a comment frame.

To create a comment frame, you need:

- QuickTime Pro (www.apple.com/quicktime/pro)
- eZediaQTI (www.ezedia.com)

You can download the eZediaQTI demo version from www.ezedia.com/products/downloads. After installing the application, you're ready to create your first comment frame. If you don't already have QuickTime Pro installed, you need to purchase and download that as well.

## Set Up and Create an eZediaQTI Project

When you launch the eZediaQTI application, it creates a new blank project for you — a large white square, which is called the workspace canvas. It is basically the frame you are working with and is where you will add interactive objects to your comment frame.

First, set the workspace canvas to the correct size. To do so, click the Attributes button on the toolbar to display the Attributes panel (see Figure 10-1).

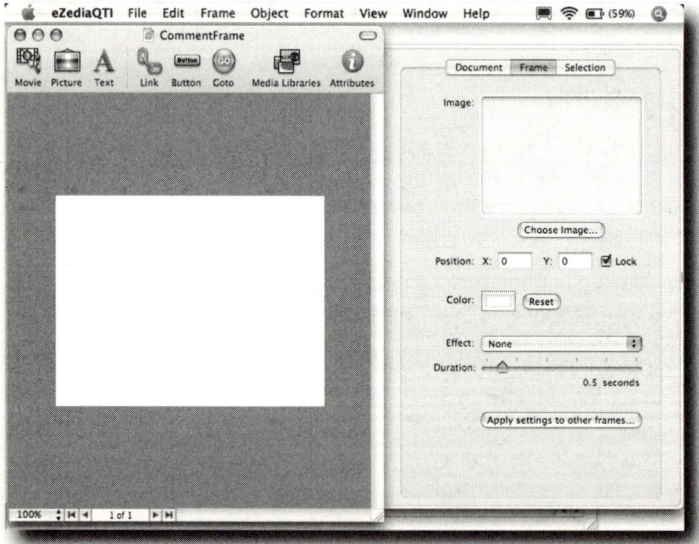

FIGURE **10-1:** eZedia's Attributes panel.

The Attributes panel enables you to adjust the attributes of the object you have selected on the workspace canvas. Select the Document tab, and you can set the overall size of the canvas. Just choose the correct size from a drop-down list (see Figure 10-2). Select the size that matches the dimensions of your video, which most likely is by 320 x 240.

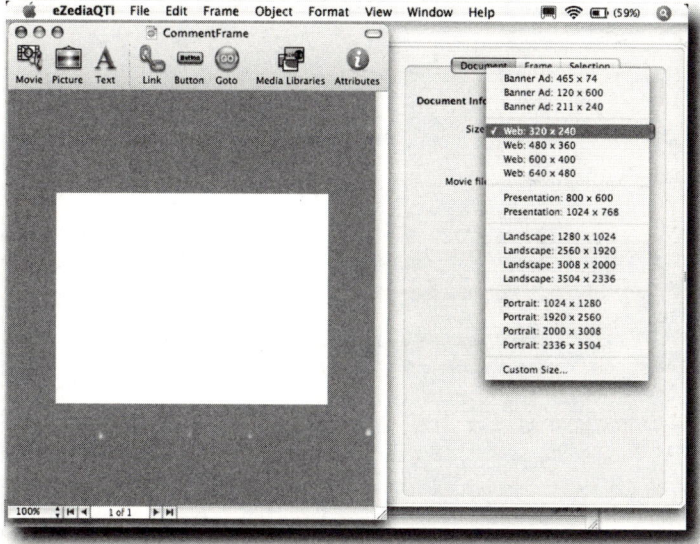

FIGURE 10-2: Setting the size of the document.

If the size you want isn't listed, select Custom Size and enter the size manually.

## Creating a Button or Link

A comment frame needs to lead to a web site, so you must add a Goto object to your document. The Goto object is the "clickable" area in your video. To add it, click the Goto button on the eZediaQTI toolbar, and then position the object where you want your button or link to appear within the frame of your video, as shown in Figure 10-3.

Next, direct the Goto object to visit your web site when clicked. To configure it, select the Goto object and locate its attributes, which are displayed on the Selection tab of the Attributes panel. Set the object's Action: Select Web Location for Go To, and enter your web site's URL in the URL field, as shown in Figure 10-4.

Once you've configured the button, adjust its appearance and title attributes by using the Attributes panel. You'll more than likely want to change the Title attribute so that the text of the button indicates that it is clickable; otherwise, most viewers won't relate to it. You can also change the text of the button by double-clicking the text, inside the frame of video you are working with. If you need to resize the Goto object so that it can hold more text, you can do so simply by dragging its edges within the workspace canvas.

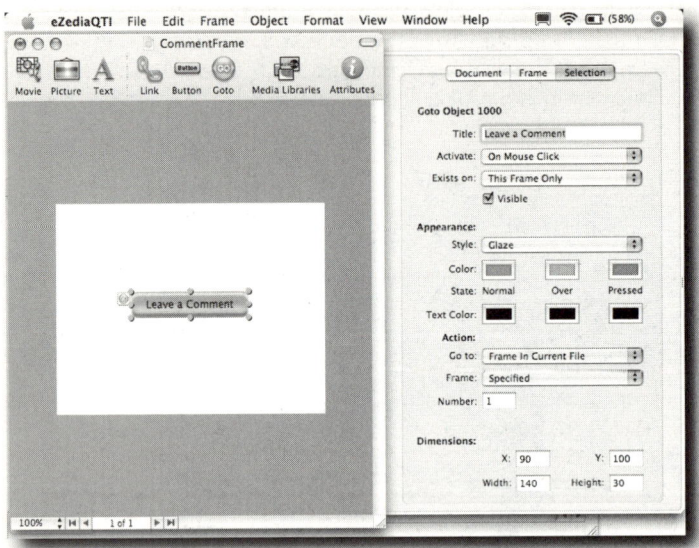

FIGURE 10-3: Placing a Goto object.

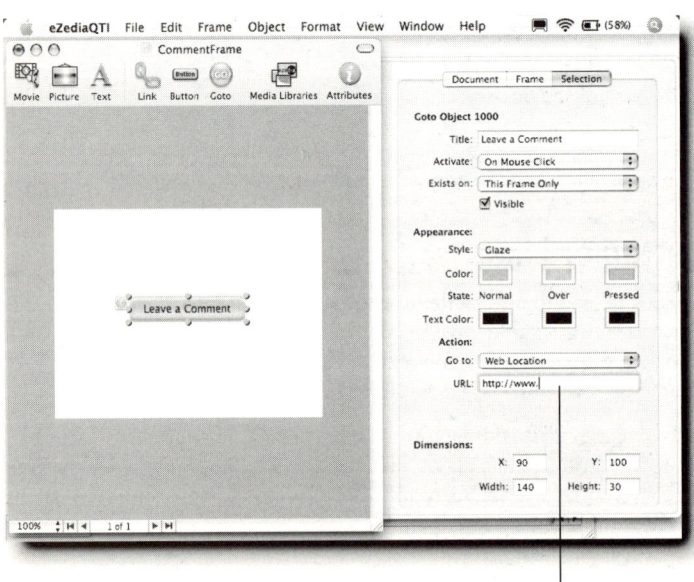

Enter your site's URL.

FIGURE 10-4: Setting the Goto object's URL attribute.

You can add some style to the button by selecting an item from the Style drop-down list, such as flat, glass, or tabs. Also, you can change the color of the button or the text by using the Color and Text Color options, and you can set different colors for the Normal, Over, and Pressed states to give the button a rollover effect.

## Export a QuickTime Video

You can't use your comment frame until it's in a format that you can work with outside of eZediaQTI, so you want to export it as a QuickTime video. To export, select File → Export Interactive Movie. Then select the location where you want to save the comment frame, enter a filename for it, and click the Save button.

If you're using the free version of eZediaQTI, you may see a dialog box explaining the limitations of the free version. After you have read the notice, click OK to continue.

By default, eZediaQTI opens the exported movie file in your web browser, where you can test it. Just close the browser when you're done.

## Adding the Comment Frame to Your Videoblog

Creating a comment frame isn't going to do you much good if you don't have a video to attach it to. So, go shoot, edit, and explore a video. When you're done, just save and compress your video in the manner that you are accustomed to (remember where you save it).

Open the comment frame (Figure 10-5) movie in QuickTime Pro. Select the eZediaQTI video window, choose Edit → Select All, and then choose Edit → Copy. This places the interactive video onto your computer's Clipboard.

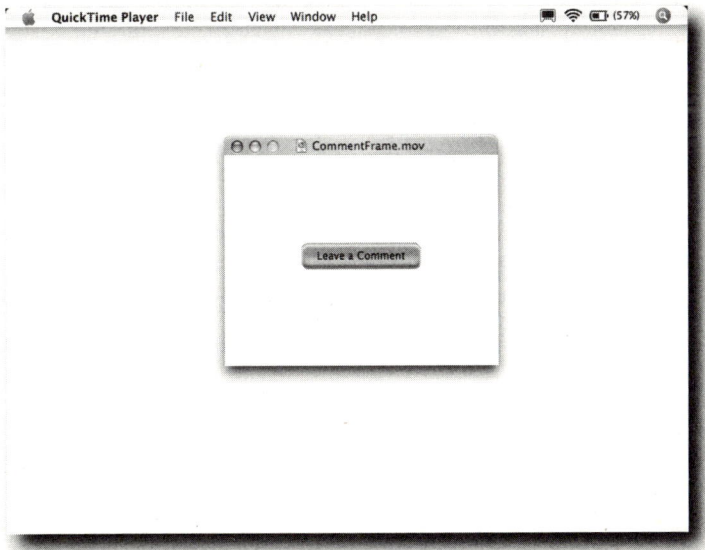

FIGURE 10-5: A comment frame opened in QuickTime.

Next, locate the video you want to add the comment frame to, and open it in its own QuickTime Pro window. You can do this by just double-clicking the video from the Finder/Explorer on your computer or selecting Open from QuickTime's File menu and locating the video.

**Tip** If your links/buttons are always going to point to the same place, you don't have to create a new eZedia project for each videoblog; just use the same comment frame for each one.

After opening your video, drag the playhead to the position at which you want to add your comment frame, which is usually the last frame of video. Finally, select Edit → Paste to place the comment frame in your video.

You now have a QuickTime Pro window that has your comment frame pasted on the end of your video. To save the video, choose File → Save As, enter a new filename, and select the Save As Self-Contained Movie File option. Click the Save button and you're done.

Congratulations! You're ready to publish your videoblog, complete with an interactive link back to your web site.

## More Cool Stuff

Change the color of the frame's background with the Color button on the Frame tab of the Attributes panel.

You can add an image to your comment frame — if you want to include a logo, for example. Just click the Picture button on the toolbar and browse to the image you want to include.

Create a clickable link on any picture by making your Goto object invisible (just uncheck the Visible option in the Goto object's attributes) and placing it on top of the image.

**Tip** If you're having problems with this, it may be because the Goto object isn't on top of the image but beneath it. To fix this, select the Goto object (check the Attributes panel to make sure you have the right thing selected), and select Object → Layers → Bring to Front.

There are all sorts of reasons you may want to add some interactive goodness to your videoblog, and this is only one of many methods to do it. Be creative. You could include links to web sites that have more information on your topic, a link to your copyright and license information, and even a button that takes the viewer home to your web site.

# Create a Rhizome Movie

Rhizome movies are shared QuickTime movies that have been developed to allow video-bloggers to make their own interactive content. A Rhizome movie (see Figure 10-6) provides a simple QuickTime movie template that already contains scripting to perform a series of interactive functions. The templates let everyone experiment with different ways to create interactive videos, without having to learn a complex piece of software or scripting language to do so.

FIGURE **10-6: A Rhizome movie.**

There are a variety of Rhizome movies available, each doing something slightly different, and anyone can download them to publish in his own videoblogs. You can download a variety of Rhizome templates from `http://hypertext.rmit.edu.au/vlog/archives/2005/08/24/rhizome-movies`.

## Why Create a Rhizome Movie?

You might be wondering why you would use a Rhizome movie template instead of just publish your own video in your blog. That's a good question, and there isn't just a single answer to it. However, many people are interested in being able to experiment with video in their blogs, whether for creative, personal, artistic, or professional reasons. Using the templates enables you to explore the interactive properties that digital video can offer.

The Rhizome templates invite you to think about storytelling by using video in different ways. For example, Rhizome One plays two different videos alongside each other continuously (see http://fauxpress.blogspot.com/2005/06/faux-press-vlog-collaboration.html for an example). Each video loops, and which one you hear is controlled by where you move your mouse in the movie.

You can make a video out of two related yet different (and looping) parts. Some people think of this as being more like music than linear video. Many people go so far as to "compose" videos that weave in and out of each other in playful ways. Others let each video offer commentary or a view on the other — imagine that one is a mother describing her daughter and the other is the daughter describing her mother. Envision the stories that can emerge as viewers hear different parts because they have moved their mouse from one to the other!

Other templates vary the speed of the video (faster or slower), allow an additional soundtrack, and let viewers stop and play each video track separately from the other. As you start playing with the templates, the old perceptions of video as an image and a sound track, forever in lockstep and always running for a set time, dissolve. The excitement is in discovering the stories you might now be able to tell and the new experiences you can share with the world.

## How to Use the Rhizome Templates

Each Rhizome template is published in the same way and uses the same set of rules or procedures for you to make your own. The template consists of a `.mov` file, an XML file, and a readme file.

The `.mov` file is the actual Rhizome movie containing the interactive scripts (known as sprites) that make everything possible. When the movie is launched (whether in QuickTime player or embedded in a web page), it reads the contents of the XML file and loads the URLs that have been listed in it. The readme file provides simple instructions for the viewer.

Here are the basic steps for using a Rhizome movie template:

1. Create the content you want to publish in the Rhizome movie. For example, two video clips and a sound track; video should be at a resolution of 160 x 120 pixels or larger.

2. Compress the videos appropriately, and place them online in your usual fashion. The files can be named however you want; the only requirements are that QuickTime must be capable of reading them and that they have a valid URL. QuickTime supports more than 50 file formats, including the following:

| | |
|---|---|
| 3DMF (Mac OS 9 & Windows) | MPEG-2 |
| 3GPP | MPEG-4 |
| 3GPP | MQV |
| 3GPP2 | M4A, M4B, M4P (iTunes 4 audio) |
| AIFF | M4V (iTunes video) |
| AMC | PDF (Mac OS X) |
| AMR | Photoshop |
| Animated GIF | PICS |
| AU | PICT |
| Audio CD Data (Mac OS 9) | PNG |
| AVI | QCP (Mac OS 9 & Windows) |
| BMP | Quartz Composer Composition (MAC OS X) |

| | |
|---|---|
| CAF (Mac OS X) | QuickTime Image File |
| DLS | QuickTime Movie |
| DV | SD2 (Mac OS 9 & Windows) |
| FlashPix | SDP |
| GIF | SDV |
| JPEG/JFIF | SGI |
| Karaoke | System 7 Sound (Mac OS 9) |
| MacPaint | Text |
| Macromedia Flash 5 | TIFF |
| MIDI | TIFF Fax |
| MPEG-1 | VDU (Sony Disk Unit) |
| MP3 (MPEG-1, Layer 3) | Virtual Reality (VR) |
| M3U (MP3 Playlist files | Wave |

3. In your text editor, open the XML file associated with your Rhizome movie.

   Here is some sample XML text for a Rhizome movie:

   ```
   <ChildMovieAddress>
     <ChildTrackOne>
        <ClipOne>media/Left.mov</ClipOne>
     </ChildTrackOne>
     <ChildTrackTwo>
        <ClipOne>media/Right1.jpg</ClipOne>
        <ClipTwo>media/Right2.jpg</ClipTwo>
        <ClipThree>media/Right3.jpg</ClipThree>
        <ClipFour>media/Right4.jpg</ClipFour>
        <ClipFive>media/Right5.jpg</ClipFive>
     </ChildTrackTwo>
   </ChildMovieAddress>
   ```

4. The XML file includes text that indicates where you need to enter the URLs to your files. It says something similar to `url/or/relative/pathto/some.mov`. That's where you put the full URLs to the files you've placed online and want to associate with this particular video.

**Tip**

Copy and paste each URL into a browser, just to make sure it is correct before you enter it into the XML file.

5. Save your file. However, do not rename it! Remember, there is a script inside the actual Rhizome movie (the `.mov` file) that loads this XML file when it launches. If you change its name, your Rhizome movie won't be able to find the file.

6. Launch the Rhizome movie in QuickTime Player. If the information in the XML file is correct — that is, the URLs work — your Rhizome movie plays as expected. Yes, even though it is not yet on the Internet. How, you wonder? Because it is reading the information you have entered and saved in the XML file. As long as you are connected to the Internet, your very own Rhizome movie loads the files that you have indicated in the XML file. How cool is that?

7. When you are satisfied with the results of your video, simply upload the Rhizome movie and the XML file to your blog publishing system in your usual way. Note that the XML files must be in the same directory as the Rhizome movie, or it will not work.

Once you've uploaded the requisite files, embed the Rhizome movie in your blog post.

## Common Questions

Because Rhizome movies are a new concept, most people have a few questions. Here are some of the most common:

**Q.** Can I rename the Rhizome movie?

**A.** Yes, you can rename this file, but make sure you keep the `.mov` extension; otherwise, your web server software and web browser won't know that it is QuickTime.

**Q.** Can I rename the XML file?

**A.** No, that must be left as is. It must also be always located in the same directory as your Rhizome movie.

**Q.** Does the Rhizome movie (and the XML file) need to be in the same directory as the video and audio that it plays?

**A.** No. You put the full address to what you want to play in the XML file; the actual material can be anywhere on the Internet.

**Q.** Why isn't there a controller for the movie?

**A.** The Rhizome movie loads other things into it and plays. The Rhizome movie itself is only one-second long. Because it loads other files into itself (like a web browser), it doesn't need its own controller.

**Q.** How many Rhizome movies can I have?

**A.** As many as you like! Remember, you cannot change the name of the XML file that each Rhizome movie points to, so it's a good idea to place each Rhizome movie in its own directory. That ensures that each movie will read its own XML file (not another movie's). If you are going to distribute more than one Rhizome movie, be sure that you keep individual XML files and their specific Rhizome movies together.

**Q.** How do I find examples of Rhizome movies?

**A.** A list of Rhizome movies is informally maintained using the rhizomeMovie tag at del.icio.us (`http://del.icio.us/tag/rhizomemovie`). Feel free to add your own work!

A list of Rhizome movies, an FAQ, and other information is also available via the web at `http://hypertext.rmit.edu.au/vlog/rhizome-movies`.

# Use Flash to Create Interactive Videos

This solution assumes you have some knowledge of working with Flash — specifically creating buttons and giving movie clips instance names — and some basic understanding of ActionScript. The following tricks involve importing your video footage into Flash and turning it into a movie object on the Stage. If you're not sure how to do this, have a peek at your Flash manual and then come back.

A lot of people are using Flash as a way to distribute video on the Internet. But Flash can do a lot more than just play video. As with Rhizome videos, video that utilizes Flash doesn't have to be a linear experience. There's a world of interactive narrative that hasn't been fully explored, and remember that your viewers will quite often be watching your video with a mouse in hand!

If you've been using Flash to build web sites or animations, you know that it's got some powerful tools for making interactive content. The following trick may provide a springboard for you to explore the multiple possibilities for interactive videos in Flash.

## Video Scrubbing

If you've seen the movie *Minority Report*, you remember the computer system allowed users to play video backward and forward at various speeds, determined by how fast or slow the user dragged the playhead (this is often called "scrubbing video"). Well, you may not have the hi-tech gloves, but you can make your very own system to scrub the image. By using a few features of Flash, you'll be able to create a video that can scrub based on the mouse position.

To start, create a Flash movie the same size as your video. For this exercise, assume a size of 320 x 240. After setting the size, place your video file on the timeline, turn the video into a movieclip symbol and give it an instance name. Next, you'll need to determine how many frames the movieclip contains. Then divide that number by the width of your movie in pixels (320 in this case), which will result in your multiplier.

For example, if your movie is 640 frames long, the multiplier would be 2. Select the movieclip, open the ActionScript window, and type the following:

```
onClipEvent(enterFrame){
   multiplier = 2;
   newFrame = Math.floor(_root_.xmouse*mutiplier);
 gotoAndStop(newFrame);
}
```

(You would replace the number 2 with whatever the multiplier for your video is.) Now you can test your video and see what happens.

## Grok the Code

Okay, so sometimes code can be confusing. The following is a more detailed explanation of the different parts. Once you understand it, feel free to tweak it.

- onClipEvent(enterFrame) — Because the video is a movieclip, it will run the code contained within the brackets continuously while the Flash movie is playing. If you want more control over the video, you can use a conditional within the code to do something like check to see if the mouse has been clicked.

- multiplier — A variable to hold the multiplier value.

- newFrame — A variable to hold a frame number, determined by the mouse position.

- Math.floor — This one is important because it rounds a floating-point (decimal) number to a whole number. Because the mouse position will return as a floating-point number and the video only has "whole" frames, the Math.floor method is used to obtain a number you can use later.

- _root._xmouse — The horizontal position of the mouse in the Flash movie. If you don't use _root_, it would be the horizontal position of the mouse in the movieclip. In this example, that's okay because the movieclip is the same size as the Flash movie. However, if you wanted to have multiple smaller movies on the screen, you might want each one to have its own control.

- this.gotoAndStop(newFrame) — Tells the movieclip to go to the frame with the same value as newFrame. If newFrame equals 30, for instance, the movieclip will go to frame 30 of the video.

## Push the Edge

A couple of ideas to explore this concept further include:

- Place two different movie clips on top of each other. Then use _xmouse to control each movie's frame position and use _ymouse to control each movie's opacity in opposite directions. This implementation gives you real-time, cross-fading from one movie to the other.

- Place invisible buttons around the screen that trigger various sound files to play. This implementation enables you to add a voiceover while a viewer scrubs around the video.

If you've previously used Flash, you've probably used buttons to navigate around a Flash movie. Navigation using hotspots is another approach you could take when using Flash and video together. What about just clicking characters in a video to find out more about them?

Once a video is a movie object, it can be treated as a frame-by-frame animation. You can use standard navigation commands like gotoAndPlay() to visit different sections. Suppose you've got a video with two people wandering about a city, and you've also captured some interviews with them. You could edit it so the interviews are all at the end of the video and then create some invisible buttons that take the viewer to the appropriate interview when she clicks them.

Why invisible? Well, rather than overlaying your pretty footage with graphics, you can place invisible buttons over the characters in the video and use normal tweening functions to follow the images if, and when, they move. This way the viewer can click a character in the video and view the character's interview. You could also use a variable to store the frame the viewer was on when he clicked, so that when the interview has finished playing, the movie takes him back to where he left off. If you create a video like this, you may want to explain to your viewer ahead of time, either in your videoblog post or through the video itself, that images within the video are clickable.

Flash opens new possibilities and concepts for visual storytelling. The only limitation is your imagination.

# Summary

Online video isn't restricted to just passive viewership. If you want to be creative with your videoblog, the sky is the limit because digital video is exceptionally malleable and enables a completely new form of expression. Even if you choose to start off using digital video for traditional storytelling, you still know that there's an entire world of interactivity to be explored, should you ever desire a new creative outlet.

# Distribution

# Hosting Your Video

T o distribute video online, your video files need to be available to anyone, at anytime. The best way to accomplish this is to have someone
else store and distribute your video on a server, which is called hosting. There are a number of ways to have someone host your video for you,
and some are even free.

## Hosting Video for Free

Once you are ready to distribute your video, it must be hosted on a server
so other people can access it. This server is usually one of many computers
stored somewhere in a data center, with a very fast connection to the
Internet (most often, multiple connections). The problem is that hosting
costs money, and it's a monthly fee that you must continue to pay. . .or else
your files are deleted and people can't download them. If you stop paying,
your videos are erased from the server and are no longer available.

## The Internet Archive

So what happens if you want to upload a video and make sure it's always
available, no matter what? Believe it or not, there are some options. The
Internet Archive (www.archive.org) is a public server that anyone can
use for free. It was created by Brewster Kahle, and its motto is "Universal
access to human knowledge."

The Internet Archive is a nonprofit organization created with the belief that
it is important to save the work being created on the web for future generations. Because the Internet is so fluid and ephemeral, much of it is being
lost each day. By permanently storing media and spidering web pages, the
Archive will give future historians a better sense of what past generations
were like.

The Archive will let anyone upload noncommercial video to its servers.
Imagine if your great-great-great grandchildren could watch videos of you,
from your own perspective. Or imagine if you were able to see little videos
from people during the Civil War. Society would have a much better perspective on history than we currently do.

As of 2006, thousands of people have already uploaded videos, photos, audio, and text files to the Archive's server. More people are doing so every day, which equates to the Archive growing at a rate of about 20 terabytes per month. You learn about how they are handling storage at www.petabox.org.

## Joining the Archive

What the existence of the Archive means to you, as a videoblogger, is free storage and bandwidth for your videos. Here's how you can use the Archive for your videoblog.

First, you'll need to get an account at the Internet Archive. To do so, go to www.archive.org and click the Join Us button on the top-right of the page.

To join, all you need to provide is a valid email address, a password, and a screen name (see Figure 11-1). After submitting it, you will receive a "library card" in your email, which will enable you to upload files to the Archive's servers.

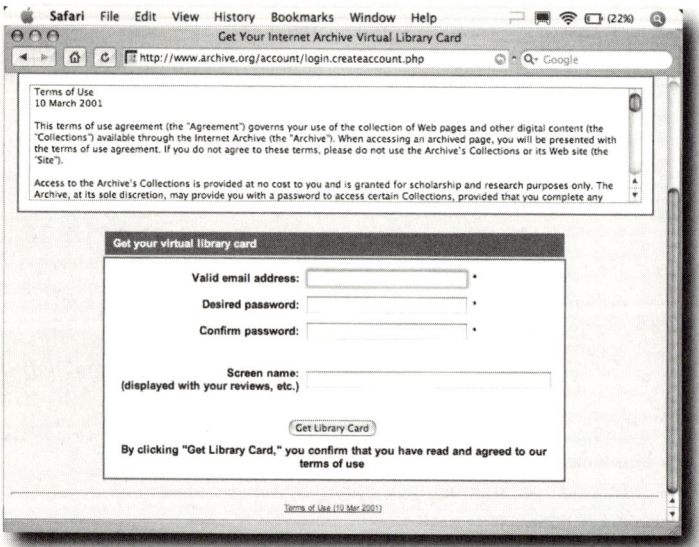

FIGURE 11-1: Joining the Internet Archive.

**Note** You can also get an account at Ourmedia.org (www.ourmedia.org), which is a "front end" to the Internet Archive. Ourmedia is targeted for collecting "personal media," whereas the Internet Archive is much broader in its collection. Both systems, however, utilize the same servers.

## Uploading a File

To upload a video to the Archive, click the Upload Your Own Movie link in the Moving Images section on the left side of the front page (see Figure 11-2).

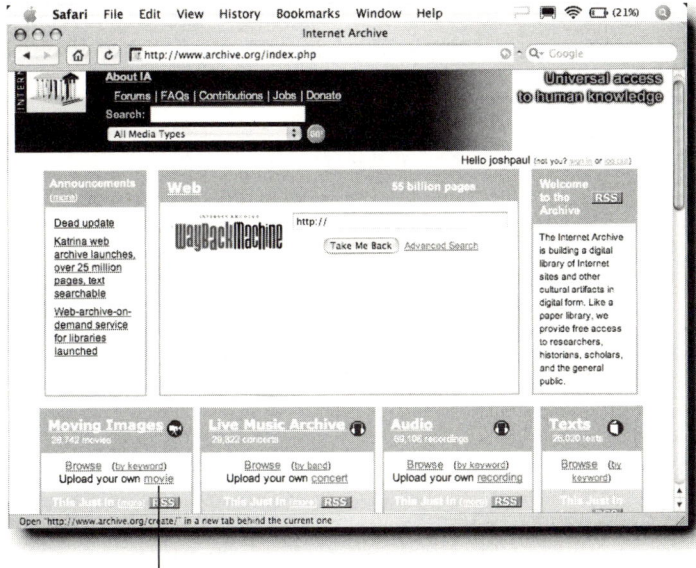

Click to upload your video.

**FIGURE 11-2: The Archive upload link.**

On the Create Item page, enter a name for the video you plan to upload (see Figure 11-3), and click the Create Item button.

Finally, upload your video, which can be as large as 2GB! If you use Internet Explorer as your browser, you can use the upload tool through the site. If you use a browser other than Internet Explorer, however, you'll have more success uploading if you use an FTP client (see Figure 11-4), as suggested by the Internet Archive.

Your uploaded file is moderated by a *curator*, who checks to see if the video contains copyrighted material. After 24 hours, you can check your Contributions (a link is on the front page) to find the direct URL to your video. You need to use this link in your videoblog post to enable people to download your video. The link will look something like this:

```
http://www.archive.org/download/LIMBO_TEASER_TRAILER/LIMBOTEASERTRAILER.mov
```

Videos uploaded with the Internet Archive (or Ourmedia) will exist as long as the Archive exists. As long as your videoblog is on the Internet, people can watch your videos.

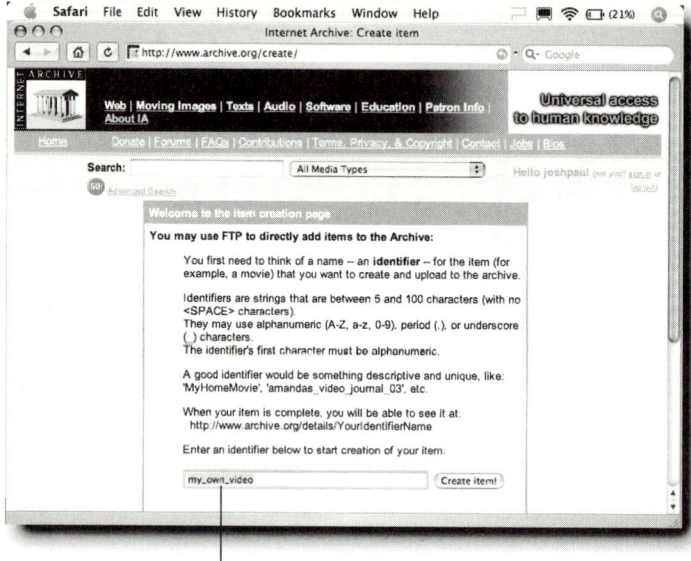

Identify your video.

FIGURE 11-3: Naming a video.

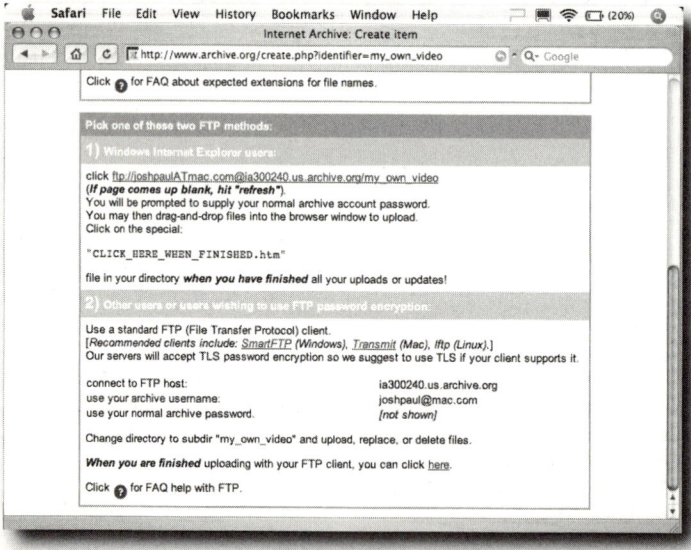

FIGURE 11-4: FTP suggestions from the Archive.

### ccPublisher

ccPublisher (www.creativecommons.org/tools/ccpublisher; free, Macintosh, Windows) is a file-upload tool that directly connects to the Internet Archive. It's a great tool that was created by Creative Commons (www.creativecommons.org).

After you download and install the program, you simply choose a video from your hard drive and follow the steps that ccPublisher walks you through to upload it. The major bonus of using ccPublisher is that it enables you to attach a Creative Commons license to your file, which communicates to the world what rights you reserve as the producer of the video.

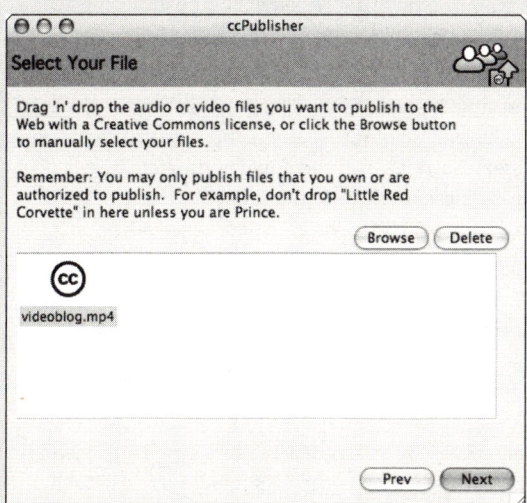

**Locating the URL for your video.**

As a producer, it's important for you to learn what rights you have for your work while still allowing people to share it. Creative Commons does this for you, in words (and symbols) that almost anyone can comprehend. ccPublisher makes the process of uploading and attaching a license nearly effortless.

Remember that the Archive is about permanent storage. Don't upload videos that you don't want to remain up forever or don't want the whole world to see. By using the Archive, you are adding to history, in addition to getting free storage.

## Using a Virtual Server

If you want to maintain complete control over your videoblog, including the type of software used to run it, the format of the video, and even the RSS feed, you need your own server.

Although that sounds expensive, a large number of web-hosting companies provide virtual servers for a very reasonable price. A favorite host for many videobloggers is DreamHost (www.dreamhost.com) and its Crazy Domain Insane hosting package.

## Signing Up

To sign up for service with DreamHost, simply go to www.dreamhost.com/shared and select a plan that suits your needs. Because you can always change your plan at a later date, you may want to select the Crazy Domain Insane plan, which is the most affordable (as of this writing, $7.95–$9.95 per month).

Then you can register a new domain, transfer an existing domain, or create a sub-domain within the DreamHosters.com site. Whichever you choose, you're on your way to having your own virtual server, a server shared among many people that allows you to have control over some of its functions. If you don't have a domain name but want one, register for one during the sign-up process.

Next, enter a username for your virtual server, as well as an initial email address. The username you select is used only to access your DreamHost account, and the email address doesn't have to be permanent. In fact, even the lowest level of service provides the capability for you to have *thousands* of email addresses.

Enter a WebID and Password, which is the actual information that DreamHost will use for your account. You'll also be required to enter your personal information, such as your address. Finally, you have to enter some payment information.

## Installing WordPress

WordPress is a flexible and popular blogging package. It is also free and an open source, which means the computer code for the application is available. DreamHost provides a one-click install of WordPress for its customers. Combined with the virtual server, it's a great solution for videobloggers.

To install WordPress, log in to your DreamHost account. Click the Goodies menu item on the left side of the screen to display a variety of tools that DreamHost provides, including its One-Click Installs. Select One-Click Installs and you get the opportunity to install WordPress by providing a little configuration information.

### Promo Codes

DreamHost often runs specials for new clients. If you're planning to sign up, do a quick search online to see if any specials are offered (they're not always listed at DreamHost). If you can't find any specials, use the promo code "vlog," which this book's authors have set up; it gives you up to $97 off the cost of the service.

### Customizing WordPress

WordPress is a very versatile piece of software, and many people contribute to its success. If you're not savvy with HTML or PHP, the computer language behind WordPress, you can still easily customize the look of your videoblog, as well as add really cool features. The creators of WordPress have allowed for themes and plug-ins, most of which are free, to be added.

For some themes and instructions on how to install them, visit:

- `http://wordpress.org/extend/themes/`

- `http://codex.wordpress.org/Using_Themes/Theme_List`

- `http://alexking.org/index.php?content=software/wordpress/themes.php`

- `http://themes.wordpress.net/theme-viewer.php`

- `http://bloggingpro.com/wordpress-theme-gallery`

For some plug-ins and instructions on how to install them, visit:

- `http://wiki.wordpress.org/Plugin`

- `http://dev.wp-plugins.org`

- `http://wp-plugins.net`

1. Select the WordPress Weblog item.

2. Enter a URL for your videoblog (leaving the field after the slash blank essentially makes WordPress your web site).

3. Enter some information for your database, including:

   - Name (for the database)

   - Hostname

   - Username

   - Password

The database information won't visually affect your videoblog. It's more for technical reasons and shouldn't ever interfere with anything you plan to do.

After entering the information, click the Install It For Me Now! button. Within 15 minutes you receive an email informing you of the installation and where to log in to complete the process.

## Configuring WordPress

When freshly installed, WordPress requires a few extra steps to work correctly. Fortunately, the steps are really simple:

1. Click the link enclosed in the email DreamHost sends upon the successful installation of WordPress. The link is similar to `http://www.domain.com/wp-admin/install.php` and leads you to a page like the one shown in Figure 11-5.

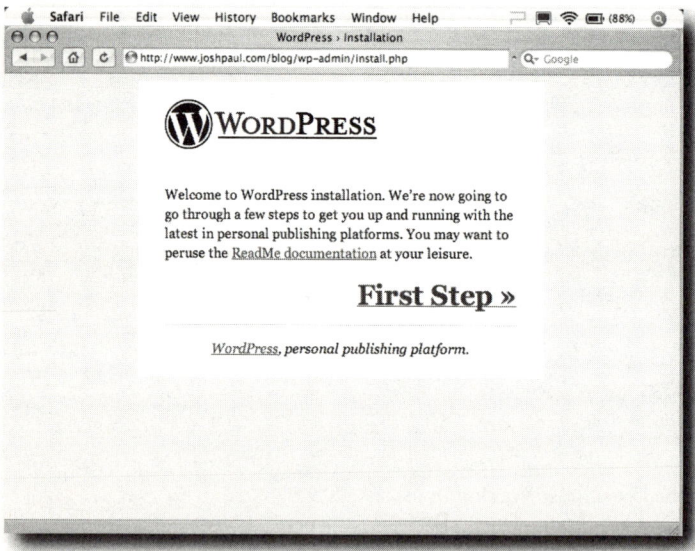

FIGURE 11-5: WordPress installation instructions.

2. Click the First Step link, which takes you to the actual first step of the installation. You'll need to enter a title for your videoblog and your email address (see Figure 11-6). Click the Continue to Second Step button.

3. The Second Step page opens (see Figure 11-7). Copy the password provided.

4. Click the log in link. Easy, huh?

5. Optionally (but recommended), change your password by clicking the Update Your Profile Or Change Your Password link. Enter your new password in the Update Password section of the page and save your changes.

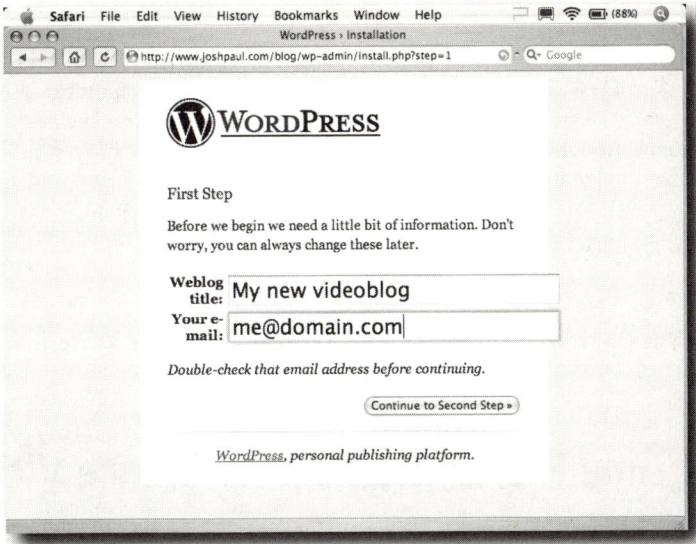

FIGURE 11-6: Configuring WordPress.

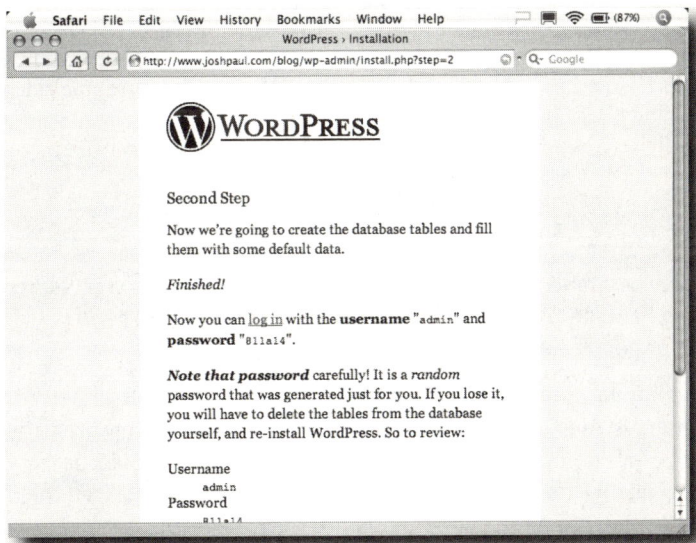

FIGURE 11-7: Completing WordPress installation.

## Posting

Obviously, you'll want to post to your new videoblog, and WordPress makes it a snap. Simply log in to your WordPress site, and click the Write button in the navigation bar. A Write Post page opens, where you can enter a title and a post. Although WordPress enables you to upload files directly, there are some limitations such as the allowed size of the file you can upload. If you have problems uploading with WordPress, use FTP or SCP to transfer your video to DreamHost.

Make sure that you embed your video correctly using HTML:

```
<a href="http://www.domain.com/path/to/video.mov" rel="enclosure">Watch</a>
```

When you're happy with your post, click the Publish button. That's it. You're now running your own virtual server, complete with storage, email, and a videoblog.

# Using QuickTime Pro to Create a Reference Video

A QuickTime reference video is like a small container that can load another QuickTime movie from any location on the Internet. Using a reference video is a simple solution that can enable you to move a video to a different server without breaking other people's links to it. It's kind of like a detour but without the confusing signs.

To create a QuickTime reference movie, you first need to obtain the URL to the full video you want to provide. For example, if you've placed a video in the Internet Archive and want people to access it, simply copy the direct URL for the video (not the page where it's embedded). Then open QuickTime Pro and select File → Open URL, type (or paste) the video's URL in the dialog box, and click OK.

### Using a Reference to Save Bandwidth

Dylan Verdi made a video, and her father, Michael, uploaded it to his web server. Dylan then linked to the video in her blog. A couple of days later, after the link had been passed all over the Internet, thousands of people linked to and downloaded the video.

To keep from exceeding his bandwidth and paying overage fees, Michael uploaded a copy of the video to the Internet Archive. The problem was that if Michael removed the original file from his server, not only would Dylan's link break (although that would be easy to fix), but everyone else's direct link to the video would break, too. So Michael replaced the original video (14MB) on his web server with a QuickTime reference movie (88KB).

When people follow the link to the video, they download only the reference video from Michael's server, and the full video loads from the Internet Archive. As a bonus, the reference video also allowed Michael to keep track of how many people accessed the video, by referring to the server's logs, even though it was no longer residing on his server.

QuickTime opens a new player window and begins to download the video from the URL you're provided. After it's fully loaded, select File → Save As. Check the Reference Movie option before clicking Save.

The new movie that you just saved is now a reference movie. Simply upload it to your web server, replacing the original file, and you're done. Now when someone accesses the file on your server, the QuickTime reference movie loads the full version from the Internet Archive.

# Distribute Video Using BitTorrent and Prodigem

Hosting video can be costly, especially if you release long or popular videos. And if you're releasing long and popular videos, well, you could wind up handing a blank check to your hosting provider. If you're like some people, you don't want to pay for hosting, but you also don't want to put your content on someone else's servers. Believe it or not, you can have your cake and eat it too. Remember the following name: BitTorrent.

BitTorrent is a popular file-sharing tool, often referred to as a peer-to-peer network, that turns your computer into a server. The files you can download using BitTorrent (called *torrents*) enable you to trade large video files without any bandwidth costs by harnessing the power of a distributed network.

**Note** BitTorrent is commonly associated with pirated videos and music. While it is true that many torrents are of copyrighted material, this has more to do with the people using BitTorrent than with the technology itself. There is a growing trend to use BitTorrent to serve up original content, and you can become part of it.

## Using BitTorrent

To use BitTorrent, you make a torrent of your video and then embed the torrent as a part of your videoblog post. When a BitTorrent user clicks the link to your torrent file, he starts downloading the video from your computer. That's pretty much how any peer-to-peer system works.

Sharing files via BitTorrent is a little more robust than doing so with other systems. Once someone has downloaded your video onto her computer, she is serving it as well. So, if a third person clicks the torrent link from your videoblog post, he starts downloading the video from your computer and the other user's at the same time!

The more people who download the video and subsequently share it, the more available it becomes. It's really a great solution, especially for people like you who want to share video.

One major caveat to using BitTorrent is that you have to "seed" your video to the network for the system to work. Seeding can be a lengthy process, requiring you to keep your connection to BitTorrent available the entire time. Fortunately, there are many sites and services to help you create torrents, but the easiest around is Prodigem (www.prodigem.com).

# Using Prodigem

The Prodigem service automates the process of creating a torrent and also "seeds" your video (does the initial hosting) to help make download speeds faster for your viewers. To use the service, you first need to sign up for an account. To do so, just go to www.prodigem.com and click the Create Account button.

## Creating an Account

Prodigem has different levels of service, some of which require a monthly fee. Other services offered include the capability to charge for people to download your content and to get more bandwidth. Initially, just sign up for a free account by clicking FREE and filling out the sign-up form.

## Uploading a Video

After logging in, click the My Content button. By doing so, you will be able to upload a video onto Prodigem's servers. Next, click "Browse" and locate the video you want to share on your hard drive. When you're ready, click the Upload button, and you'll see that your file is being sent to Prodigem.

## Creating a Torrent for the Video

To create a torrent, so that you can offer it to your audience, click the My Torrents button. This will allow you to actually make a torrent for the video you just uploaded. You should select the video, provide a title and description, and add a license, such as one from the Creative Commons. Next, click the Preview Torrent button. If everything looks good, click Create Torrent and your torrent will be created and made available to you.

## Posting a Torrent

Click the My Torrents button (again) to display a list of the torrents you've made. You can then click the torrent you want and view all of its relevant information. To obtain the URL to the torrent, right-click (or Control+click if you have a single-button mouse) the Get Torrent link, and copy the resulting link.

Once you have the torrent's URL, post to your vlog using the URL to link to the torrent. Then, whenever someone who uses BitTorrent downloads the torrent from your videoblog, he can download the related video quickly and easily.

BitTorrent and Prodigem can prove exceptionally useful should you ever produce a viral video that literally millions of people could download. Should that happen, you wouldn't have to worry about bandwidth costs or the server being shut down, because people are helping to distribute the video from their own computers. Although BitTorrent's technology is still relatively unused by the general population, it is continually being adopted. Also, some video aggregators are embracing torrents, so that you can subscribe to an RSS feed with torrents, making the whole process invisible. In the end, you and your viewers get cool videos to watch.

# Summary

Hosting can be viewed as an intimidating aspect of videoblogging. But once you take a closer look, you discover that hosting is really just serving a file from a server. . .and people have been doing that for a long time. Whether you choose to place your video on a public server, maintain your own (virtual or not), or distribute it using cutting-edge technology, you can reach a world-wide audience with relative ease.

# Really Simple Syndication

RSS is an acronym for Really Simple Syndication (sometimes called Rich Site Summary). It's a type of Extensible Markup Language (XML) that follows a specific design. It is a standardized format that enables weblogs, news sites, and other Internet content to be retrieved by Internet-connected applications, such as RSS-aware web browsers and aggregators.

## What Is RSS?

There are actually several different types of RSS (see Mark Pilgrim's Myth of RSS Compatibility at `http://diveintomark.org/archives/2004/02/04/incompatible-rss`) and a competing format called Atom (`www.atomenabled.org`). Fortunately, both RSS and Atom do the same thing: create a document describing the recent entries on a blog in a way that makes them very easy for computers to read. Thankfully, it's fairly easy for humans to read, too.

## Reading RSS

An RSS feed is composed of text, which means that it's mostly human readable. At first glance, an RSS feed may look like garbled text or even something out of *The Matrix*. Just take a look at this basic RSS feed, but don't be intimated and just look for familiar words:

```
<?xml version="1.0" encoding="utf-8"?>
<rss version="2.0">
<channel>
   <title>My Awesome Weblog</title>

<link>http://www.joshkinberg.com/blog/</link>
   <description>Welcome to My
Weblog.</description>
   <item>
      <title>This is the title of a blog
entry</title>
```

```
        <description>This is the content</description>
        <link>http://www.joshkinberg.com/blog/entry.html</link>
     </item>
  </channel>
</rss>
```

RSS organizes your blog as a `<channel>` containing an `<item>` element for each of your recent blog entries. There are typically anywhere between 15–30 recent items, although this example shows just one `<item>`. The `<channel>` must contain a `<title>`, `<description>`, and `<link>`. It may also include optional elements, such as `<author>`, `<lastBuildDate>`, `<copyright>`, and additional data known as "metadata."

Each `<item>` contains similar elements to `<channel>` that describe each of your blog entries. The RSS format is widely accepted and well understood; it enables you to easily syndicate your blog so that other computers, servers, devices, web sites, people, dogs, cats, or whatever can be notified when you update your blog and read your content across different formats, platforms, and devices. This makes your blog more portable, pushing it beyond the confines of a solitary web site.

RSS also benefits subscribers by making it easy and efficient to view content from many different web sites in one place. A user can easily scan hundreds of RSS subscriptions inside his news aggregator (a program for viewing RSS content) to quickly discover what's new and interesting. Some of the more popular aggregators include NetNewsWire (Mac OS X, $24.95; `www.ranchero.com/netnewswire`), FeedDemon (Windows, $29.95; `www.feeddemon.com`), and Liferea (Linux, free; `http://liferea.sourceforge.com`).

## RSS Provides More than Text

RSS works great for text, but what about media syndication such as the video for a vlog or the audio for a podcast? How to use standards such as RSS (which work great for text and static images to some extent) to syndicate audio/video content is being explored and hotly debated by geeks the world over.

RSS 2.0 (`http://blogs.law.harvard.edu/tech/rss`), a format championed by Dave Winer (`www.scripting.com`), deals with media syndication through the addition of an optional `<enclosure>` element. Enclosures can be added to each `<item>` (or blog entry) in your RSS feed. Here's a look at an RSS 2.0 enclosure:

```
<enclosure url="http://joshkinberg.com/blog/files/npr_vlog.mp3"
length="7771969" type="audio/mpeg" />
```

The `<enclosure>` element contains three attributes:

- `url` — An absolute link to the file
- `length` — The file size in bytes
- `type` — The registered mime-type of the file

Enclosures are similar to email attachments, enabling you to associate a file with a blog entry. While reading an RSS feed, a supporting aggregator automatically detects the enclosure file and downloads it. Moreover, an aggregator can be configured to download files via RSS enclosures on an automated schedule (say, while you are sleeping, so that the wait time for large file downloads doesn't become a usability issue). An enclosure could be any type of file, such as a PDF document, but here we're mostly talking about audio/video content.

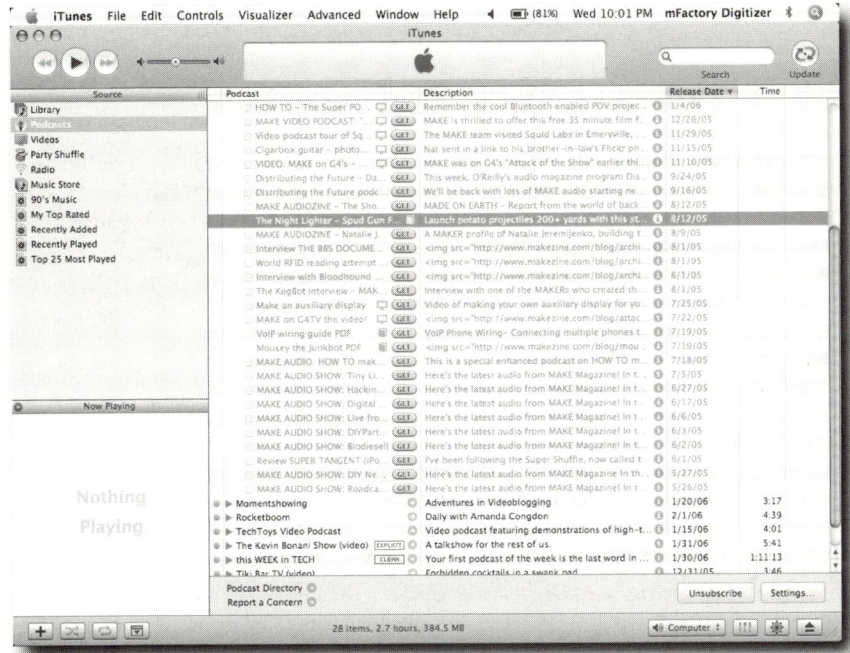

FIGURE 12-1: A PDF being distributed via iTunes. (Small icons indicate the types of files.)

The use of RSS is truly a revolution in content distribution. In essence, it's very close to micro-broadcasting — transforming a blog into your very own TV channel or radio network — available to anyone, anywhere, on demand.

Media distribution via RSS 2.0 with enclosures was essentially unused until 2004 when Adam Curry (www.curry.com) began using it to syndicate his homemade radio show, *The Daily Source Code*. Supporting aggregators, of which there were very few at the time, would automatically download the audio files and transfer them to iTunes. The user could then easily sync *The Daily Source Code* onto her iPod. Shortly thereafter, Podcasting was born.

## Beyond Podcasting

Podcasting is still in its early stages. At the moment, the term typically applies to the process of syndicating audio files via RSS 2.0 with enclosures. Even though Podcasting is audio-centric, the enclosure element in RSS 2.0 does not exclude other types of files or documents. Moreover, RSS 2.0 is not the only syndication format that supports enclosures. Atom and RSS 1.0 quickly adopted support for enclosures, each in their own way, though the element is still most prevalent in RSS 2.0, where it originated.

There have also been attempts to extend the rather simple enclosure element to something more suitable for media syndication. Media RSS is an extension proposed by Yahoo! to enable greater flexibility and added metadata for media syndication. Media RSS may be used in RSS 2.0 and Atom and can also be used to syndicate multiple files within a single `<item>`.

There are a couple key differences between the audio and video space. When dealing with audio, the MP3 format is pretty much ubiquitous — practically every audio player can play MP3s. In the video world, however, there is intense competition among companies and their incompatible proprietary formats, such as Windows Video, QuickTime, and Real. Also, video requires much more drive space and bandwidth to distribute.

## Mass Distribution

When Apple revealed that iTunes (`www.apple.com/itunes`) was going to deliver podcasts for free via the iTunes Music Store, it opened an avenue for independent audio producers to distribute their works to a very large audience (more than 30-million people have purchased iPods, and each is more than likely using iTunes). For comparison, television networks such as IFC (Independent Film Channel), DIY (Do It Yourself), and Tech TV reach approximately the same number of households.

The mechanism Apple chose to deliver podcasts was RSS because thousands of podcasters were already using it. By deciding on RSS, Apple also opened the avenue for video to be distributed (see Figure 12-2), which has worked extremely well for videobloggers. Anyone who can videoblog now has a potential audience that is larger than some cable networks can reach.

## The Future

Google and Yahoo! have both developed video search as a feature. In addition, Media RSS and the iTunes XML extensions to RSS guarantee that Internet-based video distribution is only going to get more interesting in the near future. How all of this will play out is anyone's guess . . . will iTunes become the next "network," competing with the likes of ABC, CBS, and NBC? Will Google? One thing is for sure: *You* can participate!

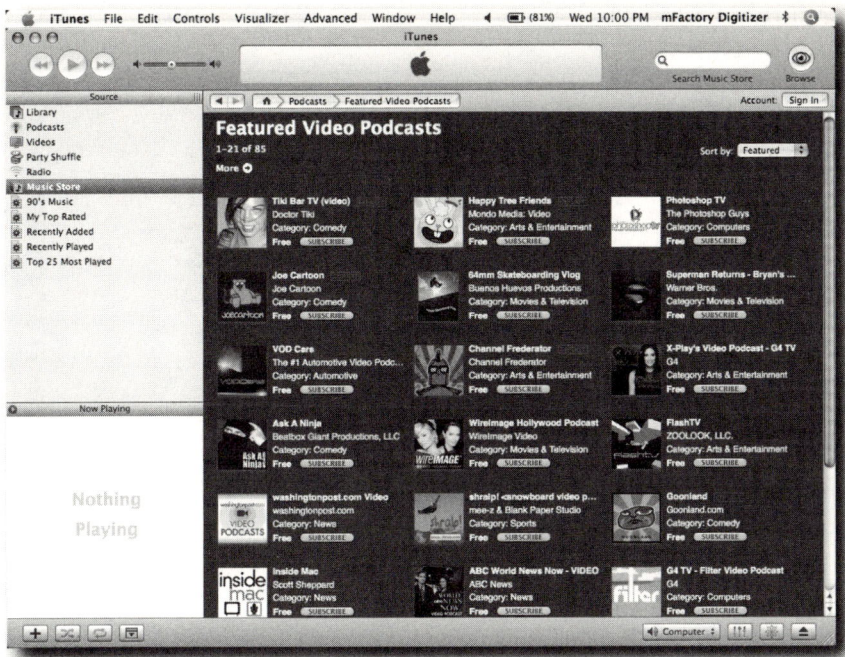

FIGURE 12-2: Video podcasts available through iTunes.

# FeedBurner: RSS Made Easy

Once you've created a blog, designed it to your liking, and added video . . . you aren't done with your videoblog. Right now, someone can type your blog's URL and watch the video on your site, but what fun is that? That's so 1999.

Videoblogging is revolutionary because anyone can subscribe to your videos and have the videos automatically sent to them anytime you create a new entry. Videoblogging enables people around the world to easily learn about each other through video.

## RSS and Aggregators

How is this subscription possible? Really Simple Syndication (RSS) and aggregators. RSS is used to notify people of new articles on a web site, and aggregators are used to collect the articles. Aggregators like Bloglines (www.bloglines.com; see Figure 12-3), NewsGator (www.newsgator.com), and Pluck (www.pluck.com) — which are all web based, meaning that you don't have to download anything — can all be used to subscribe to text-based blogs. People often compare using an aggregator to building your own newspaper out of the blogs you read (which is a bit like Netscape intended when it initially proposed the RSS concept).

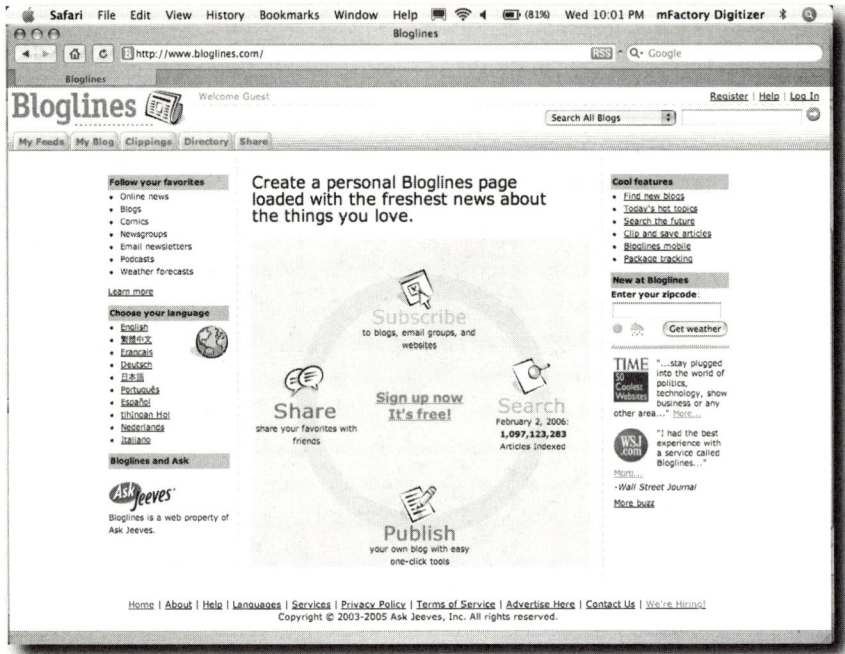

FIGURE 12-3: Bloglines is a web-based aggregator.

New aggregators such as FireAnt (www.fireant.tv; see Figure 12-4), Democracy (www.getdemocracy.org), Mefeedia (www.mefeedia.com), I/ON (http://openvision.tv/home/ion.html), and even Apple's iTunes (www.apple.com/itunes) all enable you to subscribe to video/audio blogs.

Once you have an aggregator, all you do is configure it for the videoblogs to which you want to subscribe, and it automatically downloads videos whenever new ones are posted. As a viewer, you simply wake up in the morning and watch your own "TV channel" with video that you have chosen!

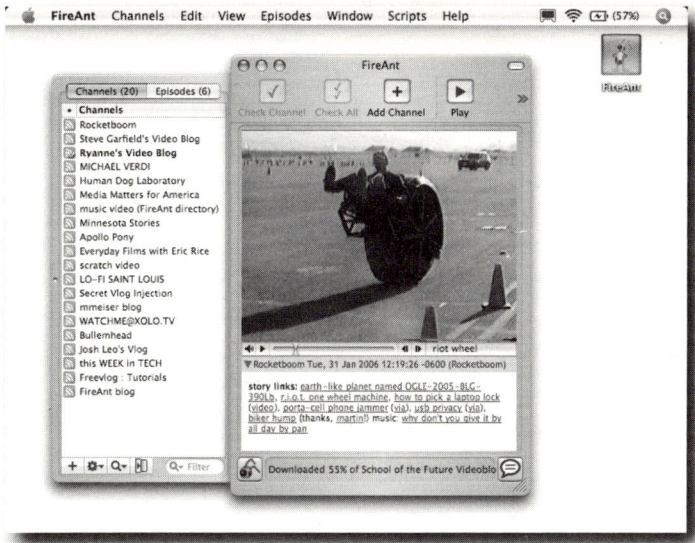

FIGURE 12-4: FireAnt is a desktop video aggregator.

## Distributing Video Using RSS

As a producer, you can now distribute your video worldwide through a videoblog. You do this with an RSS feed. But not just any RSS feed will do — after all, there are seven different versions. To successfully distribute video via RSS, you need an RSS 2.0 feed with enclosures. This format lets aggregators discover the video in an RSS feed and automatically download it.

Most blogging platforms do not automatically come with RSS 2.0 feeds with enclosures. For example, Blogger (www.blogger.com) creates an ATOM feed, which is similar to but different from RSS, and TypePad (www.typepad.com) creates an RSS 1.0 feed. So what's a videoblogger to do, short of writing her own RSS feed?

One turnkey solution is to use FeedBurner (www.feedburner.com) to create an RSS 2.0 feed with enclosures for you. Because it's a free service, it's one that many videobloggers use. Another bonus is that it can be set up in about two minutes. To use FeedBurner:

1. Point your web browser to FeedBurner (www.feedburner.com).

2. Sign up for a free account by clicking the Register link and following the necessary steps (Figure 12-5).

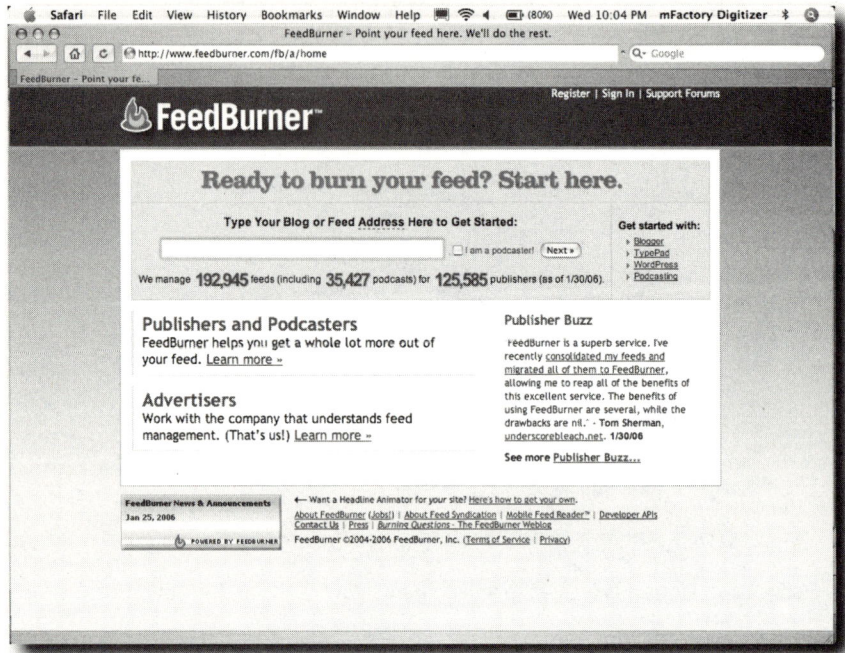

FIGURE 12-5: FeedBurner is a free RSS2 service.

**3.** Enter your blog's URL or your existing feed's URI.

**4.** Enable your new FeedBurner feed, and select the SmartCast option (check the I'm A Podcaster box), which is what adds videos as "enclosures" to your feed, allowing aggregators to automatically download your videos. (An enclosure is kind of like a letter inside an envelope — an enclosure inside your feed.)

**5.** FeedBurner gives you a new feed URI for distribution. Aggregators will need the URI to access the FeedBurner-created RSS feed.

**6.** Finally, choose Publicize to generate a "chicklet" that you can put on your blog. A chicklet is a small graphic that informs people about your feed. It comes in the form of HTML code that you add to your blog's template. Various blogging platforms let you customize the template differently.

The badge on your blog lets visitors know that your videos can be subscribed to using an aggregator. In addition, FeedBurner collects statistics so you will know how many people are subscribing to your videos. FeedBurner also offers a number of other features; some are considered "Pro" and cost money. However, the majority of the features available via FeedBurner are free.

# Create RSS Enclosures in Movable Type

Although enclosures were part of the RSS 2.0 spec when it was written in 2002, most blogging platforms do not natively add <enclosure> elements to the RSS feeds they generate. Luckily for Movable Type users, there is an excellent plug-in written by Brandon Fuller called MTEnclosures (http://brandon.fuller.name/archives/hacks/mtenclosures). MTEnclosures will discover links to media files in your blog entries and then convert them to <enclosure> elements in your RSS feed. You can also set certain filters on the plug-in — to create enclosures only for audio, only for video, or only for a specific file type, for example.

## How to Use MTEnclosures

To start using MTEnclosures, download the plug-in from http://brandon.fuller. name/archives/hacks/mtenclosures. Then upload the Enclosures.pl file to your Movable Type plugins directory. (If you discover that you don't have a plugins directory, create one in the same location as your mt.cgi file.)

**Tip**  If you're using FTP, make sure you upload using ASCII mode.

To take advantage of the new plug-in, add the new MTEntryEnclosures tag to your Movable Type RSS 2.0 template as:

```
<MTEntries lastn="15">
    <item>
        ...
        <$MTEntryEnclosures$>
    </item>
</MTEntries>
```

Once installed, the plug-in searches all URLs inside of HREFs, checking against a list of valid media file types. Simply add a media link URL to one of your blog entries; for example:

```
<a href="http://joshkinberg.com/blog/files/tornado.mov">Watch
this!</a>
```

The MTEnclosures plug-in then performs its magic to create the correct RSS enclosure elements, and your subscribers can successfully download your videos automatically.

If you have any trouble, be sure to check the Movable Type Activity Log for errors.

## Enhancing MTEnclosures

There are some extra parameters you can use to gain better control over which files and URLs will generate enclosures. For example, if you want to create enclosures for video files but not for audio, images, or other file types, you can do so by modifying the MTEntryEnclosures tag in your RSS 2.0 template like this:

```
<$MTEntryEnclosures mime_include="video"$>
```

Or if you want both audio and video files to generate enclosures:

```
<$MTEntryEnclosures mime_include="video|audio"$>
```

Or perhaps you just want to exclude images:

```
<$MTEntryEnclosures mime_exclude="image"$>
```

Sometimes you may link to remote media files on the web that are not hosted on your own server. If so, you might not want these to generate enclosures in your RSS feed. To restrict downloads only to files that are local to your or your host's server, set the plug-in's remote parameter to zero:

```
<$MTEntryEnclosures remote="0"$>
```

Remote versus Local is determined by comparing the URL of the enclosure file with the URL of your weblog, which is obtained from your weblog's configuration. Basically, if your enclosure file is being distributed from the same server as your blog, MTEnclosures can determine that the file is local. Otherwise, it will determine that the file is remote.

For more information on more advanced usage of the MTEnclosures plug-in, visit `http://brandon.fuller.name/archives/hacks/mtenclosures`.

# Fix FeedBurner to Work with WMV Files

How often have you thought, "Hey, FeedBurner is not creating enclosures for my .wmv files!"? Okay, even if you haven't, keep reading and you'll never have to. WMV files not showing up as RSS enclosures is a common problem for users of FeedBurner, but there is a solution.

The cause of the problem is likely that the server does not know the correct WMV mime-type. If this setting is not available to the web server, the server responds with a mime-type of `text/plain` whenever WMV files are requested. This is fairly common because WMV is a fairly new type.

FeedBurner relies on mime-types to create enclosures, and the correct mime-type for WMV is `video/x-ms-wmv`. If your server responds with `text/plain`, FeedBurner won't discover the video file. This occurs even if you have enabled FeedBurner's SmartCast option, which enables FeedBurner to create enclosures for any link that returns a type other than `text/` or `image/`.

You can add the correct mime-type to your server even if you don't have administrator's access. If your server is using Apache, and most are, simply create a file named `.htaccess` that defines the correct mime-type, and upload it to the same directory where you host your WMV videos. Here's how:

1. Because files that begin with a dot are traditionally hidden from view, you'll need to create a text file named `dot-htaccess`. It should include only the following line:

   ```
   AddType video/x-ms-wmv .wmv
   ```

2. Upload the `dot-htaccess` file to your server, probably by using FTP in ASCII mode, and put it in the same directory where you store your video files. You will need to add the file to every directory where you store WMV video files for distribution.

3. After placing the file, rename it `.htaccess`. If you are using a graphical tool to upload the file, it may disappear from view when you rename it. (That's okay, because files that begin with a dot are normally hidden from view.)

You should now be good to go. By adding the `.htaccess` file to the server, the server should respond with the correct mime-type for WMV files, and FeedBurner will happily create enclosures in your feed.

# Redirect an Existing Feed to FeedBurner

If you've had a blog for a while with an existing RSS feed, your readers are likely subscribed to your feed's current URL in their news aggregators. How can you painlessly migrate their requests from your old server/feed to your newly burned FeedBurner feed? Easy.

## Apache's mod_rewrite

For this hack to work, your web host will need to be Apache-based and have `mod_rewrite` installed. `mod_rewrite` is a URL rewriting engine, which basically means that it can intercept an incoming URL request and change it. Many people use this feature to make user-readable URLs while seamlessly referring the user to a buried or dynamically created page on the server. In this case, you'll use `mod rewrite` to redirect to an off-site location.

The best way to determine if `mod_rewrite` is installed is to configure the rewrite rules and see if they work. If they don't, speak to your host and find out how you can get it enabled.

## Choose Your Feed URL

Choose an easy-to-remember feed URL for your site. It must be different from any of the existing feed URLs to prevent interfering with your web-hosting software. Some examples you should *not* use are:

- `http://example.com/index.xml` (used by MovableType/Typepad)
- `http://example.com/feed` (used by WordPress)
- `http://example.com/rss.xml` (used by Radio)

Using something like `http://example.com/rss` should work well, so let's use that as the example for generating the rules.

## Generate the .htaccess File

Several blogging engines generate `mod_rewrite` rules for you, so check on your site to see if a file named `.htaccess` already exists within your blog. If it does, download it so that you can edit it. However, make sure that you rename it `dot-htaccess` or else it might become invisible to you. If it doesn't exist on your site, just open a blank text file, using Notepad on Windows or TextEdit on Mac, and type the rules.

First, you need a statement that checks for the `mod_rewrite` engine and a statement to turn `mod_rewrite` rules on for this directory:

```
<IfModule mod_rewrite.c>
RewriteEngine On
```

Next, set the base directory for the rules to operate on. If your videoblog is set up in a subdirectory like `http://example.com/blog/`, this is where you'd set that. For this instance, this example is set up in the blog subdirectory, so it'll be `/blog/` (but if it were in a directory called giggle, the base directory would be `/giggle/`):

```
RewriteBase /blog/
```

Then add a condition that redirects everyone except FeedBurner:

```
RewriteCond %{HTTP_USER_AGENT} !FeedBurner
```

This is necessary if you are redirecting your blog's regular RSS feed, because FeedBurner needs to access the original feed to do its job.

Now set up the rule that will redirect from `http://example.com/rss` to the FeedBurner URL:

```
RewriteRule ^rss$ http://feeds.feedburner.com/Example [R=301,L]
```

The special characters are significant, and if you want more details about how `mod_rewrite` rules are created, please see the mod_write URL Rewriting Guide.

In redirecting your blog's RSS feed to FeedBurner's, be aware of certain characters that `mod_rewrite` uses in special ways. For example, a period is used by `mod_rewrite` to represent *any* character. So to indicate that you want a period to be interpreted as a period, you need to "escape" it using a backslash. For example, `RewriteRule ^index\.xml$` works against anything starting with `index.xml`.

---

### Wait! I Have a Feed in WordPress!

If you already have readers subscribed to your existing WordPress RSS feed, you need to redirect them to your new FeedBurner feed using the existing RSS URL that your subscribers are using. For WordPress, there is a plug-in for working with FeedBurner-created feeds at `http://orderedlist.com/articles/wordpress-feedburner-plugin`.

For more information, see the mod_write URL Rewriting Guide at `httpd.apache.org/docs/2.0/misc/rewriteguide.html`.

After you've entered the rules, save the file as `dot-htaccess` somewhere on your computer and remember where you've saved it.

## Upload the .htaccess File

Now upload the `.htaccess` to the base directory you specified on your server. If you were editing a `.htaccess` you downloaded from your web host, delete the `.htaccess` that's already there before uploading the new one. Open your favorite FTP program and upload the file you named `dot-htaccess` to the server. Now rename the file `.htaccess`. Do not be alarmed if the file disappears from the file listing; by default, most FTP clients hide files beginning with a period.

Once you've uploaded and renamed the file, `mod_rewrite` should be activated and using the instructions you entered. If everything is working correctly, you can access your FeedBurner feed from the URL you set up. To test it, open your web browser and point it to your web site, followed by the name you gave your feed URL (for example, `http://example.com/rss`), and make sure it redirects to your FeedBurner URL.

## Finish Up

Lastly, you need to make sure all the links in your blog template that point to your RSS feed are now pointing to your new feed URL. Refer to your specific blog software documentation for how to do this, but you want to make certain you change not only the link visible on the page but also the `<link>` tags in the header that point to the RSS feed for people who use FireFox, Safari, and others to auto-find your feed address.

# Summary

RSS is an ideal solution for distributing video online because it integrates seamlessly with the web and also allows video to be obtained through other means. Also, it's easy to use. Through RSS, the Internet is capable of enabling a new medium of communication.

# Getting Video into a Web Page

**J**ust because you've managed to place video on a server doesn't mean it's a part of your videoblog. To have people watch your video, you have to embed or link to the video file. There are a few techniques to do so, and some are more technical than others, but all of them are easy to implement.

## Using the <object> Tag

Hypertext Markup Language (HTML) is the language of the web. It is made up of tags that describe to a web browser how it should display the representative content. One such tag is <embed>, which enables you to place rich media, like video, in a web page (see Figure 13-1).

Embedding a video enables you to create a more pleasant experience for your viewers and also provides you the opportunity to "brand" your videos within the context of your site. Simply using a direct link to your video forces the browser to display only the video, as shown in Figure 13-2.

Because of a patent infringement, however, Microsoft had to change the way Internet Explorer handles media, so all versions of Internet Explorer after 5.5 SP2 work only with an <object> tag. To place video in a web page successfully so that people using various browsers can view it, you need to use both the <embed> and <object> tags.

Using <object>and <embed> is pretty easy, as long as you pay attention to the details. Specifically, you need to use certain strings of text, technically labeled classids, depending on the type of video you're using. For example, if you are distributing QuickTime, you'll use a classid of 02BF25D5-8C17-4B23-BC80-D3488ABDDC6B. Don't be intimidated . . . just follow along.

FIGURE 13-1: A video embedded in a web page.

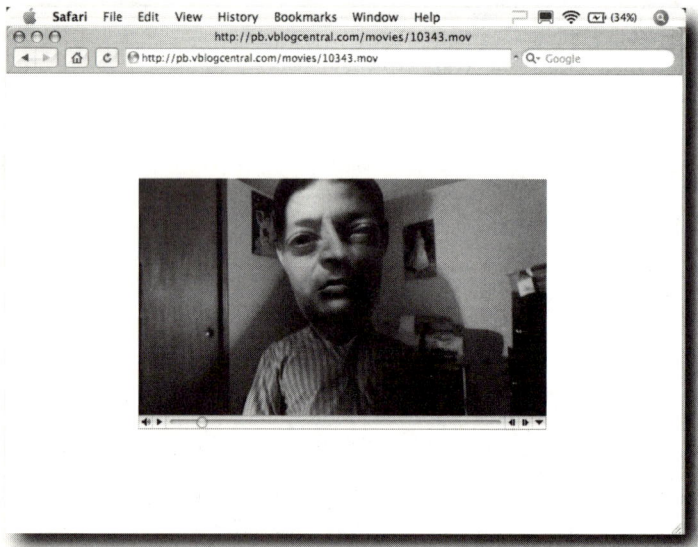

FIGURE 13-2: A video directly playing in a web page.

There are really four critical pieces of information you need to know to embed a video onto a web page:

- The type of video you're using (that is, QuickTime, Windows Media, or Flash)
- The height of the video
- The width of the video
- The URL to the video

As long as you know those, you'll have no problems.

A note regarding the occurrence of < and >: They are indicators to the web browser of the beginning of technical information, not just text. Text that occurs between <>s is called a tag and is used to give instructions to the browser. As such, it is essentially hidden from the reader. Tags usually occur in pairs, one to open and one to close. In a nutshell, it works like:

```
<tag>(some information)</tag>
```

Okay, on to the fun.

## The HTML

To embed a QuickTime video, add the following HTML:

```
<object classid="clsid:02BF25D5-8C17-4B23-BC80-D3488ABDDC6B" ⊃
width="320" height="256" codebase = ⊃
"http://www.apple.com/qtactivex/qtplugin.cab">
    <param name="src" value="my_video.mov">
    <param name="pluginspage" value=⊃
"http://www.apple.com/quicktime/download/index.html">
    <embed width="320" height="256" src="my_video.mov" ⊃
pluginspage="http://www.apple.com/quicktime/download/index.html">
    </embed>
</object>
```

**Caution**

You must add 16 pixels to the height of your video to provide room for the movie controller. For example, if your video is 320x240, enter the width as 320 and the height as 256.

To embed a Windows Media video, add the following HTML:

```
<object classid="clsid:6BF52A52-394A-11D3-B153-00C04F79FAA6" ⊃
width="320" height="240" codebase = "http:// ⊃
activex.microsoft.com/activex/controls/mplayer/en/nsmp2inf.cab">
    <param name="url" value="my_video.wmv">
    <param name="pluginspage" value=" ⊃
```

```
http://www.microsoft.com/windows/windowsmedia/">
    <embed width="320" height="240" url="my_video.wmv" ↵
pluginspage="http://www.microsoft.com/windows/windowsmedia/">
    </embed>
</object>
```

If you look closely, you'll notice that there are only subtle differences, but those differences make a huge distinction.

 On April 11, 2006, Microsoft released an update for Internet Explorer 6 that changed how the browser loads certain elements, including those that use the <object> and <embed> tags. Because of this change, viewers using the patched version of the browser will have to confirm that they want to view the video by clicking through a dialog box that states "Click to run an ActiveX control on this webpage." If you would prefer your video to load without this requirement, refer to the "Using JavaScript to Embed Video" section in this chapter. Other browsers such as Firefox (http://www.mozilla.com/firefox) and video aggregators are not affected. Understanding the Code

Examining the code line by line will help you understand it better.

First, you want to inform the web browser that there is an `object` that needs to be rendered:

```
<object
```

Then you provide the `classid` of the object so that the web browser can identify it. You can think of the `classid` as a unique identifier for a type of file, kind of like Ford is an identifier for a type of vehicle. The `classid` for each type of media is always the same:

- For QuickTime, use:

  ```
  classid="clsid:02BF25D5-8C17-4B23-BC80-D3488ABDDC6B"
  ```

- For Windows Media, use:

  ```
  classid="clsid:6BF52A52-394A-11D3-B153-00C04F79FAA6"
  ```

Next, you provide the width of the video:

```
width="320"
```

And its height:

```
height="240"
```

Finally, you provide a `codebase`, which provides a URL where the web browser can obtain more information about the object's inherent attributes. This will always be the same. You should take note of the >, because it is an indicator to the web browser of the end of the tag's information.

- For QuickTime, you'll use:

```
codebase = "http://www.apple.com/qtactivex/qtplugin.cab">
```

- For Windows Media, you'll use:

```
codebase = "http://activex.microsoft.com/activex/ ↩
controls/mplayer/en/nsmp2inf.cab">
```

You then provide additional information as parameters to the `object` tag. The parameters are indicated using `param` tags. A parameter requires a `name` and a `value`. You can think of this like a dictionary. For example, the *word* (name) car has the *meaning* (value) of "a motor vehicle with four wheels." The web browser looks at a name and finds an associated value.

Because the web browser needs to know the location, or source, of the video file, you provide the `src` or `url` parameter name and assign it the value of a URL:

- For QuickTime, you use a video file with one of the QuickTime compatible file extensions, which include `.mov`, `.mp4`, `.m4v`, and `.mpg`. The most common is `.mov`.

```
<param name="src" value="my_video.mov">
```

- For Windows Media, you use a video file with one of the Windows Media compatible file extensions, which include: `.wmv`, `.asf`, and `.avi`. The most common is `.wmv`.

```
<param name="url" value="my_video.wmv">
```

There is a large set of names available for use. One that is quite helpful for your audience is the `pluginspage`, which provides information about where they can download the necessary plug-in to view the video if they don't already have it installed. The `value` for this parameter should always be the same:

- For QuickTime:

```
<param name="pluginspage" value= ↩
"http://www.apple.com/quicktime/download/index.html">
```

- For Windows Media:

```
<param name="pluginspage" value=" ↩
http://www.microsoft.com/windows/windowsmedia/">
```

The next two sections provide an overview of QuickTime and Windows Media parameter options. Then you'll take a look at the last of the code.

## QuickTime Parameter Options

There are a variety of options you can use when embedding a QuickTime video in a web page. Following are brief descriptions of them.

| Option | Description |
|---|---|
| AUTOHREF | Automatically opens the viewer's browser to the URL specified in the HREF attribute (used in conjunction with the HREF attribute). |
| AUTOPLAY | Causes the video to start playing automatically upon loading. |
| BGCOLOR=HEX | Sets the background color of the video to the HEX value (FFFFFF, for example). |
| BGCOLOR=NAME | Sets the background color of the video to the NAME value (such as WHITE). |
| CACHE | Determines whether the viewer's browser can cache the video. |
| CONTROLLER | Indicates whether the playback control should be visible. |
| DONTFLATTENWHENSAVING | Determines how the viewer can save the video. |
| ENABLEJAVASCRIPT | Enables JavaScript control over the QuickTime player. |
| ENDTIME | Indicates at what time the video should stop playing. |
| HEIGHT | Required to determine the display height of the video. |
| HIDDEN | Controls whether the video is visible. |
| HREF | Sets the URL where the viewer's browser should open when the video is clicked. |
| KIOSKMODE | When enabled, prohibits the viewer from saving the video. |
| LOOP | Indicates whether the video should play continuously. |
| MOVEID | Used to identify a video by number when more than one may be playing. |
| MOVIENAME | Used to identify a video by name when more than one may be playing. |
| PLAYEVERYFRAME | Causes the video to play every frame so that no frames are skipped. |
| PLUGINSPAGE | A URL where the viewer can download the latest version of QuickTime. |
| QTNEXTn | A video to play after the current video ends. |
| QTSRC | Forces the viewer's browser to use QuickTime to view the video. |
| QTSRCCHOKESPEED | Restricts the speed in which a viewer can download the video. |
| QTSRCDONTUSEBROWSER | Causes QuickTime instead of the viewer's browser to download the video. |
| SCALE | Determines how to scale the video, given the height and width parameters. |
| SRC | URL required by the browser so that it can locate the actual video file. |

| Option | Description |
|---|---|
| STARTTIME | The time at which the video should start playing. |
| TARGET | Where QuickTime should open a URL. |
| TARGETCACHE | Allows the browser to cache the video prior to playing it when used in conjunction with a Movie Poster. |
| TYPE=MIMEtype | Helps the browser determine which plug-in to use; best to use video/QuickTime. |
| URLSUBSTITUTEn | Used to replace URLs in HREF tracks. |
| VOLUME | Sets the volume of the video. |
| WIDTH | Required to determine the display width of the video. |

Only three of them are required: src, height, and width. All the others are optional. A comprehensive list of the options and their implementation is available at www.apple.com/quicktime/tutorials/embed2.html.

## Windows Media Parameter Options

Microsoft also provides a variety of options to provide greater control over the embedding of video into a web page. In brief, they are:

| Option | Description |
|---|---|
| autoStart | Causes the video to start playing automatically upon loading. |
| balance | Determines how stereo audio should be played. |
| baseURL | Indicates the base URL of the video. |
| captioningID | The name of the video to display captions. |
| currentPosition | Indicates the current position of the video in seconds. |
| currentMarker | Identifies the current marker number. |
| defaultFrame | Indicates where Windows Media should open a URL. |
| enableContextMenu | Determines whether the context menu should be enabled. |
| enabled | Indicates whether the playback control should be visible. |
| fullScreen | Causes the video to play at full-screen resolution. |
| invokeURLs | Determines whether URLs should open a web browser. |
| mute | Mutes the audio. |
| playCount | Indicates how many times a video should play. |

*Continued*

| Option | Description |
|---|---|
| rate | Determines the playback rate of a video. |
| SAMIFileName | Indicates where a closed-caption file resides. |
| SAMILang | Determines the language for closed captioning. |
| SAMIStyle | Indicates the style of closed captioning to use. |
| stretchToFit | Determines to scale the video to the size of the video player. |
| uiMode | Determines the type of controls the player should display. |
| URL | URL required by the browser so that it can locate the actual video file. |
| volume | Sets the volume of the video. |
| windowlessVideo | Causes the video to display directly in the browser without the player. |

Only three of the parameters are actually required: url, height, and width. A comprehensive list of the parameters and their implementation is available at `http://msdn.microsoft.com/ library/default.asp?url=/library/en-us/wmplay10/mmp_sdk/paramtags.asp`.

## Enabling Deployment by Other Browsers

Because browsers other than Internet Explorer may not implement the `object` tag, you should also utilize the `embed` tag, which is similar but more succinct. Following is an example:

```
<object ...
    ...>
    <embed width="320" height="240" src="my_video.mov" pluginspage
= "http://www.apple.com/quicktime/download/index.html">
    </embed>
</object>
```

Here are the details:

1. Open an `embed` tag inside the `object` tag:

```
<object ...
    <embed
```

2. Provide the width and height:

```
width="320"
height="256"
```

3. Provide the source (`src` or `url`) of the video as a URL. Here are examples of `src` for QuickTime and `url` for Windows Media:

```
src="my_video.mov"
```

```
url="my_video.wmv"
```

**4.** Provide a `pluginspage` for viewers who don't have the correct plug-in installed. Here are examples for QuickTime and Windows Media:

```
pluginspage = "http://www.apple.com/quicktime/↵
download/index.html">
```

```
pluginspage="http://www.microsoft.com/windows/windowsmedia/">
```

Because this is the last option going into the embed tag, end it with a >.

**5.** To indicate to the browser that you have finished providing information for the embed tag, you simply close the embed tag, like this:

```
</embed>
```

**6.** And ensure that the object is closed, too:

```
</object>
```

As mentioned earlier, practically all HTML tags (and XML, SMIL, and so on) work the same way, with opening (`<tag>`) and closing (`</tag>`) tags. The tags are the same except that the closing one is prepended by a forward slash (/).

Whether you choose to use QuickTime, Windows Media, or both, you now have the ability to embed your video in your videoblog.

# Embedding QuickTime with a Poster Frame

A poster frame is a unique solution for presenting QuickTime within a web page. It is basically a single frame of video embedded in your videoblog that, when clicked, loads the represented video in its entirety. This solution builds on the premise of the `object` tag but requires some additional preparation.

## Creating a Poster Frame

Because a poster frame is a single frame of video (see Figure 13-3), you need to export it from the video you plan to distribute. Here's how to get started:

**1.** Open the QuickTime video file by launching QuickTime and selecting File → Open. Alternatively, you can just double-click the video file in the Finder or Explorer.

**2.** Locate a single frame of video that you want to display. Select a frame that is visually interesting to entice viewers to click and watch the video.

**3.** Click and drag the video image to the desktop. This creates a single-frame QuickTime video — a poster frame.

**4.** Rename the frame. (As always, avoid using spaces or any nonalphanumeric characters.)

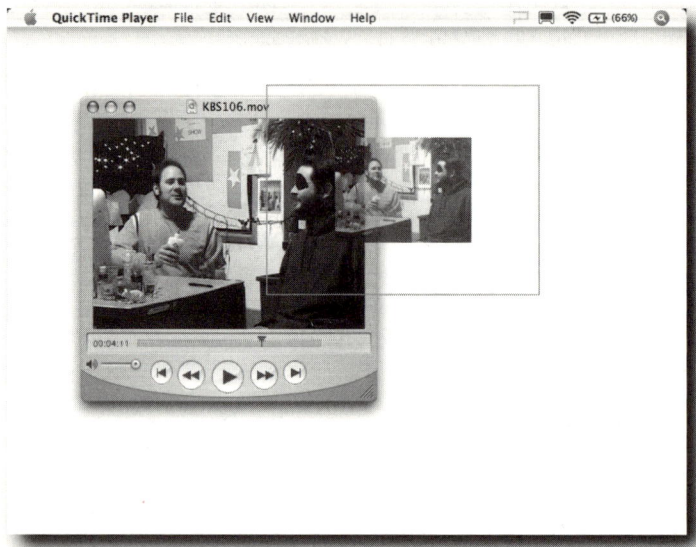

FIGURE 13-3: Creating a poster frame from QuickTime.

## Creating the HTML

To embed the poster frame, use the `object` tag, with a couple of optional parameters:

```
<object classid="clsid:02BF25D5-8C17-4B23-BC80-D3488ABDDC6B"
width="320" height="240" codebase =
"http://www.apple.com/qtactivex/qtplugin.cab">
    <param name="src" value="my_poster_frame_video.mov">
    <param name="pluginspage"
value="http://www.apple.com/quicktime/download/index.html">
    <param name="href" value="my_complete_video.mov">
    <param name="target" value="myself">
    <param name="contoller" value="false">

    <embed width="320" height="240" src="
my_poster_frame_video.mov"
pluginspage="http://www.apple.com/quicktime/download/index.html"
href="my_complete_video.mov" target="myself" controller="false">
    </embed>
</object>
```

Note that the `src` for the video is the poster-frame video, not the complete video. That's because you are embedding the poster frame that, when clicked, will load the complete video. You should also notice the optional parameters:

- `href` — Informs the QuickTime plug-in of the complete video's URL.

- `target` — Tells QuickTime that it should load the complete video over the poster frame.

- `controller` — Informs the QuickTime plug-in whether to display a video controller.

With the two video files and your HTML, you're set to embed your QuickTime video using a poster frame. Considering how simple this solution is, and how little time and effort it takes, the payoff is well worth it. Even though you have to upload two video files to your server, you probably want to use this technique for all of your videoblog posts.

# Creating a PHP Pop-up Window

Usually when you link to a `.mov` file in your web browser, it automatically plays in the browser using the QuickTime plug-in. If the `.mov` file is compressed with Fast Start enabled, it begins auto-playing while the download is still in progress. This is not the case in Internet Explorer (IE), because of the way it handles the QuickTime plug-in.

With IE, a `.mov` file does not Fast Start unless it is embedded in an HTML page; otherwise, the whole video must download before it begins playing in the browser. Luckily, this is not the case in any other web browser (FireFox, Safari, Opera, and so on). However, IE is the most widely used browser, which means that many viewers may be frustrated by the experience of watching your videoblog unless you embed the video in HTML so it can Fast Start.

Files with the `.wmv` extension, on the other hand, do not play automatically from a direct link in any browser. Instead, they launch in Windows Media Player and begin streaming. If you've ever experienced this process, you know that you could be stuck watching the video buffer indefinitely. This problem can be avoided by embedding your video in HTML, which makes viewing in the browser much smoother. To see this in action using your own video, visit `http://embedthevideo.com`.

**Tip** If you're using a blogging service that doesn't allow you to use PHP, don't worry. You can use Embed the Videos (`http://embedthevideo.com`) free pop-up creation service to resolve your predicament.

## A Little Code

The fundamental idea here is to pass the location of your video file from the URL to the script so that it can write the HTML to embed the video into the web page properly. With this solution, you need only create one pop-up window that will load any movie you throw at it, rather than creating a new HTML page for each video. So the URL query should look like this:

`http://yoursite.com/popup.php?url=http://path/to/video.mov`

The portion following the question mark tells PHP that there is a url variable and its value (=) is the location of your video file (http://path/to/video.mov). You can enable PHP to use this variable and place it into the resulting HTML embed code.

Now that you understand the basic premise, take a look at the full PHP code. In your text editor, create a new document called popup.php and type the following:

```php
<?php

if ($_GET['url'])
  $url = $_GET['url'];

// get file extension
$url_array - split("/", $url);
$filename = $url_array[sizeof($url_array)-1];
$file_array = explode(".", $filename);
$file_ext = strtolower($file_array[sizeof($file_array)-1]);

?>
```

The first statement inside the PHP block gets the url variable passed from the query string. The next set of statements determines the file extension of the video.

After this, you want to print a standard HTML header with a bit of CSS styling:

```html
<html>
<head>

<title>Video</title>

<style>
body {
  background-color: #000000;
  text-align: center;
  margin: 10px;
  padding: 0px;
  color:#CCCCCC;
  font-size:12px;
  font-family: Arial, Verdana, Helvetica, sans-serif;
}

a {
  font-size:12px;
  color:#CCCCCC;
  text-decoration:none;
}

a:hover {
  text-decoration: underline;
}

</style>
</head>
```

```
<body>

<?php

// print HTML embed code for each file type
switch ($file_ext) {
  case "mov":
  case "mp4":
  case "mpg":
  case "mpeg":
    $html =<<<END
<object classid="clsid:02BF25D5-8C17-4B23-BC80-D3488ABDDC6B"
width="320" height="256" codebase=⏎
"http://www.apple.com/qtactivex/qtplugin.cab">
<param name="src" value="$url">
<param name="autoplay" value="true">
<param name="controller" value="false">
<param name="scale" value="aspect">
<embed src="$url"
  width="320" height="256"
  autoplay="true"
  controller="true"
  scale="aspect"
  pluginspace="http://www.apple.com/quicktime/download/">
</embed>
</object>
END;

    break;

  case "wmv":
  case "avi":
    $html =<<<END
<object id="MediaPlayer1"
width="320" height="286"
classid="CLSID:22D6F312-B0F6-11D0-94AB-0080C74C7E95"
codebase="http://activex.microsoft.com/activex/controls⏎
/mplayer/en/nsmp2inf.cab#Version=6,4,7,1112"
standby="Loading..."
type="application/x-mplayer2">
<param name="fileName" value="$url">
<param name="showControls" value="true">
<param name="showTracker" value="true">
<embed type="application/x-mplayer2" name="MediaPlayer1"
  pluginspage = "http://www.microsoft.com/Windows/MediaPlayer/"
  width="320" height="286"
  showControls="true" showTracker="true"
  src="$url">
</embed>
</object>
END;
```

```
      break;
}

echo $html;

?>

</body>
</html>
```

The main logic is contained in a `switch` statement using the file extension that is parsed out in the beginning. If the file extension matches types that should use QuickTime (MOV, MP4, MPG, and so on), the script displays the video using the HTML code to embed QuickTime. If the file extension matches types that should use Windows Media Player (WMV, AVI, and so on), the script displays the video using the HTML code for embedding Windows Media.

 **Note**   You can add more file extensions and HTML <embed> blocks as needed (for embedding Flash media, for example). Don't forget to adjust the `height` and `width` attributes to reflect those of your video.

## Using the Code

A sample of the PHP page in action can be found at http://www.joshkinberg.com/blog/popup.php?url=http://joshkinberg.com/blog/files/tornado.mov.

With your dynamic page created, you just have to pop it up using JavaScript and pass the location of the video in the URL. You can do so by using the following HTML snippet:

```
<a href="http://www.domain.com/path/to/video.mov" onclick=⤸
"window.open('http://www.domain.com/popup.php?url=⤸
'+this.href,'video','width=350,height=286,top=20,left=20, ⤸
scrollbars=no,resizable=no,toolbar=no,directories=no,location=⤸
no,menubar=no,status=yes,left=0,top=0');return false>Click ⤸
to view</a>
```

Using the HTML, the only items you'll need to change are the domain and location of your video. So, you'd change:

http://www.domain.com/path/to/video.mov

to reflect the actual URL to your video file. And you'd change:

http://www.domain.com/popup.php

to reflect the actual URL of your PHP script.

If you're looking to create a more stylized viewing experience for your audience and don't want them to experience some of the inherent problems with different browsers and video formats, simply use your new-found PHP skills and a little JavaScript magic.

# Using JavaScript to Embed Video

While this book was in production, a major change occurred in the way Microsoft's Internet Explorer 6 embeds video. Although this change affects only IE6, with a specific patch applied, it nevertheless needs to be taken into account. If a viewer goes to your videoblog and wants to watch a video, she will be prompted by the browser to confirm that she wants to actually watch the video.

Unfortunately, the prompt is generic and states "Click to run an ActiveX control on this webpage." Some viewers may not understand this prompt and assume you are attempting to compromise their system and therefore might simply leave your site. This is obviously not something you want to encourage. Fortunately, through the use of JavaScript, there is a simple solution to this change.

The solution is to remove the `<object>` and `<embed>` tags from your HTML and replace them with a `<script>` tag. That tag loads an external JavaScript file with the information necessary to play your video.

## HTML

The HTML you need to use is pretty easy, as it consists of simply using a `<script>` tag. This tag informs the browser where to find the JavaScript file, which will then embed the actual video.

```
<html>
  <body>
    ...
      <script src="/path/to/embed_video.js" language="JavaScript"
type="text/javascript"></script>
...
  </body>
</html>
```

The `src` attribute of your `<script>` tag should resolve to the location where you'll be storing the JavaScript file on your web server.

## Javascript

As with the HTML, the JavaScript is fairly simple, as it is simply replacing the `<object>` and `<embed>` tags you originally had in your HTML. Basically, the JavaScript uses the document.write function to dynamically create the `<object>` tag in the viewer's web browser.

If you are using QuickTime, your JavaScript will look like:

```
// embed a QuickTime video file
document.write('<object classid="clsid:02BF25D5-8C17-4B23-BC80-⊃
D3488ABDDC6B" width="320" height="256" ⊃
codebase="http://www.apple.com/qtactivex/qtplugin.cab">\n');
document.write('<param name="src" value="my_video.mov" />\n');
document.write('<param name="pluginspage"
value="http://www.apple.com/quicktime/download/index.html" />\n');
document.write('</object>\n');
```

## Using Third-Party Tools

A variety of third-party tools are available to help you embed video using JavaScript. FreeVlog (`http://freevlog.org`) offers an online form that will create the necessary HTML for you. The form is located at `http://www.freevlog.org/popup/`. The resulting HTML works with any blog software, including Blogger.

If you are using blog software such as WordPress (`http://www.wordpress.org`), the vPIP (`http://utilities.cinegage.com/videos-playing-in-place`; free) plug-in can make embedding video a fairly simple process. Instructions for using vPIP with Blogger and WordPress are available on the site, as well as general installation instructions that work with many popular blog software packages.

More techniques for embedding video using JavaScript can be found at:

> `http://developer.apple.com/internet/ieembedprep.html`
>
> `http://msdn.microsoft.com/library/default.asp?url=/workshop/auth or/dhtml/overview/activating_activex.asp`
>
> `http://www.macromedia.com/devnet/activecontent/articles/ devletter.html`

Although it's an extra step to embed video using JavaScript, doing so ensures that your videoblog is accessible to the largest number of people.

If you are using Windows Media, your JavaScript will look like:

```
// embed a Windows Media video file
document.write('<object classid="clsid:6BF52A52-394A-11D3-B153-
00C04F79FAA6" width="320" height="240" codebase =
"http://activex.microsoft.com/activex/controls/mplayer/en/nsmp
2inf.cab ">\n');
document.write('<param name="url" value="my_video.wmv" />\n');
document.write('<param name="pluginspage" value="
http://www.microsoft.com/windows/windowsmedia/" />\n');
document.write('</object>\n');
```

After writing your JavaScript, you should save it to your web server in the location indicated in your HTML. For example, if you indicate the src of the JavaScript in your HTML as /scripts/embed_video.js, you should save your JavaScript as embed_video.js and place it in the scripts directory on your web server.

## Summary

By utilizing some of the tricks outlined in this chapter, you can present your videos in a more appealing manner. Whether you choose to embed your videos directly into your web pages or use a glitzy pop-up window, your viewers will receive a much better viewing experience. Once you've managed the basics, you may want to experiment with some of the options to really "wow" your audience.

# Find and Watch Videoblogs

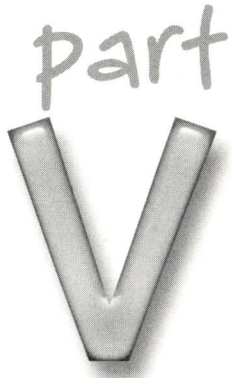

part
V

# Finding and Subscribing to Videoblogs

**B**eing a part of the videoblogging community entails producing and consuming video. From the beginning, people within the community have created tools to help others find interesting and compelling content. One of the coolest features of videoblogging, however, is being able to subscribe to videoblogs and have them delivered to you. Let's take a look at some of the tools you can use.

## Using Mefeedia

Mefeedia.com is a videoblog directory that aggregates thousands of video feeds. The site is focused on videobloggers, and it's a great way to explore the world of videoblogging. Like most video sites, Mefeedia uses *tags* to help users find videos. Tags are essentially keywords that enable you to locate videos easily by simply typing a word that describes what you're looking for.

### Browsing Using Tags

The tags are divided into various groups, such as People, Topic, Place, Language, and Event. In the Topic section, for instance, you'll find tags like "comedy" and "interactive theater." Just browsing through the groups can turn up dozens of tags that may be of interest to you, as shown in Figure 14-1.

Click a tag and Mefeedia provides lists of videos with descriptions, Mefeedia-related tags, and people who are using certain tags. At any point, you can click on person's username to see what other tags he is using, in addition to the videos he's tagged. Browsing tags is a great way to find videos that you might like and possibly even connect with someone who has similar interests to your own.

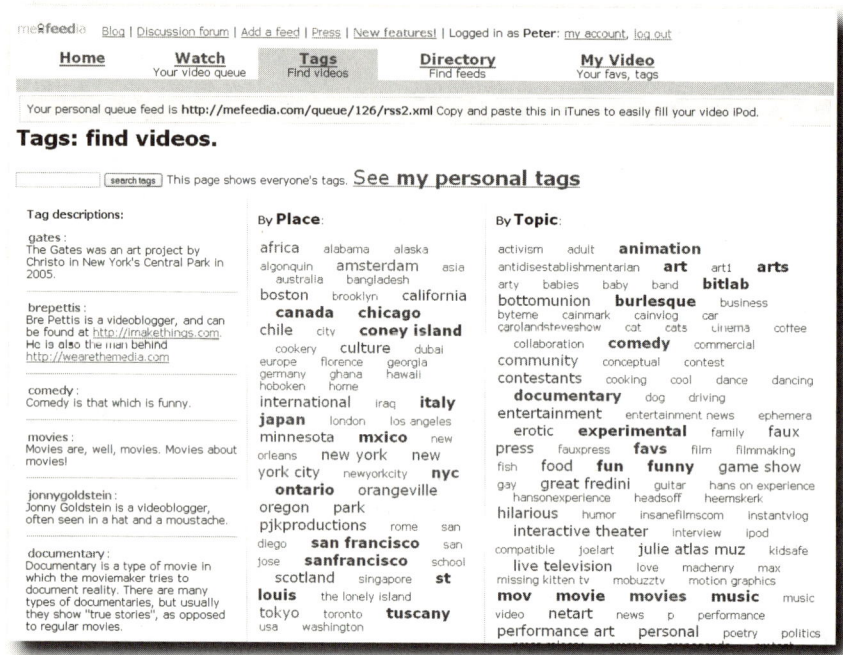

FIGURE 14-1: Tags used in Mefeedia.

# Browsing the Directory

Another way to find videos using Mefeedia is to browse the directory. When you locate and watch a video in Mefeedia, you'll notice that there is a link called Next Feed in the upper-right corner of the page. A great way to get a feeling for the variety of videoblogs available is to simply spend a few minutes clicking links and browsing through the feed details pages.

## Describing Tags

A simple keyword isn't always sufficient to describe what it is meant to represent. To overcome this hurdle, Mefeedia allows tags to have descriptions. For example, the tag "gates" has the description "The Gates was an art project by Christo in New York's Central Park in 2005."

The descriptions work like a wiki, which is where anyone can write a description for any tag and anyone can change a description, too. This open type of system works surprisingly well. The editing is moderated, and Mefeedia encourages users to write "objective" descriptions of tags.

The directory helps to order feeds by categorizing them by popularity, alphabetically, recently added, or recently reviewed. The recently reviewed ordering is particularly interesting because it includes a brief review of the video and often shows you feeds you didn't know of. The recently reviewed category is a great discovery tool when you're looking for new videoblogs.

## Subscribing to Feeds

Mefeedia makes it really easy for users to subscribe to feeds. . .lots of feeds. However, you first need to open an account and then sign in. Opening an account takes about five seconds and just requires you to enter a username, a password, and your email address.

After logging in, you can add videos to your Mefeedia queue, which is really a personal video list that you compile. Add an individual video to your queue by clicking its + Queue button.

You can also subscribe to any feed on the site by clicking the Subscribe button. Afterward, any video published within that feed is automatically added to your queue. Subscribing allows you to see all the future videos, much like subscribing to a magazine.

Mefeedia uses your queue to create a custom RSS feed. You can use this feed to watch your videos in any program that accepts RSS feeds, such as FireAnt (www.fireant.tv) or iTunes (www.apple.com/itunes). You can also use your queue as a feed to synchronize videos to an iPod (through iTunes), as shown in Figure 14-2.

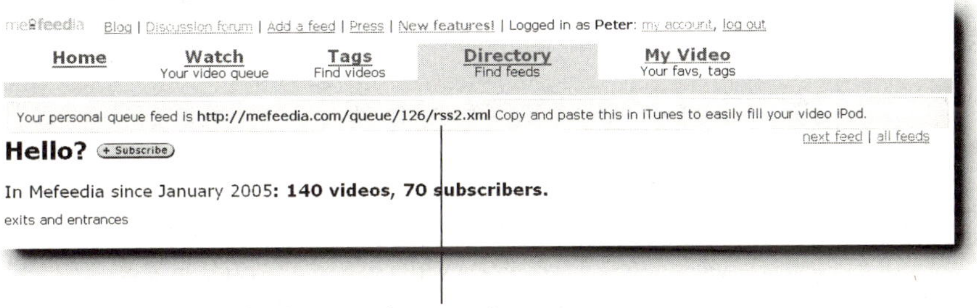

Mefeedia provides complete instructions.

FIGURE 14-2: Fill your iPod with video using Mefeedia.

Once you've added your queue's RSS feed to an aggregator (for example, iTunes), any videos you add to your queue in the future automatically propagate to the aggregator. Your queue's feed is an easy way to fill up an iPod or other portable video device. For example, Mefeedia's RSS feed works the same way with Sony's Media Manager program, if you'd like to fill up your PlayStation Portable. To take advantage of this, just click a variety of queue and Subscribe buttons, and your aggregator takes care of downloading and synching through Mefeedia's RSS feed.

Mefeedia has other feeds available, too, such as one for new tags or for recent changes to descriptions. However you choose to use Mefeedia, you're guaranteed to find videos to suit your taste and have them delivered directly to you.

# Using VlogDir and Gmail

VlogDir, as the name implies, is a directory of videoblogs. The site was launched in May of 2005 to help fill a void at a time when videoblogging culture was starting to thrive, and the importance of having services to help discover new Internet video channels was quickly becoming obvious to the community. VlogDir has helped videobloggers from around the world find each other. As the vlogosphere grew, so did the general audience interested in watching this new source of video content.

Users of VlogDir can discover, watch, and subscribe to videoblogs easily. VlogDir organizes videoblogs by categories, and the integrated search engine is capable of traversing the database treating any word — whether it's contained within a videoblog's description, name, address, or anything else associated with the vlog — as a keyword. This feature makes finding videoblogs of interest possible for almost anyone.

## Subscribing Using VlogDir

Subscribing to videoblogs through VlogDir is one of the site's primary features, and you can do so in a variety of ways. Because VlogDir supports other community projects, you can choose subscription options from other services, such as those available from FireAnt or Mefeedia.

A defining feature in VlogDir is one that enables people to subscribe to videoblogs by email so that you receive videoblog posts directly from VlogDir, via email. As email is ubiquitous, and the applications are well developed, using Gmail as an aggregator enables efficient management and organization of videos through the use of filters and labels. Subscribing to a videoblog using VlogDir's service is as easy as entering your email address on the site's Subscription page (see Figure 14-3).

When signing up, you can see a preview of how the messages will appear when you receive them in your inbox. Videoblog content can be emailed in HTML or text format and includes a download and a playback link to the video, as well as a link to the permalink (direct source of the video). In addition, VlogDir provides subscription-management options to unsubscribe, import, or change your email address. Email subscriptions work particularly well with Google's Gmail service.

## Viewing and Organizing Using Gmail

If you have a Gmail address, you can use some of its provided tools to create your own email video aggregator. To do so, go to the Gmail Settings page (Settings link at top on right) and create a new Label. Within Gmail, Labels enable you to group, sort, and effectively search your messages. Typically, you give the Label the same name as the videoblog that you want to filter (Figure 14-4). For example, if you had a subscription to pouringdown.blogspot.com, you'd set up a Label titled pouringdown.blogspot.com or just pouringdown.

Enter your email address and click Subscribe.

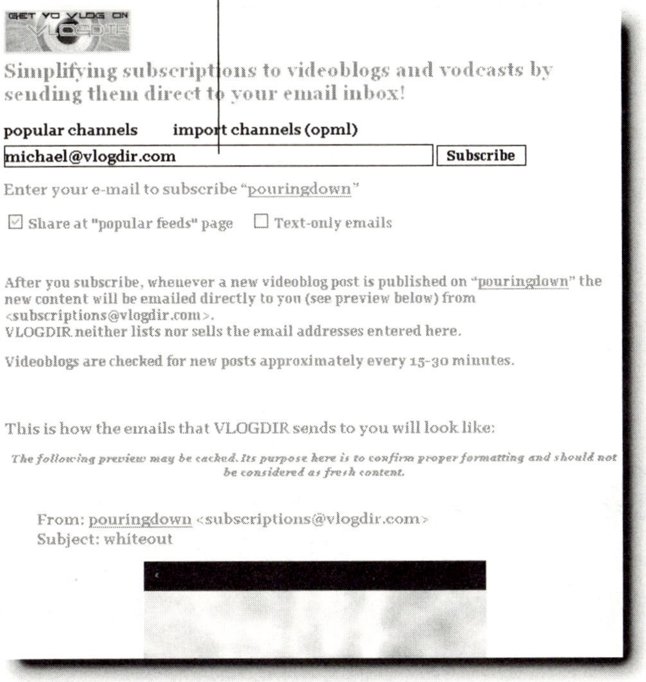

FIGURE 14-3: Subscribing to an emailed videoblog.

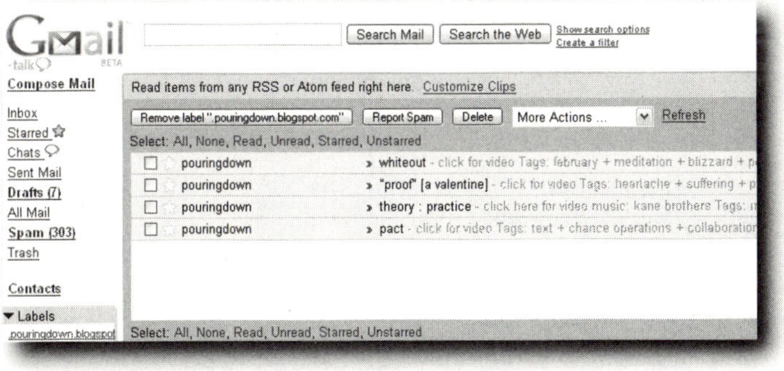

FIGURE 14-4: Videoblogs organized by Label in Gmail.

After setting up the Label, create a filter, which is like a rule that instructs Gmail to follow certain steps whenever it receives a message that matches the criteria you specify. Click the Filters link in the Settings page and select the Create New Filter option. A wizard helps specify how to filter incoming messages. To filter an incoming videoblog, all you need to enter is the name of the videoblog, as per the RSS feed's channel title, in the From field.

When you've finished setting your filter, click the Next Step button and choose the Label that you created for this videoblog. If you want your subscription to skip your inbox completely and be automatically sorted in the Label area, just choose that option.

That's it. You've now turned Gmail into a videoblog Aggregator, as shown in Figure 14-5.

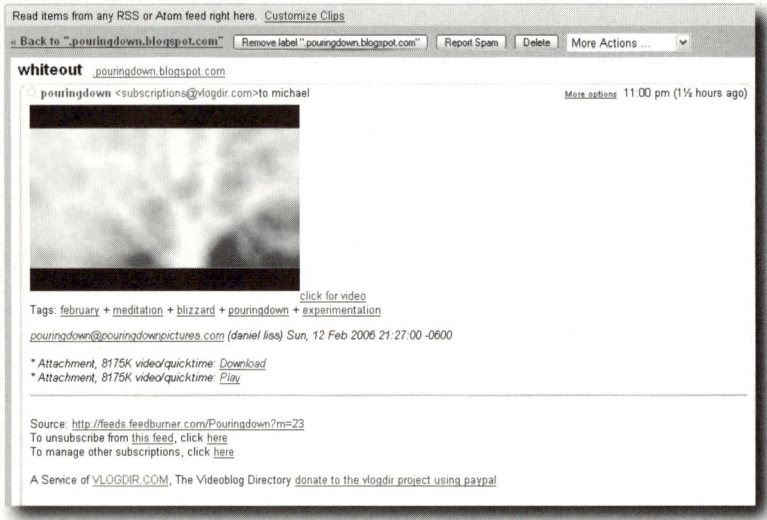

FIGURE **14-5: Viewing a video within Gmail.**

# Using I/ON

I/ON (`http://openvision.tv/home/ion.html`) is an open-source desktop program for Windows XP and Mac OS X that lets you subscribe to video feeds. It supports many types of video, including Apple's QuickTime, Windows Media, Macromedia Flash, and even Java Media. I/ON also has built-in access to Mefeedia.com, Blip.tv, Yahoo!, Flickr, WebJay, and other places where you can find videos.

## Subscribing to an RSS feed

Using I/ON, you can subscribe to any RSS 2.0 compatible feed. To add a feed to I/ON, locate the feed address and copy the feed's URL. Then select Feeds → Add RSS Feed, and paste the URL in the dialog box that appears (Figure 14-6). You can also just drag and drop any address or feed icon link directly onto I/ON.

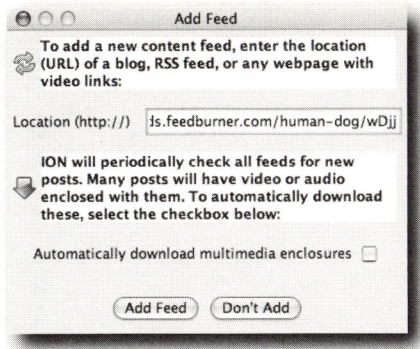

FIGURE **14-6: Adding an RSS feed to I/ON.**

If you would like I/ON to download all of the available videos for the feed, check the Automatically Download checkbox. If you would rather decide for yourself which particular videos to download, simply leave it unchecked. Finally, click the Add Feed button, and the feed will be verified and added to the channel list. You can now click any channel in the channel list to see the latest published posts and videos.

To subscribe to a videoblog included in one of the integrated directory services (Mefeedia, Blip.tv, or Vlogdir), just click any of the Add Feed to I/ON links that appear while you're browsing. You can also click any RSS link inside the I/ON browser, and I/ON will detect that it is a link to a feed and automatically subscribe.

If you aren't sure of the URL for a videoblog's RSS feed, you can enter the URL address of a page you think may be a videoblog and I/ON will parse the page. If I/ON locates an appropriate feed, it automatically attempts to subscribe to the feed or just downloads any video files found in the page itself.

## Discovering Videoblogs with I/ON

There are two basic ways to find new videoblogs to subscribe to when using I/ON. One is to use the Directory Browser, which displays a rotating list of featured feeds, as well as a selection of videoblogs from various video directories, like Mefeedia, Blip.tv, VlogDir, and WebJay. Each of these services provides different ways to browse its listing, and each provides a link to its RSS feeds, which you can use to subscribe to within I/ON.

You can also find and subscribe to new video and videoblogs using the Search tool. To discover new video and videoblogs using search, select the Search tab, enter a keyword into the search box, and click the Search button (see Figure 14-7). This returns search results from one, or all, of the available search engines.

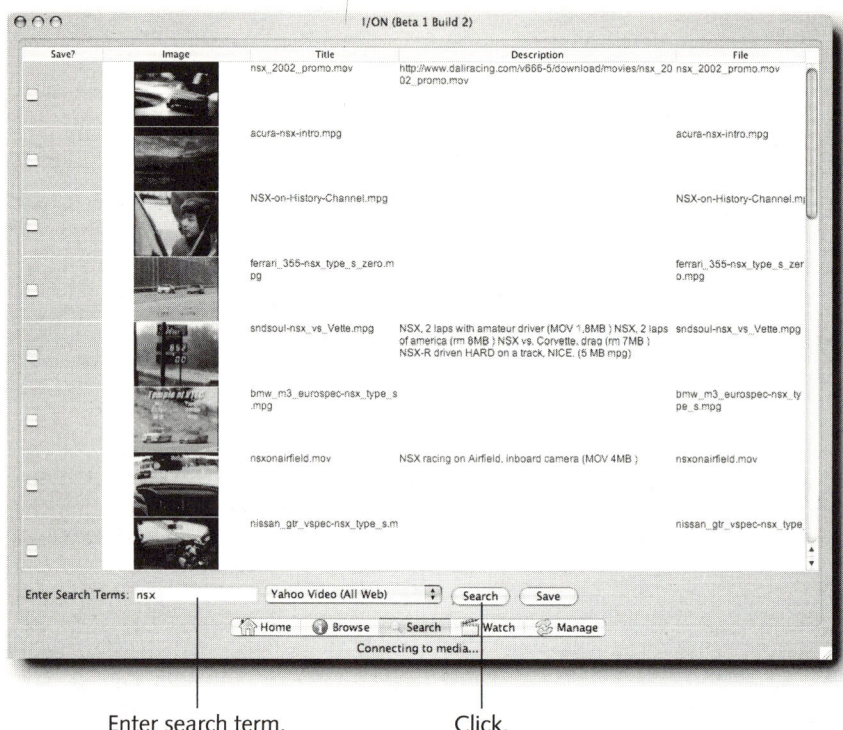

Enter search term.                    Click.

FIGURE 14-7: Searching for video using I/ON.

## Saving Videos Using I/ON

During a search, check the Save? checkbox for each video you'd like to watch, and then click the Save button. You are presented with a dialog in which to name the saved items as a channel, which will then appear in the pop-up list in the Browse tab of I/ON. This feature enables you to save a set of videos that you find and watch them at your convenience.

With its built-in access to the prominent videoblog directories, a powerful search tool, and the capability to play a variety of video formats, I/ON is a great tool to add to your videoblog arsenal. At the time of this writing, I/ON is still in early beta stages, so it is bound to be an amazing piece of software by the time it reaches a 1.0 release.

# Using iTunes

Apple is the 800-pound gorilla in the videoblogging world. Once a music player and then a music store, iTunes added the capability to receive videoblogs when it enabled its podcasting feature. Although Apple has focused on ways to sell commercial TV content, such as the television shows "Lost" and "Desperate Housewives," it also has provided a way for independent producers to distribute their videos through iTunes (although currently for free only).

## Finding and Subscribing to Videoblogs in iTunes

To find videoblogs in iTunes, click the Music Store item. After the Music Store loads, click the Podcasts link, located on the left side navigation area. Next, click the Video Podcasts button to get a listing of the featured video feeds (see Figure 14-8) that are available.

FIGURE **14-8:** Featured videoblogs.

You can find other videoblogs by using the search tool and entering "video" while using Search All Podcasts option.

When you locate a videoblog to which you'd like to subscribe, simply click the Subscribe button, and iTunes adds the feed to your Podcast library and begins downloading the most recent video.

If you come across a videoblog online that you can't locate in iTunes, you can still subscribe to it using the iTunes manual subscription feature. To add the feed, select Advanced ➔ Subscribe to Podcast (see Figure 14-9). Then type or paste the URL of the RSS feed.

Figure 14-9: Manually adding an RSS feed.

## Viewing Video in iTunes

To watch videos you've downloaded or subscribed to, click Videos on the left side of the iTunes window. Then click the video you want to view. iTunes plays the video as a small box in the bottom left corner of the window. You can detach the video from iTunes by clicking on it. The video will float over iTunes and you can resize it.

To play the video full-screen, click the Full Screen button (fifth button from the left at the bottom of the iTunes window). The Full Screen button is enabled only while video is playing, however. You can also access your videos through the Podcasts and Library items.

One drawback of using iTunes is that it does not link back to the video's original site in an obvious way, nor does it include any of the social features of some other aggregators. Nevertheless, its tight integration with the iPod is a major reason to use it.

# Using FireAnt

FireAnt (www.fireant.tv) was started in 2004 by some of the original pioneers of video-blogging and has become a powerful online "TV Guide" for video RSS channels. FireAnt takes a unique approach to searching and subscribing to videoblogs by providing a web-based directory and a desktop application that together present a great experience. The directory covers a wide range of independent and commercial content and often "discovers" videoblogs within minutes of their being created.

## FireAnt's Aggregator

The FireAnt desktop application, which is free and for both Mac OS X (see Figure 14-10) and Windows (see Figure 14-11), enables users to subscribe to videoblogs, automatically download fresh content, organize and view practically any media format, comment on videoblogs, and synchronize media to portable devices.

FIGURE 14-10: FireAnt on Mac OS X.

FIGURE 14-11: FireAnt on Windows XP.

FireAnt is exceptional for videobloggers because it supports almost every media format available, including BitTorrent files, and can synchronize to a variety of portable video devices. It also gives users many ways to organize their media, share what they find with friends, and even comment to videoblog producers. The desktop application is tightly integrated with the web-based directory, which makes for a very pleasant search, subscribe, view, and sync experience. The directory, however, can also be used by itself.

## The FireAnt Web Directory

Point your web browser to www.fireant.tv and you have complete access to the FireAnt videoblog directory (see Figure 14-12). You also can access it directly by using the FireAnt desktop application. Within the directory, you can use a simple search tool to look for videoblogs or browse them by Channel, Episode, or Location. You can even use tags to locate footage.

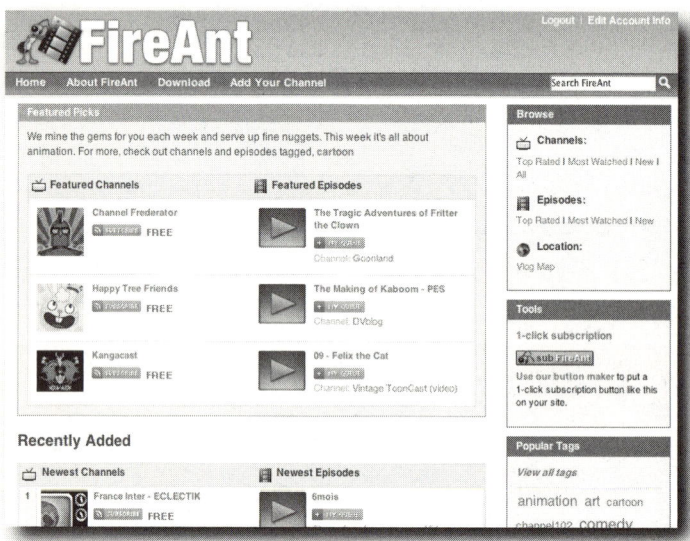

FIGURE 14-12: The FireAnt directory.

To really take advantage of all that the site has to offer, sign up for an account—all you need is a username, a password, and your email address, although you can optionally provide your first and last names, your web-site information, and your RSS feed. Once you've signed up, you can add tags to items, add videos and feeds to your queue, and rate videoblogs on a one-to-five star basis.

FireAnt creates an RSS channel for tags on the site, so if you want "funny" videos, you can subscribe to the funny tag and automatically receive videos that you or others have tagged as such. FireAnt also keeps track of what's popular in the vlogosphere as Top Rated items and Most Watched, independently of each other.

FireAnt claims to be "Buzzword Compliant," in a tongue-in-cheek sort of way. That compliance, however, has lead to a very capable and polished application for videobloggers to enjoy their peers' labors.

# Watching Rocketboom on TiVo

In 2005, Rocketboom shook the videoblogging world by announcing that it was going to be distributed on TiVo, in addition to being distributed online. Although it flew under most of the traditional entertainment companies' radars, it vibrated through the entertainment industry as well. Why? Rocketboom would appear in a TiVo user's list of shows, just like anything else.

Although distributing Rocketboom via TiVo is deemed a beta service, it sheds a ray of hope for anyone who has dreamed of producing video for television. If you own a TiVo, experience it for yourself.

## Subscribing Using TiVo

At the time of this writing, you can't subscribe to Rocketboom using your TiVo. You have to use TiVo's web site. Fortunately, it's just a formality and is really easy.

To subscribe, go to TiVo's research page devoted to Rocketboom at `http://research .tivo.com/rocketboom` and follow the onscreen directions: Enter the email address TiVo has on file for your account and your TiVo account number, select the Subscribe radio button, and click Submit. That's all there is to it.

## Viewing Using TiVo

After you've subscribed, Rocketboom is downloaded to your TiVo whenever a new episode is available. The first time you see it, a smile might appear on your face. There, next to all of these shows that cost hundreds of thousands of dollars (sometimes millions!), is Rocketboom. To watch it, just select the show and then select Play.

### TiVo Series 2

For the subscription to work properly, you need a TiVo Series 2 machine (TiVo Series 1 and DirectTV versions don't currently work). In addition, your TiVo has to be connected to the Internet, because Rocketboom isn't broadcast over traditional airwaves. If your TiVo is not connected to the Internet, don't worry. You can find directions for connecting at `http://www .tivo.com/4.9.16.asp`.

Whoever believes that you need to live in Hollywood, have an agent, make a deal with a major network, and drink double-tall-nonfat-soy-peppermint-mocha lattes to distribute a show on television is in for a big surprise.

# Reblogging Videos Using del.icio.us

Once you know how to find and subscribe to videoblogs, you can also let other people know what you're watching by using del.icio.us in a creative way. One key characteristic of the videoblogging community is its emphasis on conversation. A good way to participate in this conversation is through *re-vlogging*.

Re-vlogging is a process of taking videos created by other videobloggers and repackaging them into a new blog. This acts as a kind of "favorite videos list" that lets other people know what videos you're watching and what you find interesting. By re-vlogging, you also act as a filter for the thousands of videoblogs out there and help the good content float to the top.

## Setting Up a del.icio.us Thingy

Currently, the easiest way to set up a re-vlog is to use del.icio.us tags and have the service automatically post to your blog. The first step to do this is to set up a del.icio.us account (see Figure 14-13).

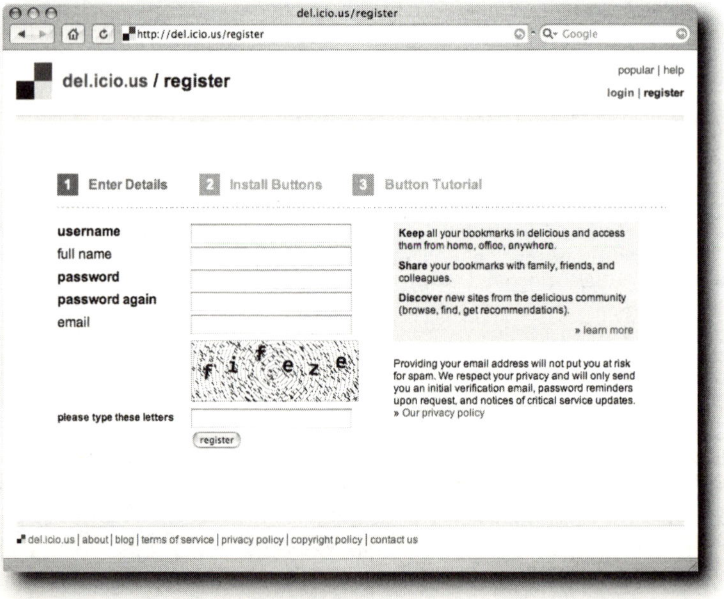

FIGURE 14-13: Signing up for del.icio.us.

Next, set up a separate blog to post all your re-vlog links to. This enables you to keep your re-vlog items separate from your original ones. (If you're not comfortable giving del.icio.us your blog's username and password — which is stored in cleartext there — create the blog with an alternate username and password.) Then set up a del.icio.us account to make the daily posts on that blog.

To create your re-vlog feed, go to the del.icio.us web site and log in. Click the Settings link in the navigation menu at the top right of the main page. The settings menu opens on the right side of the page. Under the Experimental heading, click the Daily Blog Posting link and select Add New Thingy. An Add New Thingy form appears, as shown in Figure 14-14.

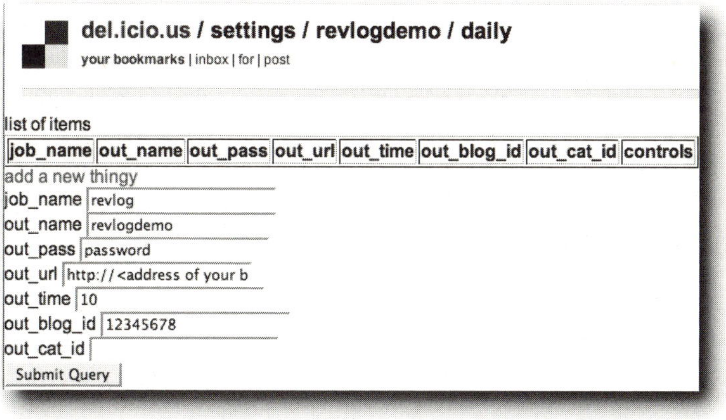

FIGURE 14-14: Adding a thingy.

If you are using the Movable Type, TypePad, or WordPress blogging software applications, fill in the fields as follows:

- job_name — Enter whatever you choose (suggestion: re-vlog).

- out_name — Enter the username to log in to your blog; account must have posting rights!

- out_pass — Enter the password to log in to your blog.

- out_URL — Enter the URL for your xmlrpc page.

    For WordPress: http://<address of your blog>/xmlrpc.php

    For Movable Type or TypePad: the mt-xmlrpc.cgi, likely located at http://<address of your blog>/cgi-bin/mt-xmlrpc.cgi

- out_time — Enter the hour in GMT that you want to the post to occur.

- out_blog_id — Enter **1**, unless you know otherwise.

- out_cat_id — Enter the ID for the category you would like the post to appear, available through the Administration interface to your blog software.

If you are using Blogger, here's what to put in the fields:

- `job_name` — Enter whatever you choose (suggestion: re-vlog).
- `out_name` — Enter your Blogger username.
- `out_pass` — Enter your Blogger password.
- `out_URL` — Enter `http://www.videoblogging.info/tools/translator/`.
- `out_time` — Enter the hour in GMT that you want to the post to occur.
- `out_blog_id` — Enter your Blogger ID. For instructions on finding it, go to `http://help.blogger.com/bin/answer.py?answer=874&topic=12`.
- `out_cat_id` — Enter any number, because it doesn't work in Blogger.

When you're finished entering your information, click the Submit Query button. The del.icio.us service then posts to your blog on a daily basis.

## Linking to Individual Video Posts

To have links appear on your blog, you must bookmark and tag them using del.icio.us. The del.icio.us bookmarklet simplifies and streamlines this process. You can obtain a bookmarklet by going to `http://del.icio.us/help/buttons` and dragging the Post to del.icio.us button to your browser's Bookmarks or Favorites toolbar.

The next time you see a video you like, go to the permalink of the post (the direct URL to the post) and click the del.icio.us bookmarklet. Doing so displays a window that contains the following fields: URL, `Description`, `Notes`, and `Tags`. The URL and `Description` fields are already filled in with the permalink and title of the post (see Figure 14-15).

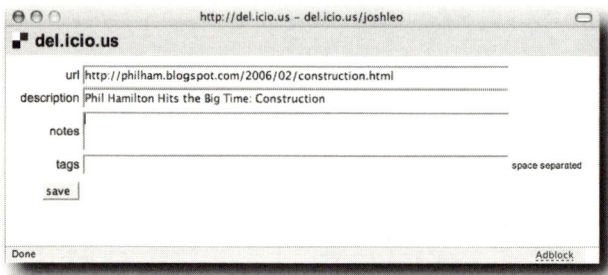

FIGURE 14-15: Creating a del.icio.us bookmark.

Because you want the feed created from your re-vlog post to have video enclosures, you must link directly to the media itself. The problem with direct linking is that you want to adhere to the videoblogging code of ethics, which is understood to allow viewers to go back to the original post. To do this, copy the permalink URL into the Notes field and then copy the actual URL of the linked media into the URL field.

Add personal comments to Notes field, too (see Figure 14-16). They help people gain some context of the video before they watch it and provide you with a reminder in the future.

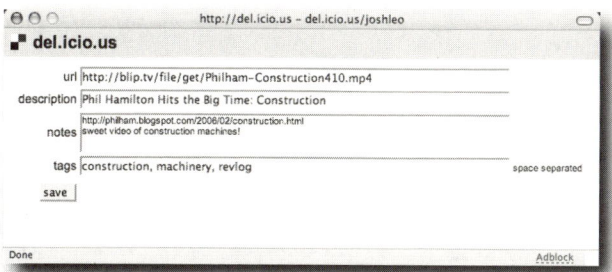

FIGURE 14-16: A tagged del.icio.us bookmark.

The final step is to tag the video, using the Tags field. You can tag the video whatever you want, based on its subject matter or the information you gain from it. Keep in mind that all videos meant for your re-vlog should include a consistent tag, such as "favorites," "revlog," or even "jimsfavs" (see Figure 14-16). When you're done, click Save.

## Creating a Feed

Once you have started a designated tag (such as revlog) for your re-vlog videos and tagged at least one video, go to your del.icio.us page and click your tag located in the right sidebar. A page displays (see Figure 14-17), presenting only the videos you've bookmarked with that tag. On the bottom of the page is an orange RSS button.

To create your feed, copy the URL of the RSS button and head over to FeedBurner (www .feedburner.com). Sign in (create an account, if needed) and paste the copied URL of the RSS feed into the blank text field on the FeedBurner front page. Check the I'm a Podcaster! checkbox, click the Next >> button, and simply follow the few steps to create a feed.

When you've finished, add a link on your newly created blog's sidebar using the URL that FeedBurner provides. The feed will reference your del.icio.us tag and enclose each video as a separate item. If you've created a del.icio.us thingy, your blog will have groupings of linked videos posted daily or whenever you add a new link to del.icio.us. Adding this simple task to your web browsing activities is a great way to keep people up to date with your video findings while online.

People can now subscribe to your favorite videos while reaping all the benefits of another filter in the vlogosphere.

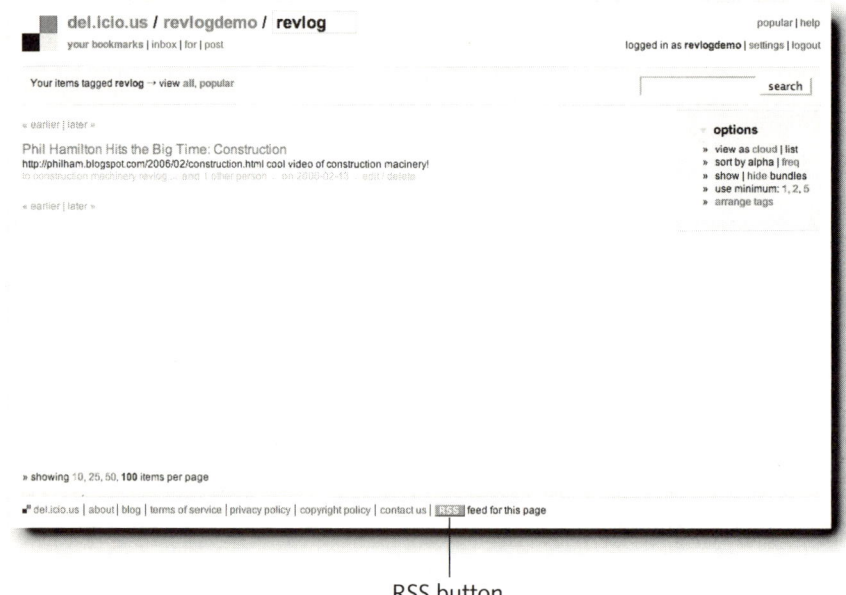

RSS button

FIGURE 14-17: A del.icio.us RSS button's at the bottom of your page.

# Summary

Finding and subscribing to videoblogs can be an eye-opening experience. There are so many different people, with different interests, expressing themselves in traditional and nontraditional ways. From video-diary entries, to videoblogs about how to mix drinks, to experimental videos, there's something for everyone. With a variety of tools at your disposal, you can easily find and watch videoblogs from around the world. Once you start using these tools, you'll discover that the convergence of computer and video entertainment is finally here.

# Watching Videoblogs

**J**ust producing and distributing videos is not enough to be a good videoblogger. You also have to keep up with other people's work. Videoblogging is a completely new art form, so seeing new styles, formats, and approaches only helps you become better at what your do. The great news is that there are many ways to watch videoblogs besides the web.

## Watch Videos on TV

You don't always have to watch videos hunched over your computer; you can watch them directly on your TV. To do so, all you need are a few pieces of inexpensive equipment:

➤ A computer with a video output (RCA or S-video) and an audio output.

➤ A television with a video input and audio input (most modern TVs come with these).

➤ Video cable.

➤ An audio cable to connect the computer with the TV (probably 2.5mm-to-RCA; see Figure 15-1).

## Setting Up

Connecting your computer to your TV is fairly straightforward, once you know what you're looking for.

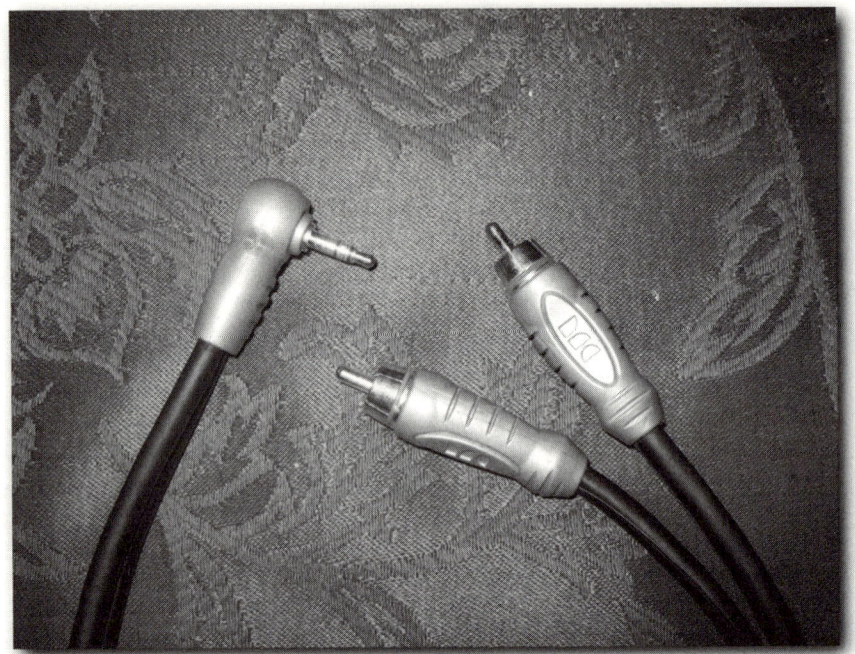

FIGURE 15-1: A 2.5mm-to-RCA stereo audio cable.

## Video

Start with your TV. First, find a video connection that is not being used. Plug one end of the video cable into the TV. The video input connection of RCA cables is yellow; the S-Video connection has five holes for pins. Figure 15-2 shows a variety of connections.

### Disclaimer

Before you buy the equipment to watch videos on your TV, there are a couple things of which you should be aware. First, because most videos are highly compressed, they are "designed" to look best within a relatively small window on a computer screen. When you blow them up to the size of a TV screen, you will often see "artifacts," and they can be somewhat blurry.

Second, because of the differences in resolution between most modern TVs and computer screens, you probably won't be able to read regular-size text at all. So it's not easy to read written posts associated with videos; you'll pretty much have to settle for just watching the videos.

Despite these limitations, you may very well fall in love with watching videoblogs on TV. The investment is small and the process is easy, so you might as well try it out and see how it works for you.

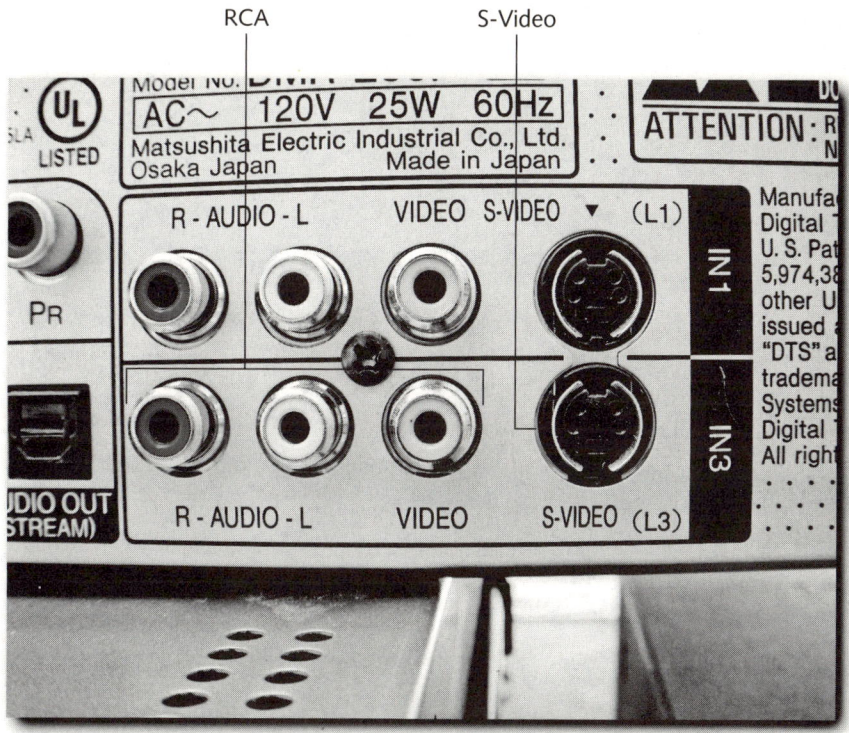

FIGURE 15-2: Various connections.

Plug the other end of the video cable into the video port on your computer (see Figure 15-3).

When you plug in, pay attention to the labels, such as Video 1 or Video 2, above the connections on your TV. New TVs are designed to handle multiple devices, and your computer will serve as just another input device. When you go to watch your videos, you'll need to make sure you're viewing the correct input.

## Audio

If you want to get the complete videoblog-on-television experience, you obviously want audio, too. To route the audio, plug one end of your audio cable to the RCA audio connections on your television, and plug the other end into your computer. More than likely, your computer has a headphone jack, which is sufficient for sending the audio to your TV.

### Uh, It Doesn't Look Right

If your computer has an S-Video input, and you notice that the input looks different from the one on your TV, don't worry. Some computers use a more advanced cabling system. You need only to make sure that the actual format for the video is the same, such as S-Video to S-Video.

S-Video

FIGURE 15-3: S-Video port on computer.

## Starting Up

After connecting all of your cables, turn on your TV and tune to the input you connected the computer to (Video 2, for example). If your computer's not running, turn it on. This is basically the same thing as hooking your computer up to a video projector, in that the TV shows exactly what is on your computer screen. When you see a mirror image of your computer's display on the TV, you're ready to watch some videos! If all you see is a blue screen, however, don't panic. The problem is probably easy to fix.

### Windows

If you see a blue screen on your Windows PC, the problem is most likely that the LCD/CRT toggle is set to show only your computer. On most PCs this can be fixed by simply pressing a function key. For example, on most Dell laptops, you'll see CRT/LCD written in little blue letters on the F8 key. In that case, hold down the function key and push F8, which will toggle the display among monitor, monitor and external screen (TV), and external screen only. The necessary function key differs among PC manufacturers, so check your manual or interactive help application to find the key you need to use.

### Macintosh

On a Mac, the most common problem is that the computer has not detected the external display. In this case, open System Preferences, select Displays, and then click the Detect Displays button, which usually fixes the problem. You'll know if the computer is detecting the external screen because the Display window will show an option for Arrangement between the Display and Color buttons. If Detecting Displays doesn't work, try setting the display to a different resolution.

## Configuring the Screens

One last thing about viewing videoblogs on the television screen is that you most likely will want to see the same thing on both your computer and TV screens, which is called *mirroring*. This enables you to use your computer monitor for setting things up and controlling the videos, if you need to, while being able to watch them on the TV.

Monitors can be set up so that each screen shows half the display, known as *screen spanning*. This is the way you might set things up for working with "dual monitors" on your computer. If you're not used to this, it can be very disconcerting to see your display spread across two screens and the mouse jump from one screen to the other as you move it. If your computer is set up this way, you will probably want to change it.

### Windows

To change your monitor set up in Windows, open the control panel and click Display. Select the Settings tab, where you will see two squares that represent monitors. The secondary monitor will have the number 2 on it. Click that monitor and then check/uncheck the Extend My Windows Desktop onto This Monitor option. If it is checked, each monitor represents a part of the display. If unchecked, they will mirror one another.

### Macintosh

To change the monitor setup on Macintosh, open the System Preferences application, select Displays, and click the Arrangement tab. You can then check/uncheck Mirror Displays, depending on your preference.

## Watching Videos

To watch videos, you basically do the same thing you would when watching them on your computer. Just launch the viewing application of your choice, and select the video(s) you want to view. A couple of options, however, are particularly good for watching videoblogs on your TV.

First, you are more likely to want to just sit back and watch several videos in a row without having to manually change from one to the next with the help of such features as playlists. Second, you will probably want to experiment with watching the videos in full-screen mode. The more popular tools for watching videoblogs, such as FireAnt and iTunes support full-screen mode, so feel free to experiment and have fun.

# Watch Videoblogs on a Pocket PC

The integrated feel, the capability to download video anywhere, and the capability to view posts from a videoblog make using a Pocket PC a great option for watching videoblogs. With a Pocket PC device, you can download videoblogs from a wireless network and view them whenever and wherever you want. Also, you can view any notes included in the videoblog's RSS feed. Plus, with integrated file management, you can automatically delete videoblogs after you've viewed them.

## Configuration Tips

For a Pocket PC to be suitable for watching videoblogs, it should have at least 256MB of storage capacity, which will store a small number of videoblogs (5–10). If you'd like to store more videos, you should consider purchasing a larger storage card, such as a 1GB to 2GB.

Given the current state of videoblogging, it's reasonable to have a video file size of 50MB or even 100MB; keep this in mind when producing videos for your videoblog. In addition, the playback capabilities on modern portable devices are suitable for high-quality video playback. Be aware, however, that some Secure Digital cards may not be fast enough to play back your video. For reasonable performance, you want a fast card running at least 32x speed.

## iPod Encoding

Many videobloggers, and those producing video for an RSS feed, are encoding video geared toward the iPod, which has a very specific set of video-decoding capabilities. Therefore, most of the video you acquire will probably be encoded in either H.264 (also known as AVC) with audio in AAC or using another MPEG-4 encoder, such as 3ivx or DivX. If you want to play iPod-targeted video on a Pocket PC, you need to download and install third-party playback software. You can determine the type of codec used by opening the video file in your media player and checking the video's properties.

Currently, only one player available for the Pocket PC is capable of playing iPod-targeted videos: TCPMP (`http://tcpmp.corecodec.org`), version 0.71b or later. Audio and video playback is possible with either an "unofficial" plug-in (meaning the license fees to the AAC Patent holders are not being paid) or with a commercial version of TCPMP that includes the AAC plug-in.

## Playing Videos

So you've managed to download a ton of videoblogs. Where do you start? The easiest way to play videos on your Pocket PC is to use the file-management capabilities within the Pocket PC itself. To do so, simply launch the video player program, watch the videos, and then delete the video files when you are done with them.

By using the file-management features, you can develop a routine of playing and deleting, but that requires some effort and consistency in your video-watching life. With file management, you play a videoblog, and when it's done, you play the next one while deleting the first one. Prior to playing the next video in your list, you can choose to keep it or to delete it later.

## Portable Media Players

There are portable media players other than the Pocket PC, such as Archos' AV500 ($499.00),Creative's Zen Vision ($379.00), and even Apple's video-enabled iPod ($299.00). Most of these players provide large amounts of storage, ranging from 30GB to 100GB. Although these media players cannot download videoblogs directly like a Pocket PC can, combined with a desktop-based aggregator they can synchronize videoblogs to your portable video device to be viewed while "on the go."

## Using FeederReader

You can treat a Pocket PC as a video player with removable memory and transfer all videos using a card reader. Or you can use the ActiveSync application to connect directly to your Pocket PC and synchronize your videos between your desktop computer and your Pocket PC. But, to really take advantage of videoblogs on a Pocket PC, you want to consider using an aggregator, such as FeederReader (www.feederreader.com; $9.00).

You can install FeederReader into RAM or on a memory card. (Putting it on a memory card leaves you more RAM for running other applications.) To install FeederReader, use CabInstl (www.s-k-tools.com/util.html; free), as shown in Figure 15-4, which allows you to install the FeederReader CAB file onto your memory card. Or you can install FeederReader using the desktop installer application provided with your Pocket PC.

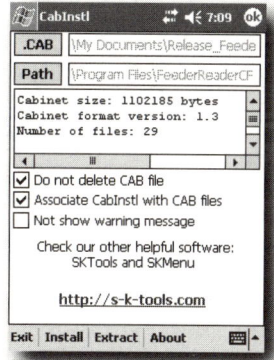

FIGURE 15-4: Using CabInstl.

After FeederReader is installed, you can add a new feed (Figure 15-5) by selecting the Add Feed menu item and entering the feed's URL.

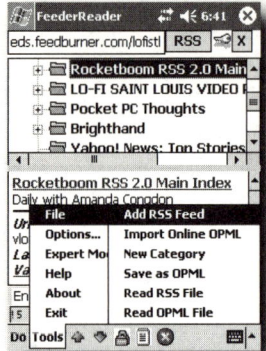

FIGURE 15-5: Adding a new feed.

Once you've added feeds that interest you and arranged them into categories, select Update Feeds. When that process completes, select Update All Enclosures (Figure 15-6) to download all enclosures — the videos — from the feeds. Note that FeederReader downloads several videoblogs at once, so that if one videoblog has a timeout, the others continue to download.

FIGURE 15-6: Updating enclosures.

## Using the Internet

To use an aggregator like FeederReader, the Pocket PC must have a connection to the Internet. Usually such a connection is through WiFi, a cell phone (using Bluetooth, IR, or a direct-link cable), or ActiveSync with Internet Passthrough turned on. Although a PC is not required, it is sometimes helpful to connect with ActiveSync to take advantage of a true broadband connection.

Most recently manufactured Pocket PCs come with integrated WiFi, either the 802.11B standard or the faster 802.11G standard. Both B and G versions are faster than home broadband speeds, so it more than likely won't matter which one you have. WiFi combined with a broadband connection is the most preferred method for downloading videoblogs.

Remember that videoblogs can be as short as 10MB, but they can easily top 100MB, too. Keeping this in mind, some cell-phone connections, such as GPRS, access data at rates ranging from 20Kb per second to 50Kb per second. Based on this, a 20MB file could take one to two hours over a GPRS connection, compared to less than five minutes using a broadband connection, as shown in Figure 15-7.

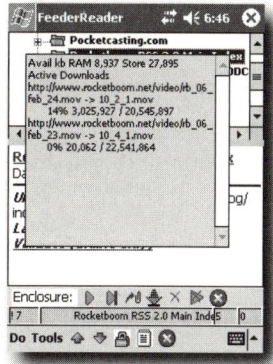

FIGURE 15-7: Downloads in progress.

One thing crucial to a Pocket PC, but less so for a desktop PC, is a "resume" capability for enclosures. More often than not, the Internet connection on a Pocket PC is much less reliable than that of an Ethernet-connected desktop PC. In addition, you may be in a position to download for only a few minutes as you breeze through a WiFi Hotspot on the road. In these cases, you probably want to avoid having to restart any enclosure downloads from the beginning. Being able to resume a download means that the next time you have an Internet connection, your Pocket PC will begin downloading the file from the point it left off at.

Automated file management is implemented in FeederReader with the Enclosure toolbar (Figure 15-8). Just bring up the Enclosure toolbar and tap the Play icon to play a videoblog.

FeederReader works with any media that the Pocket PC can display or play, so it launches the appropriate player for the enclosure (Figure 15-9) and lets you continue reading other RSS feeds. In addition, you can watch videoblogs while you continue to download more!

To go to the next enclosure or videoblog, tap the Delete–Play Next icon. Doing so automatically deletes the previous videoblog, giving you more room to download videoblogs. Once you get the hang of it, working with the Download, View, and Delete icons is really efficient. If you want to save the video, simply click the Play Next icon.

FIGURE **15-8:** The Enclosure toolbar.

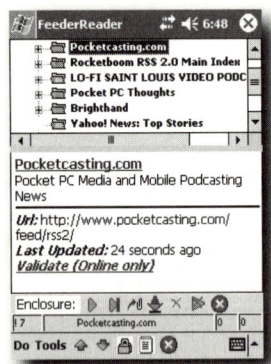

FIGURE **15-9:** Enclosures in
FeederReader.

## Keeping Up to Date

Video downloading and viewing technology is advancing quickly for the Pocket PC, Smart-
phone, and other devices as well. New specifications are being defined, and new capabilities are
being added continuously. Here are some links you can use to keep track of what is going on
with Pocket PCs and podcasting:

- www.pocketcasting.com—News dedicated to Pocket PC media and mobile devices.

- www.pocketpcthoughts.com—Generic forum and news site for all things
  Pocket PC.

- www.brighthand.com—News, reviews, and forum site for handheld devices.

- www.mobilitytoday.com—News, reviews, and forums on mobile devices.

As technology moves from simple podcasts to podcasts with integrated and more advanced features, the Pocket PC is perfectly positioned to adapt to the landscape. It will require more development from vendors, as well as more development on the videoblogging tools, but there will be greater functionality as standards continue to develop.

# Watch Videoblogs on a Windows Media Center PC

Over the last few years, new applications have been developed that enable people to navigate and manage their expanding digital media collections, as well as play and record live TV. These applications sport a "10-foot" interface that allows navigation from a sofa using a remote control. Some examples of this class of software are Windows Media Center (`www.microsoft .com/windowsxp/mediacenter/default.mspx`), TiVo (`www.tivo.com`), the Linux-based Myth TV (`www.mythtv.org`), and Apple's Front Row (`www.apple.com/imac/ frontrow.html`).

## Windows Media Center

One of the more popular media management/personal video recorder software packages is Microsoft's Windows Media Center (Figure 15-10). This software comes bundled on many PCs marketed as high-end media systems.

FIGURE 15-10: Windows Media Center.

Watching videoblogs using the Media Center's built-in My Videos section is easy. Just install a videoblog aggregator like FireAnt (`www.fireant.tv`; free), and then add its video-download folder to the My Videos section of the Media Center (Figure 15-11). As the aggregator downloads new video, it becomes available in My Videos.

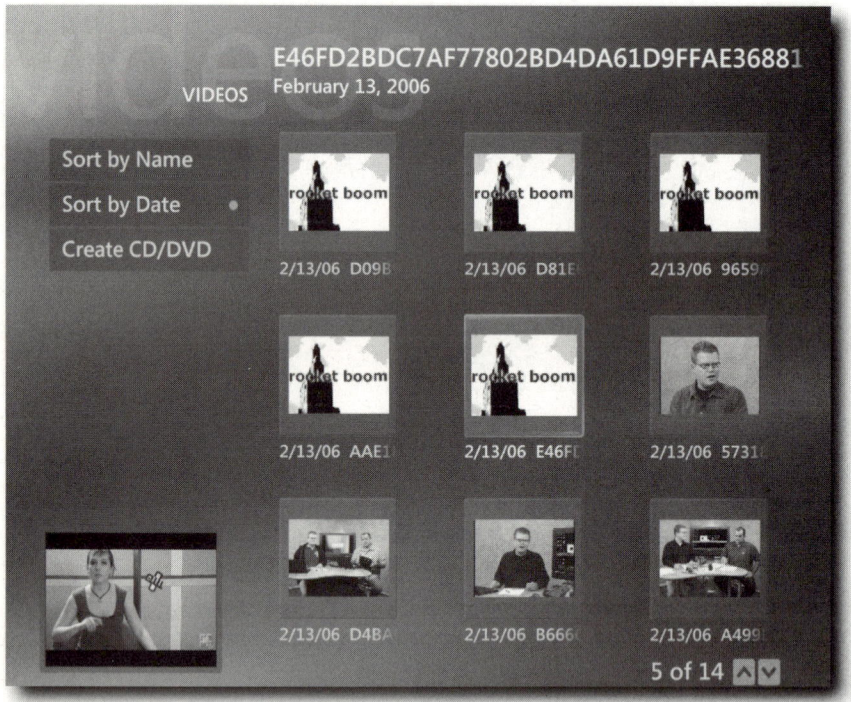

FIGURE 15-11: Videos on a Windows Media Center.

There are a couple of drawbacks. First, Media Center's built-in player supports only video that is compatible with Microsoft's Windows Media Player. Because many videoblogs are produced using Apple's QuickTime format, including all videoblogs compatible with the video iPod, you won't be able to watch these videos with Media Center's built-in player. Second, some people might not like choosing a video from a long list of unorganized files. Because of this, it's not a very TV-like experience.

## TVTonic

For folks looking for a more sofa-friendly experience, there is TVTonic (`www.tvtonic.com`; free). TVTonic has the added benefit of allowing QuickTime video playback within Media

Center, if you have the QuickTime player installed. Once TVTonic is installed, it can be accessed via the More Programs or the Online Spotlight sections of Media Center.

One of TVTonic's main benefits is that it enables you to watch, subscribe to, and manage videoblog subscriptions, all with a remote control within one application. You subscribe to videoblogs in the Add Channels section, which features popular videoblogs in addition to high-quality video feeds exclusive to TVTonic. It also enables you to add any RSS feed from the web through a simple one-click process. Once you subscribe to a feed, it shows up as a channel in TVTonic's My Channels (Figure 15-12) screen, and the video starts downloading in the background.

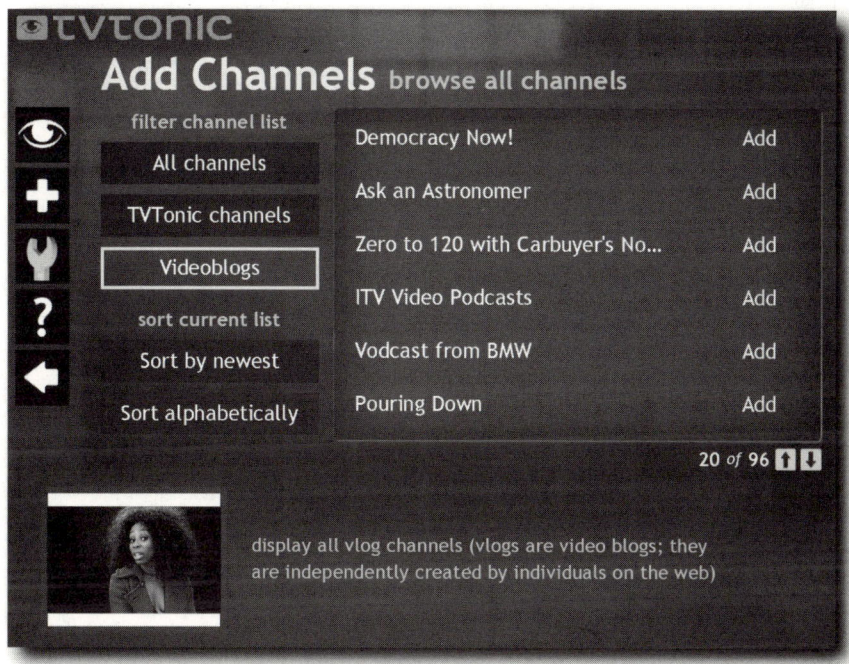

FIGURE 15-12: Videoblogs listed in TVTonic.

Once a few channels have been subscribed to, and a few videos downloaded, watching videoblogs in TVTonic is simple. When you launch TVTonic, you're taken to the default My Channels screen (see Figure 15-13), and video starts playing right away, picking up where you last left off. Selecting a channel button plays all videos in that channel, one after the next, in reverse chronological order. Or you can dig down into the channel and select individual videos.

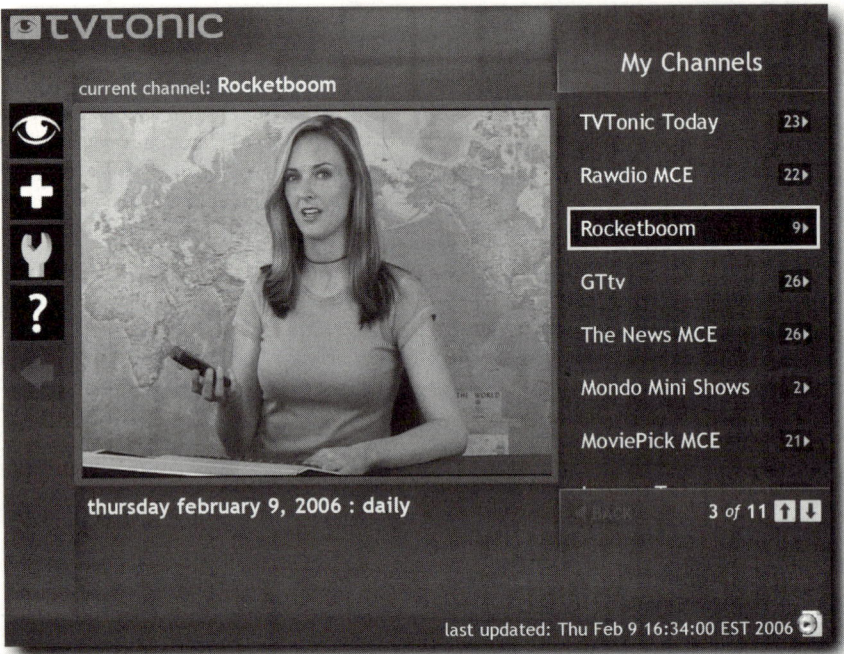

FIGURE 15-13: Channels within TVTonic.

TVTonic also aggregates your newest video into a special channel called TVTonic Today, which enables you to play all the newest videos from compatible feeds. TVTonic provides a Web Link button that's always displayed under videoblog media; it links back to that video's homepage in a separate browser window so that you can comment on a video at any time and participate in the videoblog experience.

You can also manage disk-space usage for each channel. The Disk Cache Settings (Figure 15-14) screen provides an overview of how much space is allotted for the entire service and how much space is currently being used. You can also see how much disk space each channel is using. Selecting a channel reveals a simple slider interface that enables you to set the disk usage for that channel so that you don't run out of drive space. Be aware, however, that if you reach your drive limit, no additional videos will be downloaded until others are deleted.

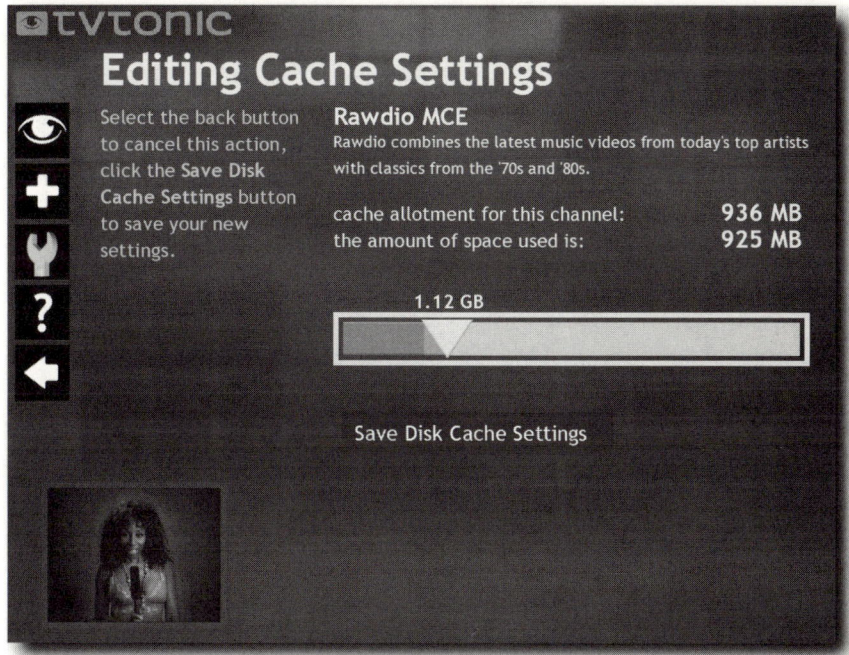

FIGURE 15-14: Changing a channel's cache.

## RSS Readers

There are a few Media Center-compatible RSS readers available that also handle video and audio enclosures. These applications function much like desktop RSS readers but are navigable with a remote control and provide the "10-foot" experience.

NewsGator Media Center Edition (www.newsgator.com; free–$49.95/year), shown in Figure 15-15, doesn't require any additional software and is available via the Online Spotlight section of the Media Center. NewsGator's main function is to act as a newsreader, but it can also handle videoblog enclosures. When an item in the RSS feed list view has a video enclosure, it's marked with a video icon. When you select a video item, a button appears in the left-hand navigation section that allows you to play the video.

Two other RSS readers, mNewsCenter (www.embeddedautomation.com/EAHAmNews Center.htm; $19.99) by Ian Dixon, and MCE RSS Reader (http://mcerssreader .oabsoftware.nl; free) by OABsoftware, provide similar functionality but do require you to install software. These newsreaders handle text, audio, and video and are a good choice if you want all your RSS in one place.

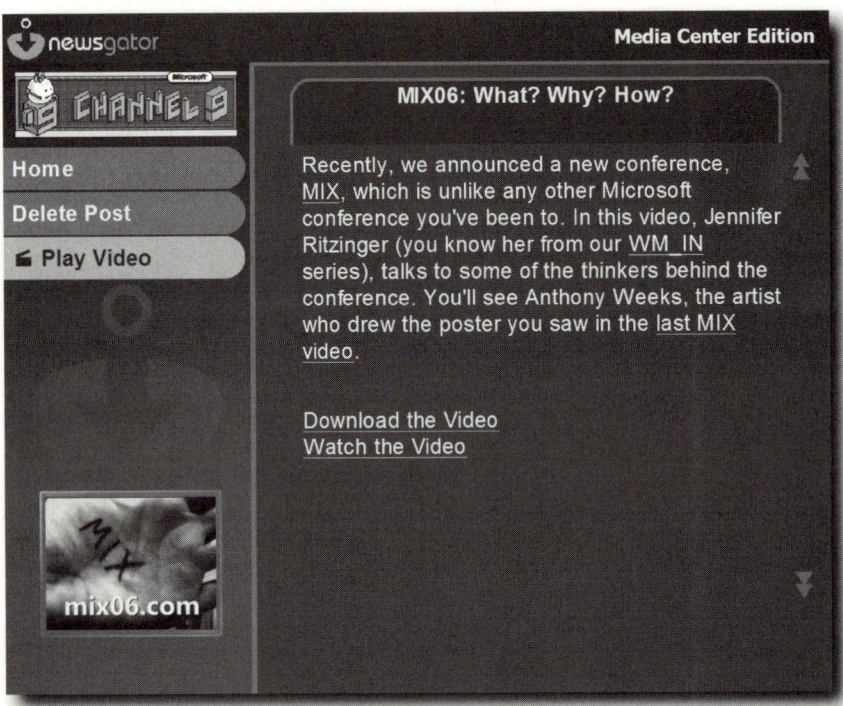

Recently, we announced a new conference, MIX, which is unlike any other Microsoft conference you've been to. In this video, Jennifer Ritzinger (you know her from our WM_IN series), talks to some of the thinkers behind the conference. You'll see Anthony Weeks, the artist who drew the poster you saw in the last MIX video.

FIGURE 15-15: NewsGator MCE.

## Media Center Plug-ins

Media Center has a plug-in architecture that many independent developers have taken advantage of to create numerous add-on applications. One developer, mcesoft (www.mcesoft.nl), has created two plug-ins specifically to download and play video from two popular videoblogs: Rocketboom (Figure 15-16) and Rebell.tv. If you just want to watch Rocketboom (www.rocketboom.com) or the German-language Rebell.tv (http://intervention.ch/vlog), the mcesoft plug-ins are a perfect fit.

Windows Media Center combined with RSS readers and plug-ins enable people to watch "old media" (such as network or cable TV) to incorporate independently produced videoblogs into their TV diet in just a few clicks. By incorporating videoblogs alongside traditional media, these new applications "flatten" the media-viewing experience for creators and viewers alike. Similar to the egalitarian web, where anyone can have a web site and compete with the big players, new software and devices are making it possible for anyone to compete for living-room television. More and more videoblogs are being created with a main focus on an RSS feed. These videobloggers are interested in having their content distributed to devices that connect to home entertainment systems.

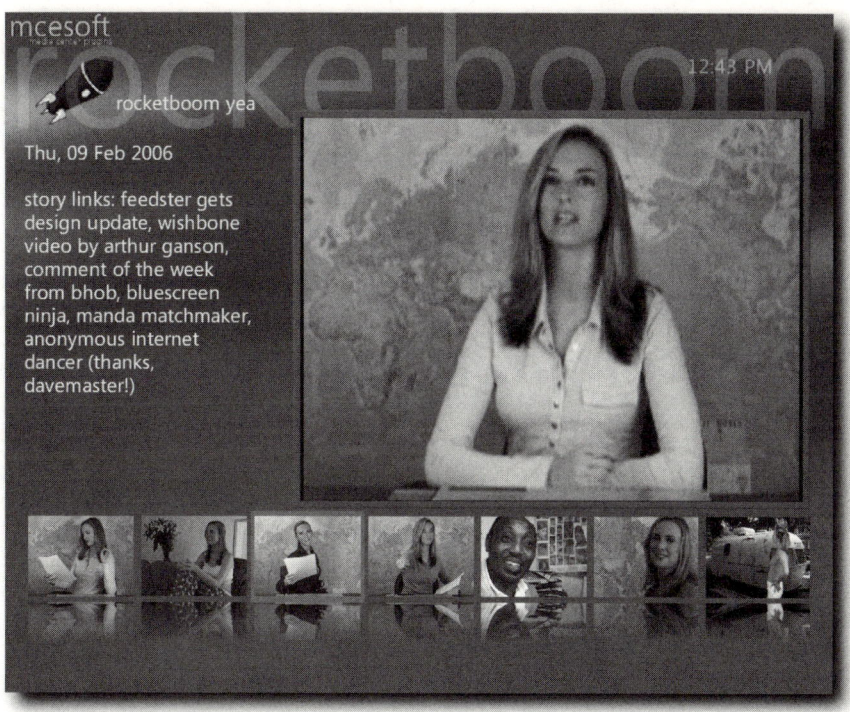

FIGURE 15-16: mcesoft's Rocketboom plug-in.

# Summary

As a videoblogger, you know that you (and everyone else) can produce video that people can watch on their computers. Through creativity and ingenuity, software developers are creating ways for people to watch your videos on their TVs. As videoblogging grows out of the realm of "alpha geeks" and finds its way into the mainstream, video entertainment as most people know it will change dramatically.

# Customizing Your Videoblog

The visual aspect of your videoblog is the first interaction a potential viewer has with you and your videos. By customizing its appearance, you have the opportunity to attract viewers who might otherwise pass it by as just another blog.

## Create a Vlogroll

The vast majority of blogs have a list of other blogs in a sidebar. The list is representative of the blogs that the author reads on a regular basis and is called a *blogroll*. In reality, it's a great way for bloggers to promote each other.

Many blog software packages make it exceptionally easy to create a blogroll, while others require you to do it manually. Some blog packages even extend the metaphor to include Xhtml Friends Network (XFN) information. (You can learn more about XFN at `http://gmpg.org/xfn`.)

In its simplest form, however, a blogroll is a list of links. In the video-blogging sphere, people *vlogroll* each other (see Figure 16-1).

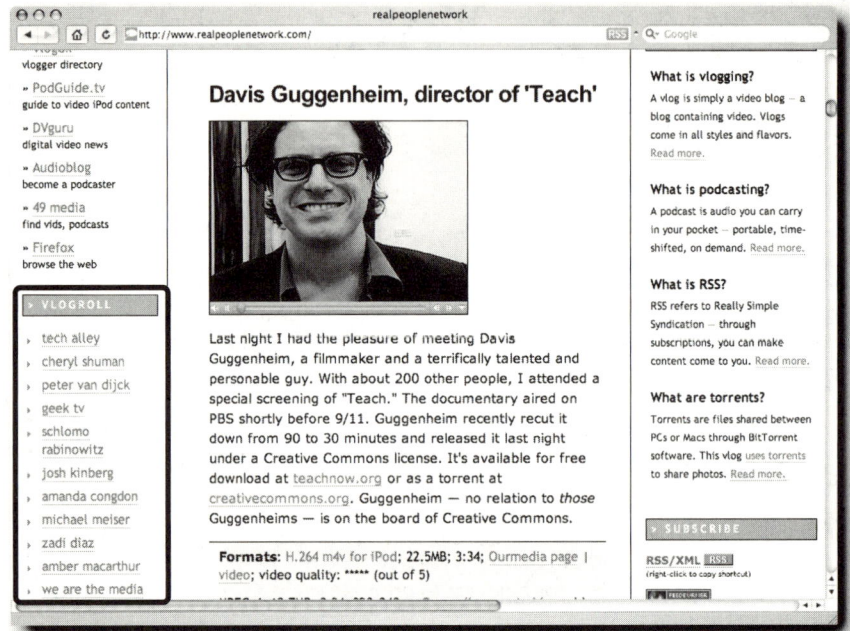

FIGURE **16-1:** A vlogroll.

You can use your blog software's built-in tool (if possible), hand- build a list using HTML, or use Videoblogging Universe's unique vlogroll-creation tool (`http://videoblogging-universe.com/vlogroll`) to create a vlogroll for your videoblog.

## Using Blog Software

Blog software such as Blogger, TypePad, and WordPress all include an easy way to create a vlogroll. Often, all you need to do is type the URL to the site you want to link to and a name for the link (see Figure 16-2).

## Creating an HTML List

To build a vlogroll using HTML, create an unordered (un-numbered) list of links. The HTML tag for an unordered list is `<ul>`. Then, for each link in the list, create a list item, (using the `<li>` tag). Finally, to create a link, use the `<a href>` tag. For example, to create a vlogroll for "90 Seconds of Dave," "Eric Rice," and "FreeVlog," the HTML would be:

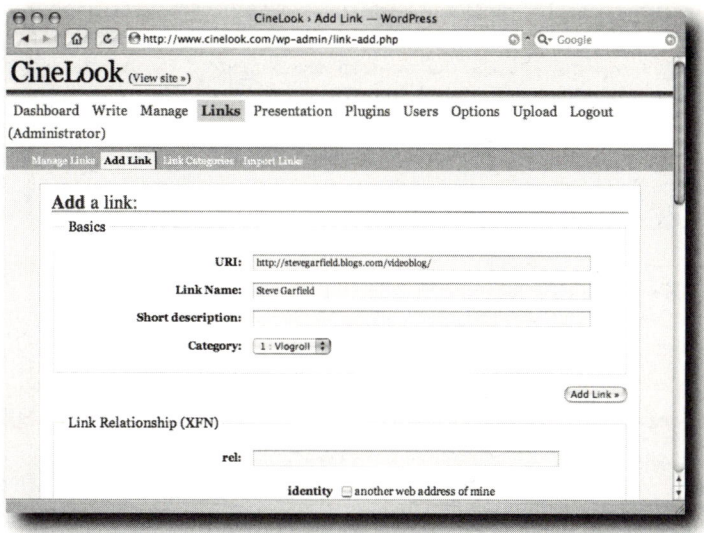

**FIGURE 16-2:** Adding a vlogroll link in WordPress.

```
<ul>
   <li>
      <a href='http://davemedia.blogspot.com/'>
      90 Seconds of Dave
      </a>
   </li>
   <li>
      <a href='http://blog.ericrice.com/blog/TVVideo'>
      Eric Rice
      </a>
   </li>
   <li>
      <a href='http://freevlog.org/wordpress/'>
      FreeVlog
      </a>
   </li>
</ul>
```

## Using Videoblogging Universe

For a really distinctive vlogroll, try Videoblogging Universe's vlogroll tool. What makes the vlogroll unique is that it is a visual list of videoblogs, in addition to the links. Beyond that, whenever a user places his mouse over one of the videoblog images, the video plays! It really has to be experienced to be appreciated. (Print just doesn't do it justice!)

To use the tool, point your web browser to `http://videoblogging-universe.com/ vlogroll`, check off the videoblogs that you'd like to have in your list, and click the Submit button. You'll receive a snippet of HTML that you can use to create your vlogroll, as well as a sample of what the vlogroll will look like (see Figure 16-3) and how it will work.

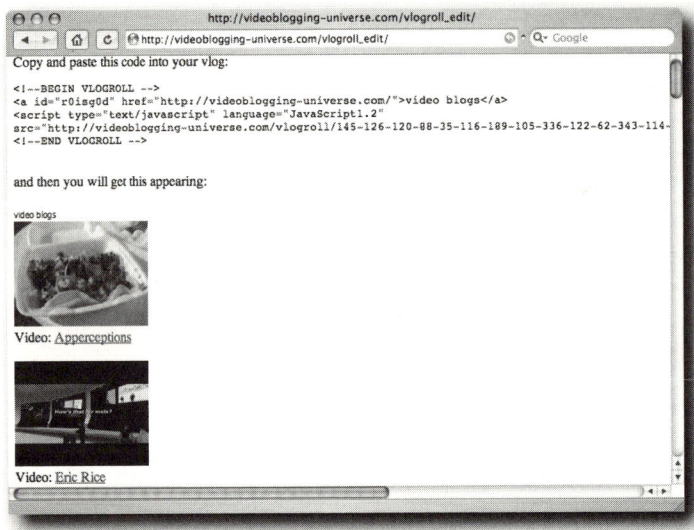

FIGURE 16-3: A vlogroll as created by Videoblogging Universe.

Placing a vlogroll on your site not only jazzes it up; it also informs your viewers about the videoblogs you find interesting.

# Watermark Your Videos

If you've watched television in the last few years, you've no doubt seen a network watermark. It's often a small, slightly transparent logo located in a corner of the screen. Although you don't have to follow this convention, it works quite well and is well tolerated by viewers.

Your watermark can be as simple as a line of text or as elaborate as a color logo, although you should take care not to overpower your video image (Figure 16-4). The best way to accomplish this is to limit the size of the watermark and add a little transparency to it. For reference, flip through a few channels on your television and see how the various networks apply their watermarks.

Use your editing software to create your watermark. When you have completed your project, but before you export it for the web, add a video layer to your timeline.

Watermark

FIGURE 16-4: A visual watermark.

Then import the watermark file and place it within the new video layer. Make sure it runs the length of your timeline. Otherwise, you'll have a section of video that isn't covered by your identifier.

**Tip**   If you are using QuickTime Pro, you can take your complete watermarked video and make it "clickable." To accomplish this, just add an HREF track that opens a particular web page when the video is clicked. You can learn about how to implement an HREF track in Chapter 7.

When you're satisfied with the overall look and placement of your watermark, you can export your video for distribution, knowing that anywhere it travels, viewers will know where it came from.

## Apple iMovie and Windows Movie Maker Tips

Apple iMovie and Windows Movie Maker do not have built-in ways to create watermarks. As usual, however, third parties have devised methods to do so.

For iMovie, the "picture in clip" plug-in (`www.imovieplugins.com/plugs/pictinclipstat.html`; $1.50) from cf/x enables you to select an image and place it as an overlay on your video. You can also control the image's location, transparency, and framing.

For Movie Maker, Rehan of RehanFX (www.rehanfx.com) has provided instructions on creating a watermark at `www.rehanfx.org/customtc.htm`. You'll also find a wealth of information about getting the most out of Movie Maker throughout the site.

# Add a Theme to WordPress

WordPress is one of the more popular blog packages available. You can use it for free at www.wordpress.com, find a hosting provider that offers it as an easy install (such as DreamHost at www.dreamhost.com), or download the software to run on your own server at www.wordpress.org. Because WordPress is widely distributed and easy to customize, a large number of users have contributed easy-to-integrate themes to the community. These themes alter the appearance of the blog without affecting the contents.

You can locate themes using the following web sites:

- http://wordpress.org/extend/themes
- http://codex.wordpress.org/Using_Themes/Theme_List
- http://alexking.org/index.php?content=software/wordpress/↩ themes.php
- http://themes.wordpress.net/theme-viewer.php
- http://bloggingpro.com/archives/category/wordpress-themes

## Browsing Themes

Some sites offer a "theme browser," such as the one at Alex King's site: www.alexking.org/software/wordpress/theme_browser.php. A theme browser such as the one shown in Figure 16-5 enables you to see a sample of what the theme looks like, without having to download and install it.

Theme browsers are a great way to experience all the different "looks" available for WordPress, making it easier for you to decide on a theme to use for your videoblog. When you find a theme you want to use, simply download the theme's file, usually as a .zip archive. Then install it.

## Installing a Theme

After downloading a theme file, you need to upload it to your server. If the theme file is archived, such as in a .zip file, extract it. Uploading your theme requires a file-transfer tool.

---

### WordPress.com

If you are using WordPress.com for blogging, you cannot install your own theme. However, you'll quickly discover that a large selection of themes has been preinstalled for you to use. Each theme offers its own customization options.

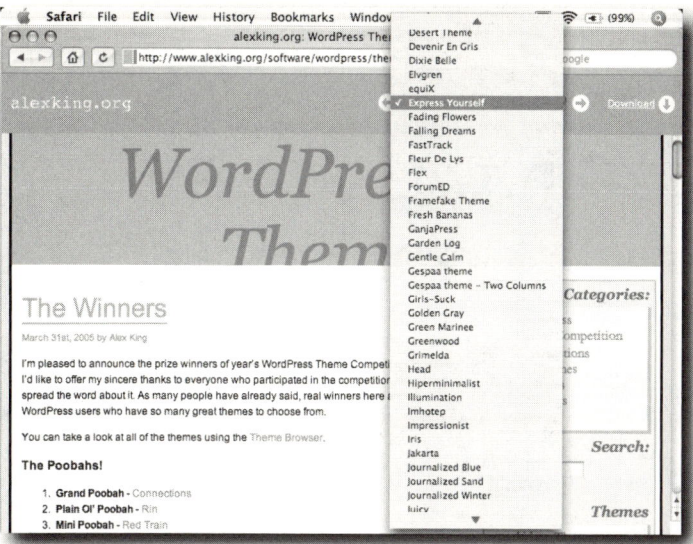

FIGURE 16-5: Using a theme browser.

The most popular tool for transferring files is the File Transfer Protocol (FTP), and a number of applications are available to help you use it. If you are using Windows, a good FTP client is FileZilla (http://filezilla.sourceforge.net; open source, free), and for Mac OS X there is CyberDuck (http://cyberduck.ch; open source, free). You can also use the built-in FTP tool by using command on Windows or Terminal on Mac OS X.

To upload and install a theme, launch your FTP client, enter the username and password for your server, and log in. Then place the theme files inside the themes folder, which is located in the wp-contents folder of your WordPress installation. If you discover that there is no themes folder, create it. Once you've placed the theme files, you've installed your theme. Easy, huh?

## Activating a Theme

To activate an installed theme, log in to your blog (using an Administrator's account). Click the Presentation link, which enables you to see the various themes you have available. Locate the theme you want to use and click its link. It becomes the active theme.

Finally, click the View Site link to see how your site has changed. The beauty of it is that it's instant and you can change the theme as often as you want.

Figures 16-6 and 16-7 show examples of themes.

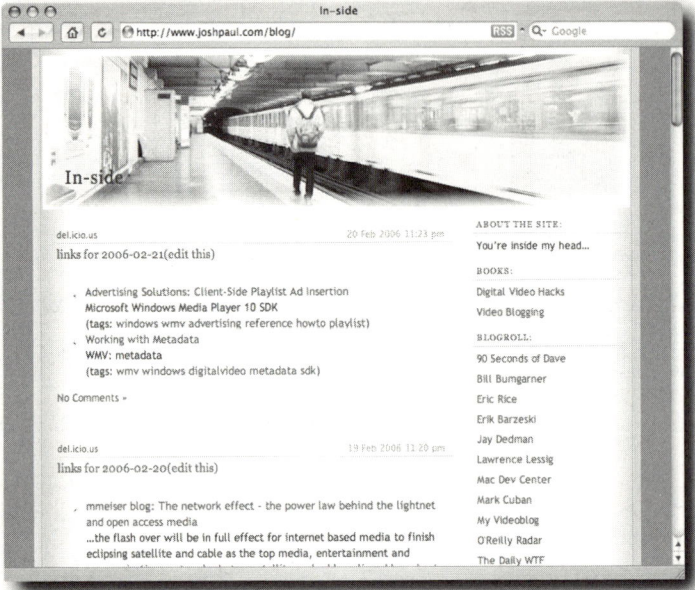

FIGURE 16-6: The FastTrack theme.

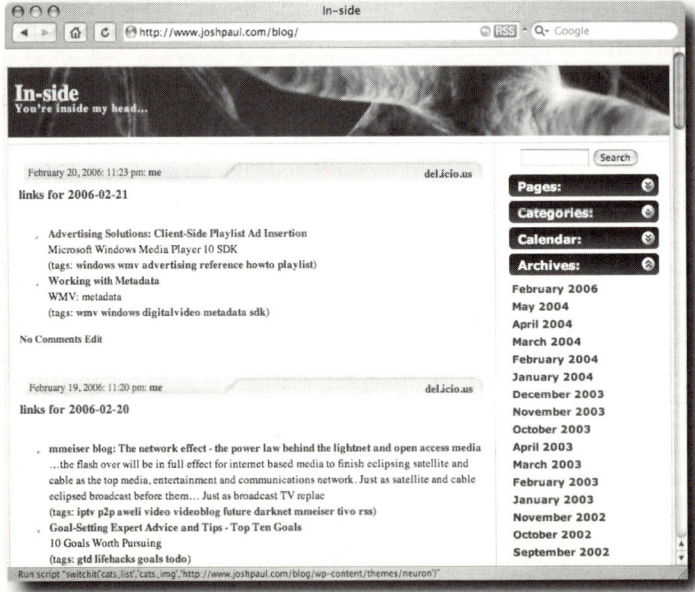

FIGURE 16-7: The Neuron theme.

# Create a Visual Archive

Practically every blog has an archive available, usually on the sidebar of the site (see Figure 16-8). An archive enables people to browse previous posts. A videoblog is more of a visual medium, though, so to make browsing your archives easier for your viewers, you can create a visual archive that they can quickly browse.

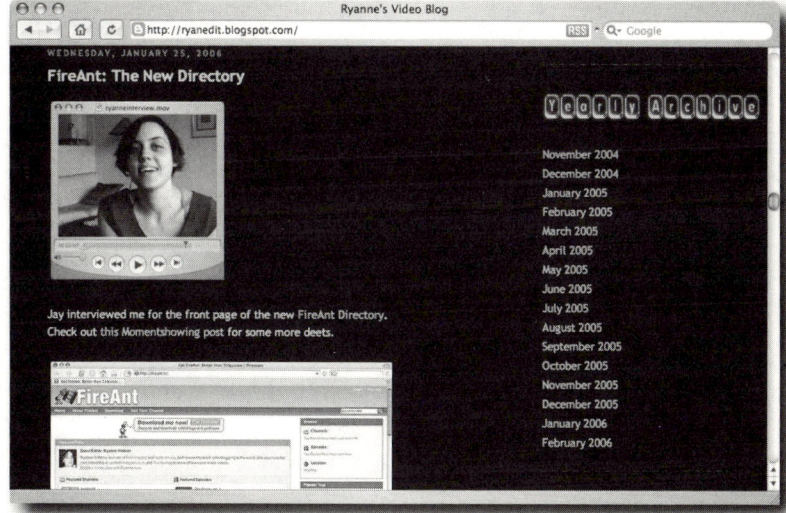

FIGURE 16-8: A textual archive on a videoblog.

Creating a visual archive can be a tedious and technically difficult process, but Peter Van Djick of Mefeedia (www.mefeedia.com) decided to make the process easy for just about anyone. Also, he made it so that although Mefeedia creates the visual archive, it can be embedded on any web site, including your videoblog.

To use Mefeedia's visual-archive tool, you need a Mefeedia account. If you don't have one, create one; then log in to the site.

Mefeedia must be aware of your videoblog, so add it to the directory if you haven't already. To add your feed to Mefeedia's directory, simply click the Add a Feed link at the top of any page and enter your blog's RSS URL. Next, click the Add This RSS Feed button, and Mefeedia takes care of the rest.

## Find Your Feed ID

To create a visual archive using Mefeedia's tool, you need to know your Feed ID. To find it, click the Directory link in the navigation section of the page, and look for your feed using the supplied search form.

When you find your feed, click the More Info link just below the information for your blog. Then look at the URL in your browser, which should be something like this: `http://Mefeedia.com/feeds/5903`.

Notice the number at the end of the URL (5903 in this example). That's the Feed ID and is the number you need to create your visual archive.

**Note** At the time of this writing, Mefeedia's working on an easier way for users to create a visual archive. When it's finished implementing the feature, you'll be able to simply find your feed and click a Get Thumbs for This Feed on Your Website link. This will return a page with the relevant information.

## Create the Archive

Click the My Video link in the navigation bar, and the My Videos page (see Figure 16-9) displays a list of the videos in your queue, videos you've tagged, and your favorite videos. Click the Instant Archive link on the left side of the screen to create your visual archive.

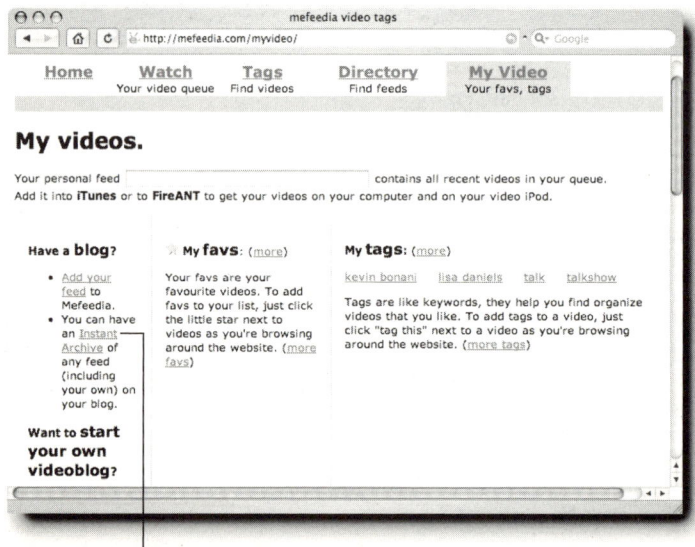

Instant Archive link.

FIGURE 16-9: The My Videos page.

On the resulting page (see Figure 16-10), enter your Feed ID in the designated box and click the Use This Feed ID button next to it. Then copy the HTML that Step 2 supplies.

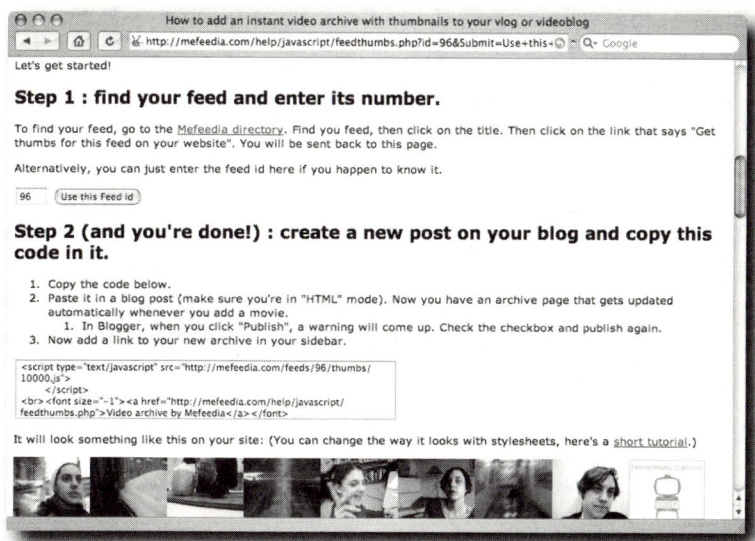

FIGURE 16-10: Creating a visual archive using a Feed ID.

## Place the Archive on Your Site

Now create a New Post (or New Page, if your software provides for it) for your videoblog and paste in the HTML. The code looks similar to this:

```
<script type="text/javascript" src="http://mefeedia.com/feeds/5842/thumbs/
10000.js"></script><br/><font size="-1"><a href="http://mefeedia.com/help/
javascript/feedthumbs.php">Video archive by Mefeedia</a></font>
```

Publish the Post/Page and view it in your browser. Figure 16-11 shows an example result.

After verifying that your visual archive works as expected, copy the complete URL for the post. Because the URL is a direct link to your visual archive, using it as a link enables people to easily view your archive in the future. To add the post as a link, edit your blog's sidebar to include it as:

```
<a href="http://the.post.url">Video Archive</a>
```

As a bonus to Mefeedia's creating the archive for you, the site constantly updates the visual images contained in the archive — it requires no maintenance on your part. Considering how easy Mefeedia makes it to create a visual archive, and the impact that it creates, every videoblogger should take a few minutes to produce one.

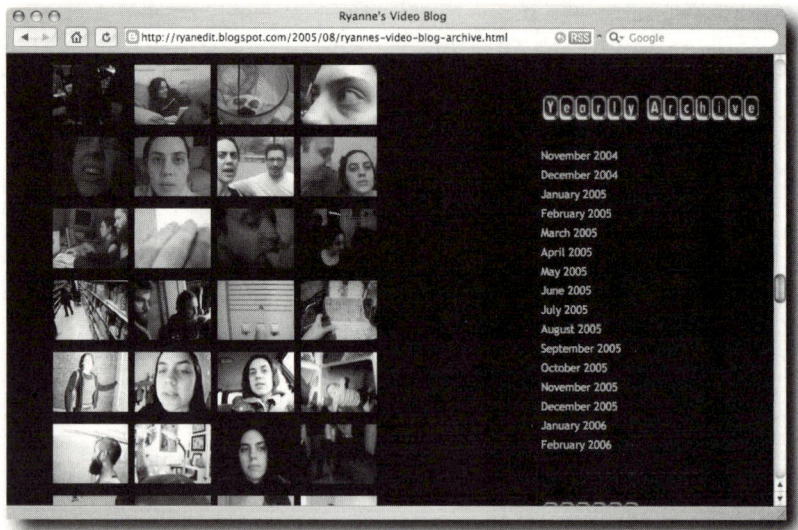

FIGURE 16-11: A visual archive on a videoblog.

## Summary

There are a variety of ways for you to customize the appearance of your videoblog. From creating a list of other videobloggers to creating a visual archive of your footage, changing the visual aspect of your videoblog is an easy, fun, and creative way to extend the theme of your videos to a web page.

# Pimp Your Vlog

part

VI

# Tagging To Make Videos Stand Out

**M**uch like keywords, tags help describe content with metadata (data about data). Many of today's popular search engines use the same concept to effectively find Web pages. However, images and video pose a unique problem because metadata is not directly embedded inside the media; it is contained in the web page that embeds the media.

## Tagging in Mefeedia

After you've created and posted video to your blog, you more than likely want people to watch. You can help make your videos easier to find on the web by *tagging* them in different services. Tagging labels photos and videos with simple, descriptive keywords, alleviating the problem of identifying them. Tagging can also help to group similar videos together.

## Understanding Tags

You can use various kinds of tags to group movies together in different ways. Perhaps you want to indicate the names of the people who appear in your videos. For example, if you wanted to find videos that Josh Leo appears in or is mentioned in, you can search using the `joshleo` tag at a site like Mefeedia—`www.mefeedia.com/tags/joshleo`. Figure 17-1 shows the result of such a search.

Tags can be topical, like the name of a city: `http://mefeedia.com/tags/newyorkcity`. Events are also good candidates for tags because you can group all videos of an event around a tag. In 2005, "The Gates," an art event by Cristo in New York's Central Park, was recorded by a group of videobloggers. The videos were tagged with `gates`, and you can find these videos at `http://mefeedia.com/tags/gates` (see Figure 17-2)—there are orange flags everywhere!

FIGURE 17-1: Videos with Josh Leo.

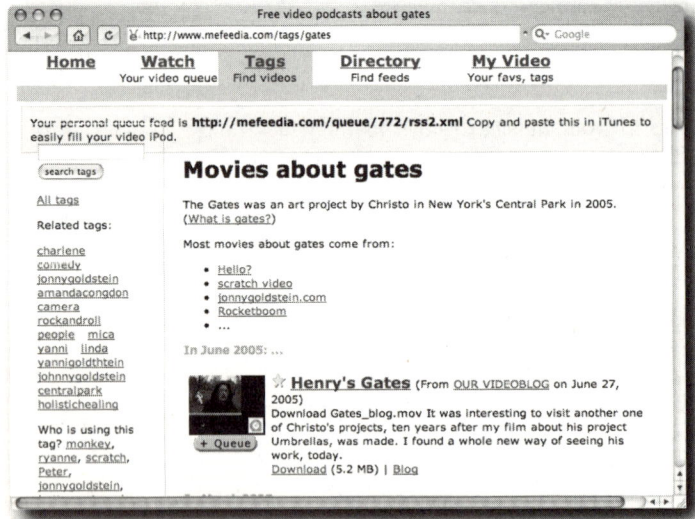

FIGURE 17-2: Videos from the Cristo art event.

Tags can be created to mark any event or subject you want. For example, in 2005 a group of videobloggers decided to make a videoblog every day of the week and called this "Videoblogging Week 2005." The resulting videos can be found at `http://mefeedia .com/tags/videobloggingweek2005`.

As you can probably tell, tags are very flexible in their use.

## How to Tag

Applying a tag depends on the system you are using. Most systems adhere to a simple standard that uses `rel="tag"` in HTML, which is explained more in "Using Technorati Tags," later in this chapter. If you aren't comfortable with HTML or you want to tag other people's videos, you can use Mefeedia's tagging tool.

Tagging in Mefeedia is accomplished by logging in to the site and simply browsing videos (fun!). A Tag This! button appears below every video you watch. When clicked, it reveals a simple tagging interface (see Figure 17-3). Just enter a comma-separated list of tags, click the TAG! button, and Mefeedia handles the rest.

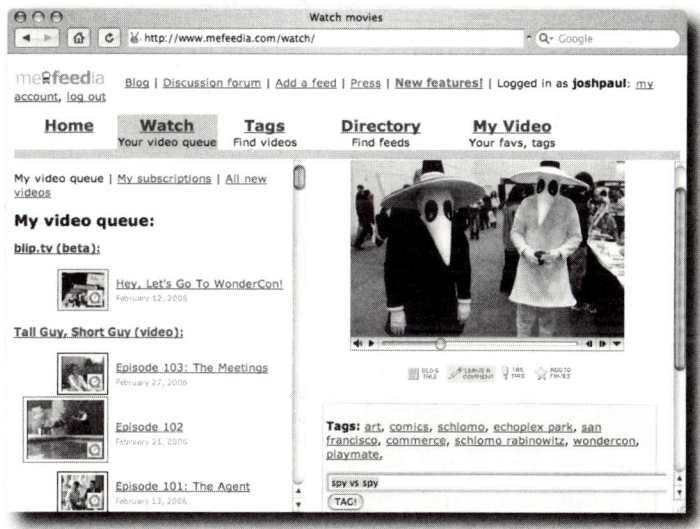

**FIGURE 17-3: Tagging in Mefeedia.**

In Mefeedia, navigate to the My Tags section to see a list of your tags and a list of the videos you've tagged. The My Tags page is the easiest way to find videos you've already seen, and you can use it to organize videos you want to recall later.

## Tags and Spaces

Some tag services don't allow spaces in tags—Mefeedia does. So you can create tags called `Peter Sellers`, and `I hate these videos`, and they'll show up at:

    http://mefeedia.com/tags/peter_sellers/

    http://mefeedia.com/tags/i_hate_these_videos/

Note the underscores; spaces get turned into underscores in the URL. Also, notice that capitals are removed, so all tags are lowercase throughout the system. Other tag services require you to enter the underscores instead of spaces.

## Browsing Tags

You can also browse other people's tags using Mefeedia. Browsing tags lets you view what other people have been tagging and can be useful in finding new videos and videobloggers. Just browse around the tags by clicking links to related tags and watching the related videos.

Mefeedia has a unique feature that enables users to write descriptions for tags. The descriptions make the tags more understandable, especially in the case of tags with obscure meanings. For example, the tag "videobloggingweek2005" doesn't completely describe the related videos (unless, of course, you're already "in the know"), but `http://mefeedia .com/tags/videobloggingweek2005` (see Figure 17-4) explains it.

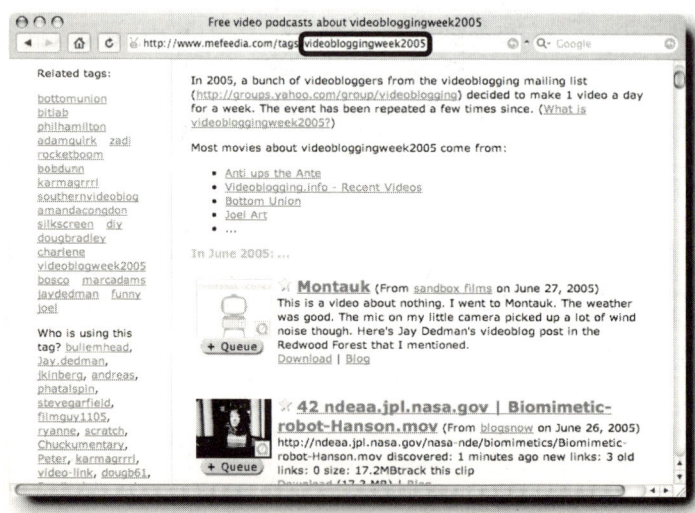

FIGURE 17-4: videobloggingweek2005 and its description.

The description shows up on the tag's related page.

In Mefeedia, anyone can edit the description of a tag, and the idea is that you write these descriptions objectively. It works somewhat like a wiki, so you can go a tag page, click Edit Description, and add your changes. Everyone can then view the changes. It's a collaborative environment. Most directories and video services have similar tagging systems, although not always as full featured.

# Geotag a Videoblog

Believe it or not, you can add geographical data to your videos. This is often called getting *mapped* or *geotagged*. Geotagging is the process of associating geographical information with various types of media such as web sites, RSS feeds, and rich media, especially video. Videobloggers can use these geographic tags (geotags) to add more context to their web sites, as well as to their individual videos and videoblog posts. Geotag data consists of latitude and longitude coordinates, although it also supports altitude and location names.

As a result of the complexity of embedding metadata into a video file, geotags normally remain in text format external to the video. There are currently several ways to geotag content, including adding geotags to a web page as well as to a specific element within a web page. The same is true for an RSS feed, in that both the feed and each item in the feed can contain geotags.

The easiest way to get your site geotagged is to submit it to VlogMap.org, a community map that displays the locations of videobloggers worldwide (Figure 17-5).

FIGURE 17-5: Videoblogs from around the world.

### Why Geotagging Is Important

Imagine searching for a video about the Pike Place Market in Seattle. Currently, the only way you might be able to find this content is to search for the keywords "video" and "pike place market." The problem with this is that these words will not be found in the video but rather inside a page or caption that only relates to the video.

As more audio, video, and rich media is placed onto the web, it will become increasingly important to make your media easy to find. By geotagging, you can help make this a reality.

To get your videoblog on the map, visit the home page at `www.vlogmap.org` and click on the Submit link at the top. Complete the form on the Submit A Video Blog page and then click Submit New Video Blog. The process is as simple as providing your videoblog's name, a link to your videoblog, and the location on a map, specifically the latitude and longitude coordinates. By submitting to VlogMap, you are effectively geotagging your videoblog site, making it easier for others to find it.

## Geotagging Your Content

Following is a barebones example of the geotag elements, in which X represents longitude, Y represents latitude, and Z represents the optional altitude value. So, if you shot a video at the Statue of Liberty, you would use:

```
<geo:long>40.69016</geo:long>
<geo:lat>-74.04492</geo:lat>
<geo:alt>0</geo:alt>
```

To geotag, find the longitude and latitude of the location you want to represent, most likely where your video was acquired. A quick way to find the longitude and latitude of a location is to use a GPS receiver. Given that the majority of people don't have access to a GPS receiver, however, there is a great list of resources available at `http://jan.ucc.nau.edu/~cvm/latlon_find_location.html`.

According to the World Wide Web Consortium (W3C), the basic geo vocabulary was created as "an informal collaboration" and is "not currently on the W3C recommendation track for standardization." That just means that it is not standardized for professional Geographic Information Systems (GIS) use. The web community has adopted geotags, however, and support is on the rise.

### Geotagging a Web Page

To associate a location with an entire web page, use the `<meta>` tag in the page's `<head>` element:

```
<meta property="geo:lat">40.69016</meta>
<meta property="geo:long">-74.04492</meta>
```

If you want to see a map of where the web page originated, you can go to `http://maps.google.com` and enter `40.69016, -74.04492`.

Figure 17-6 shows an example of a Google-mapped location.

FIGURE 17-6: Mapping a geotag.

## Geotagging an HTML Element

In addition to defining a web page's geolocation, specific elements inside an HTML document can also contain geotags by using the tag in combination with the namespace declaration and a `display:none` style, like this:

```
<span xmlns:geo="http://www.w3.org/2003/01/geo/wgs84_pos#"
style="display:none">
  <geo:lat>40.69016</geo:lat>
  <geo:long>-74.04492</geo:long>
</span>
```

The namespace declaration (`xmlns:geo="http://www.w3.org/2003/01/geo/wgs84_pos#"`) is not needed if it has been defined in a parent element.

---

### Tech Talk

The prefix `geo:` is defined by the RDFIG Geo namespace at:

```
http://www.w3.org/2003/01/geo/
```

Namespaces are used in HTML and XML to expand the markup elements. The preceding namespace defines the various geo elements that can be used in your markup.

### Geotagging an RSS feed

RSS feeds support two levels of geotagging: the feed as a whole and the individual posts. The overall feed can define the geo:lat and geo:long tags to specify a "base" location. In addition, individual posts can contain the geo:lat and geo:long tags to define the location of particular item.

The basic structure is the same as tagging an entire page, but you must remember to declare the namespace. Here is a complete RSS example, displaying the use of the geo namespace and both types of geotagging (feed and individual post):

```
<?xml version="1.0" encoding="UTF-8"?>
<rss version="2.0"
xmlns:geo="http://www.w3.org/2003/01/geo/wgs84_pos#">
  <channel>
    <title>VlogMap.org</title>
    <link>http://www.vlogmap.org/blog/</link>
    <description>The World of Video Blogs</description>
    <geo:lat>47.612</geo:lat>
    <geo:long>-122.328</geo:long>
    <item>
      <title>The Statue of Liberty</title>
      <link>http://www.nps.gov/stli/</link>
      <geo:lat>38.8974</geo:lat>
      <geo:long>-77.0363</geo:long>
    </item>
  </channel>
</rss>
```

The first link of the feed declares the XML version and encoding. The second line is where the namespace is declared, which aids in the actual geotagging. Next, the channel starts, followed by the title, link, and description tags. You'll notice that the geo:lat and geo:long tags follow, which are for the latitude and longitude numbers for the channel.

After the latitude and longitude are declared for the channel, items can follow. This feed contains only one item, which has the title of The Statue of Liberty. Once the title is provided, the link for the item is given, along with the geo:lat and geo:long tags.

# Tagging Videos as "geovlogged"

geotagged is a tag that has been gaining support in both Flickr (www.flickr.com) and del.icio.us (http://del.icio.us), but VlogMap.org started a more specific tag called geovlogged. The purpose of tags is to make items easier to find and to group similar links together, so it made sense to create a tag to help gather all of the videoblogs that have been geotagged. Any link to a videoblog, or even a video that's stored in del.icio.us using the geovlogged tag, should include the geo:lat=X and geo:long=Y elements.

## Using Google Earth to Browse Videoblogs

Many people agree that one of the best software projects released in 2005 was Google Earth (`http://earth.google.com/downloads.html`; free). The application combines satellite imagery and geographic information with the capability to "fly around" 3D terrain and buildings. The really great engineers at Google enabled Google Earth with the capability to add external data, which the application calls a Network Link.

With the Network Link files available from `www.vlogmap.org/google_earth.php` (download the `.kmz` files), you can use Google Earth to browse videoblogs. It's really something that has to be experienced to be appreciated, but if you'd like a sample of what it's like (and what can be done creatively), visit `http://randomshow.com/archives/9-Wonderful-World.html`. It is a wonderful world.

# Adding Technorati Tags

Technorati (`www.technorati.com`) is a web site that tracks blogs . . . a lot of blogs. In fact, according to the site, "Technorati is the authority on what's going on in the world of weblogs." It tracks 28.9 million sites as of this writing. It does so by using tags to help locate and organize blog posts, such as those tagged with `privacy` (Figure 17-7).

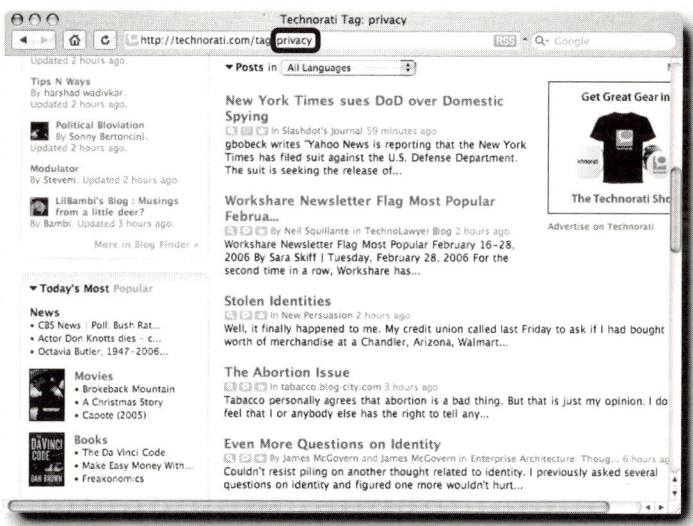

FIGURE 17-7: Technorati's list for "privacy."

### Automating Technorati Tags

Because Technorati focuses on blogs, it has been designed to take advantage of the more popular blog packages. Therefore, if you're using WordPress, TypePad, or MovableType for your blogging software, you can use Categories within your posts to work as tags. For example, if you set up a Category for Privacy, you could check it whenever you create a post related to privacy. Technorati treats Categories as tags.

Technorati is a membership-oriented site, but you don't have to be a member to take advantage of its indexing features. You simply need to add compatible tags with each of your videoblog posts.

## Adding a Tag

To add a tag to a videoblog post, you have to enter a small amount of HTML for every tag you want to associate with. For example, to associate a post with the tag `Privacy`, you would add the following HTML:

```
<a href="http://technorati.com/tag/privacy" rel="tag">Privacy</a>
```

You can tag using any word or combination of words, including ones you make up, although it is highly recommended that you use "video" and "videoblog" as tags for any videoblog posts. Do so simply by using the following HTML:

```
<a href="http://technorati.com/tag/video" rel="tag">Video</a>
<a href="http://technorati.com/tag/videoblog" rel="tag">Videoblog</a>
```

You can also create multiple word tags by using a + between each word. For example, a tag for "ice cream" would be `ice+cream`:

```
<a href="http://technorati.com/tag/ice+cream" rel="tag">Ice Cream</a>
```

Technorati is not case sensitive, so you don't need to be concerned with capitalizing words. You can read more about the tagging feature in Technorati at www.technorati.com/help/tags.html.

If you have multiple blogs, or simply want to be a little creative, you may want to create a tag using your name. By doing so you'll have a searchable, listable Technorati tag with your name, and you'll wind up having a page on Technorati's site! Granted, other people could use your name as a tag, too, but the incentive is probably pretty low (unless, of course, you're a subject of the post they're tagging).

# Summary

Until computers are advanced enough to identify the subjects of a video and recognize the words in the audio, a human must add this identifying information as an extra step through tagging. With exponential amounts of video being produced and placed online, it is important to ensure that your content can be found easily.

# Letting People Know About Your Feed

For the most part, people won't just stumble across your videoblog. How can you help people find you? Well, you can always tell your friends and family about your videoblog, hoping that they pass the word along to their friends, and so on. You can also make announcements on user groups like the Yahoo! Videoblogging Group's newsgroup. But those approaches can only go so far.

Fortunately, there are a variety of free tools that you can use to publicize your videoblog to the world.

## Getting Listed in Videoblog Directories

Directories are popular places for people to find videoblogs. Specifically, they find them through directories such as VlogMap (www.vlogmap .org), VlogDir (www.vlogdir.com), Mefeedia (www.mefeedia.com), and FireAnt (www.fireant.tv). Passing your videoblog's information along to these directories is easy.

### VlogMap

One of the first places to put your RSS feed is VlogMap. The site was launched in early 2005, when Google opened up its mapping system for savvy developers to use. When using VlogMap, you can see where videobloggers are all over the world (see Figure 18-1). To do so, just click one of the thumbnails; you're provided site and feed information regarding who is videoblogging in that area. Using VlogMap a great way to meet people locally or see life in parts of the world that you may never visit.

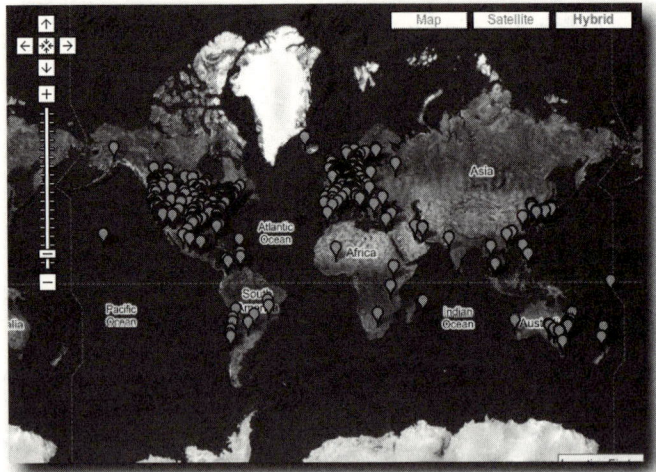

FIGURE 18-1: VlogMap.

To add your feed, simply click the Submit link in the toolbar on the front page. The resulting form (see Figure 18-2) walks you through the process of placing your feed on the map. It even allows you to click a map to gather your latitude and longitude.

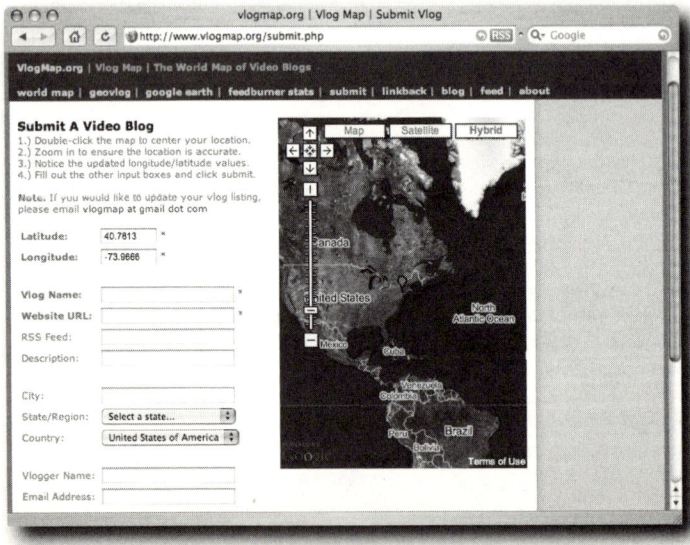

FIGURE 18-2: Submitting a videoblog.

All submissions are moderated, but they are usually added to the directory within 24 hours.

## VlogDir

VlogDir is one of the few directories available that is specific to videoblogs. It is designed to help promote original, independent video content and is open to everyone. To be listed in the VlogDir, go to www.vlogdir.com and click GET YO' VLOG ON! on the front page. Then fill in the requested information (see Figure 18-3), and click "Submit Vlog." It's really that easy.

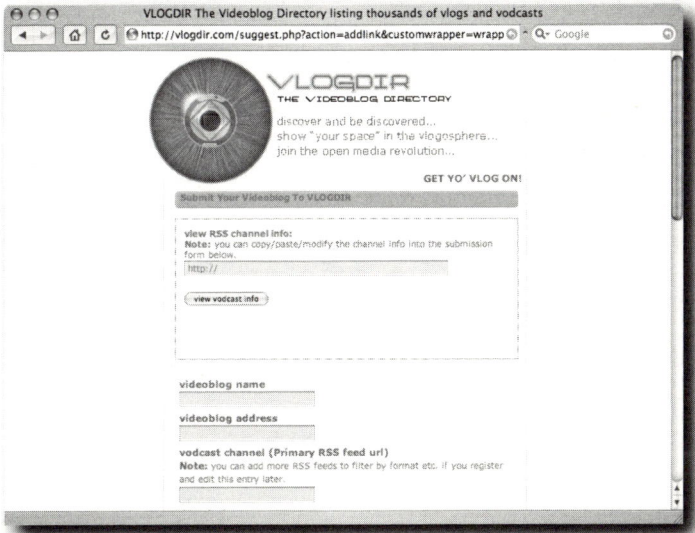

FIGURE 18-3: Submitting to VlogDir.

## Mefeedia

Run by one of the original members of the Yahoo! videoblogging group, Peter Van Dijck, Mefeedia has one of the largest collections of video feeds available. To be listed in Mefeedia, go to the home page and click the Add A Feed link at the top of the page. The Add a Videoblog to Mefeedia page opens, as shown in Figure 18-4.

After you've added your videoblog to the directory, you can go to your feed page and click the Promote This Videoblog link. Mefeedia has several promotional ideas for you (see Figure 18-5).

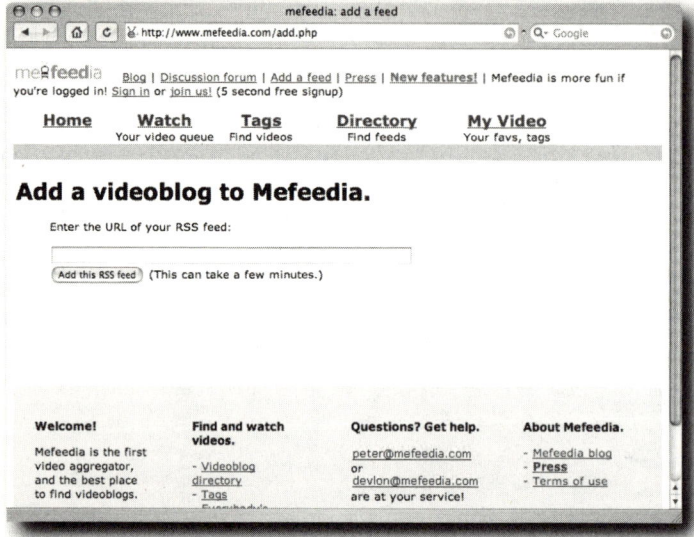

FIGURE 18-4: Mefeedia.

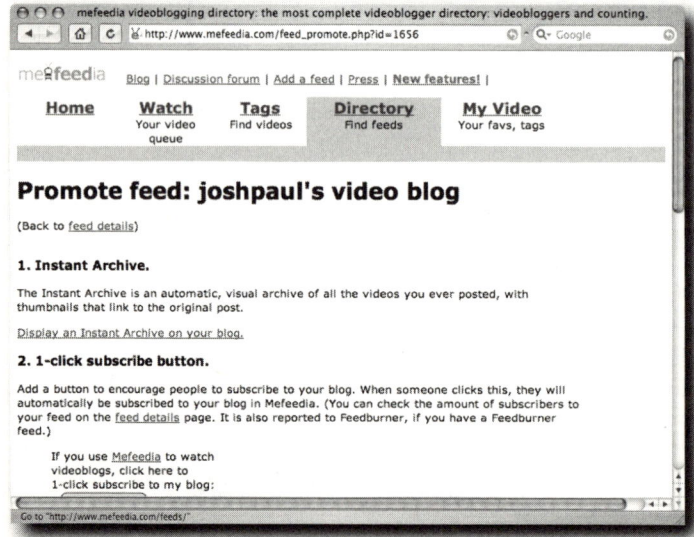

FIGURE 18-5: Promotional help from Mefeedia.

Besides creating a visual archive, which is very cool, you can also copy the provided HTML code to add to your blog's sidebar. The code provides a link that will automatically subscribe someone to your Mefeedia feed whenever he clicks it.

## FireAnt

FireAnt is similar to iTunes but is open to more video formats and is more interactive. FireAnt makes it easy to add your feed and put a one-click button on your sidebar. To add your feed, log in (or sign up for an account if you don't have one, and then log in), go to Add Your Channel (see Figure 18-6), and submit your feed through the supplied form. If you want to, you can also attach tags to your feed so people can more easily find your videos.

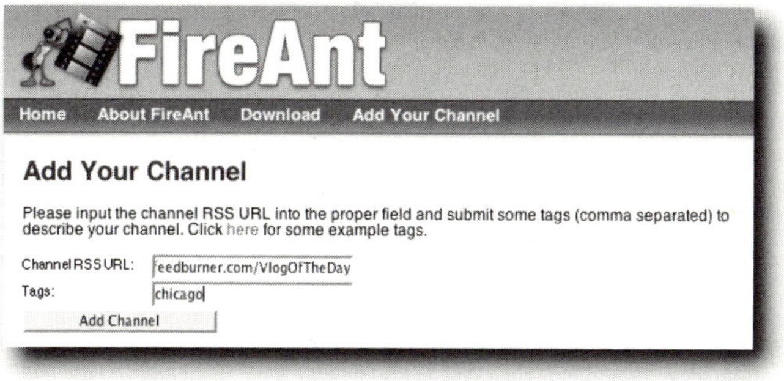

FIGURE 18-6: Adding a channel in FireAnt.

The cool thing about FireAnt is that it's also hooked into an aggregator that automatically downloads videos to which people subscribe. So being listed in FireAnt also helps you reach those people who are using the FireAnt aggregator . . . and a lot are.

Getting listed in directories is a fast, easy way to make your videoblog simple to find.

# Pinging Directories

There are a lot of blog directories on the Internet, and the vast majority of them have made it easy to inform them of when you've updated your videoblog through a process called *pinging*. Pinging involves direct communication with the directory, informing it that there is new content.

To make a blogger's life easier, most blog software takes advantage of the ping feature made available through various directories. If your software doesn't allow you to ping directories, or you're limited in how it pings, you can always use some third-party services such as Technorati (www.technorati.com), ping-o-matic (http://pingomatic.com), or FeedBurner (www.feedburner.com) to accomplish your goal.

## Using Your Blog Software

Pinging can be accomplished automatically by following some basic instructions, depending on the blog software you are using.

### TypePad

After logging into your account, select "Create a Post" to make a new post. Then click the Customize the Layout of This Page link and locate the Post Screen Configuration dialog box. Click the Custom radio button, and then check the TrackBack URLs to Ping checkbox.

Once you've enabled the TrackBack area, enter the URLs you'd like to ping in the Send a TrackBack To These Addresses text area. For your convenience, a list of directory URLs is provided at the end of this section. Finally, click the Save button.

### Movable Type

Although similar to TypePad — it's built from the same foundation — Movable Type offers a different way to ping directories. After you've logged in to your site, select the Settings tab, and click the New Entry Defaults link. On the resulting page, near the bottom, locate the Publicity/Remote Interfaces section. Finally, check the appropriate boxes for the services you would like to ping and then save your changes.

### WordPress

While logged in to the WordPress administration console, select the Options tab from the navigation menu. Then select the Writing sub-menu item, and enter the directory URLs that you want to ping in the Update Services text area, near the bottom of the page. Save your changes.

### Blogger

To enable Blogger to ping, log in to your account and click the Change Settings icon. Then add your blog to Blogger's listings by selecting Yes from the Add Your Blog To Our Listings? section, and save your changes. Blogger then automatically pings the major directories, such as Technorati.

After you've added tags and published a post, you'll more than likely want to inform Technorati, the largest blog-tracking directory. If you don't ping Technorati, the site won't visit your videoblog, and it won't update its information accordingly.

If you are a member of Technorati, you can click Update Ping for your blog. To ping Technorati manually, visit www.technorati.com/ping.html (see Figure 18-7), enter your blog's URL in the provided space, and click the Ping! button.

If your blog software enables you to ping directories, you can automate the process of informing Technorati about new posts by adding http://rpc.technorati.com/rpc/ping to your directory list. By doing so, you won't have to visit Technorati's ping page every time you create a new post.

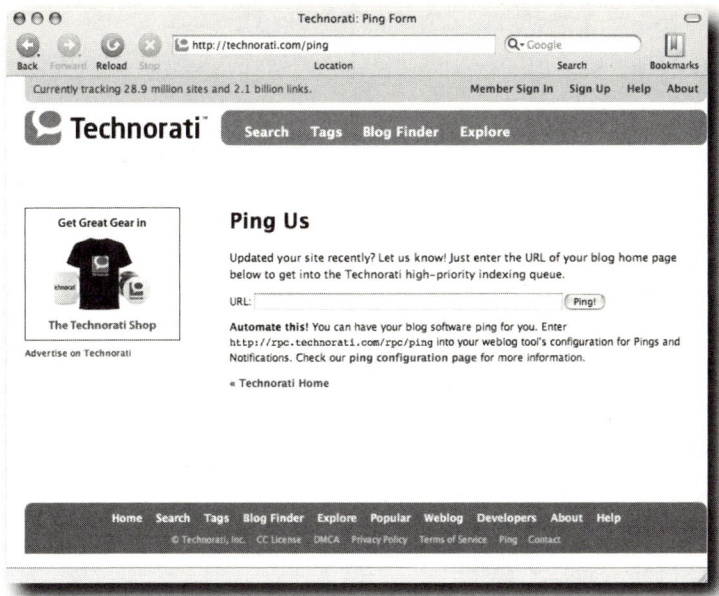

FIGURE 18-7: Pinging Technorati.

## Using Ping-O-Matic

The site Ping-O-Matic will ping a group of directories in one fell swoop. The only required information is your videoblog's name and URL (see Figure 18-8) and the directories you want pinged. You can also provide your videoblog's RSS feed, but that's completely optional.

## Using PingShot from FeedBurner

FeedBurner offers a free service called PingShot (www.feedburner.com/fb/a/ publishers/pingshot) that will ping an undisclosed list of third-party directories. The beauty of the service is that it allows directories to become a part of the service by registering. To quote FeedBurner:

> "Everyone can play. It's kind of like tag or Marco Polo, but without all the running around and yelling."

As new directories come online, they can simply register with FeedBurner to be notified when your videoblog is updated (kinda cool, huh?). To take advantage of PingShot, log in to your FeedBurner account and select the Publicize tab. Then just activate PingShot and join in on the big game.

**FIGURE 18-8: Ping-O-Matic ready for service.**

Pinging blog directories is one of the easiest ways to expose your videoblog to the world. Considering that it's free, too, setting up your software to ping whenever you update your site is an investment that is well worth the time.

## Directory URLs

You need to know the correct URLs to ping various directories. Here's a fairly complete list, obtained through WordPress.com:

- http://1470.net/api/ping
- http://api.feedster.com/ping
- http://api.moreover.com/RPC2
- http://api.my.yahoo.com/RPC2
- http://bblog.com/ping.php
- http://blog.goo.ne.jp/XMLRPC
- http://blogmatcher.com/u.php
- http://bulkfeeds.net/rpc
- http://coreblog.org/ping/

- http://ping.bitacoras.com
- http://ping.blo.gs/
- http://ping.bloggers.jp/rpc/
- http://ping.blogmura.jp/rpc/
- http://ping.feedburner.com
- http://ping.myblog.jp
- http://ping.syndic8.com/xmlrpc.php
- http://ping.weblogalot.com/rpc.php
- http://ping.weblogs.se/
- http://rpc.blogrolling.com/pinger/
- http://rpc.icerocket.com:10080/
- http://rpc.newsgator.com/
- http://rpc.technorati.com/rpc/ping
- http://rpc.weblogs.com/RPC2
- http://topicexchange.com/RPC2
- http://trackback.bakeinu.jp/bakeping.php
- http:// blogdigger.com/RPC2
- http://xmlrpc.blogg.de
- http://xping.pubsub.com/ping/

If you want to target videobloggers specifically, ping videoblogging.info at www.videoblogging .info/ping.

# Getting Listed in iTunes

Apple's iTunes (www.apple.com/itunes) is possibly the biggest opportunity for videobloggers to break into the mainstream because it's installed on every current Macintosh computer and is more than likely used by every person who owns an iPod (more than 30 million people). People can locate and subscribe to videoblogs through iTunes, so it's worthwhile to be listed in the iTunes directory. Getting listed is easy and free.

---

### A WordPress Plug-in

If you are using WordPress (www.wordpress.org) for your blog software and you are going to distribute your videoblog via iTunes, you may want to evaluate the WP ipod-catter plug-in available at www.garrickvanburen.com/wpipodcatter. The free plug-in adds a few features that iTunes honors, such as the running time of your video posts, whether a video contains explicit language, and more categories. It is a well-thought-out plug-in and is under active development.

---

To submit your videoblog to iTunes for listing, launch the iTunes application and go to the Music Store (see Figure 18-9) by clicking the aptly named icon on the far-left side of the screen. You'll need an Apple ID to submit your feed. If you've ever purchased music or videos using iTunes, you have an account. If not, you need to create one (it's free).

Click to go to Music Store.

Click to access Podcasts.

FIGURE 18-9: iTunes Music Store.

Locate the Podcasts link in the Inside the Music Store section on the left side of the store's interface. Click it to enter the Podcasts section of the store (see Figure 18-10). Then click the Submit a Podcast link in the Inside the Music Store section.

Submit a Podcast link.

**FIGURE 18-10: Podcasts.**

iTunes' Submit Podcasts page opens (see Figure 18-11). Enter the URL to your videoblog's RSS feed (see Figure 18-11), and click the Continue button. The iTunes application will contact and verify your feed's validity.

After submitting your feed, choose a podcast category for your video (see Figure 18-12). Unfortunately, at the time of this writing, there is no Videoblog category, so you may want to follow what other videobloggers have done and select the Audio Blogs category. This oversight will hopefully be corrected in future versions of iTunes.

Once you've finalized your selection and made sure everything is acceptable, simply click the Submit button. Within a few hours to a few days, you'll receive an email informing you whether your videoblog has been accepted (the majority are) and, if it has, giving you the URL for people to access your videoblog through iTunes.

FIGURE 18-11: Submitting a podcast.

FIGURE 18-12: Selecting a category.

# Creating a 1-Click Subscribe Button

Aggregators automatically work with RSS feeds because that's what they're designed for. But you may want to create a way for people to subscribe to your videoblog using a specific aggregator such as iTunes (www.apple.com/itunes) or FireAnt (www.fireant.tv).

## iTunes

If you've submitted your videoblog to iTunes and received an approval email, you just need to create a link on your blog that will launch iTunes and subscribe a viewer. The URL provided by iTunes looks similar to this:

```
http://phobos.apple.com/WebObjects/MZStore.woa/wa/viewPodcast?id=124901921
```

To create the link, use the following HTML, replacing the URL with the one provided by iTunes:

```
<a href= "http://phobos.apple.com/WebObjects/MZStore.woa/
wa/viewPodcast?id=124901921">Subscribe Using iTunes</a>
```

Your link may end with &s=xxxxxx, which is an identifier used by iTunes. Unfortunately, the ampersand is not XHTML compliant. Being compliant is only significant to those who want to adhere to web standards; it won't affect how people see your site. If you want to be compliant, substitute &amp for the &, or simply remove the last portion of the URL, beginning with the ampersand.

If you don't want to submit your feed through iTunes, or if your feed is rejected, you can still create a link using Mefeedia's 1-Click subscription tool.

## Using Mefeedia's 1-Click Buttons

Mefeedia provides a tool that creates a 1-Click button you can place on your videoblog to allow people to subscribe to your site through iTunes, even if you're not listed in the iTunes directory. Access the tool at http://mefeedia.com/help/javascript/itunes.php.

To create a button, you need your Feed ID (see Figure 18-13). As discussed in Chapter 16, you can find the Feed ID through the Mefeedia directory at http://mefeedia.com/feeds by clicking the Get Info link. If your videoblog isn't listed in Mefeedia, simply submit it using the form at http://mefeedia.com/add.php.

Enter your Feed ID in the appropriate box and click the Use this Feed ID button. A small amount of HTML code is created for you. To place the 1-Click button on your site, just copy the supplied code and paste it into your blog's template. Mefeedia provides everything, including the small "chicklet" graphics.

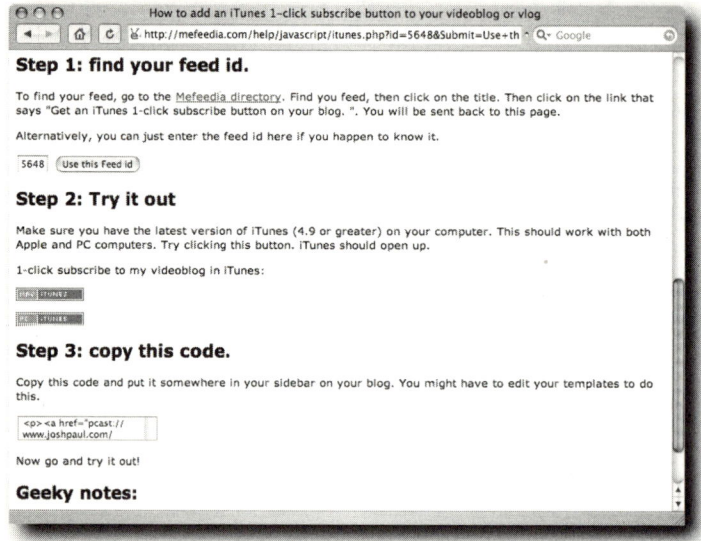

FIGURE **18-13:** Creating a button using Mefeedia.

## FireAnt

FireAnt (www.fireant.tv) is a very popular video-aggregation application that can use standard RSS feeds to subscribe to video. If you'd like to cater to viewers who are using FireAnt or help promote the application, you can create a 1-Click subscription button at http://fireant.tv/buttonmaker.

Once on the FireAnt 1-Click Subscription Button page (see Figure 18-14), enter the URL for your videoblog's feed and click the Make Button button.

Then copy the resulting HTML code and paste it into your blog. When someone visiting your site clicks the button, his FireAnt application automatically subscribes to your feed.

One-click buttons are a great way to help people subscribe to your feed, while still catering to those who just visit your site.

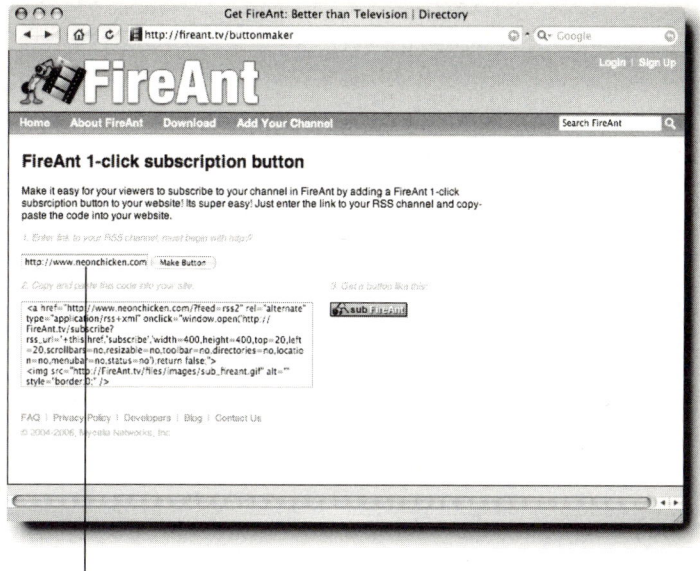

Enter your vlog's URL.

FIGURE 18-14: Creating a button using FireAnt.

# Summary

Complete strangers are likely to find your videoblog not only through typical search engines such as Google and Yahoo! but through directories as well. To reach people who may be looking for the type of content you're producing, continually update your listing in the various blog directories around the Internet. Fortunately, that's easy to accomplish, and most blogging software includes features to make it automatic.

# Tracking Statistics

**P**ractically every videoblogger is interested in the size of his or her audience. Every server maintains logs of people who visit it, and most hosting providers supply this information in an easy-to-digest way. Still, you may want to maintain your own statistics or organize the information using a different method than that provided by your host.

## Using StatCounter

One popular way to gather statistics is to use a counter on your web site. Counters record the number of visits to your site. There are numerous counter services available, and one that has gained some popularity with videobloggers is StatCounter (`www.statcounter.com`).

StatCounter offers a basic, free service to people who have web sites that have fewer than 250,000 views per month. The company also offers paid services, ranging from $9.00 to $29.00 per month, aimed at web sites that get millions of page views per month.

## Creating a Counter

To start using a StatCounter counter, first sign up for an account. Then StatCounter walks you through the process of creating a counter, called a Project, that suits your personal preferences. The first selection you'll have to make is what type of Project you want to create (see Figure 19-1). As of this writing, there is only one available, the Standard StatCounter, but two additional services are under development for more advanced uses: Advanced StatCounter and E-Commerce StatCounter.

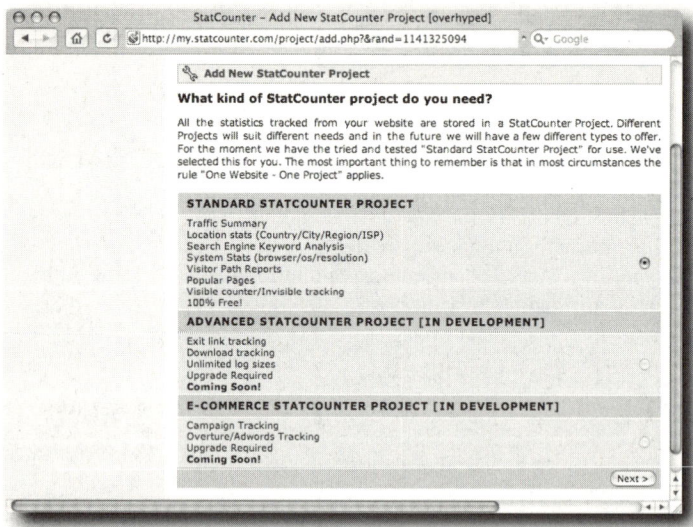

**FIGURE 19-1: Creating a Project.**

After making your selection, click Next to begin configuring your counter. The configuration options on this page are:

- Website Title — Title of your web site; used by StatCounter for organizational purposes.

- Website URL — URL of your web site.

- Category — A category in which to include your web site; used by StatCounter for organization.

- Timezone — Time zone that you want your logs to reflect.

- Maximum Visit Length — Amount of time between visits to be considered a unique visit from a viewer. For example, if your Maximum Visit Length is set for 45 minutes, and a viewer watches a video, goes to another site, and returns to watch another video in less than 45 minutes, the two visits are considered only one unique visit.

- Log Size — Number of visitors to maintain on your log; doesn't affect long-term statistics. In your logs, you can view details for the number of visitors you enter here.

- IP Blocking — If you have your own server and IP address, place the IP address here to avoid corrupting your statistics.

- Public Stats — Enable this feature if you'd like the general public to be able to view your statistics.

Click Next. Then select how you want to display your counter (see Figure 19-2), if at all. If you want to keep statistics quietly or maintain the look of your site, you can select to use an invisible counter. Otherwise, your options are to use a visible counter, a visible counter on your homepage, or a button to represent that you're using StatCounter. Which you select is a personal choice.

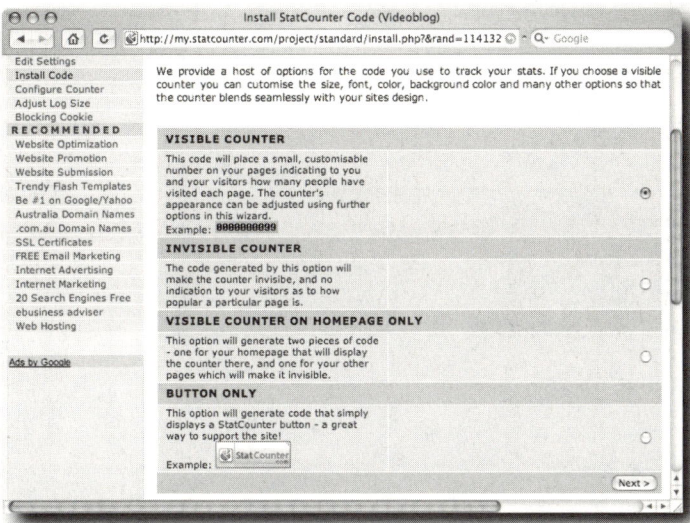

FIGURE 19-2: Selecting a counter type.

Click Next and select the type of HTML to use (see Figure 19-3). Unless you're concerned about remaining compliant with web standards, such as XHTML, simply leave the default values selected. Before proceeding, make sure that you have chosen the correct setting for whether your site uses frames; it more than likely doesn't.

Click Next. Finally, indicate whether you're using a web page editor, such as DreamWeaver or GoLive. If you're just planning to insert the counter into your blog software, simply indicate that you're not using an editor.

When you're finished configuring your Project, StatCounter supplies you with a snippet of HTML that you can use to gather statistics.

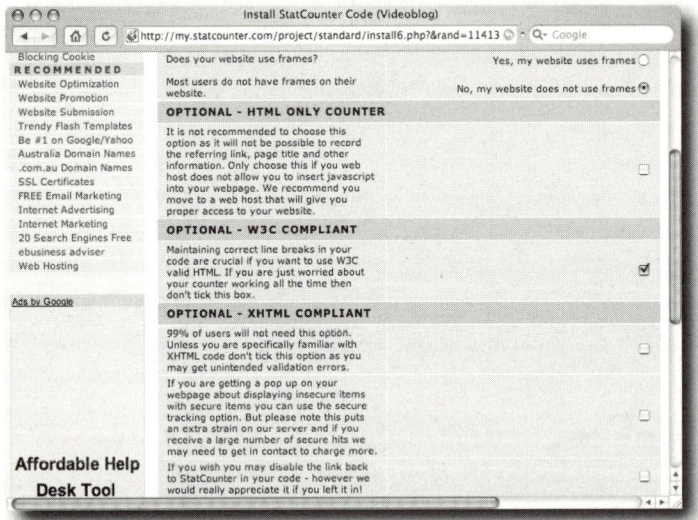

FIGURE 19-3: Selecting an HTML style.

## Using a Counter

To use your newly created counter, copy the supplied HTML and place it in between the
<body> and </body> tags on your web page(s). If you're using an invisible counter, place
the HTML just before the </body> tag, or just after the <body> tag, on your web page. If
you're using a visible counter, keep in mind the layout of the page, and place it at the bottom
of the web page by inserting the HTML just before the </body> tag. The resulting HTML
will look similar to the following:

```
<html>
  <body>

  ...

  <!-- Start of StatCounter Code -->

  <script type="text/javascript" language="javascript">
  <!--
  var sc_project=1341260;
  var sc_invisible=1;
  var sc_partition=12;
  var sc_security="66e40499";
  //-->
  </script>
```

```
<script type="text/javascript" language="javascript" src="http://
www.statcounter.com/counter/counter.js"></script>
   <noscript><a href="http://www.statcounter.com/" target="_blank"><img src=
"http://c13.statcounter.com/counter.php?sc_project=1341260&amp;java=0&amp;
security=66e40499&amp;invisible=1" alt="how to add a hit counter to a
website" border="0"></a></noscript>

<!-- End of StatCounter Code -->

</body>
</html>
```

Once placed, anytime someone visits one of your pages, StatCounter adds the information to your log. At any point, you can log in to your StatCounter account and view your statistics, as shown in Figure 19-4.

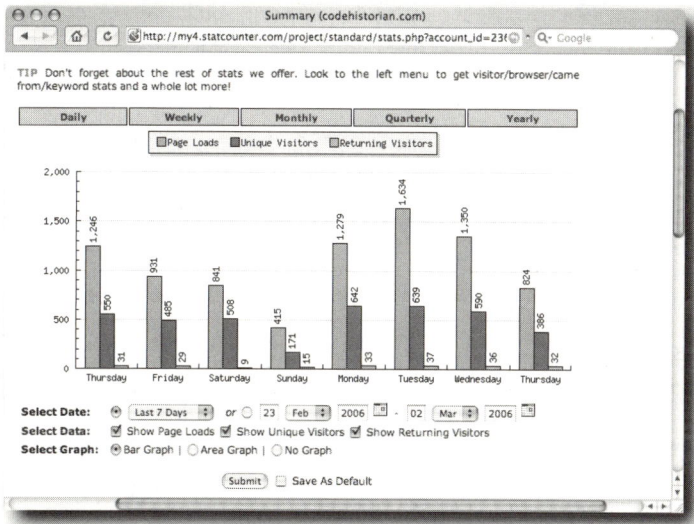

FIGURE 19-4: StatCounter-gathered statistics.

# Logging Video Downloads

If you've uploaded your video to a hosting service that doesn't provide statistical reports, it can be difficult or impossible to know how many times your videos are downloaded. That's often the price of using a free service — it provides the storage and bandwidth but not the report on how popular your videos are.

## Logging External Files

If you are hosting your videoblog on a server that provides you with statistics but hosting your video elsewhere, you can create a little logging application for yourself. With a slight modification of your URLs and a few lines of code, you can garner some meaningful statistics.

The idea is that instead of using a URL like `http://hosted-service.com/videoblog .mov`, which points to an external server that hosts your video(s), you would use a URL like `http://your-site.com/hit.php?http://hosted-service.com/videoblog.mov`. Using the updated URL, when a browser or aggregator requests the file, your server logs the request and responds with a message that says, "I found what you are looking for; it's somewhere else. Go there instead." Technically speaking, the response is status code `200 - OK`, which the browser interprets as a 302, redirecting the browser or aggregator to another site.

## The Code

There are two good solutions for logging visits prior to redirecting your viewers. One uses Perl and the other uses PHP; the part of the URL that occurs after the ? helps direct viewers to the actual video file.

To use Perl, create a file called `hit.cgi` in your server's cgi-bin directory, and add the following code to it:

```
#!/usr/bin/perl
print "Location: " . $ENV{QUERY_STRING} . "\n\n" ;
```

When linking against this file, your URLs will look much like: `http://your-site.com/hit.cgi?http://hosted-service.com/videoblog.mov`.

To use PHP, create a file called `hit.php`, and include the following code:

```
<?php header("Location: " . $_SERVER['QUERY_STRING'] . "\n\n"); ?>
```

When linking against the PHP file, your URLs will look much like: `http://your-site .com/hit.php?http://hosted-service.com/videoblog.mov`.

If you want to track the downloads from the web page separately from the downloads that happen via the enclosure in an RSS feed, you can create two different versions of the script. Name one `hit.cgi` and use it for web pages, and name the other `enc.cgi` and use it for enclosures.

Using this method for gathering statistics is not foolproof, because anyone can see what the "real" URL of the file is and simply request it directly. That's okay. This method is meant primarily as an easy way to try to gather more accurate statistics by separating file downloads. It's also handy that the log file, and any reports you run against the log file, will contain the actual URLs of the videos, not just the URL that the viewer used. This can help greatly in determining the most popular videos you have distributed.

# Reading a Log File, Live!

How would you like to watch how people browse your videoblog? Well, Natalia Bazhenova created a great application called Log RSS Creator that enables you to view visits on your site, live! Using PHP, MySQL, and an RSS reader, you can examine how people are using your site, while they are using it.

## Installing Log RSS Creator

Using the application requires that you have privileges to install software on your videoblog's server. You can download Log RSS Creator from Natalia's web site at www.fh54.de/ Log_RSS. Unarchive the application and place the files in a folder on your blog server. Then run the install.php script by visiting your web site at the appropriate location (Figure 19-5), such as http://www.my_site.com/Log_RSS/install.php.

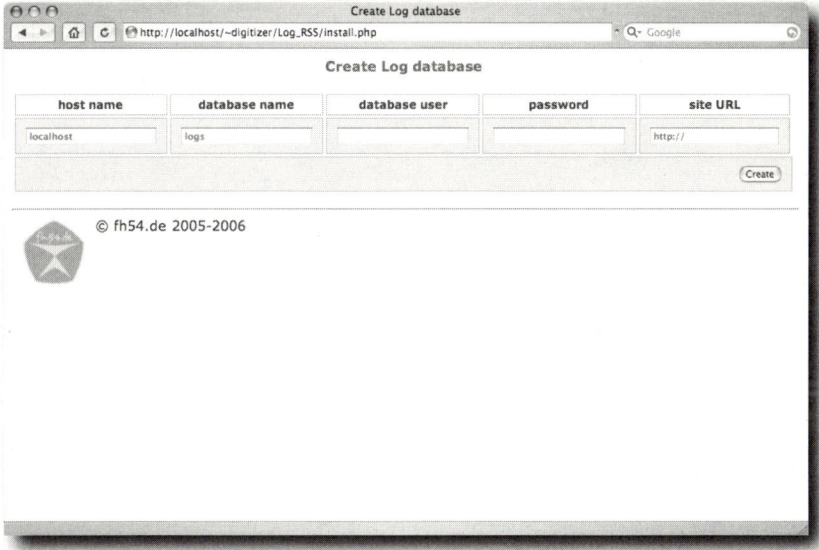

FIGURE 19-5: Installing Log RSS Creator.

The application creates two tables in your MySQL database and also creates a file named parameters.php. Then, for any pages that you want to keep an eye on, include the inc_log_sql.php file by adding <? include '/path/to/Log_RSS/ inc_log_sql.php'; ?> to your PHP for the specific page.

The code for the file looks like this:

```php
<?

$str=str_replace(basename(__FILE__),"parameters.php",__FILE__);

include $str;

$link = mysql_connect($hostname, $username,$password);

mysql_select_db($dbname) ;

$ip=$_SERVER['REMOTE_ADDR'];

$ref=empty($_SERVER['HTTP_REFERER']) ? '-' : $_SERVER['HTTP_REFERER'];

$browser=empty($_SERVER['HTTP_USER_AGENT']) ? '-' : $_SERVER['HTTP_USER_AGENT'];

$querystring=$_SERVER["QUERY_STRING"];

$page=str_replace("?".$_SERVER['QUERY_STRING'],"",$_SERVER['REQUEST_URI']);

$isRobot=0;

$query="select name from log_browsers where isRobot=1";

$result=mysql_query($query);

while ($rows=mysql_fetch_array($result)) {

    if (eregi($rows["name"],$browser)) {$isRobot=1;break;}

}

//if (mysql_num_rows($result)>0) $isRobot=1;

$host=gethostbyaddr($ip);

if ($ip!=$own_host) {

    $query = "insert into log_mysite
(time,ip,page,querystring,ref,browser,host,isRobot) values ('".date("y.m.d
H:i:s")."','".$ip."','".$page."','".$querystring."','".$ref."','".$browser."','"
.$host."','".$isRobot."') ";

    @mysql_query($query);
}

@mysql_close($link);

?>
```

After you've installed everything and included the appropriate PHP code, point your browser at your site and click around. Then open an RSS reader and use the URL provided by the Log RSS application to watch the logging occur, live.

## Using Log RSS Creator

While viewing the logs, you'll quickly notice that a variety of information is available to you (see Figure 19-6). The title of each entry is the domain or IP address of the visiting computer. The number in parenthesis next to the title is the number of pages the specific visitor has viewed. Below each title is a list of the web pages that the computer has visited. The More Info link provides detailed information about the specific visit.

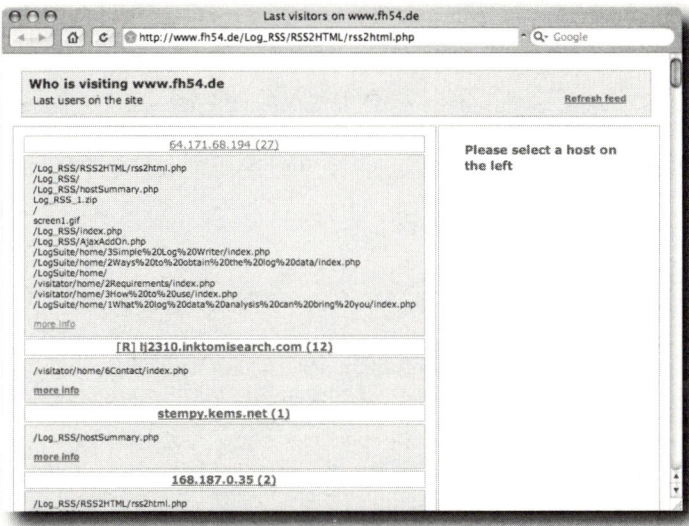

FIGURE 19-6: Viewing a live logging session.

You'll also probably notice, at some point, a title that begins with an [R]. This designation indicates that the visiting computer is probably a robot, such as the automated systems used by Google and Yahoo! to index the web.

Using the Log RSS Creator application is a fun and interesting way to analyze how your audience is using your site and which files are of most interest to them.

# Logging External Files Using AJAX

Viewing traditional logs is one thing, but many videobloggers host their blog on one server and their video content on another, so they have to deal with two log files. Over the past year, Asynchronous JavaScript and XML, also known as AJAX, has become a major buzzword in the online world. Through the use of AJAX, it's possible to gather and view statistics in real-time using your web browser.

A little AJAX trickery provided by Natalia Bazhenova, along with xaJax (`http://xajax project.org`) and Log RSS Creator with AJAX add-on (`www.fh54.de/Log_RSS/ AjaxAddOn.php`), will enable you to gather statistics on external files, as well as on the files residing on your server. The external files can include videos, images, documents, and even links to pages outside your site.

## Implementing an AJAX Client

In addition to Log RSS Creator, you need the AJAX implementation for PHP xaJax, available from the project's homepage at `http://xajaxproject.org`. After downloading and installing xaJax, create your client code by simply adding the following in the `<head>` of your web pages:

```
<?php
require($_SERVER["DOCUMENT_ROOT"]."/global/inc_log_sql.php");

logUrl();

require($_SERVER["DOCUMENT_ROOT"]."/global/xajaxlog/sqlWriteCommon.php");

$xajax->printJavascript("/global/xajaxlog/");
?>
```

Note that you have to change the relative URL to the appropriate PHP files as needed.

Then add the following just before the `</body>` tag in your pages (yes, that's at the bottom of your page):

```
<script language="JavaScript" src="/global/xajaxlog/addAjaxLogging.js"
type="text/javascript" ></script>
```

Once implemented, you can enable the AJAX logging feature by simply adding the `logging` attribute (shown in bold) to a link, like this:

```
<a href="http://www.neonchicken.com/" logging="1" target="_blank">⤶
Neon Chicken</a>
```

By setting `logging` to 1, you turn on the logging feature. Setting the `target` to `blank` enables the logging to occur accurately. You can always create nonlogged links by not adding the `logging` attribute.

## Implementing an AJAX Server

To implement the AJAX server portion of the logging application, copy the `parameters.php` file, which is created during the installation process, into the `global` directory of your installation. You'll find the `global` directory inside the `AjaxAddOn` directory. If you notice that the `global` directory doesn't exist, simply copy it from the unzipped package to your web server, and then copy the `parameters.php` file into it.

In this application, all of the logging scripts are located in the `global` directory. In addition, all of the AJAX files are located in the `xajaxlog` directory, which is inside the `global` directory. This structure is important; don't change it or you'll break the application.

After everything is installed, simply run your RSS reader, open your log's feed, and watch your log files roll by in full AJAX style.

# Using Aweli to Determine Views

Gathering statistics for downloaded videos can help determine how popular your videoblog is. Unfortunately, gathering statistics for downloaded videos doesn't reveal information about whether people are actually viewing your videos. This is because RSS aggregators, search engine robots, and other automated systems can skew the numbers by accessing your files automatically. Aweli (`www.aweli.com`) provides a service to help overcome this problem.

Aweli's service, which is in beta as of this writing, gathers statistics about the number of views your video's had instead of the number of times it's been downloaded. This is exceptionally helpful in ascertaining whether people are actually watching your videos. Aweli doesn't require you to store your video on its servers or paste any HTML in your blog.

## Using Aweli

To use Aweli's service, first sign up for an account at `http://www.aweli.com`. Then download the V2 application using the link provided in your sign-up email. Launch the application and configure it to use your Aweli username and password.

Next, select File ➜ Open and choose a video that you would like to enable. (You can also drag and drop a video onto the application's window.) Finally, click the Enable button (Figure 19-7). As of this writing, Aweli is supporting only QuickTime files. However, the company is working on integrating with Windows Media and Flash.

After a short processing period, depending on the size of your video and the speed of your computer, your video is enabled, and you can upload it to a server and distribute it as you would any other file.

Click.

FIGURE 19-7: Enabling a video to use Aweli.

## Viewing Statistics

To view your statistics, simply log in to Aweli's site. Any videos that you've enabled using V2 are listed, as shown in Figure 19-8, along with some additional information (such as the video's length in seconds). Most important, however, are the number of views.

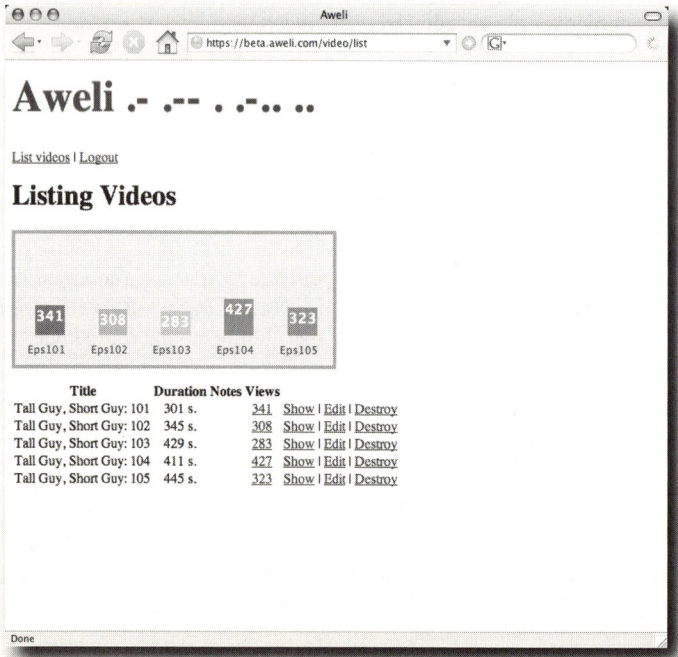

FIGURE 19-8: Viewing statistics gathered by Aweli.

Aweli enables you to search through your statistics and drill down to get a clearer picture of your audience. In addition, you can export the information in a variety of ways, including to a comma-separated file for use with Excel. Combined with the statistics gathered from other logging methods, you can glean a much more comprehensive image of your audience, what they like and don't like, and how often they come back for more.

# Summary

Producing video and distributing it online is the major part of videoblogging. If you're hoping to discover what your audience enjoys so that you can cater to them, gathering statistics can go a long way in helping you achieve that goal. It's also nice just to know that people *are* watching your videos.

# Making Money

**P**utting so much work into creating and posting videos to your blog, an obvious question you may ask yourself is "How do I get paid?" The quick answer is simple: No one knows. . .yet.

You should ask yourself how much money you want to make. You may want to earn a living videoblogging, but you should evaluate the landscape and determine whether that's realistic. Maybe you just want to make enough money to pay for your videotapes and server space. Whatever your goal is, there are some semiproven ways to make money, including seeking donations from your viewers, inserting advertising on your videoblog or on your videos, or selling merchandise such as branded T-shirts.

## Using PayPal for Donations

If you get hooked on videoblogging, you might realize that it's a more expensive hobby than you originally thought because small costs such as videotapes and hosting add up over time. Regular bloggers have these issues as well, and a common concept in the blogging world is that of the virtual "tip jar." You often see small badges (graphic links) or text links in bloggers' sidebars or within their posts pointing to donation pages, Amazon Wish Lists, and similar services. Asking for voluntary donations is a much-used, nonintrusive way of asking for financial support of your otherwise free blogging adventures.

One way to seek donations is to use a PayPal (`www.paypal.com`) button on your site. If you're not already a PayPal member, simply point your browser at the company's site and sign up for a free account.

### Creating a Button

To create a Donation button, sign in to your PayPal account. Then do the following:

1. Select the Merchant Tools tab in the navigation menu at the top of the page.

2. Click the Donations link.

3. The Donations page (see Figure 20-1) opens. Enter a few items of information, some of which are optional:

   - Donation Name/Service — A name for the service you've provided.

   - Donation ID/Number — An identifier for the donation you're receiving, in case you seek donations on different sites using the same PayPal account.

   - Amount — The suggested amount of the donation.

   - Currency — The currency you'd like to receive the donation in.

   - Country — The default country to be selected for the user when donating.

   It's suggested that you at least fill in the Donation Name/Service.

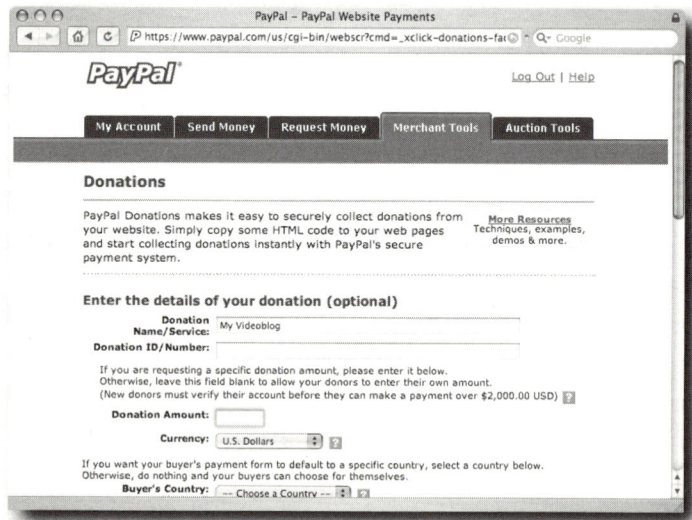

FIGURE 20-1: Configuring a PayPal button.

4. Select a look for your button. PayPal provides a graphic by default, but you can provide your own by entering a URL that points to it.

5. Decide whether to use encryption to secure your link (see Figure 20-2). This is highly recommended, although if you elect to encrypt, use some of the additional options such as the look of the payment page, the URLs that a user is forwarded to after a successful or cancelled transaction, an additional note for the user upon donating, or the option to use a different email address to receive the donations.

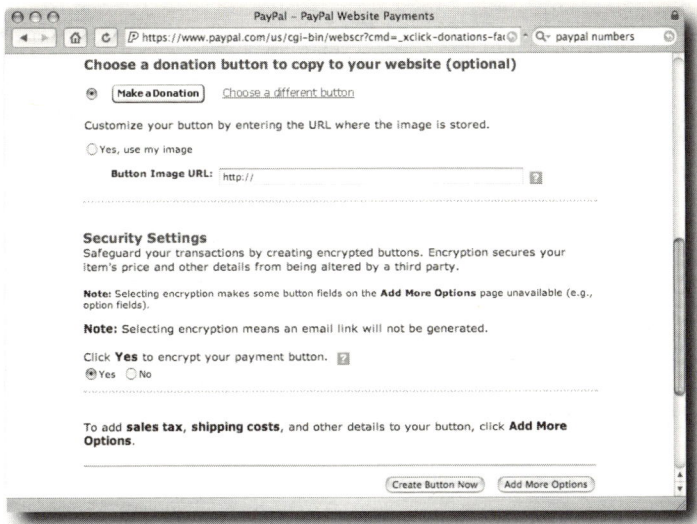

FIGURE 20-2: The PayPal button configurator.

**6.** If you choose to secure your button, click Create Button Now. Otherwise, click the Add More Options button, configure the additional parameters, and then click Create Button Now.

**7.** You are provided with a small amount of HTML that you can add to your videoblog to ask for donations. Copy the HTML to a text document and save it on your computer.

## Adding the Button to Your Site

To put the Donation button on your site, log in and add the HTML to your blog template, or place it on your blog's sidebar if possible. The HTML will look similar to this:

```
<form action="https://www.paypal.com/cgi-bin/webscr" method="post">
<input type="hidden" name="cmd" value="_s-xclick">
<input type="image" src="https://www.paypal.com/en_US/i/btn/x-click-but21.gif"
border="0" name="submit" alt="Make payments with PayPal - it's fast, free and
secure!">
<input type="hidden" name="encrypted" value="-----BEGIN PKCS7-----
/9j/iKG4Thia/Oflx4TdL+IFJBAyPK9v6zZNZtBgPBynXb048hsP1612vi0k5Q2JKiPDsEfBhGI+HnxL
XEaUWAcVfCsQFvd2A1sxRr67ip5y2wwBelUecP3AjJ+MDwiM4cJxbgvMd17GoT4qqjF+kBtX+FwQYIGO
Zz/sWRjPRq9DFu93Jwzwb+se4w1x5gCyu0+iciHsrA3RRaZep4nib+sSrOnG50QUk/w09pfudrxjqHiT
gCFlo55dUii3nI=-----END PKCS7-----">
</form>
```

Figure 20-3 shows a PayPal Donation button on a videoblogger's site.

## Sites of Interest

There are a lot of services available online that provide ways to seek donations. Here are some places worth checking out:

- Amazon Associates—www.amazon.com
- BitPass—www.bitpass.com
- CaféPress—www.cafepress.com
- DropCash—www.dropcash.com
- PayPal—www.paypal.com

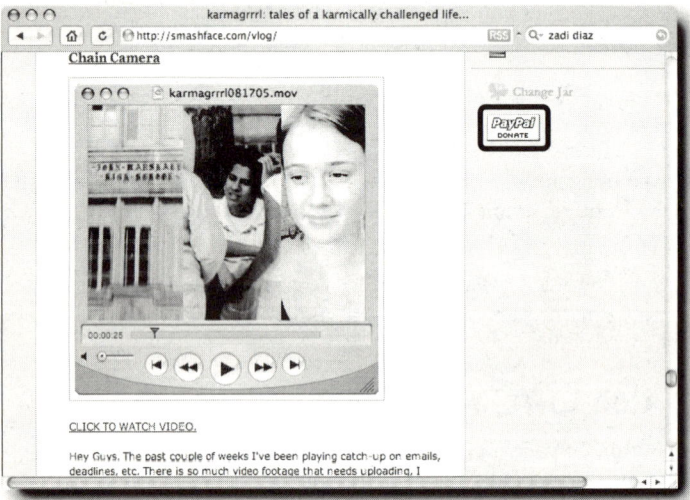

FIGURE 20-3: A videoblog using a PayPal Donation button.

Once you've placed your HTML, the Donation button you configured appears on your site. Whenever someone clicks it, he'll be taken to PayPal where he can donate money to you. Upon receiving a donation, you get an email confirming it, and the amount is added to your PayPal account balance.

# Getting Paid, Videoblogging Style

Bloggers and videobloggers use these "tip jar" services in the same way, by placing a badge or a text link on their blog. Videobloggers, however, have an additional obstacle. A large number of viewers do not use a web browser to follow videoblogs — they use a video aggregator such as FireAnt (www.fireant.tv), iTunes (www.apple.com/itunes), or Mefeedia (www.mefeedia.com) instead. Video aggregators remove your videos from the web page, and, as a result, tip-jar badges are not shown along with the video. The result is that you don't get paid when you could have.

## Using rel="payment"

Fortunately, FireAnt and Mefeedia (and hopefully others soon) have found a way to solve this problem for you. You can add a bit of extra text to your donation link so that both aggregators will recognize it as a payment indicator and give it special attention when playing your video. For example, Mefeedia inserts a $ Support Blogger box below your video (see Figure 20-4) while it's playing.

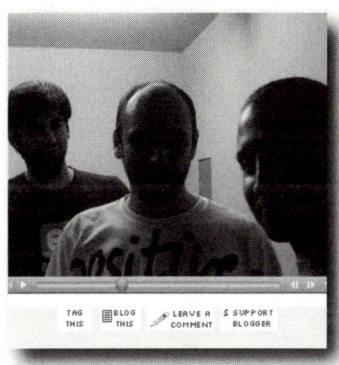

FIGURE 20-4: Mefeedia displaying a Payment button.

The extra bit you have to add to your link for it to become a Payment button is a rel attribute with a value of payment. For example, where you would normally type:

```
<a href="http://www.dropcash.com/campaign/torrez/a_test/">Send me
some cash!</a>
```

use:

```
<a href="http://www.dropcash.com/campaign/torrez/a_test/"
rel="payment">Send me some cash!</a>
```

The only difference is the `rel="payment"` text. That's it! By adding it, you are creating a link called a "payment link," which is displayed by many video aggregators to inform viewers that donations or payments are appreciated. It can't be put in your sidebar to work as expected; the payment link has to be part of a blog post.

In addition to the `rel="payment"` part of the link, you can use the `title` attribute to provide a description of the kind of payment you're seeking. For example:

```
<p>
I created a Cafépress Store today where you can <a
href="http://www.cafepress.com/" rel="payment" title="Bob's
Cafépress Store">buy my stuff</a>.
</p>
```

Video aggregators use the `title` value to provide viewers with more information about payment links.

## Using the Payment Link Creator

If you aren't comfortable creating payment links by hand — after all, the links won't work if you make a typo — there is an online generator that can set up payment links for you: the Payment Link Creator (see Figure 20-5). It was built by Andreas Haugstrup Pedersen and is located at `www.solitude.dk/archives/payment`.

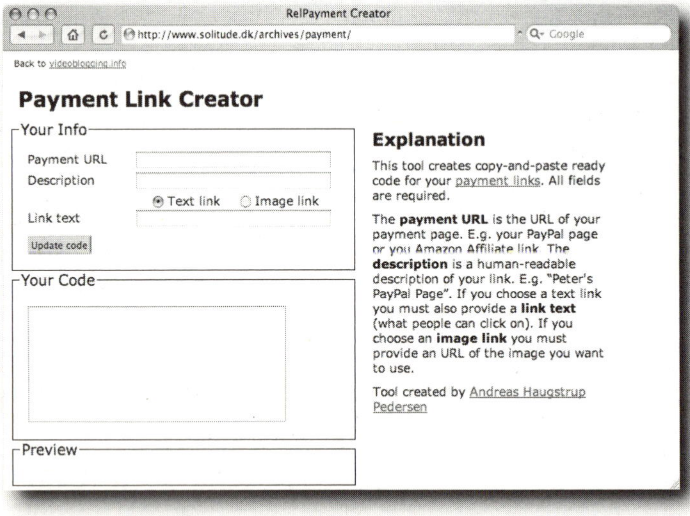

FIGURE 20-5: The Payment Link Creator.

To use the Payment Link Creator, simply enter your payment URL (your DropCash Campaign URL, Amazon Wish List URL, and so on), a description, and text for the link.

Then click the Update Code button, and the generator gives you finished code that you can copy and paste directly into your blog entry.

## Payment Links for Support

Payment links do not have to be about you and your costs. Any cause that you deem worthy can be the target. If you are interviewing a music group, you can create a payment link to a page where your viewers can buy the band's CDs. Or you can create payment links to your best friend's online shop.

Basically, you can point the link to the place you feel your viewers can support you best. Only your imagination sets the limit. Also, you can create payment links that don't involve money, such as to an online petition for a local political cause.

## Payment Links in Feeds

If you want your videoblog to have a payment link within each post, (but only in the RSS feed, not in the blog post itself), you can customize your feed template. Depending on the blogging software you are using, this can be quite easy. With WordPress, Movable Type, or other software that lets you edit the RSS feed template, you just need to add a payment link, similar to the following:

```
<a href="http://tinkernet.org/support/" rel="payment" title="Support
tinkernet">Support tinkernet</a>
```

Place the code at the bottom of the `<description>` and/or `<content:encoded>` section of your template. It allows the text of your blog post to show up with the payment link right below it. Aggregators use the link found in the feed, and it won't show up on each and every post on your videoblog.

## Keeping Expectations Real

Clicking a payment link is completely voluntary, so you won't get rich overnight. Even if you do have viewers, you can't be sure that they will click your links. You have to keep your audience in mind when you start asking for donations. Placing payment links on every videoblog entry most likely won't yield as good a response as placing links on select entries only.

Also, keeping the topic of a payment link related to the topic of a video will yield better results than generic donation links. For example, a link to a CD of the music you used in your video is more likely to result in a sale of the CD (and a potential commission) than a standard PayPal donate link.

# Using Google's AdSense

An exceptionally popular way of making money from a videoblog is through Google's AdSense (www.google.com/adsense). The service provides individuals and businesses the opportunity to generate revenue by placing a dynamic advertising banner on their web sites. In a nutshell, if someone visits your web site and clicks a link provided by AdSense, you get paid.

The primary feature that makes AdSense great is that the advertising it delivers is context-based, whenever possible. This means that if you create a post on your videoblog about Porsche cars, the advertising will most likely relate to Porsche cars. Ultimately, this type of targeting results in higher click-throughs, which is good for you because that's how you'll get paid. (It's good for Google and the advertiser, too!)

Figure 20-6 illustrates Google's ads across the top of a blog.

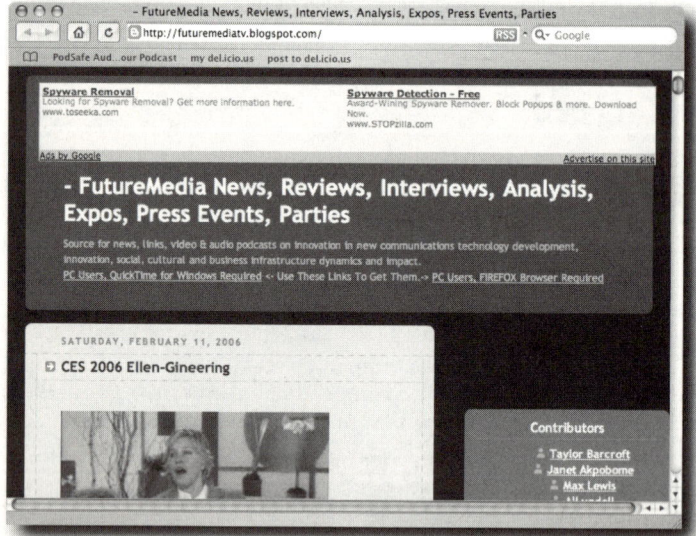

FIGURE 20-6: A videoblog with Google AdSense ads.

## Signing Up

To get started with AdSense, go to www.google.com/adsense and sign up for an account. You need to enter a little information, most of which is pretty standard, such as your name, address, and email address. However, two items need explanation: Account type and Product(s).

For Account type, you have a choice of either Individual or Business. The basic rule is that if you are an individual or a business with fewer than 20 employees, sign up for an Individual account. In practice, the only difference is who the payee is on any checks written by Google to you.

For Product(s), the options are AdSense for Content and/or AdSense for Search. Unless you want to integrate Google's search into your web site, just check the AdSense for Content box.

After you've filled out the required information and agreed to the various terms of service, click the Submit Information button. You'll then have to wait up to 72 hours for Google to accept or reject your application. More often than not, you'll get an approval email with a link to proceed with your sign up.

## Configuring Your Service

After you've been accepted to AdSense, log in to your account and select the AdSense Setup tab. Choose the service you want to use (most likely, this will be AdSense for Content), and then use the supplied forms to configure your ads, including the color so that they will fit in with the overall theme of your videoblog.

You can also create channels, which are a way for you to gather some statistical data about your site. You can create either URL channels, which track information across your entire site, or custom channels, which can help you track how well certain topics, site pages, or even color schemes generate click-throughs.

Another nice feature of the AdSense service is Alternate Ads. It enables you to run other ads, whether from another advertiser or your own, whenever the Google service can't match an ad to your content.

Ultimately, if you're going to use AdSense, it is highly recommended that you read through Google's AdSense Support site (www.google.com/support/adsense). There you can find information on the best ways to increase click-throughs through Optimization Tips, how to get your site "found" by Google, and other very useful information.

After you've configured your ad service, Google provides you with a small amount of HTML that you need to place on your videoblog. The HTML looks similar to:

```
<script type="text/javascript"><!--
google_ad_client = "xxx-1234567890987654";
google_ad_width = 728;
google_ad_height = 90;
google_ad_format = "728x90_as";
google_ad_type = "text_image";
google_ad_channel ="0000000000";
google_color_border = "003366";
google_color_bg = "000000";
google_color_link = "FFFFFF";
google_color_url = "99FFCC";
google_color_text = "99FFFF";
//--></script>
<script type="text/javascript"
  src="http://pagead2.googlesyndication.com/pagead/show_ads.js">
</script>
```

## Tracking Your Performance

After you've placed the HTML, anyone visiting your site will see an ad delivered by Google, and any time someone clicks a link, you'll be paid. At some point, you'll want to log in to your account to see how your site is performing. Fortunately, Google offers a variety of reports on your site's performance (even at hourly intervals, should you want them).

The amount of money you make depends on how much the advertisers are willing to pay, how much traffic your site generates, and how many people click the ads.

# Running Ads with Revver

Revver (www.revver.com) is a service that places advertisements in your videos and shares the profits from clicks with you. The advertisement, or "RevTag," is placed at the end of each video you upload. To use the service, you upload your video to the company's server, link to the video from your blog, and wait for people to click the link placed at the end of your video.

## Getting an Ad

To add a RevTag to your video, you need to sign up for a Revver account. To do so, point your browser to www.revver.com, click the Register button, and fill out the supplied form. Make sure you to use a valid email address because Revver sends your login information to the email you provide.

After logging in, select the My Videos tab on the top toolbar. You can then upload videos that are less than 10MB using the form on the upload page (see Figure 20-7). If you need to upload files over 10MB, you must download the Revver Upload Tool, which is available in Macintosh, Windows, and Java versions.

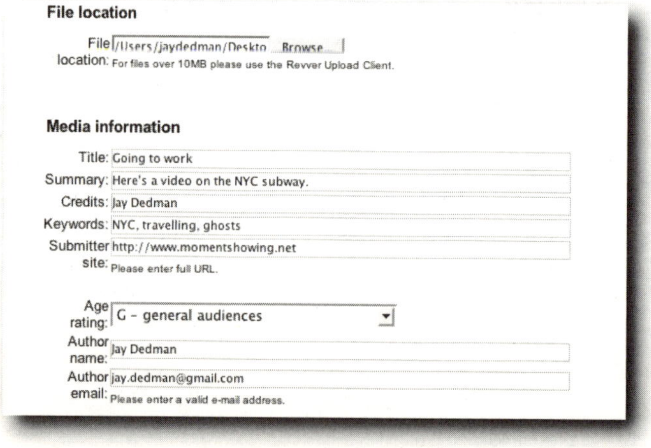

FIGURE 20-7: Revver's upload page.

You can also choose the kinds of ads you do not want associated with your work. If you don't want tobacco advertisements attached to your video, for example, you can omit them from contention.

## Linking to Your Video

Revver checks your uploaded video to make sure it's not copyrighted material owned by someone else, like an episode of "The Simpsons." Once cleared, you can simply link to the video from your blog. As Figure 20-8 shows, there are a few options on how you can link to your video, including directly to the file, by using a Revver-branded player, or by using a thumbnail of your video.

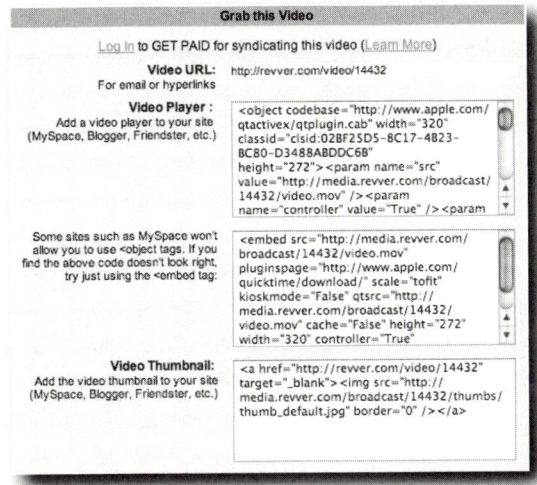

FIGURE 20-8: Optional ways to link to your video.

When the advertisement is displayed and someone clicks the screen, a page opens in the viewer's web browser to the site that paid for the ad. You are paid only if someone clicks the ad. Through IP address observation, Revver knows if the same computer is clicking the links repeatedly, so don't try to cheat the system.

Be aware that to make any money, you need hundreds or thousands of people to click the advertisements. Also, Revver deletes videos that aren't getting much traffic. But this service is free and plays fair with you, the creator. Who knows? You may one day create a viral video and be able to cash out.

# Auctioning Ad Space with eBay

If your videoblog becomes popular, you may want to explore offering advertising via an auction. Rocketboom (www.rocketboom.com) did exactly this in February 2006 using eBay (www.ebay.com) and setting the stage for others to follow. When the auction ended, the winning bid was for $40,000.00 for five days of advertising (see Figure 20-9).

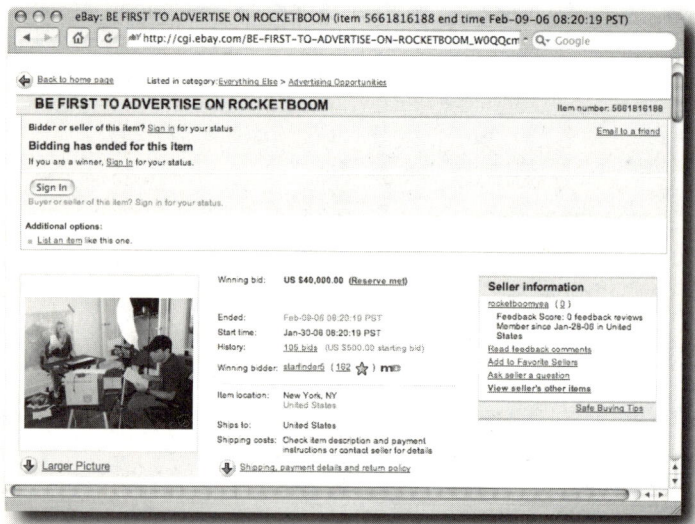

FIGURE 20-9: Rocketboom's eBay auction page.

## Starting an Auction

To start an auction, you need an account with eBay. After signing in, click the Sell button in the navigation bar. Select Online Auction (see Figure 20-10) for the way to sell, and click the Sell Your Item button. Then follow these steps:

1. Select a category for the auction. For your category, select the Everything Else radio button, and then click the Continue button.

2. On the next page, select Advertising Opportunities (see Figure 20-11), and click the Continue button.

3. Enter a title and description. You can optionally enter a subtitle as well. Definitely use the words *video*, *blog*, and advertise, because they will help people in the eBay universe find your auction easier; For example: Videoblog Advertising, Reach 250,000 People Daily Using Video, Advertise Your Product in My Video.

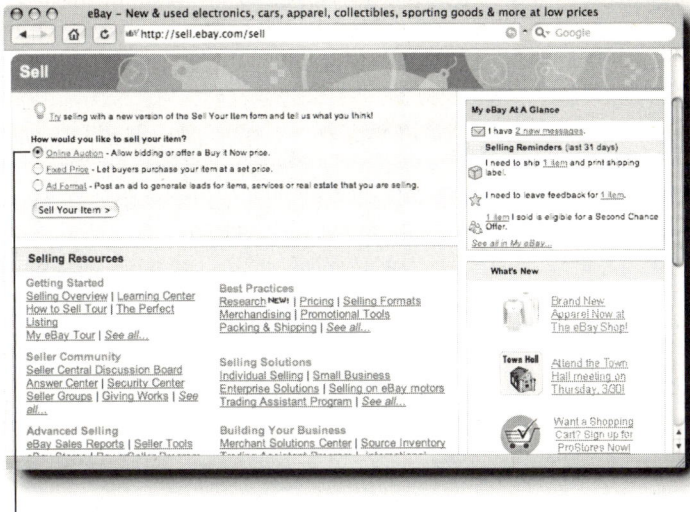

Choose Online Auction.

FIGURE 20-10: Starting an eBay auction.

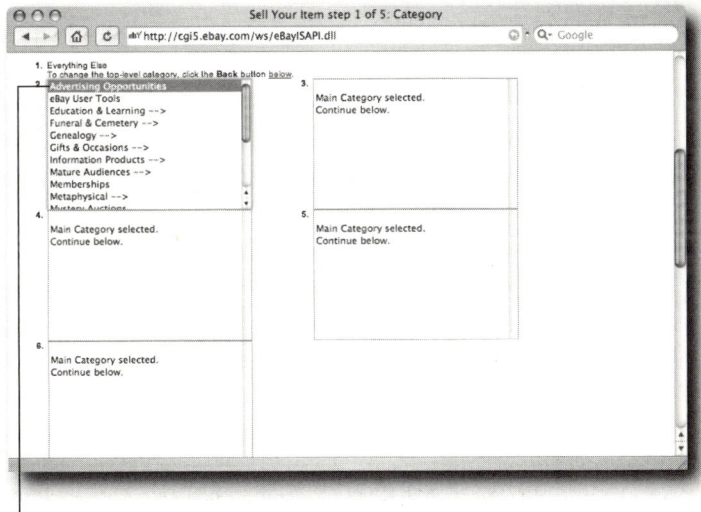

Choose Advertising Opportunities.

FIGURE 20-11: Selecting the Advertising Opportunities option.

4. Set your Starting Price and Reserve Price, as well as the option to donate a portion of the sale to charity. You also need to select how long your auction will run for (1–10 days) and the Quantity available. If you plan to sell more than one ad "slot," you may want to try offering more than one item.

5. You can also add pictures to your auction. For example, you can add screenshots of your video(s). Other options include setting the layout, various themes, ways to increase your auction's visibility on eBay, and even a visit counter. Those are all personal choices.

6. Select what payment options the winning bidder(s) will have. The options are all very straightforward, and PayPal is the eBay payment option of choice. Unless you'll be shipping something, there's no need to fill out any of the shipping items. You can also set up Payment Instructions, in case there are certain requirements you need fulfilled for legal reasons.

7. Review your auction information and make any adjustments necessary. When you're satisfied with the way your auction is going to be presented, click the Submit Listing button.

Auction on!

## Advertising the Auction

Your first foray into advertising using your videoblog could well be the advertising of your auction. What a great way to learn what works and what doesn't, huh? How you choose to advertise your auction is really up to you, but because people are watching your videos, you'll probably want to mention the auction in one of your posts.

## Inserting the Advertising

Depending on the agreement you have with your advertiser, the insertion of the ad can vary. You might obtain a "commercial" video from the advertiser that you just place at the beginning, middle, or end of your video. You might have to create the advertisement for the advertiser or possibly even perform a product placement.

Whatever approach you take, take a minute for yourself, sit back, and enjoy the fact you've just started your own ad-supported video network . . . just like the major television networks.

# Summary

As of this writing, companies such as Apple and Google are selling videos on a pay-per-download basis. So far, the only content that people seem to be paying for are traditional TV shows. Other companies are experimenting with placing ads before, after, and during the videos. Still, it isn't clear whether people are willing to watch ads on web video.

What is known is that people seem willing to pay for video content that is posted regularly, has a predictable format, and visits the same topic each time. That may sound a lot like traditional television, but videoblogging is a whole new art form, and you can help determine its future.

# Getting Involved

The world of videoblogging is a global community of entertainment, education, and communication. By taking part, you make videos so other people will watch, and you watch other people's videos. You are a producer and a consumer.

Videoblogging is an extremely new art form, offering innovative and exciting ways to tell stories, communicate ideas, and show our lives using an audiovisual (and sometimes interactive) medium. Every week, new technology becomes available that makes videoblogging easier and more powerful.

With so much change, and so much room for growth, how do videobloggers keep up with everything? By talking to other videobloggers and helping each other out, everyone benefits.

## Producing Regularly

Many videobloggers become discouraged early on when they don't have a large audience. The funny thing is, the more consistent a videoblogger is in releasing video, the larger his audience becomes over time.

One of the best ways to get involved in the videoblogging community is to regularly produce and distribute video. Whether you choose to upload a video every day, every week, or every month is a matter of how much time you can commit. Ultimately, the key to staying motivated and consistently producing video is to have fun doing it.

**Interview with Kent Nichols of Ask a Ninja (www.askaninja.com)**

*What motivated you to create a videoblog?*

We were frustrated by the gatekeeper mentality of traditional Hollywood. I've always been an iconoclast, and I believe that you should create your own institutions instead of seeking outside validation from those that preceded you.

Video over RSS allows us to do that. We create the content, and then it immediately gets to our audience. It is a direct connection, much like theater in that respect. In TV or film production, you shoot something and then it takes months or years before you get audience feedback. We shoot something Monday and post it on Wednesday and get feedback instantly.

*What keeps you going? Why?*

Ultimately, it's that connection to the audience. Getting an email from a kid who's a huge fan or watching a mashup of our shows someone has done is thrilling to us. And it truly is the consistency of the content that keeps our audience growing.

And right now there is a lot of confusion in Hollywood on how to utilize this vast new tool in a positive way. And there is confusion on the Internet side of how to produce great content. What keeps us going is that we see how those two sides are going to meet and we want to be there first.

*Anything you'd like to say to new videobloggers?*

When we started Ask a Ninja, we purposely set the production quality low so we would not feel so much pressure to make an epic production each week. And we've improved it slightly each week. So that would be my advice—if you're comfortable doing a minimovie every week, then do it, but realize that it's tough at every level to consistently produce quality podcasts.

Also, if you see a podcast out there and you feel that you could do better—do it! Use resources like this book and freevlog.com to put together your own podcast on the cheap. There is nothing stopping anyone anymore from producing good-enough quality video for mass consumption.

The key is being able to do it consistently, and there's no magic to that, other than just buckling down and doing the work.

# Troubleshooting and Helping

Every videoblogger, including those who have Ph.D.s, has trouble with some part of the videoblogging process at some point. Whether it's signing up for an account for blog software, trying to compress a video, uploading a file to the Internet, or lighting a scene, videobloggers encounter hurdles and problems daily. It's just part of the process.

Troubleshooting is just the manner in which you discover the root of any given problem and then methodically develop a solution. The great part about troubleshooting is that once you've solved a problem, you can usually identify it and help others in a similar (or exact same) situation.

This is where online groups come in. Not only can you ask for help in troubleshooting a problem, but you can also help others in need of your knowledge. It takes less than a minute to create or join a group online, and often it's free.

# Joining Online Groups

In the world of the Internet, there are groups for everyone and everything, and videoblogging is no exception. Online groups are great because you can bring like-minded people together from around the world. You can create your own groups at Google (`http://groups .google.com`), Yahoo! (`http://groups.yahoo.com`), and a number of other sites on the Internet. As of this writing, Yahoo! alone has 14 groups devoted to videoblogging in some way (see Figure 21-1).

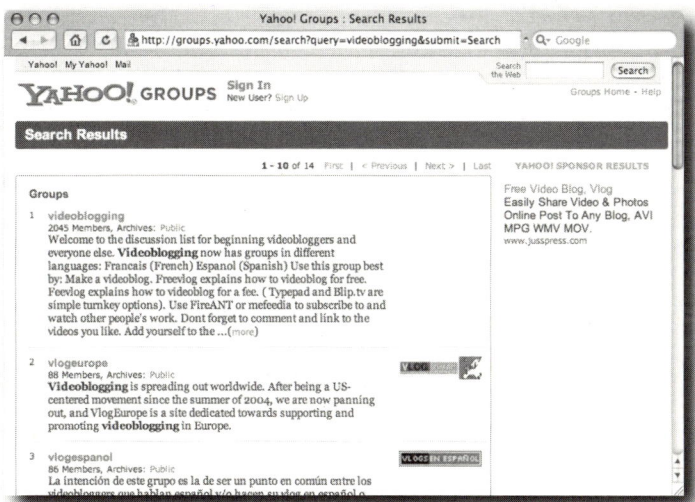

FIGURE 21-1: Yahoo! videoblogging groups.

The largest and most active videoblogging group is the aptly named *videoblogging*. You can find out more about the group—and join—at `http://groups.yahoo .com/group/videoblogging`. The Yahoo! group is primarily an email list, where very passionate people discuss the how, what, and why of placing video on the web. In less than 18 months, the group generated more than 36,000 messages. You can tell that the people in the group have a lot to say.

The Yahoo! videoblogging group started in the spring of 2004 and has become a place that houses the original people who pushed videoblogging development (and continue to push it). Their motto is "The newest person is the most important," so the group is a great place to join and ask the most basic of questions. Also, the group's membership comes from around the world, so there is always someone online to help at any hour.

Members of the group love to discuss, in depth, how they envision the evolution of video on the web. It's truly an exciting time for independent video creators, and the members of this group are at the forefront. There is also a group in French at `http://groups.yahoo .com/group/francevlogging` and in Spanish at `http://groups.yahoo .com/group/vlogespanol`.

Joining an online group also helps you gain an audience. By getting help and helping other people, you get a reputation. This is one of the great features of the Internet. The community is your audience, so you are judged by your actions.

Groups also help to build communities in the real world. If you wanted to, you could join an online group just for videobloggers in your town (or you could create one if it doesn't exist). The most important aspect of being part of a group is staying active and helping to foster a productive community through open communication.

# Attending Conferences

Because videoblogging is still in its infancy, there aren't a lot of conferences yet. However, there are a few throughout the year, scattered around the world. Also, online meetings occur regularly.

## Vloggercon

The biggest conference—and the original—is Vloggercon (`www.vloggercon.com`). Vloggercon is planned around a particular theme every year to focus the daily sessions (see Figure 21-2), and there are sessions for everyone, from beginner to expert.

Conferences are a great way to learn about what's new in the videoblogging world, as well as to meet face to face the people you see online daily.

---

### Videoblogging Vloggercon

What would a conference about videoblogging be if it wasn't videoblogged? Sure enough, Vloggercon 2005 was videoblogged, and you can find the videoblog at `http://vloggercon .blogspot.com`. On the site, you can view a few of the sessions that took place and read what some of the attendees thought about what was happening.

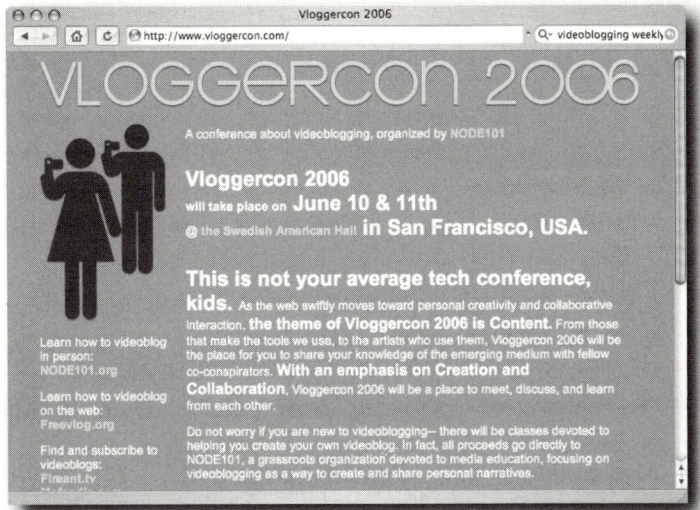

FIGURE 21-2: Vloggercon web site for 2006.

## Flash Meeting

In addition to joining online groups and attending conferences, there is a weekly Flash meeting, organized by Markus Sandy (`http://apperceive.blogs.com`). This meeting is a videoconference and online chat that anyone can join, even if you don't have a camera.

The videoconference site is `www.voxmedia.org/wiki/Videoblogger_Videoconferences` (see Figure 21-3), which is where you can find out how to join the next meeting. You can also view past videoconferences, as every meeting is archived.

The videoblogging community is composed of a wide variety of people. Through conferences in person and via video, videobloggers connect and share their visions of what videoblogging is . . . and what it will be.

FIGURE 21-3: Web site for Videoblogger videoconferences.

# Summary

You've got this book, and you've got the knowledge at your fingertips to videoblog. There are only two words for you:

Just videoblog!

Do it. Record your vision of a television show or your children's birthdays or a sunset. Whatever you want to show the world, do so. The number of people videoblogging around the world is continuing to grow daily. Join the fun.

# Index

# How to take it to the Extreme.

If you enjoyed this book, there are many others like it for you. From *Podcasting* to *Hacking Firefox*, ExtremeTech books can fulfill your urge to hack, tweak and modify, providing the tech tips and tricks readers need to get the most out of their hi-tech lives.

 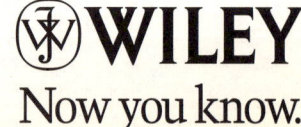